FoxPro®
The Master Reference
2nd Edition

FoxPro®
The Master Reference
2nd Edition

Robin Stark
Shelley Satonin

Windcrest®/McGraw-Hill

SECOND EDITION
FIRST PRINTING

© 1992 by **Robin Stark and Shelley Satonin**.
First edition © 1991 by **Robin Stark and Shelley Satonin.**
Published by Windcrest Books, an imprint of TAB Books.
TAB Books is a division of McGraw-Hill, Inc.
The name "Windcrest" is a registered trademark of TAB Books.

Printed in the United States of America. All rights reserved. The publisher takes no responsibility for the use of any of the materials or methods described in this book, nor for the products thereof.

Library of Congress Cataloging-in-Publication Data

Stark, Robin.
   FoxPro : the master reference / by Robin Stark and Shelley
Satonin.—2nd ed.
     p.   cm.
   Includes index.
   ISBN 0-8306-2582-8
    1. FoxPro (Computer program)   2. Data base management.
I. Satonin, Shelley. II. Title.
QA76.9.D3S72   1991
005.75'65—dc20   91-23484
                                                           CIP

TAB Books offers software for sale. For information and a catalog, please contact
TAB Software Department, Blue Ridge Summit, PA 17294-0850.

Acquisitions Editor: Ron Powers
Technical Editors: Sandra L. Johnson and Patti McCarty
Production: Katherine G. Brown
Book Design: Jaclyn J. Boone
Cover: Sandra Blair Design and Brent Blair Photography, Harrisburg, PA.

WP1

Contents

Introduction   xi

1   The FoxPro User Interface   1

Interface windows   1
    Interface menus
    Using menus with the keyboard
    Using menus with a mouse
    Dialog boxes
    Alerts
    Text editing in the Interface
    Cursor movement
    Selecting text
    Deleting text

The menu system   8

The File menu   9
    File New...
    File New Database
    File New Program
    File New File
    File New Index
    File New Report
    File New Label
    File Open...
    File Close
    File Save
    File Save As...
    File Revert
    File Printer Setup...
    File Print
    File Quit

The Window menu   37
    Window Hide
    Window Move

  Window Size
  Window Zoom
  Window Cycle
  Window Color...
  Window Command
  Window Debug
  Window Trace
  Window View
The Browse menu 51
  Browse Browse
  Browse Grid Off
  Browse Unlink Partitions
  Browse Change Partition
  Browse Size Field
  Browse Move Field
  Browse Resize Partitions
  Browse Toggle Delete
  Browse Append Record
The Database menu 57
  Database Setup...
  Database Browse
The Browse menu 64
  Browse Append/Change
  Browse Grid Off
  Browse Unlink Partitions
  Browse Change Partition
  Browse Size Field
  Browse Move Field
  Browse Resize Partitions
  Browse Toggle Delete
  Browse Append Record
  Browse Append From...
  Database Copy To...
  Database Sort...
  Database Total
  Database Average
  Database Count...
  Database Sum...
  Database Calculate
  Database Report...
  Database Label
  Database Pack
  Database Reindex
The Edit menu 83
  Edit Undo
  Edit Redo
  Edit Cut
  Edit Copy
  Edit Paste

>   *Edit Clear*
>   *Edit Select All*
>   *Edit Goto Line...*
>   *Edit Find...*
>   *Edit Find Again*
>   *Edit Replace and Find Again*
>   *Edit Replace All*
>   *Edit Preferences*
>   The Record menu   91
>   *Record Append*
>   *Record Change*
>   *Record Goto...*
>   *Record Locate...*
>   *Record Continue*
>   *Record Seek...*
>   *Record Replace*
>   *Record Delete...*
>   *Record Recall...*
>   The System menu   98
>   *System About FoxPro*
>   *System Help...*
>   *System Macros...*
>   *System Filer...*
>   *System Calculator*
>   *System Calendar/Diary*
>   *System Special Characters*
>   *System ASCII Chart*
>   *System Capture*
>   *System Puzzle*
>   The Program menu   118
>   *Program Do...*
>   *Program Cancel*
>   *Program Resume*
>   *Program Echo*
>   *Program Step*
>   *Program Talk*
>   *Program Compile...*
>   *Program Compile*
>   *Program Generate*
>   *Program FoxDoc*
>   *Program FoxGraph...*

2 FoxPro commands   123

Alphabetical listing of commands   123

3 FoxPro SET commands   247

Alphabetical listing of SET commands   247

4	FoxPro functions	267
	Alphabetical listing of functions 267	

5	System memory variables	389
	Alphabetical listing of system memory variables 389	

6	FoxPro programming	399

Using the editor   399
 Editing keys
 Indentation
 Copying and moving text
 Other features
Modular design programming   401
 Setting up the FoxPro environment
Memory variables   402
 Memory variable and fields
Decision making   404
Loops   405
The People sample application   405
 A simple program for maintaining the file
 The Main program
 The Insert program
 Insert using arrays
 The Edit program
 Edit with arrays
 The Delete program
 Report
 Crit
 Dest
 Labels
 Packem

7	Using the Screen Builder	429

Designing a custom screen   429
Starting the Screen Builder   430
Designing the screen   431
Saving the screen   438
Creating a second screen   438
Generating code   440
Running a program   441
Other control objects   442
Design screen commands   443

8	Using the Menu Builder	445

Designing a custom menu   445
Starting the Menu Builder   446

      Designing the screen   446
      Saving the menu   451
      Generating code   451
      Running the menu   452
      Running a program generated from screen border   452

9   Using the RQBE window   455
      Setting query conditions   455
      Opening the RQBE window   456
      Selection criteria   459
      The SQL SELECT command   461
      Running the query   462
      Joining multiple databases   462
      Saving the query   462
      Exiting the RQBE window   463

10   The 10 most important additions to FoxPro 2.0   465
      Increased speed   465
      SQL-SELECT   465
      RQBE window   466
      The Rushmore technology   466
      Improved index files   466
      Extended version   466
      Screen Builder   466
      Menu Builder   467
      Application Program Interface   467
      New commands and functions   467

Appendices

A   Setting parameters with CONFIG.FX   469

B   Color schemes and color pairs   473

C   System menu names   477

D   Foxhelp categories   481

     Index   483

Introduction

I WILL NEVER FORGET THE DAY THAT MY COPY OF FOXPRO ARRIVED. LIKE MOST FoxPlus users, I had been anxiously awaiting this new product. As any FoxPlus or FoxBASE user knows, the Fox products have always been exciting—just the improved speed had made FoxPlus much better than comparable systems.

I couldn't wait to try out the program for myself. On that fateful day that the package from Fox software arrived, and I loaded it on to my system, my heart just sank. This new program seemed so different than FoxPlus!

Fortunately, once I practiced a little with the new user interface, and got the hang of it, things started to look up. I realized that Fox had made some major improvements with this newest member of the FoxBASE family. The new design of the Interface is much easier to use. The menu and screen builders allow beginners to create the types of programs that until now, only an experienced programmer could write. And finally, the new commands that create bounce-bar and pop-up menus are a FoxBASE programmer's dream.

Well, it didn't take long for me to decide on the goal of this book. *FoxPro 2.0: The Master Reference* is to help anyone who has felt at all intimidated by Fox's package of six manuals. We realized that there had to be an easier way to explain this program. In many ways we have attempted to "cut out the fat" from the manuals. We have streamlined certain topics without eliminating any of the important aspects of this program.

For instance, in explaining the required syntax of each command, we do not print the command with a long list of optional clauses and arguments. This method of listing all possible options can confuse users, especially those new to dBASE. Instead, we display the simplest syntax of the command, and then list all options along with examples of both simple and complex usage.

The layout of the book is also streamlined. Instead of many different sections, this book is divided into five main sections, namely:

The user interface
FoxPro commands
FoxPro functions
Creating programs
Using the Menu Builder and Screen Builder

This book contains plenty of reference information regarding each of these topics. In fact, with this book by your computer, you should never again have to wade through the FoxPro reference manuals. Our goal was to make a simpler, easier-to-use reference, while still providing all of the information a user would need. If you are new to dBASE-style database managers, this book should help you move from novice status to confident user. If you are experienced with Fox products, but just new to FoxPro, this book will help you get up and running with the new features in no time. And no matter what type of user you are, *FoxPro 2.0: The Master Reference* will be the easiest way to find the most answers.

With the advent of FoxPro 2.0, introduced in late 1991, the program (and this book!) have gone through some major enhancements. FoxPro is now much faster and uses less memory. Other additions that result in improved speed are the Rushmore Technology, which causes query selections to perform faster, and compact index files, which process index functions much faster. The Screen Builder and Menu Builder are easy-to-use program generators that allow you to design screens with all the controls (pop-up menus, buttons, and menu bars) of a sophisticated system. The SQL SELECT command is a very powerful command that can take the place of five or six standard commands. In addition, there are over 100 new and enhanced commands and functions. See the last chapter for a list of the 10 most important additions to version 2.0.

1

The FoxPro User Interface

THE FOXPRO USER INTERFACE IS THE BEST PLACE FOR A BEGINNER TO BECOME FAMILIAR with database management. The User Interface lets you work entirely from pop-up menus, selecting commands and functions with a few keystrokes or mouse movements. With the Interface, you can design your database, create reports and mailing labels, and perform a wide variety of operations that formerly required programming skills.

Interface windows

When you start FoxPro, the *sign-on screen* appears, as shown in Fig. 1-1. This screen has the FoxPro logo, a Command window, and a menu bar. If you know the commands and functions you want to use, you can simply type them in the Command window to execute their actions. If you are just learning FoxPro, you will find it easier to work with the menus in the View window.

When you choose View from the Window menu (choosing menu options is discussed later), the View window in Fig. 1-2 opens.

The program and the Text, Report, and Label Layout windows can be opened from the File menu when you choose the Open option. If you have several windows open at once, their names will all be listed on the Window menu, with the frontmost window selected. You can move another window to the front by selecting it from the menu. Windows can be sized, moved, and manipulated in other ways. For details, see the Window menu section in this chapter.

You can scroll to see information that is not showing in the window. With a mouse, click the arrows at either end of the scroll bar along the edge of the window. To view information more rapidly, drag the diamond-shaped thumb. Click once in the page up or page down area to see the preceding or following page.

2   The FoxPro User Interface

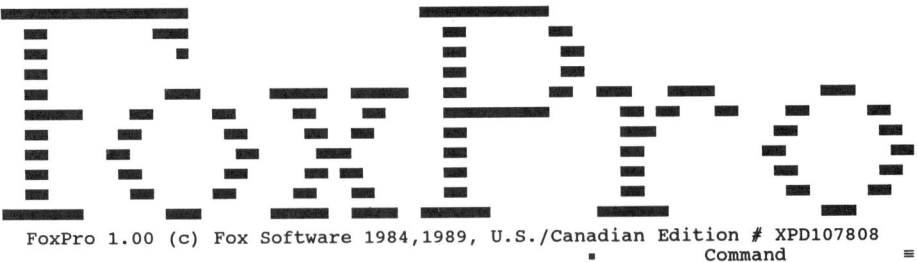

Fig. 1-1. Sign-on screen.

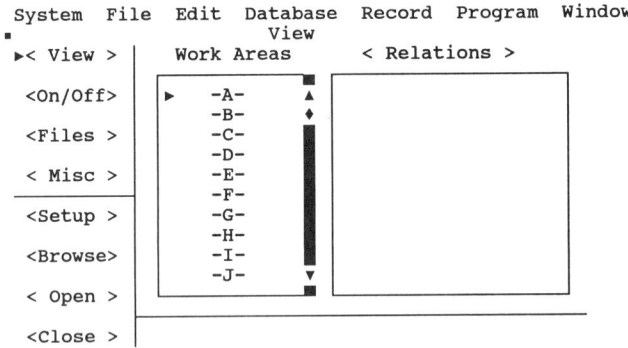

Fig. 1-2. View window.

With the keyboard, use the arrow keys to scroll, and PgUp and PgDn to move up or down one page. Press the Home key to go to the top of the window, and End to go to the bottom.

Interface menus

You can type commands in the Command window if you are already familiar with FoxPro's programming language. For beginners, the menu bar is the door to operating FoxPro's database management system.

Each menu shown in the menu bar consists of a list of menu options that you can select to run operations. The menu bar changes depending on what you are doing in the interface.

When you select a menu, a list of options appears beneath it. Some of the options might appear dimmed, and you cannot select them. These items are disabled because some other operation must be performed before they can be chosen.

Some of the menu options are followed by an ellipsis (...). This indicates that a dialog box will appear when you select the option. A *dialog box* asks you for further information about the activity you want to perform. Some of the items in a dialog box might also include an ellipsis. This means another dialog box, or a *radio box*, will appear if you select the option. In a radio box, you "switch on" the radio button for an item by selecting it.

Using menus with the keyboard

You can perform FoxPro operations from the keyboard or with a mouse. Some functions are easier with the mouse; others can be done more quickly when you know the keystrokes and you do not have to look up from your work to find items on the screen.

To open menus with the keyboard, press Alt or F10 and the hot key for the menu. The hot key is highlighted and is usually the first letter of the menu name. To select a menu option from the menu, press the item's hot key, or use the Up and Down arrow keys to highlight the option you want and then press the spacebar. If you want to leave the menu without selecting an option, press Esc, Alt, or F10.

Once you are familiar with interface menu options, you can select them by pressing Alt or F10, the menu hot key, and the option hot key without stopping to look at the menu. Some menu items can be selected from the keyboard by pressing the Ctrl key and a function key. These special shortcut keys are listed to the right of the menu options on the menu listing.

Using menus with a mouse

If you loaded a mouse driver when you installed FoxPro, you can use a mouse to move around and execute actions in the interface. With a mouse installed and attached to your computer, the sign-on screen appears with a pointer box instead of a flashing cursor.

To open a menu with the mouse, point to the menu name and hold down the mouse button. To select an option on the mouse, continue holding down the mouse button and drag the pointer to the option you want. When you release the button, the action is performed, or, if the item has an ellipsis, a dialog box appears.

Dialog boxes

When you select a menu item that is followed by an ellipsis, a dialog box appears. Dialog boxes also appear during other operations that require more information from you. You can press Esc to exit the dialog box without providing any information.

To move around a dialog box with the keyboard, press Tab until the control you want is highlighted. You can point to the control you want with the mouse. Each type of control in Fig. 1-3 has its own requirements for executing an action. These are described in the following paragraphs.

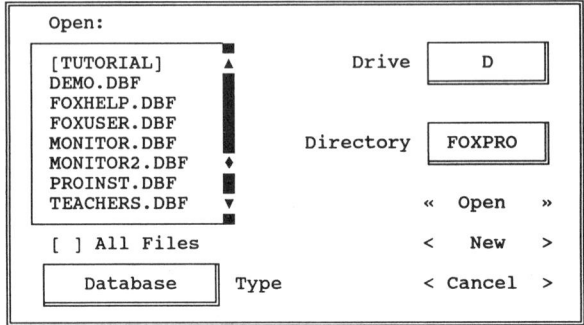

Fig. 1-3. Open file box with scrollable list.

Scrollable list *Scrollable lists* usually contain items such as directories, files, or fields. To scroll down the list, click the arrow at either end of the scroll bar or use the Up and Down arrows. You can use PgUp and PgDn to see more pages in the list, as well as Home and End to move to the top and bottom of the lists. Pressing the first letter of the item you want takes you to the first item in the list that begins with that letter.

Select the item by clicking on it with the mouse or pressing the spacebar when it is highlighted.

Radio button A *radio button* is a pair of parentheses followed by text. Only one radio button in a group can be chosen at a time. Figure 1-4 shows four radio buttons.

Click the radio button with the mouse to choose it, or press the spacebar when the button is highlighted. When the button is on, a bullet appears inside the parentheses. When you choose a radio button, any other previously chosen button in the group is automatically deselected.

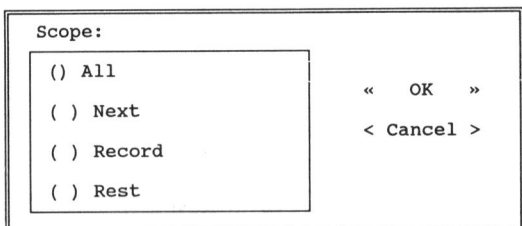

Fig. 1-4. Scope box with radio buttons.

Check box   A *check box* is a pair of square brackets followed by text (see Fig. 1-5). When a check box is highlighted, you can turn on and off its settings by clicking with the mouse or pressing the spacebar. When a setting is turned on, an X shows in the check box.

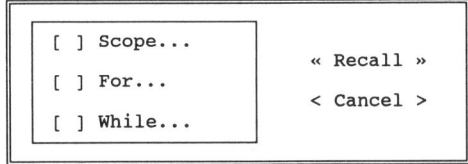

Fig. 1-5. Check boxes in a dialog box.

If the text is followed by an ellipsis, choosing the check box opens a dialog box. When you complete the dialog box and choose OK, the check box shows an X. More than one box can be checked at one time.

Text box   A *text box* (Fig. 1-6) is an area where you can enter text. Point to the text area with the mouse, or Tab to it from the keyboard and then enter text.

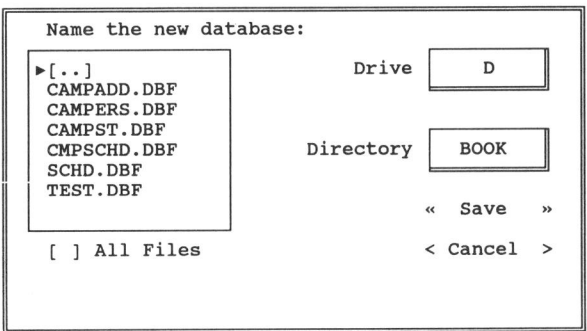

Fig. 1-6. A Save As dialog box with a text box.

Pop-up control   A *pop-up control* is a rectangle with double right and bottom borders. The text to the left of the rectangle tells you what type of information pops up when you highlight the pop-up control and hold down the mouse button or press the spacebar. To select an item in the pop-up, drag to it with the mouse and release the mouse button, or use the Up and Down arrows to highlight the item and press the spacebar.

You can also use PgUp and PgDn to scroll a long list of pop-up items. The Home and End keys take you to the top and bottom of the list. If the list is alphabetized, you can press the first letter of the item you want, and FoxPro will highlight the first item that begins with that letter.

Text Button   *Text buttons* are enclosed in angled brackets. Selecting the text inside the brackets executes the action described or opens a dialog box if there is an ellipsis after the text. Some text buttons must be highlighted or pointed to and then selected by pressing Enter or clicking with the mouse. If the text button has an underlined letter, pressing that letter will execute the action.

The double-bracketed text button is the default, and you can choose it by clicking anywhere inside the dialog box with the mouse or by pressing Ctrl – Enter.

Alerts

If you ask FoxPro to do something impossible, or if you start to do something that will destroy information, an alert appears to warn you or tell you of your error. You can remove the alert from the screen by clicking the mouse button or by pressing any key with the exceptions of the function keys and the Ctrl, Shift, or Alt keys.

Text editing in the Interface

You can edit text in FoxPro's Program, Text, Memo Command, and Report Layout windows, and in dialog boxes. Some text editing procedures can be accomplished with menu options (i.e., Cut, Copy, and Paste on the Edit menu), and others use cursor movement keys.

Cursor movement

To edit text, you must place the cursor where you want to make changes. In Insert mode, the cursor looks like a flashing underscore. When you type a character, it appears at the cursor position, and existing text is moved one character to the right. In Overwrite mode, the cursor is a flashing box. When you type text in Overwrite mode, existing text is replaced by your entry. The Insert key toggles between Insert and Overwrite modes.

With the keyboard, use any of the movement keys described as follows:

Key	Moves cursor
→/←	One character to the right/left.
↑/↓	Up/down one line.
PgUp/PgDn	Up/down one window of text.
Home/End	To the beginning/end of the current line.
Ctrl – →/←	One word to the right/left.
Ctrl – Home/End	To beginning/end of text.

With a mouse, you can move the cursor by pointing or by scrolling using the scroll bars at the right and bottom edges of the window. To use the scroll bars, click on the appropriate arrow or drag the thumb to scroll quickly. Then point and click on the cursor position you want.

When the cursor is in the desired position, type the text you want to enter. FoxPro automatically wraps words at the end of each line. Press Enter to start a new paragraph.

Selecting text

When you want to move or copy blocks of text, you must first select the text. Place the cursor at the beginning of the text you want to select. The keystrokes for selecting are listed here. They are the same keystrokes for cursor movement, with the Shift key added. To use the selection keystrokes, press and hold each necessary key until the final key is pressed. For instance, to select a word, hold down Shift, press and hold Ctrl, and press the appropriate arrow:

Keys	Selects
Shift – ←/→	One character at a time.
Shift – ↑/↓	One line at a time.
Shift – Ctrl – ←/→	From the cursor to the beginning/end of the word.
Shift – Ctrl – Home/End	From the cursor to the beginning/end of the text.
Ctrl – A	All text.

To deselect text, press any cursor movement key.

The same techniques can be performed quite easily with the mouse. First place the cursor in the starting position. Then:

Mouse action	Selects
Double-click	A word.
Triple-click	A line.
Double-click, drag	Word by word.
Triple-click, drag	Line by line.
Reposition cursor, Shift – click	All text from original cursor location to Shift – click location.

To deselect text with the mouse, drag back over selected text before you release the mouse button. After releasing the mouse button, Shift – click at the position in the text where you want the selection to end. Deselect all selected text by placing the pointer outside the selected text and clicking.

Deleting text

Three keys can be used to delete text. Press Backspace to delete the character immediately to the left of the cursor. If text is selected, Backspace deletes the entire selection.

Ctrl – Backspace deletes the word in which the cursor is positioned. When the cursor is in a blank space following a word, Ctrl – Backspace deletes the space and the word.

Delete erases the character that the cursor is on. If text is selected, Delete erases the selection.

The menu system

Now that you know how to get around FoxPro's User Interface, you are ready to begin executing actions. This section covers each menu separately, starting with the menu you are most likely to use first, and continuing in this order:

    File menu
    Window menu
    Database menu
    Edit menu
    Record menu
    System menu
    Program menu

The beginning of each menu section has a short tutorial designed to help you get a feel for the uses of the menu options. Following that, each menu option is defined in the order that it appears on the menu.

The File menu

The options on the File menu let you create, save, open, close, and print your files. For practice, create a new file to keep track of the campers attending the Sierra Sylvestri Summer Camp as shown in Fig. 1-7.

Fig. 1-7. The File menu.

```
New...
Open...
Close

Save
Save as...
Revert

Printer Setup...
Print...

Quit
```

First, open a new file. Choose New from the File menu: press Alt – F, then Enter, or point to the File menu with the mouse and release the button on the New option. You should see that the Database radio button is selected. Choose OK to open a new database file. A structure box appears. Describe the fields you want to include in your database:

1. Type Fname in the text box and press Tab.
2. Press Tab again to accept the Character description.
3. Type 12 in the Width column and press Enter.
4. Type Lname, press Tab twice, and enter 12 as the width.
5. Type City and press Tab twice.
6. Enter 12.
7. Type Age and Tab once.
8. Press the spacebar in the Type column. Select Numeric from the pop-up to indicate your entries in this field must be numeric.
9. Enter 2 in the Width column.
10. Type Camp, press Tab twice, and enter 17 in the Width column. Choose OK, and a Save dialog box appears. Type Campers in the text box and choose Save.

Now you have a named database with five fields, but there are no records in it. Select Yes in the message box to display an append screen in which you can enter records into the Campers database. You can see your field names on the left side of the browse screen. Enter five names into the database, as shown in Fig. 1-8. Notice that it is not necessary to press Enter in the Age field because FoxPro automatically moves the cursor to the next field when the current field is filled.

10   The FoxPro User Interface

```
       System   File  Edit   Database   Record   Program   Window   Browse
                             View
  ▪                                     CAMPERS
    Fname  Sherry
    Lname  Stone
    City   Sorana Beach
    Age    12
    Camp   Bumblebee Brigade
    Fname  Wally
    Lname  Taylor
    City   Provo
    Age    13
    Camp   Lemur Lodge
    Fname  Bo
    Lname  Travis
    City   New Orleans
    Age    11
    Camp   Woodpecker Wigwam
  ↔
```

Fig. 1-8. New database with records entered.

Close the append window by choosing File Close. This does not actually close the Campers file; try opening it and see what happens:

1. Choose File Open.
2. Select Campers from the menu.

As you can see, FoxPro will not allow you to select the Campers file. That is because it is already open. If you want to see the records again, you can choose Browse from the Database menu, or Append from the Record menu, or a number of other options that will display the contents of the Campers file. Because the Campers file is already open, you will not need to indicate the file name every time you want to perform an action.

To close the Campers file, choose View from the Window menu and select the Close text button, or, if you are finished working in FoxPro, choose Quit from the File menu.

Each option in the File menu is described in the following sections.

File New...

File New lets you create a new file in FoxPro. As shown in Fig. 1-9, selecting it opens a dialog box with a list of radio buttons.

Indexes depend on databases for their information, so you cannot create any of these files unless a database is currently open. If there is no database

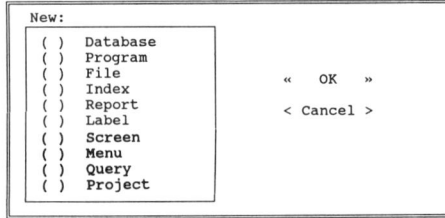

Fig. 1-9. New File dialog box.

open, this radio button will not be available. The other options—Screen, Menu, Query, and Project are explained in later chapters.

Choose Cancel to exit the dialog box without creating a new file. Choose OK after you have selected a file type that you want to create.

File New Database

When you choose the Database radio button in the New File dialog box an empty Structure dialog appears.

You define the fields you want to include in your database in four columns in the text box. Type the name of the first field under the Name heading. When you press Enter, the default field type and width appear. Tab to the Type column to select a field type from the pop-up. Type options are:

Type	Specifications	Width restrictions
Character	Any type of data	Up to 254.
Numeric	Numeric data only	Up to 20, including the ± sign and decimal.
Date	Dates only	8.
Logical	Accepts T or F	1.
Memo	Any type of data	Expands to accept data entered; limited only by memory available.
Float	Scientific data	Up to 20, including the ± sign and decimal place.

Enter the width and decimal places, if applicable. Figure 1-10 shows the Campers.dbf structure.

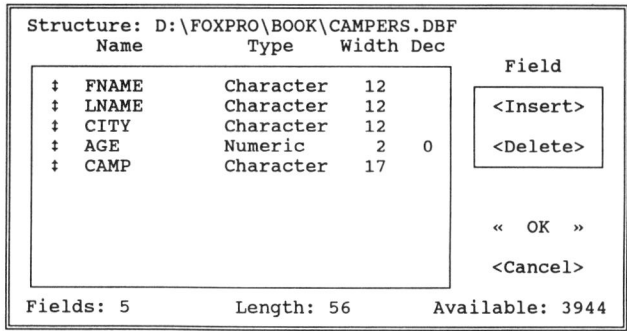

Fig. 1-10. Structure dialog box for Campers.dbf.

You can insert and delete fields in the database structure. To insert a field, place the cursor on the field above which you want to add a new field. Choose the Insert text button with the mouse, or choose the Insert option from the Structure menu that was added to the menu bar when you opened the Structure box. A field named Newfield appears with a character type and a width of 10. Type the field name, select the type, and enter the width you want for the field. To delete a field, select it and choose the Delete text button or menu item.

You can also change the order the fields are listed in the database. With the keyboard, Tab to the double-headed arrow to the left of the field you want to move and press the spacebar. Use the arrow keys to move the field to a new position, and press the spacebar to fix the field in place. With the mouse, point to the appropriate double-headed arrow and drag it to its new position.

When you are finished defining the database structure, choose OK. A Save dialog box appears. Type the new name of the database in the text box and choose Save. A message box appears, asking if you want to input data records now. Choose No to return to the Interface screen.

If you choose Yes, an Append screen appears. You can also access this screen by choosing Append from the Record menu or Browse from the Database menu. To append records, type data in the appropriate fields, and press Enter to move to the next field. A blank record is always added to the existing list of records.

When you append records, a Browse menu is added to the menu bar. The options on this menu let you view your database in different formats and edit your records. See the section about Browse in the Database menu discussion for further information on browsing records.

See also: Database Browse p. 63
File Save As p. 35
Record Append p. 92

File New Program

When you choose the Program radio button in the File New dialog box an empty programming window appears. Enter your program in the window and save the file. It will automatically be given a .PRG file extension. See chapter 6 for information on programming.

File New File

Choose the File radio button to display an empty text editing window named Untitled. Enter any text in the window and then save the file and close the window. No extension is assigned to the file name unless you specify one.

File New Index

The Index radio button is only enabled if a database is currently open. Indexing (Fig. 1-11) allows you to set the order of records in the active database (you can activate one of several open databases in the View window).

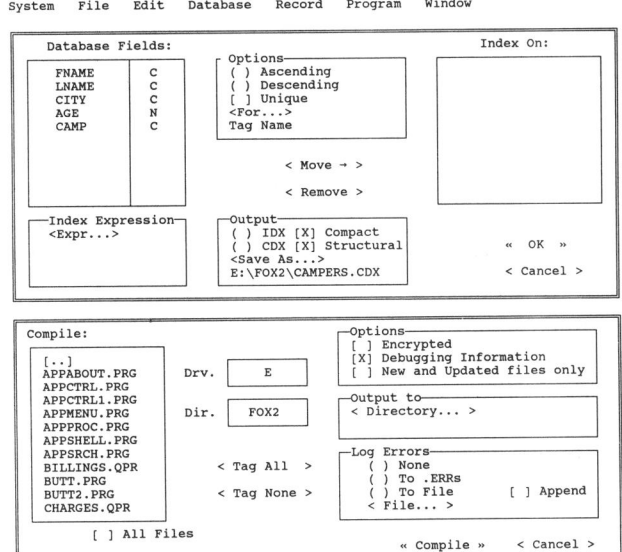

Fig. 1-11. Index dialog box.

When you select the Index radio button, the Index dialog box appears. Two types of indexes can be created. *Single index files* track one sort order (for instance Lname). *Multiple index files* (.CDX) maintain a group of sort orders (for instance, Lname order, Zip order, and Camp+Lname order). The dialog box includes a list of all the field names in the database. To indicate the field on which you want the database indexed, select the field in the list or type the field name in the text box to the right of the Expr... text button. If, for example, you type Lname, the index will order the campers alphabetically by last name. If you select the Expr... text button, the Expression Builder appears. Choose the field name from the scrollable list. If the file is a multiple index file (the .CDX radio button is checked), you must enter a tag name for this index. If the file is a single index file (the .IDX radio button is checked), you must enter a file name for the index file. Enter Name as the tag for the Lname index. You must then choose Move to move the Lname field into the Index list. Choose OK. The field name on which the index is sorted is called the *index key*.

- [ ]Unique If you only want the first record with the index key to appear in the index, check the Unique check box.
- For... If you want to specify other criteria for including specific records in the index, choose the For... text button. When you choose For..., the Expression Builder appears.

The *Expression Builder* lets you build expressions that FoxPro recognizes as commands to execute specific actions. Some expressions are simple: a field name is an expression when it is used to indicate the index key.

Complex expressions combine a number of variables to express a command. They might include combinations of field names, memory variables, constants, functions, and operators. The expressions you build when you choose the For... and While... text buttons will often be somewhat complex.

The Expression Builder makes it easy for you to build these complex expressions. When you need an expression, you can type it in the text box and choose Verify to make sure it is a valid expression. Then you can choose OK. But if you are not sure how each of the elements of the expression must be entered, you can use the pop-ups to help you create the expression.

When you open the Expression Builder, an Expression menu is added to the menu bar. This menu contains the items in the Expression Builder. This allows you to select items in the Expression Builder by pressing the hot keys on the keyboard as an alternative to selecting them in the dialog box.

The Math, String, Logical, and Date options each contain pop-up lists of functions available for use in building expressions. (See chapter 2, FoxPro Commands, and chapter 4, FoxPro Functions, for descriptions of commands and functions.) When you choose an item from one of these pop-ups, it is entered in the expression box. For example, if you wanted to index the campers in the Campers database, but you only wanted to include those campers over the age of 11, you would need a FOR... expression indicating the field name in which age appears, a logical operator, and the comparison value. These elements, Age, >, and 11, are shown in the example in Fig. 1-12.

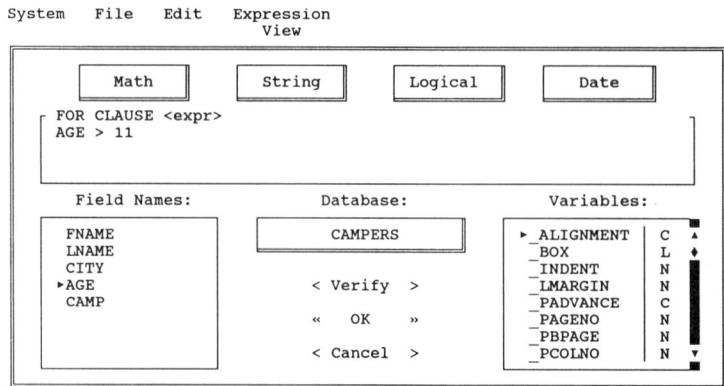

Fig. 1-12. The Expression Builder.

When you enter an item in the Expression box, whether by typing or by selecting it from a pop-up, you can use standard editing techniques to edit the expression. You can combine selecting items from list boxes and pop-ups with typing the data you need.

The Fields list contains the field names of your database. The Variables list contains the memory variables available for use in your expressions. When you choose a variable from the list, it is added to the expression in the expression box. Variables are usually used when you are programming in FoxPro.

The Database pop-up shows the database currently being indexed. The Database pop-up menu contains all the databases currently open. Change databases by selecting a new name from the pop-up menu.

Choose Verify when you have completed entering your expression and you want to verify that it is valid. Choose OK to save your changes and return to the Index dialog box. If you have created a For... expression, make sure the For... box is checked, and choose OK. You only need to name the index file if the .idx button is chosen. Otherwise, the default name of the multiple (.CDX) index file is the same as the data file. For this example, save it as a .CDX file.

See also: Window View p. 44

File New Report

Use the Report radio button to design custom report forms (Fig. 1-13).

When you select the Report radio button, a report layout window appears. Above the layout window, you will notice that the Report menu has been added to the menu bar. The window name, Untitled, has the .FRX report extension.

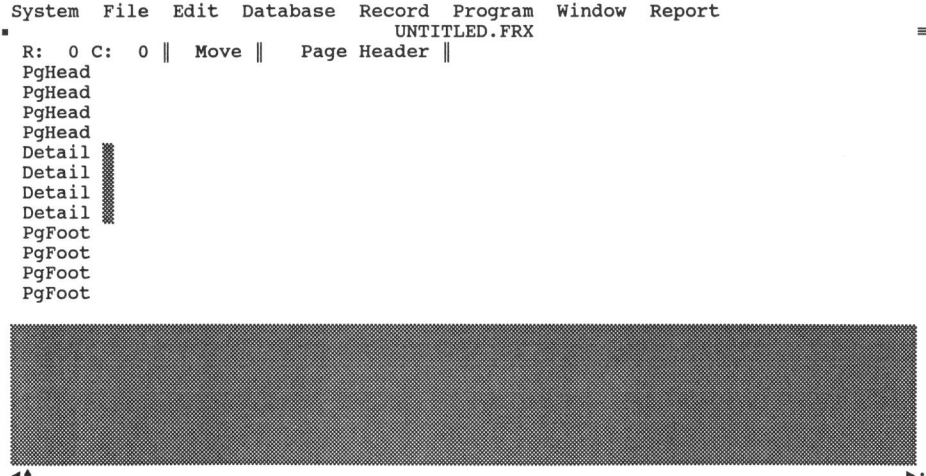

Fig. 1-13. Blank Report Layout window.

At the top of the layout window, a status bar indicates the row and column in which the cursor is located, followed by the current activity. The last piece of information is the band where the cursor is located.

Three bands are listed down the left side of the layout window. Other bands will become available as you add objects to the layout by choosing options on the Report menu. Bands can be expanded or shrunk by choosing Add Line or Remove

Line from the Report menu. The only limit is the maximum number of lines possible in a report definition: 255.

Following is a description of the layout bands.

- *Title*   The Title band contains information that appears at the top of the report. It can be a simple title or a paragraph. Information in the Title band is printed only once.
- *Page Header*   A Page Header appears at the top of each page of the report. Your Page Header might include the date, the title, and the page number. Some of this information is fixed, and some is variable.
- *Group Header*   If you break items on the report into groups, each group can have a heading to identify it.
- *Detail*   The Detail band makes up the body of the report. This information comes directly from records in your database(s), or from calculations performed on those records. If this information is grouped, the Detail band can also contain Group Headers and Footers.
- *Group Footer*   A Group Footer can contain summaries and/or subtotals for each group listed under a Group Heading.
- *Page Footer*   Page Footers perform the same function as Page Headers, but do so at the bottom of the page. You might prefer to list page numbers, for instance, at the bottom as a Footer.
- *Summary*   The Summary appears once at the end of the report. It can contain summary information taken from calculations, or text.

As shown in Fig. 1-14, the Report menu under File New lets you indicate the information you want to display in your report.

To create a simple report that uses some of the Report menu's features, first open the database that the report will be based on. In this example, use the

```
Report
┌─────────────────────────┐
│ Page Layout...          │
│ Page Preview...     ^I  │
├─────────────────────────┤
│ Data Grouping...        │
│ Title/Summary...        │
│ Variables...            │
├─────────────────────────┤
│ Box                 ^B  │
│ Field               ^F  │
│ Text                ^T  │
├─────────────────────────┤
│ Add Line            ^N  │
│ Remove Line         ^O  │
├─────────────────────────┤
│ Bring to Front      ^G  │
│ Send to Back        ^J  │
│ Center                  │
├─────────────────────────┤
│ Quick Report...         │
└─────────────────────────┘
```

Fig. 1-14. The Report menu.

Campers database. Now, open a new report file by turning on the Report radio button in the File New dialog box. The Report layout window will appear.

Suppose you want a report that lists campers alphabetically by camp and shows each camper's age. Call the report "Sierra Sylvestri Camp Report." To enter this title, choose Title/Summary from the Report menu. Check the Title Band box and choose OK.

Now type the title. Notice that the current activity to the right of the row and column numbers says Text. If you try to use the arrow keys to move the cursor down, FoxPro beeps. When you finish entering text, you must press Enter to return to Move mode.

The title will look better in the center of the page. Select the title by placing the cursor anywhere on it and pressing the spacebar or clicking with the mouse. Now choose Center from the Report menu and press Enter. The Title might not look like it is in the center of your screen, but FoxPro knows to center it between the right and left margins.

Pretend this is a very long report, and that you want to see today's date at the top of each page.

1. Put the cursor in the top PgHead band and choose Field from the Report menu. Choose Expr... and an Expression Builder appears.
2. Open the Date pop-up and choose DATE( ) from the list.
3. Choose OK in the Expression Builder and the Expression dialog box. You will see DATE( ) at the top of your layout window.
4. Choose Page Preview from the Report menu. You can see that today's date is now showing where DATE( ) appears in the report. Choose Done to return to the layout window.

Add two more headers that you will want to see at the top of each page. The left column of the report should be headed "Campers by Camp" and the right column will be "Age." Place the cursor in the bottom line of the PgHead band and type the two headings.

To group the campers by camp, you must first be sure the database is indexed on the Camp field. Use File New Index to create an index tag for the Campers database. Choose Window View and make sure the index bullet is showing in front of the Campers file name, indicating the index is active. If it is not, use the Setup button to choose the Camp index order.

To create the Camp grouping, place the cursor in the detail band:

1. Choose Data Grouping... from the Report menu.
2. Choose Add, and the Group Info dialog box appears.
3. Pick Group... to bring up the Expression Builder.
4. Select Camp from the field list and choose OK.
5. Choose OK again in the Group Info box, and again in the Group box, where Camp is now listed as shown in Fig. 1-15.

```
System  File  Edit  Database  Record  Program  Window  Report
                                      CAMPERS.FRX                              ≡
 R:  0 C:  0 ‖ Move ‖          Title ‖
 Title                                Sierra Sylvestri Camp Report
 PgHead ▒DATE()
 PgHead ▒
 PgHead ▒
 PgHead ▒Campers by Camp                              Age
 ┌1-camp
 ┌1-camp   camp
 Detail ▒
 Detail ▒trim(FNAME)+" "+LNAME                         age
 └1-camp
 PgFoot ▒
 PgFoot ▒
 PgFoot ▒
```

Fig. 1-15. A Report layout.

Creating a data grouping causes records to be grouped, but it does not automatically print the name of each group. To do that, you must add the camp field to the grouping band. Place the cursor in the band that says 1-camp:

1. Choose Field from the Report menu.
2. Pick Expr... to open the Expression Builder.
3. Select Camp from the Expression Builder.
4. Choose OK and return to the layout window.

In each group, you want to list the campers' first and last names. In the detail band:

1. Select Field from the Report menu.
2. Pick Expr... to open the Expression Builder.
3. Choose TRIM( ) from the STRING pop-up.
4. Choose Fname from the fields list.
5. Move the cursor to the right of the right parenthesis and type + " " + .
6. Choose Lname from the fields list.

This expression trims the blank spaces from the end of the Fname field, adds a space, and adds the Lname field. Without the TRIM( ) function, names would look like this:

Bo   Travis
Sherry   Stone

Enter as in the width box, choose OK, and return to the layout window. Press Ctrl – I to choose Page Preview, and you will see the names are showing correctly.

Add the Age field using the Field option and the Expression Builder. If you forgot to place the cursor in the right position first, select the Age field and use the arrow keys to put it where it belongs. Now press Ctrl – I to see the report. It should look like Fig. 1-16.

```
System  File  Edit  Database  Record  Program  Window  Report
■                            Preview
------------------------------------------------------------------------
07/24/90                 Sierra Sylvestri Camp Report
 Campers by Camp                           Age

 Bumblebee Brigade

 Sherry Stone                              12

 Lemur Lodge

 Wally Taylor                              13
 Miles Walker                              12

 Woodpecker Wigwam

 Bo Travis                                 11
 « Done »   < More >   Column:   0
◄♦                                                                      ►
```

Fig. 1-16. Page Preview of a report.

Because the report has four detail bands, the names are triple-spaced. The extra bands would be helpful if you were printing the camper's city, or other information under their name, but because the lines are not being used, they just leave too much space between each name. Delete one of the blank detail bands by moving to an empty band and pressing Ctrl – O (you could also choose Remove from the Report menu). Repeat this step on the other blank detail band. To insert an extra line at each grouping, move to the 1-camp area and press Ctrl – N.

When you want to print a report, use the Report option in the Database menu. If you make changes in a previously saved report and decide you want to go back to the saved version, use the FileRevert option (see below) to do so.

After creating a new report, save it through the File Save As dialog box. It asks if you also want to save the environment information. This saves not only the report but the open databases and indexes you used to create the report so that you can open them all again by selecting a single file name. If you save the report by itself, it has an .FRX extension.

If you want to use a report that you created in an earlier version of Fox-BASE + or another compatible program, it will be listed in the File Open dialog box with an .FRM extension.

When you are ready to run your report, use the Report option on the Database menu.

The Report menu options are described in detail here.

See also: Database Report p. 78
            File Open p. 33

Report Page Layout   The options in the Page Layout dialog box in Fig. 1-17 let you determine where the report will print on a page:

- Page Length   Enter the number of lines you want in your report.

- **Top/Bottom Margin** Type the number of blank lines you want at the top and bottom of the report.
- **Printer Indent** This is the left margin. Enter the appropriate number of characters.
- **Right Margin Column** Enter the right margin, measured from the left margin. The maximum width of a report is 255 columns.
- **Save** Automatically saves the environment information with the report.
- **Clear Automatically** Does not save the environment information with the report.

```
Page Layout:

   Page length    (rows):   66         «   OK   »
   Top margin     (rows):    0
   Bottom margin  (rows):    0         <  Cancel  >

   Printer indent (columns):    0
   Right margin column:    80
```

Fig. 1-17. Page Layout dialog box.

Choose OK when you have the settings you want. Choose Cancel or press Esc to close the dialog box without changing the settings.

Report Page Preview After you have created your report, you can preview the report before printing it. When you choose Page Preview, the top of the first page of your report appears. All data is displayed in correct locations as in Fig. 1-18, but type styles such as bold, italic, or underline will not appear.

If the report is wider than your screen, scroll to see the remaining informa-

```
System   File   Edit   Database   Record   Program   Window   Report
                                  Preview
-------------------------------------------------------------------------------
                        Sierra Sylvestri Camp Report
07/24/90


Campers by Camp                         Age

Bumblebee Brigade

Sherry Stone                            12

Lemur Lodge

Wally Taylor                            13
Miles Walker                            12

Woodpecker Wigwam

Bo Travis                               11
   « Done »   < More >   Column:   0
```

Fig. 1-18. Page Preview of a report.

tion. To view successive pages, choose More in the lower left corner of the window. Choose Done to return to the layout window.

Shortcut key: Ctrl – I

Data Grouping... This option lets you group records on the report. To do this properly, you must index or sort the database on the same expression you want to use for the grouping. Otherwise groups will be separated as they occur in the database. For example, in Fig. 1-19, if the Campers database is indexed on the Lname field but the data grouping is the Camp field, campers will be listed alphabetically on the report with spaces between groups each time the Camp field value changes.

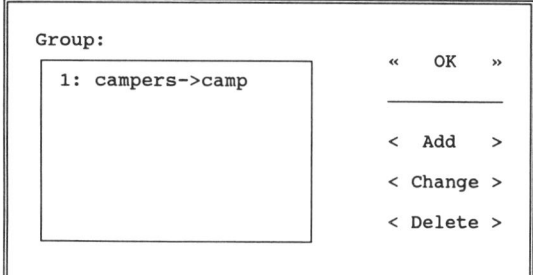

Fig. 1-19. Data Grouping dialog box.

When you choose Data Grouping..., the Group dialog box appears:

- Add   Choose Add to add a new grouping. The Group Info dialog box appears.
- Group...   Choose Group... to indicate the expression to group on in the Expression Builder. Create the Group expression and choose OK (Fig. 1-20). In the previous example, Camp was the expression used to group records on the report.
    - ~[ ]Swap Page Head   If you want Group Headers to appear at the top of each page instead of Page Headers, check the Swap Page Header box. When you do this, the New Page box is automatically checked. Each new group is printed on a new page.
    - ~[ ]Swap Page Footers   Swap Page Footers works the same way. The Group Footer is printed at the bottom of the page instead of the Page Footer.
    - ~[ ]New Page   You can check New Page by itself to start a new page each time a new group begins. In this case, Page Headers and Footers print as usual.
    - ~# of rows following header   Sets the number of rows that follow each group's heading. In Fig. 1-16, one row followed each group's header.

Choose OK when your selections are complete. You can add up to 20 groups to a report, with each group breaking down records within the higher group.

```
Group Info:

< Group... > Campers->camp            «    OK    »
Options:
                                      <  Cancel  >
[ ] Swap Page Header
[ ] Swap Page Footer
[ ] New Page
[ ] Reprint Header
[ ] Reset Page Number
```

Fig. 1-20. Group Info dialog box.

To change or delete a group, select the group in the Group box and choose Change or Delete. Choose OK when you are ready to see your groups in the report layout.

Report Title/Summary You can add a title or summary to your report with this option. This dialog box shown in Fig. 1-21 is subdivided into two sections:

- [ ]Report Title In the dialog box, check Title Band if you want to add a title. Because your title can be anything from a word to pages of introductory paragraphs, you can check the New Page box if you want the title to print on a separate report.
- [ ]Report Summary The Summary check box works the same way. If it is checked, you can also check the New Page box if you want the summary to print on a separate page at the end of the report. Choose OK to confirm your selections, or Cancel to exit the dialog box without making changes.

The cursor now appears in the Title or Summary band, and you can type the appropriate text. You can also simply type in the title while placed in the page heading area.

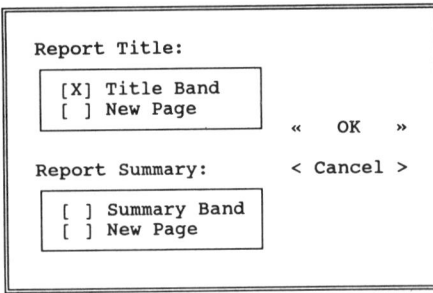

Fig. 1-21. Title/Summary dialog box.

Report Box You can draw boxes and lines on your report with the Box option as shown in Fig. 1-22. To create a box, move to where the top left corner of the box will go. Choose Box from the menu. Use the arrow keys to drag the box and shape it as desired. You can only change the bottom right corner. Press Enter when you are finished.

With a mouse, click and drag in the desired position until the box is the size you want. Release the mouse button to fix the box in place.

Fig. 1-22. Box dialog box.

```
Box:
  ( )  Single line          «  OK      »
  ( )  Double line
  ( )  Character...         <  Cancel  >
  ( )  Panel
```

To create a line instead of a box, just use a single arrow key, or drag in a single direction.

To change the format of the box, select the box by pressing Enter or clicking with the mouse. In the Box dialog, you can turn on the Single Line or Double Line radio buttons, or you can choose Character... and select some other character to make up the border of the box. Panel places a wide band around the box.

If the box is entirely within the Detail band, the Float as Band Stretches check box is also available. When you check this box, your box will stretch to accommodate field data inside. Otherwise, it will remain the same, and data that does not fit will spill over the borders.

You can move a box the same way you move any objects in the Report layout window. Select the box and use the arrow keys to move it, and press Enter when it is in the right position. Or drag it with the mouse and release the mouse button when it is in place.

To resize the box, place the cursor on the border and press Ctrl – spacebar or Ctrl – click. While the box blinks, use the arrow keys or drag the mouse to adjust the right and bottom sides of the box. Press Enter or release the mouse button to fix the size.

To delete a box or line, select it and press the backspace or delete key.

Report Field Use the Field option to place a field on your report. When you choose this option, a Report Expression dialog box appears as shown in Fig. 1-23. To edit the format at an existing report field, move to the field and press Enter.

Fig. 1-23. Report Expression dialog box.

```
Report Expression:
  <   Expr... >
  <  Format... >                          Width:    0
  [ ]  Style...        [ ]  Suppress
  [ ]  Calculate...    [ ]  Stretch Vertically
  [ ]  Comment...      [ ]  Float as Band Stretches
            «    OK    »       <  Cancel  >
```

Expr... Type an expression in the Expr... text box, or choose the box to bring up the Expression Builder. You can select a field or create a more complex expression with the pop-ups. In the earlier example, you built the expression

TRIM(FNAME)+" "+LNAME to show the first and last names in one column of the report. Select OK when you have entered your expression in the text box.

Format... Choose the Format... text button to format the field. In the Format dialog box in Fig. 1-24, you can create a format template by entering characters in the Format text box. Eleven characters (listed next) can be used to indicate a format. Any other characters typed in the Format text line will appear themselves in the format on your report.

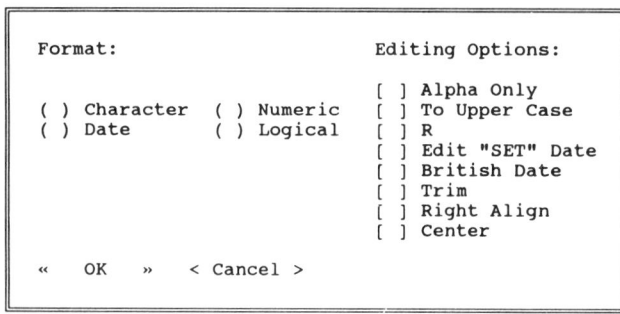

Fig. 1-24. Format dialog box.

Format characters	Description
A	Displays only alphabetic characters.
L	Displays only logical data.
N	Displays only letters and digits.
X	Displays any character.
9	Displays only digits for character data. Displays digits and signs for numeric data.
#	Displays digits, blanks, and signs.
$	Displays fixed dollar sign in front of numeric value.
$$	Displays floating dollar sign in front of numeric value.
*	Displays asterisks in front of numeric value. Can be used with $ for check protection.
.	Specifies decimal point position.
,	Separates digits left of the decimal point.

Below the Format text line, four radio buttons determine whether the field appears as a Character, Numeric, Date, or Logical field.

The right half of the dialog box contains Editing Options. These change according to which radio button is currently selected. The formatting options for each type of field are listed here.

Character field option	Description
Alpha Only	Displays only alphabetic characters.

To Upper Case	Converts all characters to uppercase.
R	Displays nonformat characters, but does not store them.
Edit "SET" date	Uses current SET DATE format to edit date data.
British Date	Edits data as a European (British) date (dd/mm/yy).
Trim	Removes leading and trailing blank spaces.
Right Align	Prints data flush right in field.
Center	Centers data in field.

Numeric field

Left Justify	Left justifies all data in field.
Blank If Zero	Does not print if field output is 0.
(Negative)	Displays negative numbers in parentheses.
Edit "SET" Date	Uses current SET DATE format to edit date data.
British Date	Edits data as a European (British) date (dd/mm/yy).
CR if Positive	CR (credit) appears after the number if the number is positive.
DB if Negative	DB (debit) appears after the number if the number is negative.
Leading Zero	Prints all leading zeros.
Currency	Displays currency format (as specified in View or SET CURRENCY command).
Scientific	Displays data in scientific notation.

Date field

Edit "SET" Date	Edits data using the current SET DATE format.
British Date	Edits data as a European (British) date (dd/mm/yy).

No editing options are available for logical data.

[ ]**Style...** The Style... dialog box in Fig. 1-25 contains a list of check boxes that determines the style of your field output in the report. Some of these text styles might not be available, depending on your printer. The styles you check will not appear in Page Preview.

[ ]**Calculate** In the Calculate dialog box in Fig. 1-26, you can choose a calculation to be made on the field entered in the Expr... text box.

Fig. 1-25. Style dialog box.

```
Style:     [X] Normal
           [ ] Bold
           [ ] Italic          «   OK   »
           [ ] Underline
           [ ] Subscript      < Cancel >
           [ ] Superscript
           [ ] Condensed
           [ ] Double
```

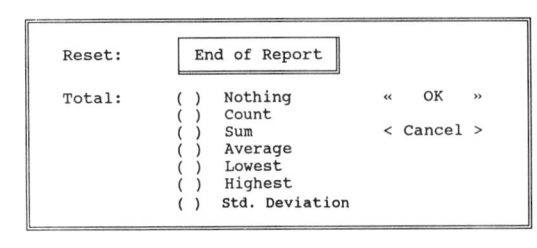

```
    Reset:     End of Report
    Total:     ( ) Nothing          «    OK    »
               ( ) Count
               ( ) Sum              < Cancel >
               ( ) Average
               ( ) Lowest
               ( ) Highest
               ( ) Std. Deviation
```

Fig. 1-26. Calculate dialog box.

The Reset pop-up contains the options End of Report, End of Page, and any groupings you have created. Choose one of the options to determine where the calculation will be made in the report. When a calculation is made, the total is "reset" to zero.

The radio buttons list the calculations that you can make on the field.

- Select Nothing if no fields are to be calculated.
- Count counts the number of times a field appears. For example, in a Camp grouping, the ages of the campers might be 12 and 13, but the count will be 2 because the Age field appears twice.
- Sum adds the values of the field. In the example above, the sum is 25 if you have selected the group in the reset pop-up.
- Average computes the arithmetic mean of the field values.
- Lowest and Highest display the lowest or highest value in the group, page or report.
- Std Deviation   Returns the square root of the variance.
- Variance   Returns a number that shows how far apart the numbers are. The variance is 0 if all the numbers are the same.

Width   When you choose an expression, a width is automatically entered in Width. You can change the width by entering a new value.

- [ ]Stretch Vertically   If you check Stretch Vertically, the field on the report will stretch if the data does not fit. It is a good idea to make a habit of checking this box. If you have a memo field in your report, you must check Stretch Vertically.
- [ ]Suppress Repeated Values   This is similar to the Unique check box you encounter in other areas of FoxPro. When you check this box, only the first occurrence of the value will appear on your report. This value does not appear for other records.
- [ ]Float as Band Stretches   This is useful if you have checked the Stretch Vertically box for another field that is very likely to overflow the line in the report. When you place the current field on the line directly below the stretched field in the report, you can check Float as Band Stretches to prevent the field from printing over data from the stretched field.

When you have completed your selections in the Expression box, choose OK to confirm them and return to the layout window. Press Esc or choose Cancel to leave without making changes.

Your expressions appear in the layout window, and you can move them around just like other objects. Some expressions might appear cut off (if the expression takes more space than the field length), but you can use Page Preview to see that the full expression is active.

To move a field, select it and use the arrow keys or drag it with the mouse to the desired position. Press Enter or release the mouse button to fix it in place.

To size a field, place the cursor in the field and press Ctrl – spacebar, or Ctrl – click with the mouse. Use the arrow keys or drag the mouse to shrink or enlarge the field. Press the spacebar to fix the field size, or release the mouse button.

Shortcut key: Ctrl – F

Report Text   You will find it is not actually necessary to use the Text option on the menu. Choosing this option changes the current activity in the layout window from Move to Text, but this happens if you simply begin typing text without choosing the option first.

You can type text anywhere you like in the layout window. Press Enter when you finish, and the activity changes from Text to Move. Now the text is treated as an object, and it can be moved or styled. If you want to edit text, simply place the cursor where you want to edit and start typing.

To move text, select it and use the arrow keys or drag it with the mouse to move it to the desired location. Press Enter or release the mouse button to fix it in place. You can move text objects to other files using the Cut and Paste options on the Edit menu.

To delete text, place the cursor on it and press Del.

A Text dialog box appears when you place the cursor on the text and press Enter. If you check Float as Band Stretches, the text will move as necessary if the field above it is stretching to accommodate data (this commonly happens with memo fields).

The Style... dialog contains a list of styles you can use. Their availability depends on the capabilities of your printer. When you select a style, it does not show in the Page Preview.

Choose OK when you have made your selections, or Cancel to close the dialog box without making changes.

Shortcut key: Ctrl – T

See also: Edit Copy *p. 86*
              Edit Cut *p. 86*

Edit Paste p. 86
File Revert p. 35
Report Field p. 23

Report Add Line/Remove Line Use these options to add lines to or remove lines from any band in the report.

To add a line, place the cursor on the line above which you want the line added and choose Add Line. You can add as many lines as you like.

If you prefer to add lines below the cursor, press Shift while you open the Report menu. This changes the Add Line option to Add Line After.

To remove a line, place the cursor in the line you want to delete and choose Remove Line. If an object is on the line, FoxPro asks if you want to delete objects on the line. If you choose Yes, the line and the object are deleted. If you choose No, you are returned to the layout window without making any changes.

Shortcut key: Add Line Ctrl – N
Remove Line Ctrl – O

Report Bring to Front/Send to Back If expressions or objects overlap on your screen, you can use these options to change the item that appears in front of the other.

Shortcut key: Bring to Front Ctrl – G
Send to Back Ctrl – J

Report Center You can center any object on the report with this option. Select the object and choose Center from the Report menu. The object is centered according to the settings you entered in the Page Layout dialog box.

To center a field on the page, you must also use the Center formatting option in the Format dialog box of the Field option.

See also: Report Field p. 23
Report Page Layout p. 19

Report Quick Report... If the Detail band of the report layout window is empty, you can use Quick Report... to create a report using a few simple dialog boxes. When you choose Quick Report..., the dialog box in Fig. 1-27 appears.

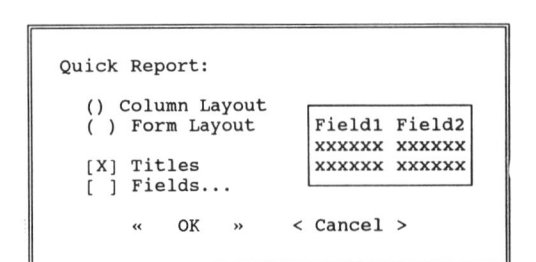

```
Quick Report:

  () Column Layout
  ( ) Form Layout      Field1 Field2
                       xxxxxx xxxxxx
  [X] Titles           xxxxxx xxxxxx
  [ ] Fields...

         «   OK   »    < Cancel >
```

Fig. 1-27. Quick Report dialog box.

The radio buttons determine whether your fields are displayed horizontally (Column) or vertically (Form). In Column layout, any fields that do not fit on the page are omitted. In Form layout, the Detail band stretches to accommodate all the fields. The radio buttons are:

- [ ]Title If you check the Title box, field names will appear as titles above or next to the field data. In Column layout, titles appear in the Page Header band, unless there are other objects in the Page Header band. In Form layout, titles appear in the Detail band next to the corresponding field.
- [ ]Fields... Select the fields you want to appear in the report from the Fields... dialog box. All the fields in your current database are listed in the Database Fields box shown in Fig. 1-28. The current database is shown in the Database pop-up. Open the pop-up to see a list of all open databases.

```
       Database Fields:                              Selected Fields:
   FNAME    | C | 12 | 0
   LNAME    | C | 12 | 0       < Move → >
   CITY     | C | 12 | 0       < All  → >
   AGE      | N |  2 | 0
   CAMP     | C | 17 | 0       < Remove >

                                < Clear  >

           Database:
                                                    <Cancel >
           CAMPERS
                                                  «   OK   »
```

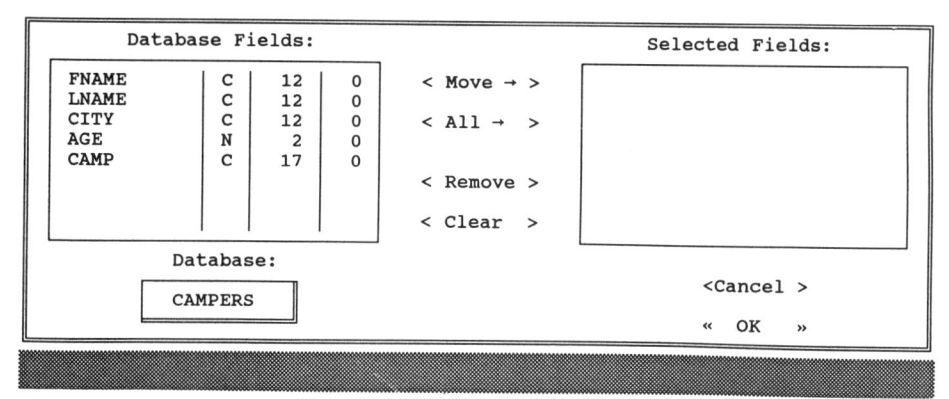

Fig. 1-28. Quick Report Fields dialog box.

To select a field for your report, choose that field, and press Enter or choose Move. The field is moved into the Selected Fields box. To put all the fields in the report, choose the All text button.

To remove a field from the Selected Fields box, select that field in the box and choose Remove. Choose Clear to remove all fields from the Selected Fields list.

Choose OK when you have selected all the fields you want. To exit the dialog box without choosing fields, press Esc or choose Cancel.

Fields added to the report with Quick Report can be sized and moved just like fields added with the Fields option.

File New Label

The Label option lets you set the format of labels by choosing a predefined format or designing your own. Because labels pull their information from a database file, this option is disabled if there is no database open.

When you select Label, an Untitled label layout window opens and the Label menu is added to the menu bar. The layout includes FoxPro's default label settings. You can see the settings described in the Remarks text box in Fig. 1-29.

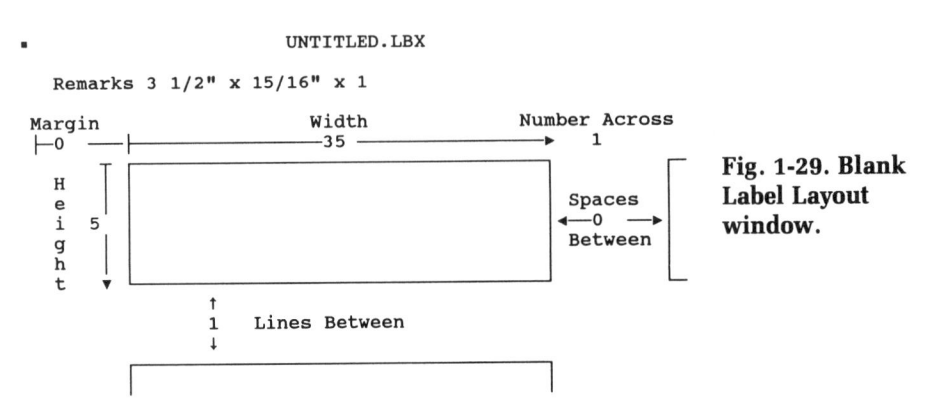

```
•                    UNTITLED.LBX

   Remarks  3 1/2" x 15/16" x 1
  Margin            Width           Number Across
  ├─0 ──┤          ─35 ─────────►        1
        ┌─────────────────────────────┐ ┐
     H  │                             │ │  Fig. 1-29. Blank
     e  │                             │ │  Label Layout
     i 5│                          Spaces│ window.
     g  │                          ◄─0─►│
     h  │                          Between
     t ▼│                             │ ┘
        └─────────────────────────────┘
              ↑
              1  Lines Between
              ↓
        ┌─────────────────────────────┐
        │                             │
```

The Margin and Width in characters are also preset, as well as the Height in lines. When the labels are "1 across" (there is one column of labels on each page), the Number Across is 1. This Lines Between label shows 1 line.

You can use the options on the Label menu to change the layout and specify the information you want to print on your labels. When you have defined your label, the best way to save it is through the File Save As dialog box. Labels receive an .LBX extension. It asks if you also want to save the environment information. This saves you having to open both the label file and the database file next time you want to work with the label.

When you are ready to generate labels, use the Label option on the Database menu.

See also: Database Label *p. 80*

Label Page Preview   After you have defined the contents of your labels, choose Page Preview to see how they look with the actual field information in them (Fig. 1-30). To scroll through labels that do not show on the screen, choose the Move text button. If your layout includes columns that do not appear on the screen, use the scroll bar or the arrow keys to scroll to the right or left. To return to the layout window, choose Done.

Label Expression...   This option lets you define the contents of your labels with an Expression Builder. If you know the fields and commands you want to use, you can simply type them in the label in the layout window. If not, choose Expression... to call up the Expression Builder (Fig. 1-31).

The label layout in Fig. 1-31 includes typical label contents. If you build these expressions in the Expression Builder, the name of the database and an

```
                        Preview
             Sherry Stone
             665 Glanite St.
             Sorana Beach, CA   92037

             Wally Taylor
             15 Grieg Way
             Provo, UT   23412

Fig. 1-30. Label Page
Preview.     Bo Travis
             135 Nosegay Rd.
             New Orleans, LA   54323

             Miles Walker
             4 Longacre Dr.
             Pahrump, NV   89005
             « Done »   < More >    Column:    0
```

Fig. 1-31. Label contents.

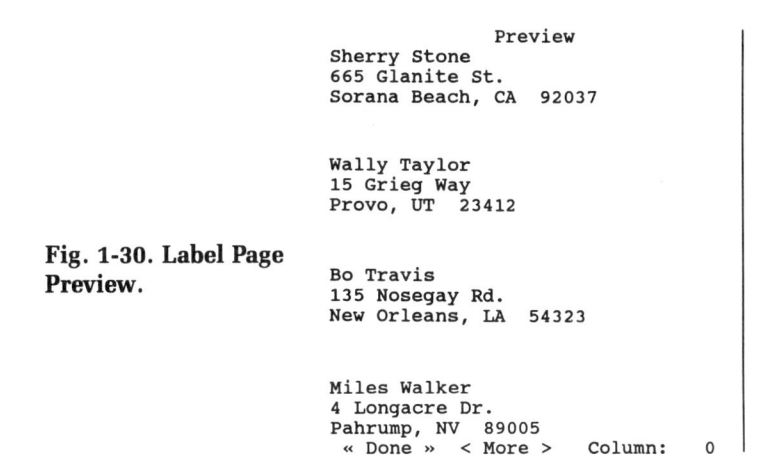

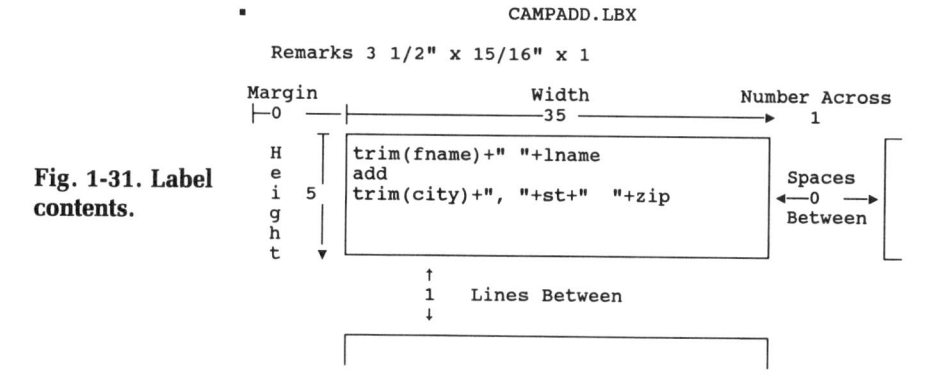

```
                          CAMPADD.LBX
       Remarks 3 1/2" x 15/16" x 1
   Margin              Width              Number Across
   |—0 —|              —35 —                   1
         H   | trim(fname)+" "+lname |
         e   | add                   |         Spaces
         i 5 | trim(city)+", "+st+" "+zip |    ←—0 —→
         g   |                       |         Between
         h   |                       |
         t   |                       |
                        ↑
                        1    Lines Between
                        ↓
```

arrow will precede the field names. You do not need to type the database name—FoxPro automatically pulls fields from the active open database.

You can find the TRIM( ) function in the String pop-up in the Expression Builder. Without the TRIM( ) function, the first name would take up the same number of character spaces as the length of the Fname field. In other words, Bo Travis would print

Bo   Travis

Commas and spaces are considered text, so they must be surrounded by quotation marks. When you combine text and fields, use plus signs to link them together. You can also enter the field names separated by commas. The entry Fname, Lname would give the same result as the entry in Fig. 1-31.

Label Layout When you choose Layout from the Label menu, a list of pre-defined label formats appears. If you select one of the listed formats (Fig. 1-32), it is applied to the label in the layout window.

```
3 1/2" x 15/16" x 1
3 1/2" x 15/16" x 2
3 1/2" x 15/16" x 3
4"   x 1 7/16" x 1
3 2/10" x 11/12" x 3 (Cheshire)
6 1/2" x 3 5/8 Envelope
9 7/8" x 7 1/8 Envelope
3"   x 5 Rolodex
4"   x 2 1/4 Rolodex
```

Fig. 1-32. Label Layout formats.

If none of these formats satisfies your needs, you can create your own formats by typing over an existing format in the list. There are a few guidelines for label formats:

Height	Can be from 1 to 255 lines.
Margin	Can be from 0 to 220 columns.
Width	Can be from 1 to 255 spaces.
Number across	Can be up to 120.
Spaces between	Can be as many as 120.
Lines between	Can be from zero to 120.
Remarks	Can include a brief note describing your layout.

Label Save Layout... To save your custom layout, choose Save Layout... from the Label menu. A Save As dialog box appears as in Fig. 1-33.

```
Save As:  3 1/2" x 15/16" x 1

    «  OK  »           <Cancel>
```

Fig. 1-33. Label Save Layout dialog box.

The Remarks in your layout format appear in the Save As box. You can accept the Remarks, or type something else over them.

If a layout with the same description already exists, FoxPro asks if you want to overwrite it. Choose Yes if you want to replace the existing layout with the new one. Otherwise, choose No to return to the Save As dialog box.

Press Esc or choose Cancel to leave the Save As dialog box without saving the layout. Keep in mind that saving the layout is not the same thing as saving the contents of your label. You must use File Save or File Save As to save your label contents in the defined layout.

See also: File Save p. 34

Label Delete Layout... When you choose Delete Layout..., a Delete dialog box appears. Select the layout you want to delete and choose Delete. To leave the dialog box without deleting a layout, press Esc or choose Cancel.

File Open...

When you choose File Open, the dialog box shown in Fig. 1-34 displays a list of files or directories along with other options.

The first time you choose File Open, the default drive and directory appear in their pop-ups. All files or directories under the displayed parent directory are listed in the scrollable list box. If you change the drive or directory, the change will remain current throughout this FoxPro session unless you change it.

Fig. 1-34. File Open dialog box.

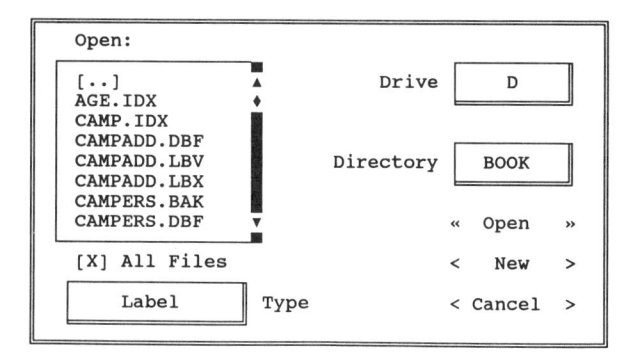

```
Open:
[..]
AGE.IDX
CAMP.IDX
CAMPADD.DBF
CAMPADD.LBV
CAMPADD.LBX
CAMPERS.BAK
CAMPERS.DBF

[X] All Files

Label     Type

Drive      D
Directory  BOOK

«  Open  »
<  New    >
< Cancel  >
```

Change drives by opening the pop-up and selecting a new drive. Change parent directories by selecting from the directory pop-up. To change subdirectories, choose the subdirectory in the scrollable list box. The subdirectory name appears in the directory pop-up, and all the files in that directory appear in the list box.

The files in the list box all contain the file extension for the file type displayed in the type box. For example, when Database is selected in Type, all files listed show the .DBF extension. To change file types, open the Type pop-up. Selecting each file type generates a different kind of action.

- Database   When you select the Database radio button and open a file, a database file is opened in the current work area (selected in the View window). If a database is already open in that area, it is closed before the new database is opened.
- Program   With the Program button selected, a program file is opened in a text editing window.
- File   This radio button causes a text file to be opened in a text editing window.
- Index   This button is only enabled if there is a database already open in the current work area. When you open an index, a bullet appears before the file name showing in the work area of the View window. If another

index is already open for this database, it is closed before the new one is opened.

You can open more than one index at a time by using the Setup... option from the Database menu or the Setup text button in the Browse window.
- Report   When you open a Report file, the report appears in a Report layout window.
- Label   Opening a Label file displays the file in the Label layout window. If you have created label files in other applications, they are also available in the Open File dialog, with an .LBL extension instead of FoxPro's .LBX extension.
- The other file options—Screen, Menu, Query, and Project—are explained in later chapters.

Once you have selected the appropriate file type, choose the file you want from the list box and choose Open. If you want to open all the files in the current directory, check the All Files check box. This opens all file types, not just the type selected in the Type box.

To create a new file, choose New. This dialog box is described under File New. To exit the dialog box without opening a file, choose Cancel.

See also: File New p. 10
              Window View p. 44

File Close

Choose this option to close the active window. This does not necessarily close the file associated with the window, as in the case of the View window. When you use File Close to close the View window, the files listed in the work area list remain open.

Mouse users can also close a window by clicking on the close box in the upper left corner of the window.

See also: Window View p. 44

File Save

This option saves any changes you have made to items in the active window (not any open windows behind it). The document remains open.

If the active document has not yet been saved or named, the Save As dialog box appears when you select Save. Save is disabled if you have made no changes since the document was last saved or when a window other than an editing window is frontmost (e.g., Browse, Command).

See also: File Save As p. 35

File Save As...

In the Save As dialog box in Fig. 1-35, you can name and save a new file, or rename and save a current file under the new name.

To name a new file, type the name in the text box and select Save. If the file has already been named, that name will show in the text box. If this is the first time the file has been saved, its new name appears at the top of the window and the file is saved. If you are renaming an existing file, that file is closed and the new title appears at the top of a new text editing window. If you have made changes since you last saved the old file, those changes appear in the new file, but not in the old one.

```
                    Save View as:
                    ►[..]                    Drive      D
                      CAMPREPO.VUE
Fig. 1-35. File Save As                      Directory  BOOK
dialog box.
                                                  «  Save   »

                    [ ] All Files                 <  Cancel >
```

Fig. 1-35. File Save As dialog box.

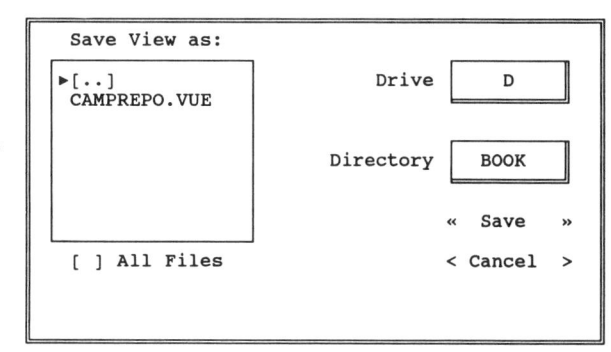

If you are saving a text file, you must type the .TXT extension if you want it included in the file name. Program files are automatically assigned a .PRG extension.

If you choose Save As... when the View window is active, you can save the current environment as a .VUE file. This file contains settings such as names of all files in use, relations that have been established, etc.

To exit the Save As... dialog box without saving or renaming a file, choose Cancel or press Esc.

See also: Window View p. 44

File Revert

If you have made changes to the currently displayed memo field or text, program, report, or label file since it was last saved, you can choose Revert to discard those changes and revert to the last saved version of the file.

Before it replaces the current version, FoxPro asks if you want to discard the changes. If you choose Yes, the document reverts to the old version; if you choose No, the current changes remain on screen.

File Printer Setup...

This dialog box lets you choose the print device for printing (Fig. 1-36). It is not available when you are browsing a database, when the View window is open, or when you are setting up a label.

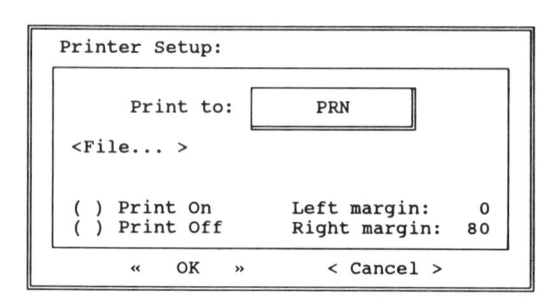

```
Printer Setup:

     Print to:   |   PRN   |
  <File... >

  ( ) Print On      Left margin:    0
  ( ) Print Off     Right margin:  80

       «   OK   »       < Cancel >
```

Fig. 1-36. Printer Setup dialog box.

Select a print device from the Print to pop-up menu, or select PRN to "print" to a file.

If you choose the File text button, a list of files appears. Select the file you want to print to.

You can disable printing by choosing the Print Off radio button, or select Print On to print.

Choose OK when you have selected the settings you want, or choose Cancel to exit without changing the current settings.

File Print

You can print a window or file using the Print option. The Print dialog box contains a Windows pop-up from which you can select the contents of the clipboard, the Command window, any open editing window, or the currently defined user window.

To print a file that is currently unopened, choose the File... text button and select the file to be printed.

When the Line Numbers box is enabled, checking it will automatically add line numbers to the output.

Choose OK to print your selection, or Cancel to exit without printing.

File Quit

The Quit option ends your FoxPro session and returns you to the system prompt or menu.

The Window menu

The Window menu (Fig. 1-37) lets you change the look of your windows on the screen and move them around so you can see what you are doing.

Fig. 1-37. The Window menu.

```
Hide
Move      ^F7
Size      ^F8
Zoom ↑    ^F10
Zoom ↓    ^F9
Cycle     ^F1
Color...

Command   ^F2
Debug
Trace
View
```

To use some of the options on the Window menu to change the Command window on the FoxPro sign-on screen, first move the window to the top left of the screen. From the keyboard:

1. Press Alt – W to open the Window menu.
2. Press M to select the Move option.
3. Use the arrow keys to move the window around. Try pressing PgUp and PgDn. Press Home and End to move the window to the left and right edges of the screen. Now use the keys to put the Command window at the left of the screen.
4. Press Enter to fix the window in place.

If you have a mouse, you do not need to use the menu options to move the window. Simply click on the window title and drag it to the middle of the screen. Now make the Command window bigger. From the keyboard:

1. Press Alt – W to open the Window menu.
2. Press S to select the Size option.
3. Use the arrow keys to make the borders stretch to the full size of the screen.
4. Press Enter to fix the size of the window.

With a mouse, you can skip the menu and click on the size control in the lower right corner of the window. Drag the frame until the Command window covers the screen.

You can hide the Command window, too. Hiding a window does not mean it is closed, it just means that it is not visible. To hide the command window:

1. Open the Window menu by pressing Alt – W or pointing to Window with the mouse.
2. Select Hide by pressing the spacebar or releasing the mouse button.

The Command window disappears. To make a hidden window reappear, choose the name of the window from the menu window. System windows like the Command window are always listed on the Window menu; other window names appear as they are opened.

To see the Command window again:

1. Open the Window menu.
2. Select Command. Use the ↓ to highlight the option, then press the spacebar, or drag the mouse to Command and release the button. The Command window reappears.

If you have more than one window open on the screen, you can size the windows so they all fit on the screen. This does not work very well if you have several windows. Another way to work with many windows open is to put one behind the other. Try this with the View window.

First, open the View window. Open the Window menu and select View. The View window opens in front of the Command window.

Because the Command window keeps track of all your operations, you might want to have a look at the commands you have executed. To do this, select Command from the Window by pressing Ctrl – F2 (the hot key). Now the Command window is in front of the View window.

Another way to change windows is to use the Cycle option. When you choose Cycle, the current window moves to the back and the next window is visible. This is handy when you have several windows on the screen because you can save opening the menu to select each window—just press Ctrl – F1 to see the next window.

The remaining Window options, in addition to the ones just covered, are described in detail in the following sections.

Window Hide

You can hide a window if you want to remove it from view without closing it. A hidden window continues to be listed at the bottom of the Window menu.

When you select Hide from the Window menu the active window is hidden from view. If you have more than one window open, you can hide them all by pressing the Shift key when you choose the Window menu. This replaces the Hide option with Hide All. Use the Show All option to unhide the windows.

To unhide a single window, choose the name of the window from the Window menu. System windows such as View and Command are always listed as options on the Window menu.

See also: Window Command p. 43
 Window View p. 44

Window Move

When you want to move a window around the screen, select the Move option from the Window menu. The border of the active window flashes and you can use the arrow keys to move it. PgUp and PgDn move the window to the top or bottom of the screen, and Home and End move it to the left and right edge of the screen. When the window is where you want it, press Enter to fix it in place.

If you have a mouse, you can move a window by clicking on its title and dragging the window to the location you want.

Shortcut key: Ctrl – F7

Window Size

Size lets you change the size of the active window. When you select Size from the Window menu, the border of the window flashes, and you can use the arrow keys to move the bottom and right borders in or out to size the window. Press Enter to fix the size of the window.

To size a window with the mouse, simply click on the size control in the lower right corner of the window and drag the border to the size you would like.

Shortcut key: Ctrl – F8

See also: Window Zoom *p. 39*

Window Zoom ↑

Zoom ↑ lets you enlarge the current window to fill the screen. If the window is already full size, Zoom shrinks it to its last size.

With a mouse, you can zoom a window by clicking on the zoom control in the upper right corner of the window.

Shortcut key: Ctrl – F10

See also: Window Size *p. 39*

Window Zoom ↓

Zoom ↓ lets you minimize the current window to one line tall by 16 characters wide.

With a mouse, you can minimize by double-clicking on the title bar of the window.

Shortcut key: Ctrl – F9

Window Cycle

Use Cycle when you want to cycle through your open windows. Each time you choose Cycle, the front window moves to the back and the following window becomes active and visible. Windows cycle in the order they were opened.

Shortcut key: Ctrl – F1

Window Color...

The Color menu option opens a dialog box called the Color Picker. This dialog box shown in Fig. 1-38 lets you determine the colors or intensity of menus, window, dialogs, alerts, etc.

```
System   File   Edit
                            12:23:45 pm   ←──( ) 7 Hot keys
                           CUSTOMER NAME  ←──( ) 2 Text box        ┌─────────┐
                                                                   │ Windows │
                Command                    ←──( ) 5 Title, idle    └─────────┘
      DO myprog■          Trace      ≡    ←──( ) 4 Title, active   «    OK    »
                  @ 1,16 GET customer     ←──( ) 1 Normal text
                  READ                    ←──( ) 6 Selected text   <  Cancel  >
      Ge          <Cancel> <Resume>       ←──( ) 9 Enabled ctrl.
                          .                                        <  Load... >
      _____            ←──( ) 8 Shadow
      «Topics» <Next> <Previous>          ←──( ) 10 Dsabl'd ctrl.  <  Save... >
                                          ←──( ) 3 Border
                                                                   <   Help   >
                  X X X X X X X X
                  X X X X X X X X
                » X X X X X X X X «
                  X X X X X X X X
                  X X X X X X X X                                  [X] Shadow
                  X X X X X X X X
                  X X X X X X X X                                  [ ] Blink
                  X X X X X X X X
```

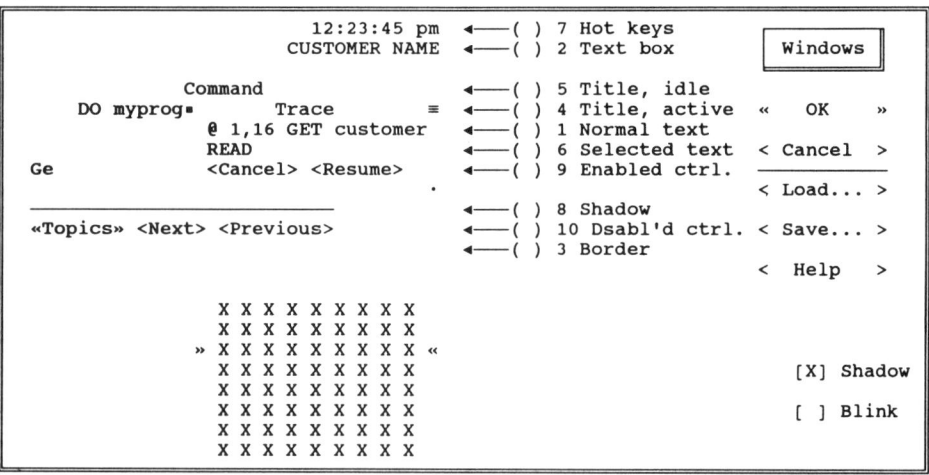

Fig. 1-38. Color Picker dialog box.

The pop-up at the upper right of the Color Picker selects the "scheme" you want to change. When you select the scheme pop-up, a list of schemes appears. The abbreviations apply to the following:

Option	Description
Usr Winds	User windows (SET colors).
Usr Menus	User menus (SET colors).
Menu Bar	Menus on the menu bar.
Menu Pops	Menu pop-ups.
Dialogs	Dialog boxes and system messages.
Dlog Pops	Pop-up controls and scrollable lists in dialogs.
Alerts	Alerts.

Windows	System windows.
Wind Pops	Menu pop-ups and scrollable lists in windows.
Browse	Browse window.
Report	Report Layout window.
Scheme 12-16	Reserved.
Scheme 17-24	Available for user applications.

When you select an option from the pop-up, the radio buttons in the dialog buttons adjust to reflect the available items in that scheme. Any selections you make elsewhere in the dialog box apply to that scheme only.

Load... Choose the Load... text button to see the list of available color sets. If your computer is not listed, choose a similar computer and choose Load. Choose OK from the Color Picker and look at the new colors for the scheme you selected. You can continue changing color sets until you find the one you like.

Modifying color sets If none of the color sets listed in the Load scroll box suit you, you can modify the existing color sets. To make major changes to a color set or to define a new set, see the SET command in chapter 3 on FoxPro SET commands. You can use the color palette in the lower portion of the Color Picker to choose color pairs.

A *color pair* is a combination of a background and a foreground color. Each X in the palette represents a foreground color, and the block behind it represents its background color. Color pairs for each scheme are listed in Table 1-1.

Once you have selected the scheme you want to modify, you can assign color pairs to each of the radio buttons showing in the Color Picker. When you select a radio button, the current color pair for that button appears selected in the color palette. To change the color pair, choosing another pair (use the arrow keys to move to the pair you want, and press the spacebar, or click on the pair with the mouse).

[ ]Shadow Three check boxes are also available to fine-tune your color scheme. If you check the Shadow box, shadows are added and the Shadow radio button appears. You can then select it to adjust your color pairs.

[ ]Bright When you choose Bright, 128 new color pairs become available if your monitor is EGA/VGA (you will not see the Bright check box if you do not have a color monitor). If you have a color monitor but you do not have a Bright check box, go to the Command window and type SET BLINK ON. Now the Bright check box should appear in the Color Picker.

[ ]Blink Choose Blink to make objects identified by your radio buttons blink. If you do not have a Blink check box, go to the Command window and type SET BLINK ON.

After you have selected all your color schemes, choose the Save... text button. Type a new name for the color set in the dialog box that appears, and choose Save.

Table 1-1. Color table by radio button.

Color scheme	User window (scheme 1)	User menus (scheme 2)	Menu bar (scheme 3)	Menu pop-ups (scheme 4)	Dialogs (scheme 5)	Dialog pop-ups (scheme 6)	Alert (scheme 7)	Windows (scheme 8)	Window pop-ups (scheme 9)	Browse (scheme 10)	Report (scheme 11)
Color pair											
Status/Hot key (7)	Clock		Hot keys	Hot keys	Hot keys		Hot keys	Hot keys		Current record	Band A, empty
Enhanced text (2)	GET fields	Enabled option	Enabled pads	Enabled option	Text box	Enabled option	Text box	Text box[1]	Enabled option	Current field	Report field
Message (5)	Title, idle	Message						Title, idle		Title, idle	Title, idle
Title heading (4)	Title, active	Menu titles						Title, active		Title, active	Title, active
Standard text (1)	SAY field		Disabled pads	Disabled option	Normal text	Disabled option	Normal text	Normal text[2]	Disabled option	Other records	Text & B full
Selected (6)	Selected item	Selected option	Selected pad	Selected option	Selected item	Selected option	Selected item	Selected text	Selected option	Selected text	Selected item
Enabled control (9)					Enabled control		Enabled control	Enabled control			Band A, full
Shadow (8)	Shadow	Shadow		Shadow	Shadow	Shadow	Shadow	Shadow	Shadow	Shadow	Shadow
Disabled control (10)					Disabled control		Disabled control	Disabled control			Band B, empty
Border	Border	Border		Border	Border	Border[3]	Border	Border	Border[3]	Border[4]	Border

1 For the View window and the Label Layout window only.
2 For the View and Label Layout windows, this color pair controls static text.
3 The background and foreground color of a scrollable list is the background color of color pair 3. The foreground colors are not bright. Thus, if you select a bright foreground for color pair 3, it will still be the color of the scrollable list border.
4 For windows with grids using scheme 8 or 10, the grid background is the background of color pair 1. The grid lines (foreground) is the background of color pair 3.

When you have finished assigning and saving color sets, exit the Color Picker by choosing OK. If you do not want your changes to be saved, exit by choosing Cancel.

See also: SET BLINK, p. 247

Window Command

Select Command to display the Command window on your screen. The Command window displays all the actions you generate when you make menu selections in the interface. You can also execute options by typing in the Command window.

Scroll the Command window to see previously executed actions. You can re-execute an action by highlighting the action and pressing Enter.

Shortcut key: Ctrl – F2

See also: Window Hide p. 38

Window Debug

The Debug option opens a window (Fig. 1-39) in which you can monitor values of variables and expressions and set break points in programs you have written.

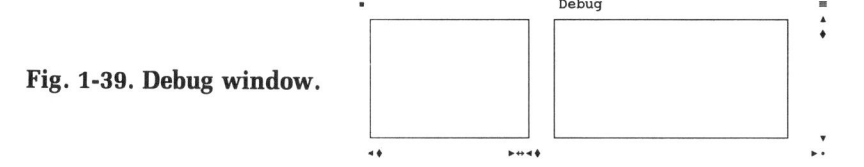

Fig. 1-39. Debug window.

To monitor values, Tab to the left partition of the window, or click there with the mouse. Type the variables and expressions you want to monitor. When you execute your program, the Debug window displays these values. You can type up to 16 debugging variables in the Debug window, and they can be related to more than one module or program.

A break point column separates the left and right partitions of the Debug window. To set a program break, mark a spot on the column by clicking to the right of the variable or expression that sets the break condition. With the keyboard, Tab until you see a highlighted block in the break point column, and use the ↑ and ↓ to move the block next to the variable or expression you want. Press the spacebar and a bullet appears to indicate a break point is set. You can remove a break point by clicking on it or pressing the spacebar when the cursor is positioned on it.

The program is suspended when the value of a variable or expression at a break point changes, and the message Do suspended appears on the screen. If the Trace window is not already displayed, it appears and you can change the values of the variables. You can choose Cancel or Resume from the Program menu or from the Trace window to cancel or resume execution of the program.

See also: Program Cancel *p. 118*
Program Resume *p. 118*
Window Trace *p. 44*

Window Trace

You can watch your program running in the Trace window shown in Fig. 1-40. Each program line is highlighted as it is executed.

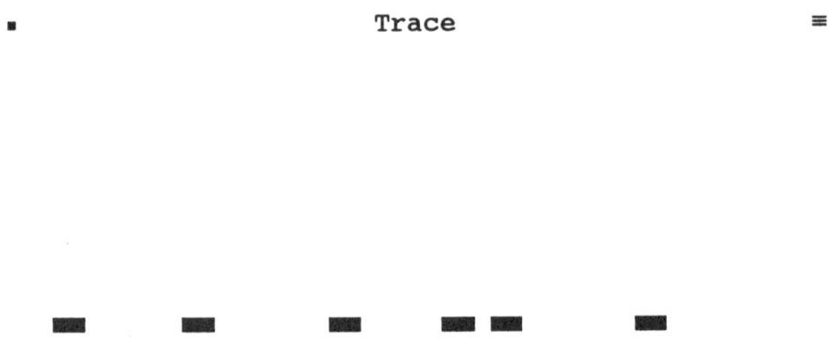

Fig. 1-40. Trace window.

You can set break points in the Trace window to suspend program execution. Position the cursor on the desired line and click with the mouse or press the spacebar to set a break point. A bullet appears to the left of the line, and the program will stop running when the break point is reached. You can choose Cancel or Resume from the Program menu or by selecting the text buttons in the Trace window. To remove a break point, click or press the spacebar on that line.

If you press Esc while a program is running, a dialog box appears. Choose Cancel, Suspend, or Ignore to continue execution. If you suspend execution, you can resume by choosing that option from the Program menu.

See also: Program Cancel *p. 118*
Program Resume *p. 118*
Window Debug *p. 43*

Window View

The View window is your master control center. From the View window, you can select work areas, open files, and set switches. To open the View window shown in Fig. 1-41, select View from the Window menu. Four text buttons are always in the upper left corner of the View window.

View   The View button is available when you are in one of the panels called up by On/Off, Files, or Misc. Selecting View closes the current panel and displays the View window.

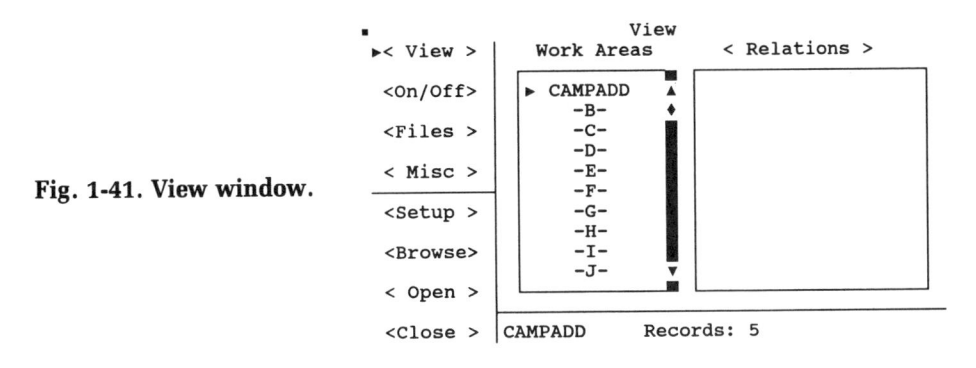

```
                          View
             ►< View >   Work Areas         < Relations >
                        ┌─────────────┬──────────────────┐
             <On/Off>   │ ► CAMPADD ▲ │                  │
                        │    -B-    ♦ │                  │
             <Files >   │    -C-      │                  │
                        │    -D-      │                  │
             < Misc >   │    -E-      │                  │
                        │    -F-      │                  │
Fig. 1-41. View window. │    -G-      │                  │
             <Setup >   │    -H-      │                  │
                        │    -I-      │                  │
             <Browse>   │    -J-    ▼ │                  │
                        │             ■                  │
             < Open >   │                                │
                        ├─────────────┴──────────────────┤
             <Close >   │CAMPADD      Records: 5         │
                        └────────────────────────────────┘
```

On/Off The On/Off panel contains 26 check boxes with setting controls for FoxPro. When you check a box, the command is set. For example, Help makes FoxPro Help available to you. These controls are shown in Fig. 1-42, and the commands are described under SET commands in chapter 3.

Files The Files panel (Fig. 1-43) allows you to change certain default settings. The Default Drive pop-up displays the current default drive. Select the pop-up to see a list of available drives, and choose the one you want to use.

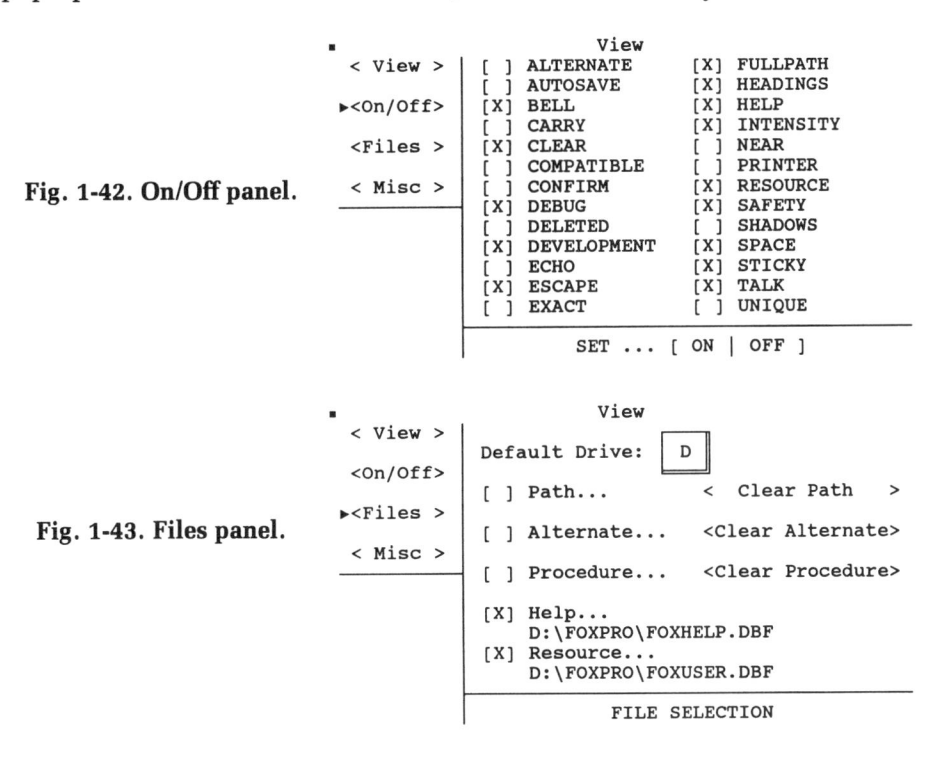

```
                                  View
             < View >    [ ] ALTERNATE      [X] FULLPATH
                         [ ] AUTOSAVE       [X] HEADINGS
             ►<On/Off>   [X] BELL           [X] HELP
                         [ ] CARRY          [X] INTENSITY
             <Files >    [X] CLEAR          [ ] NEAR
                         [ ] COMPATIBLE     [ ] PRINTER
Fig. 1-42. On/Off panel.  < Misc >    [ ] CONFIRM        [X] RESOURCE
                         [X] DEBUG          [X] SAFETY
                         [ ] DELETED        [ ] SHADOWS
                         [X] DEVELOPMENT    [X] SPACE
                         [ ] ECHO           [X] STICKY
                         [X] ESCAPE         [X] TALK
                         [ ] EXACT          [ ] UNIQUE
                         ─────────────────────────────────
                                  SET ... [ ON | OFF ]
```

```
                                  View
             < View >    Default Drive:  [ D ]
             <On/Off>
                         [ ] Path...       < Clear Path   >
             ►<Files >
Fig. 1-43. Files panel.  < Misc >    [ ] Alternate...  <Clear Alternate>

                         [ ] Procedure...  <Clear Procedure>

                         [X] Help...
                             D:\FOXPRO\FOXHELP.DBF
                         [X] Resource...
                             D:\FOXPRO\FOXUSER.DBF
                         ─────────────────────────────────
                                     FILE SELECTION
```

[ ]Path... In the Path dialog box, you can specify a directory path for FoxPro to search through to find a file that is not in the default directory. Choose the drive, directory, and/or subdirectories from the pop-up and the scrollable list.

The path you choose is displayed at the top of the box. When the path is correct, choose Select, and the path appears in the Files panel. You can deactivate this path by choosing the Clear Path text button.

[ ]**Alternate...** Use the Alternate dialog box to specify a file where you want the screen output to be saved. In the Alternate dialog box you can choose a file from the scrollable list or type a file name in the text box. Then choose Open.

The alternate file name appears in the Files panel. In the On/Off panel, check the Alternate check box to direct screen output to the alternate file. To close and deactivate the alternate file, choose Clear Alternate. The Alternate check box in the On/Off panel is automatically unchecked.

[ ]**Procedure...** This check box is for programmers who want to specify a procedure file to be searched when doing a program. The Procedure dialog box has a file list from which you select a procedure file. Then choose Open.

The name of the procedure file is shown in the Files panel. Choose Clear Procedure to deactivate and close the procedure file.

[ ]**Help...** In the Help dialog box you can indicate the name of the help file you want to be displayed when you press F1 or choose Help from the System menu. The default file is FOXHELP.DBF.

Select the file you want from the list box and choose Open. The file name appears in the Files panel, but you must check the Help box in the On/Off panel to enable the help file.

[ ]**Resource...** You can indicate the resource file you want to use with FoxPro in this dialog box. This is a file that contains resource information such as window size and location, color sets, text file preference settings, etc. You can create additional resource files for different color schemes.

Choose a file from the list box in the dialog box and choose Open. The resource file name appears in the files panel. Check the resource check box in the On/Off panel (you cannot edit the resource file when this box is checked).

Misc The Misc panel (Fig. 1-44) contains a variety of check and text boxes for determining certain formats and values in FoxPro.

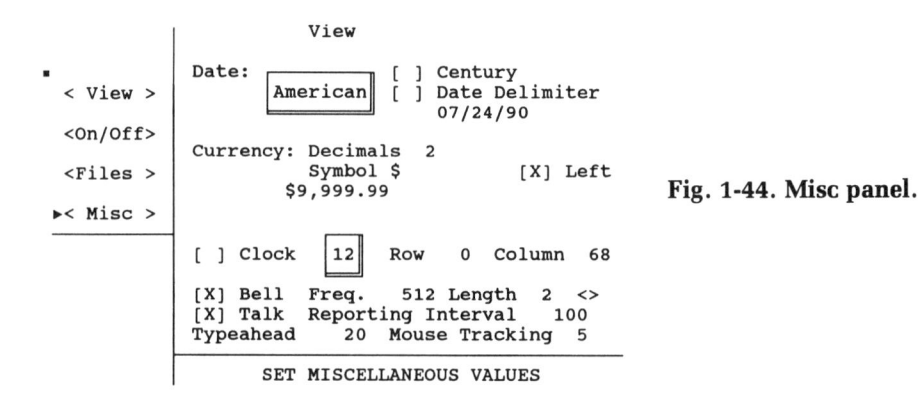

```
                      View
         Date:  ┌──────────┐  [ ] Century
< View >        │ American │  [ ] Date Delimiter
                └──────────┘      07/24/90
<On/Off>
         Currency: Decimals   2
<Files >           Symbol  $              [X] Left
                   $9,999.99
►< Misc >

         [ ] Clock  │12│  Row   0  Column  68

         [X] Bell   Freq.    512 Length   2   <>
         [X] Talk   Reporting Interval    100
         Typeahead    20  Mouse Tracking  5
         ─────────────────────────────────────
              SET MISCELLANEOUS VALUES
```

Fig. 1-44. Misc panel.

Date The Date pop-up contains a list of date formats from which you can choose. When you select a new date format, the date to the right of the pop-up is displayed in that format.

Checking the Century check box to the right of the pop-up causes the date to be displayed with all four digits in the year. Check Date Delimiter when you want to position the cursor in the displayed date and type a delimiter character (in the current date format, the slash is the delimiter).

Currency For currency formats, indicate the number of places to follow the decimal point in the Decimals box. Type the symbol you want to use in the Symbol box, and check the Left check box if you want the symbol to appear at the left of a currency value. A sample of your currency format is shown below the text boxes.

[ ]Clock Check the Clock box if you want a clock to appear on your screen. In the pop-up, select a 12-hour or a 24-hour clock, and indicate the row and column where you want the clock to appear in the text boxes.

[ ]Bell When you make an error in FoxPro, a bell will sound if the Bell check box is checked in Misc or in the On/Off panel. You can change the frequency (19 to 10,000) and the length (1 to 19) of the bell's tone. Choose the musical notes to hear the bell you have described.

[ ]Talk When the Talk box is checked, processing status information is displayed at regular intervals on your screen. The default Reporting Interval is 100, but you can specify an interval from 1 to 32,767.

Typeahead If you are a fast typist, you might want to increase the Typeahead value. This is the number of characters that can be held in the typeahead buffer. The buffer "remembers" the characters you have typed that have not yet appeared on the screen. The range of values from 1 to 32,000 can specify up to a maximum of 128 characters.

Mouse tracking This box lets you adjust the sensitivity of your mouse pointer. At 1 the pointer is least sensitive; the setting of 10 gives maximum sensitivity.

View work areas Before you can work with a database, you must select one of the 10 work areas listed in the View window as shown in Fig. 1-41. Move the cursor to the letter you want and press the spacebar. The diamond now points to that letter. You can then open a file, and you can open as many files as there are work areas.

Setup The four text buttons in the lower left region of the View window can be used when you want to work with a database in a work area.

The View Window Setup dialog box is just like the Setup dialog box on the Database menu. The Setup dialog lets you modify the structure of a database, add or remove indexes, or determine the display format of the database.

If no database is open when you choose Setup, an Open File dialog box appears so you can select and open a database. Then the Setup dialog box in Fig. 1-45 appears.

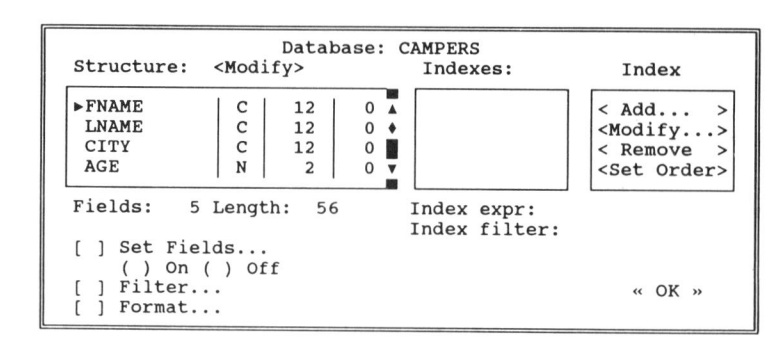

```
              Database: CAMPERS
Structure:  <Modify>         Indexes:           Index
 ▶FNAME       C | 12 | 0 ▲                    < Add... >
  LNAME       C | 12 | 0 ♦                    <Modify...>
  CITY        C | 12 | 0                      < Remove  >
  AGE         N |  2 | 0 ▼                    <Set Order>

Fields:    5 Length:   56     Index expr:
                              Index filter:
 [ ] Set Fields...
     ( ) On ( ) Off
 [ ] Filter...                              « OK »
 [ ] Format...
```

**Fig. 1-45.
Setup dialog
box.**

Structure The Structure list box in the upper left portion of the dialog box lists the fields in your database. Displayed beneath it are the number of fields and the total length of the fields.

To change the structure of the database, choose the Modify text button and the Modify Structure dialog box appears. This is the same dialog box that is used in the New option on the File menu. To add fields to the bottom of the list, type the field name, choose a field type, and enter the width and decimal places, if applicable.

Choose the type of field by pressing the spacebar in that column and selecting the type from the pop-up. Type options are:

Type	Specifications	Width restrictions
Character	Any type of data	Up to 254.
Numeric	Numeric data only	Up to 20, including the ± sign and decimal.
Date	Dates only	8.
Logical	Accepts T or F	1.
Memo	Any type of data	Expands to accept data entered; limited only by memory available.
Float	Scientific data	Up to 20, including the ± sign and decimal place.

You can insert fields by placing the cursor on the field above which you want to insert a field and choosing the insert text button, or Insert from the Structure menu. A Newfield appears in the selected position, and you can type the field name you want and choose the other specifications.

To delete a field, select that field and choose the Delete text button or the Delete option from the Structure menu.

To save your changes, choose OK. Answer Yes in the dialog box that appears if you want to make the changes permanent, or No to return to the Setup dialog box without saving them. To exit the Structure dialog box without saving changes, choose Cancel.

Indexes The names of any currently open indexes appear in the Indexes box in the middle of the Setup dialog box. An index rearranges your database according to specifications you choose. A database can have 25 index files open at a time, but only one at a time can be active. There can be no more than 25 indexes open for all 25 work areas in the View window. When an index is open with a database, a bullet appears next to the database name in the work area.

Add... Choose the Add... text button to call the Open File dialog box, where you can select the index you want and choose Open. The index name appears in the Indexes list box. The list includes .IDX and .CDX (multiple index) files.

You can continue to open indexes for the current database. The index with a bullet next to it controls the database order.

When you choose an index name in the Index list box, the Index expression and filter appear in the text boxes below the list. The Index expression is the field name on which the database is indexed. The filter is described in a later section.

If you want to create a new index, select New in the Open File box. When the Index dialog box (Fig. 1-46) appears, indicate the expression that will determine the order of the database by typing the field name in the Expr... text box, or by selecting the field from the scrollable list.

```
                        INDEX ON:
                        ┌──────────────┬───┐
                        │ FNAME        │ C │
                        │ LNAME        │ C │             «   OK   »
                        │ CITY         │ C │
                        │ AGE          │ N │           < Cancel >
Fig. 1-46. Index dialog box.    │ CAMP         │ C │
                        └──────────────┴───┘

                        <Expr...>

                        [ ] Unique
                        <For... >
```

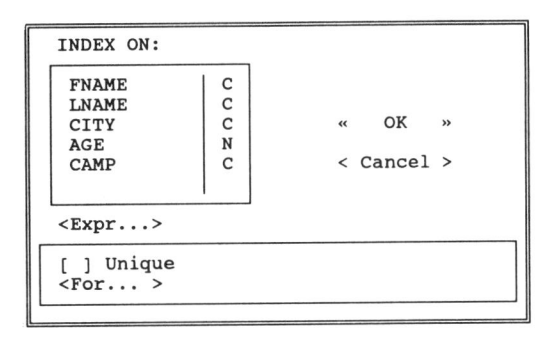

If you want the indexed database to include only one record for each index value, check the Unique check box. The database will then display the first record of each database type. For example, checking Unique in the Camp index would cause only one camper from each camp to appear on the list.

You can also limit the records shown in the indexed database by including a For clause in your index key expression. You can type the For clause in the For text box, or create the For clause in the Expression builder. For example, if you wanted to see only campers from Pahrump, you could use the For clause City = "Pahrump".

When your index selections are complete, choose OK. The Save As dialog box appears. Type a new file name (FoxPro automatically assigns the .IDX extension to index files) and choose Save. The new index name now appears in the Indexes box of the Setup dialog box.

Modify... If you want to change the key on which an index is sorted, select that index in the Index box and then choose the Modify text button in the Index box. This calls up the Index dialog that you used when you created the index. Change the key expression by selecting a new field name from the list box, or create a new For clause as you did before. Choose OK when you have made the modifications you want, and answer Yes if you want to save the changes permanently.

Remove Open indexes appear in the Indexes box in the Setup dialog box. When you select an index in the list and choose Remove, the index name is removed from the list and closed.

Set Order When more than one index is open for the current database, the active index is displayed with a bullet next to its name in the Index box. To use a different existing index to order your records, choose the index in the Index list and select Set Order.

If you choose the Index that is currently active, or if there is only one index open, the Set Order text button appears as No Order. If you choose No Order, none of the indexes is used to order the records in the database. They appear in the order they were originally entered.

[ ]**Set Fields...** The Set Fields dialog box shown in Fig. 1-47 lets you determine which fields will show when your database is displayed.

```
   Database Fields:                              Selected Fields:
  ┌─────────────────────────┐                   ┌─────────────────┐
  │ FNAME   │ C │ 12 │ 0 │    < Move → >        │                 │
  │ LNAME   │ C │ 12 │ 0 │                      │                 │
  │ CITY    │ C │ 12 │ 0 │    < All  → >        │                 │
  │ AGE     │ N │  2 │ 0 │                      │                 │
  │ CAMP    │ C │ 17 │ 0 │    < Remove >        │                 │
  │         │   │    │   │                      │                 │
  │         │   │    │   │    < Clear  >        │                 │
  └─────────────────────────┘                   └─────────────────┘
      Database:
      ┌─────────┐                                     <Cancel >
      │ CAMPERS │
      └─────────┘                                    «  OK   »
```

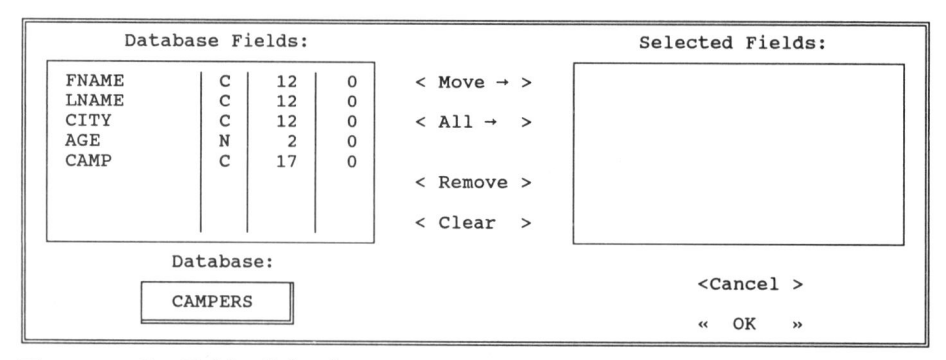

Fig. 1-47. Set Fields dialog box.

The current database is named in the Database box in the lower left corner of the Set Fields dialog box. Change databases by selecting another from the pop-up menu. All the fields in the current database appear in the Database Fields list box. Initially the Selected Fields box is empty. This is where the fields you choose will be displayed. The four text buttons in the middle of the box determine the display of the database:

- Move   Move puts the selected database field into the Selected Fields box (if Move is disabled, it is because you have not selected a field yet).
- All   To display all the fields, choose All (or exit the dialog box by choosing Cancel).

- Remove   Use the Remove button after selecting a field in the Selected Fields box to remove it from the selected display. This button is only enabled if you have selected a field in the box.
- Clear   Clear deletes all fields from the Selected Fields box. When you have selected the fields you want to display, choose OK. To exit the dialog without selected new fields, choose Cancel.

In the Setup dialog box, you need to select the appropriate radio button to make your selected display work. To show only the fields specified in the Set Fields box, turn Set Fields on. To display all the fields in the database, turn Set Fields off.

[ ]**Filter...**   You can filter out specified records for processing in your database. Choose Filter and enter the condition that filters out records in the Expression Builder (see File New for details on the Expression Builder). For example, if you only want to process records on campers from the Bumblebee Brigade, the filter expression would be Camp = "Bumblebee Brigade".

When you display your database, only the records that meet the filter condition appear. The other records still exist, they are just not shown. To remove the filter, uncheck the Filter... check box.

[ ]**Format...**   If you have created a user-defined format file using the Program menu, you can assign a format to a database for data input. Choose the Format check box and select the form from the scrollable list in the Open File dialog box. Then choose Open.

When the Format... box is checked in the Setup dialog box, the new format appears whenever you select Append or Change from the Browse menu to add records to the database.

See also: File New p. 10

<**Browse**>   When you select the Browse text button (one of the four buttons in the lower left of Fig. 1-41), a Browse window appears showing the active database. The database appears in the last format used: Append mode or Browse mode.

When you choose this option, the Browse menu is added to the menu bar. *(The rest of the Window View options follow the discussion about the submenu Browse.)*

The Browse menu

The options on this menu (shown in Fig. 1-48) let you view your database in different formats and edit your records. The Browse menu appears in the menu bar when you select Browse from Window View, when you append records with the Record Append option, and when you select Browse from the Database menu.

52 *The FoxPro User Interface*

```
Browse
┌─────────────────────────┐
│ Browse                  │
│ Grid Off                │
│ Unlink Partitions       │
│ Change Partition    ^H  │
├─────────────────────────┤
│ Size Field              │
│ Move Field              │
│ Resize Partitions       │
├─────────────────────────┤
│ Goto...                 │
│ Seek...                 │
│ Toggle Delete       ^T  │
│ Append Record       ^N  │
└─────────────────────────┘
```

Fig. 1-48. The Browse menu.

Browse Browse

If you open the Browse menu while you are in Append mode (fields are listed vertically), this option is available. It will become Change when you choose it. Choosing Browse changes the format of your database so that fields are listed horizontally, as in Fig. 1-49.

```
                         CAMPERS
 Fname     │ Lname    │ City         │ Age │ Camp
───────────┼──────────┼──────────────┼─────┼──────────────────
 Sherry    │ Stone    │ Sorana Beach │  12 │ Bumblebee Brigade
 Wally     │ Taylor   │ Provo        │  13 │ Lemur Lodge
 Bo        │ Travis   │ New Orleans  │  11 │ Woodpecker Wigwam
 Miles     │ Walker   │ Pahrump      │  12 │ Lemur Lodge
 Axl       │ Rose     │ Dearborn     │  14 │ Woodpecker Wigwam
```

Fig. 1-49. Records shown in Browse mode.

Press the Tab key to select successive fields to the right. When you Tab on the last field, the cursor moves to the first field in the database. The ↑ and ↓ move from row to row, and PgDn and PgUp move page by page. Press End to move to the end of your entry in a field, and press Home to move to the first character in the field. You can also use the scroll bars on the right and bottom of the Browse window.

You can edit and add records in the Browse window. To return to Append mode, choose Change from the Browse menu.

Browse Grid Off

In Browse mode, fields are displayed in a grid. To remove the vertical lines from the grid, choose Grid Off from the Browse menu. When you select this option, it changes to Grid On. Choose Grid On to replace the vertical lines.

Browse Unlink Partitions

If you have used Resize Partitions to create partitions in your Browse window, you can choose Unlink Partitions to display a vertical scroll bar in both partitions. This allows you to scroll each partition independently of the other. When you choose this option, it changes to Link Partitions.

Browse Change Partition

When you have two partitions, choosing Change Partition lets you activate the currently inactive partition by moving the cursor into that partition.

Shortcut key: Ctrl – H

See also: Browse Resize Partitions p. 53

Browse Size Field

You can change the width of your fields with this option. In Browse mode, choose Size and use the ← or → to stretch or shrink the selected field. Press Enter to fix the size of the field.

Browse Move Field

You can relocate a field by selecting it and choosing Move Field from the Browse menu. Use the arrow keys to drag the field to its new position and press Enter. You can move a field in Browse or Append mode.

Browse Resize Partitions

You can partition the Browse window so you can scroll part of the database while the other portion stays in place. This is useful when you want to scroll through several fields but you want to keep the name field (usually at the left end of the database) in view.

When you choose Resize Partitions, a flashing window splitter appears. Use the ← or → to move the splitter to the right of the fields you want to remain in view, and press Enter. The splitter stops flashing.

See also: Browse Change Partition p. 53

Browse Toggle Delete

When you want to remove a record from the database, you must mark it for deletion. Select the record to be removed and choose Toggle Delete. You will see a bullet at the beginning of the record. When you pack the database using the Database Pack option, the record will be deleted.

Shortcut key: Ctrl – T

See also: Database Pack *p. 81*

Browse Append Record

Append Record adds a blank record to the end of the database. You can use this option while in Append or Browse mode.

Shortcut key: Ctrl – N

Open   Choose Open from Window View to display a dialog box with a list of database files. The Drive pop-up tells you which drive you are using. Select it and press the spacebar to list all available drives. The Directory pop-up displays the current directory. You can change directories by opening the pop-up list and selecting a new directory, or by selecting the directory from the list box, if it is listed.

The list box contains the database files in the current directory. Notice that all the files have the .DBF extension. This indicates that they are database files. You cannot open other kinds of files with the Open option in the View window; you must use the File Open menu option.

If you want to open all the files in the directory, check the All Files box. Otherwise, select the database you want and choose Open. Choose Cancel to exit the dialog box without opening a file.

When you open a database, the name of the database appears in place of the letter designating the work area you selected.

Close   When you select Close from Window View, the database in the selected work area is closed and the letter name reappears.

Relations   The Relations box in Window View gives you the ability to relate more than one database based on a common reference point. A relation temporarily connects records so you can view all relevant information on one record at once.

For example, Sierra Sylvestri Campers have scheduled activities for each day at the camp. Setting up a relation between the list of campers and the schedule of activities can save some scanning for a camper who wants to know what activity is scheduled for today.

To set relations, first open the controlling database in the topmost free work area. This is the database to which another database will be related. The controlling database can be indexed or sorted in any order. In the example shown in Fig. 1-50, Campers is the controlling database, and it is indexed on Lname for the campers' convenience.

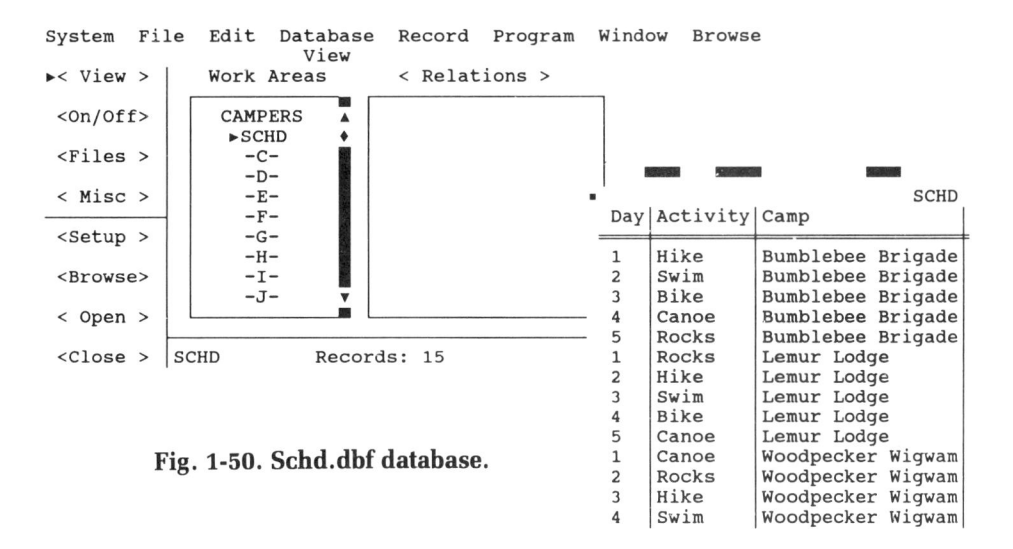

```
System  File  Edit  Database  Record  Program  Window  Browse
                        View
►< View >     Work Areas        < Relations >

<On/Off>      CAMPERS  ▲
              ►SCHD    ♦
<Files >      -C-
              -D-                                              SCHD
< Misc >      -E-                        Day│Activity│Camp
              -F-
<Setup >      -G-                         1 │Hike    │Bumblebee Brigade
              -H-                         2 │Swim    │Bumblebee Brigade
<Browse>      -I-                         3 │Bike    │Bumblebee Brigade
              -J-                         4 │Canoe   │Bumblebee Brigade
< Open >                                  5 │Rocks   │Bumblebee Brigade
                                          1 │Rocks   │Lemur Lodge
<Close >     SCHD       Records: 15       2 │Hike    │Lemur Lodge
                                          3 │Swim    │Lemur Lodge
                                          4 │Bike    │Lemur Lodge
                                          5 │Canoe   │Lemur Lodge
     Fig. 1-50. Schd.dbf database.        1 │Canoe   │Woodpecker Wigwam
                                          2 │Rocks   │Woodpecker Wigwam
                                          3 │Hike    │Woodpecker Wigwam
                                          4 │Swim    │Woodpecker Wigwam
```

Next open the related database in the work area directly below that of the controlling database. Figure 1-50 shows, for example, the Schd database with the activity schedule. The related database must be sorted or indexed on the field that will be used to relate the two databases. Because the field they have in common is Camp, the Schd database is indexed by Camp (it was also previously sorted by Day).

Now select the Campers database and choose the Relations text button. The file name Campers appears in the Relations box with a diamond pointing to it. This indicates that it is the controlling database.

Select the related database, Schd, and enter or select the field name Camp in the Expression Builder. Choose OK, and you will see an arrow point from the Campers file name to the Schd file name in the Relations box, as in Fig. 1-51. This shows the direction of the relation.

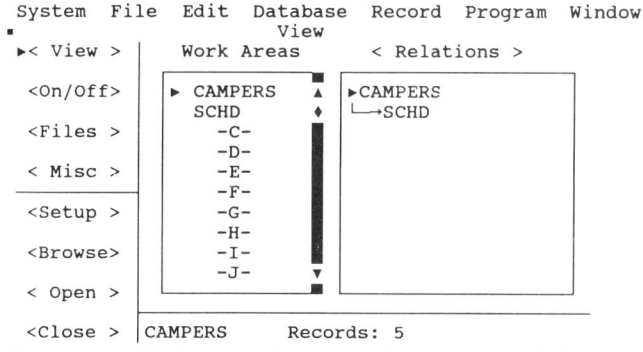

```
       System  File  Edit  Database  Record  Program  Window
                          View
       ►< View >     Work Areas        < Relations >

       <On/Off>    ► CAMPERS  ▲     ►CAMPERS
                     SCHD    ♦      └─►SCHD
       <Files >      -C-
                     -D-
       < Misc >      -E-
                     -F-
       <Setup >      -G-
                     -H-
       <Browse>      -I-
                     -J-      ▼
       < Open >

       <Close >    CAMPERS    Records: 5
```
Fig. 1-51. Relations set between Campers and Schd.

You can continue relating databases in this manner, as long as you have common fields, and the related database is indexed or sorted on the related field.

To see how the relation works, browse the Campers database. Suppose that it is day 1 and that camper Axl Rose wants to know what he will be doing today. Select his name in the Campers database. Now return to the View window and select the Schd work area. Choose Browse. When the Browse window opens, the first record with Woodpecker Wigwam, Axl's camp, is highlighted. According to the information in Fig. 1-52, Axl and the other Woodpeckers will be canoeing today.

CAMPERS

Fname	Lname	City	Age	Camp
Sherry	Stone	Sorana Beach	12	Bumblebee Brig
Wally	Taylor	Provo	13	Lemur Lodge
Bo	Travis	New Orleans	11	Woodpecker Wig
Miles	Walker	Pahrump	12	Lemur Lodge
Axl	Rose	Dearborn	14	Woodpecker Wig

SCHD

Day	Activity	Camp
1	Hike	Bumblebee Brigade
2	Swim	Bumblebee Brigade
3	Bike	Bumblebee Brigade
4	Canoe	Bumblebee Brigade
5	Rocks	Bumblebee Brigade
1	Rocks	Lemur Lodge
2	Hike	Lemur Lodge
3	Swim	Lemur Lodge
4	Bike	Lemur Lodge
5	Canoe	Lemur Lodge
1	Canoe	Woodpecker Wigwam
2	Rocks	Woodpecker Wigwam
3	Hike	Woodpecker Wigwam

Fig. 1-52. Related records in related databases.

If you want to change the *relational expression* (the field name that connects the databases), you can do so by selecting the related database and choosing a new field name.

To remove relations, choose the related database in the Relations list. When the Expression Builder appears, erase the field name from the expression box and choose OK.

The Database menu

The Database menu (Fig. 1-53) contains options that let you manipulate entire databases in a variety of ways.

Fig. 1-53. The Database menu.

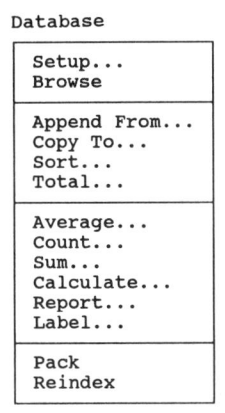

```
Database

Setup...
Browse

Append From...
Copy To...
Sort...
Total...

Average...
Count...
Sum...
Calculate...
Report...
Label...

Pack
Reindex
```

Use the Campers database you created with the File menu to use some of the options on the Database menu. First, open the Campers database using File Open or the Open text button in the View window.

Now choose Setup from the Database menu. Use the Setup dialog box in Fig. 1-54 to create an index file for the Campers file:

1. Choose Add.
2. Select New in the File Open box.
3. Select the .idx radio button, as this will be an .IDX file.
4. In the Index dialog box, select Lname and choose OK.

Fig. 1-54. Database Setup dialog box.

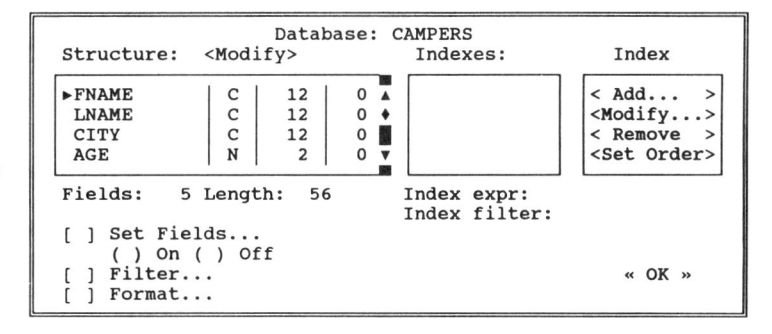

```
                    Database: CAMPERS
    Structure:  <Modify>        Indexes:            Index
    ►FNAME        C   12   0 ▲                    < Add...   >
     LNAME        C   12   0 ♦                    <Modify...>
     CITY         C   12   0 ■                    < Remove  >
     AGE          N    2   0 ▼                    <Set Order>

    Fields:   5  Length:  56       Index expr:
                                   Index filter:
    [ ] Set Fields...
        ( ) On ( ) Off
    [ ] Filter...                                  « OK »
    [ ] Format...
```

Lname is the index expression on which the index will be ordered. To name the index file, type Lname in the Save as... text area at the bottom of the dialog box. FoxPro automatically assigns the .IDX file extension. Then choose OK.

Now you can see the index name, Lname, in the Setup dialog. It has a bullet in front of it. This indicates it is the active index. Browse the database to see how the index works.

Two types of indexes can be created. Single index files track one sort order (for instance, Lname). Multiple index (.CDX) files maintain a group of sort orders (for instance, Lname order, Zip order, and Camp + Lname order). If the file is a multiple index file (the .cdx radio button in the index dialog is checked), you must enter a tag name for this index. If the file is a single index file (the .idx radio button is checked), you must enter a file name for the index file.

When creating tags in multiple index file, you must then choose Move to move the field into the Index list.

Choose Database Browse. The campers are listed in alphabetical order by their last names.

Sorting a file is different from creating an index. Press Esc to close the Browse window and choose Sort from the Database menu (Fig. 1-55).

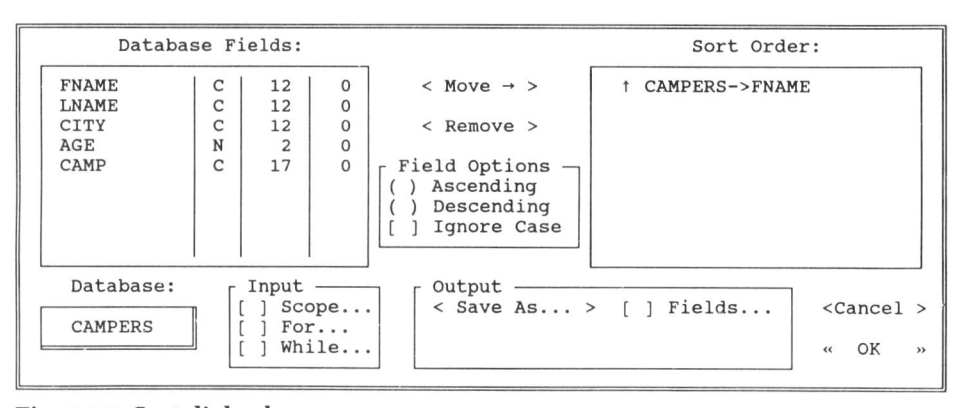

```
  Database Fields:                                Sort Order:
  FNAME      C   12   0      < Move → >      ↑ CAMPERS->FNAME
  LNAME      C   12   0
  CITY       C   12   0      < Remove >
  AGE        N    2   0
  CAMP       C   17   0    ┌ Field Options ─┐
                           │ ( ) Ascending  │
                           │ ( ) Descending │
                           │ [ ] Ignore Case│
                           └────────────────┘

  Database:       ┌ Input ──────┐  ┌ Output ───────────────────┐
                  │ [ ] Scope...│  │ < Save As... >  [ ] Fields...   <Cancel>
  CAMPERS         │ [ ] For...  │  │
                  │ [ ] While...│  │                            «  OK  »
```

Fig. 1-55. Sort dialog box.

Sort the Campers database on the Fname field.

1. Highlight the Fname field and press Enter. It appears in the Sort Order box.
2. Make sure the Ascending radio button is on.
3. Enter Fname in the Save As text box. Indexes and sort files do not have to be named with the same name as their index or sort expressions, but it is one way to keep them straight. When you create indexes and sort files for several databases, you will want to use names that reflect both the original database and the index key, if possible.
4. Choose OK.

If you were to browse the Campers database now, you would still see the names alphabetized by last name. That is because sorting creates a whole new file. To see the Campers file sorted, use File Open to open the Fname file. Notice that it has the .DBF file extension, just like a normal database.

Now choose Browse from the Database menu. The campers are in order by first name.

Find out the average age of the campers.

1. Choose Average from the Database menu.
2. Enter Age in the Expr text box.
3. Choose OK.

You will see the average age in the lower left corner of your screen.

Now you are ready to find out more about the additional elements involved in Setup, Sort, and the other options on the Database menu.

See also: File New p. 10
File Open p. 33
Window View p. 44

Database Setup...

Set up the current work area with this option. It performs the same functions as the Setup text button in the View window. If no database is open when you choose Setup, an Open File dialog box appears so you can select and open a database. Then the Setup dialog box in Fig. 1-56 appears.

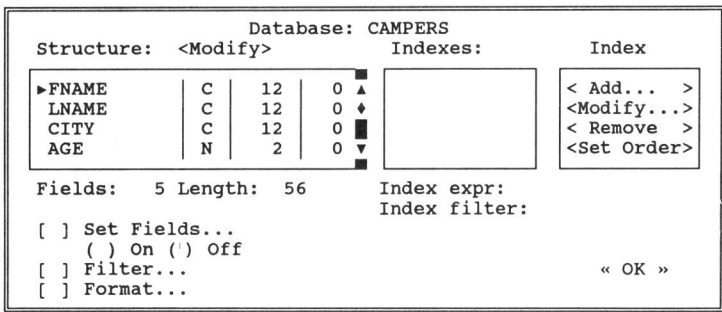

Fig. 1-56. Setup dialog box.

```
                      Database: CAMPERS
       Structure:  <Modify>         Indexes:            Index
       ►FNAME       C   12   0                      < Add...  >
        LNAME       C   12   0                      <Modify...>
        CITY        C   12   0                      < Remove  >
        AGE         N    2   0                      <Set Order>

       Fields:  5  Length:  56         Index expr:
                                       Index filter:
       [ ] Set Fields...
           ( ) On  (•) Off
       [ ] Filter...                                  « OK »
       [ ] Format...
```

Structure The Structure list box in the upper left portion of the dialog box lists the fields in your database. Displayed beneath it are the number of fields and the total length of the fields.

Modify If you want to change the structure of the database, choose the Modify text button, and the Modify Structure dialog box appears as shown in Fig. 1-57. This is the same dialog box that is used in the New option on the File menu.

You can add fields to the bottom of the list by typing the field name, choosing a field type, and entering the width and decimal places, if applicable.

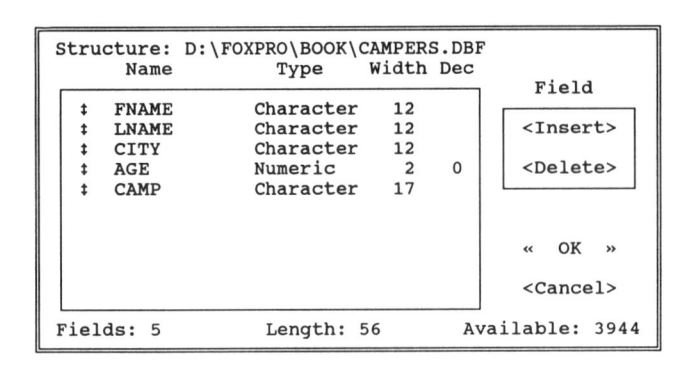

```
Structure: D:\FOXPRO\BOOK\CAMPERS.DBF
        Name            Type        Width  Dec
                                                   Field
    ↕   FNAME           Character     12
    ↕   LNAME           Character     12           <Insert>
    ↕   CITY            Character     12
    ↕   AGE             Numeric        2    0      <Delete>
    ↕   CAMP            Character     17


                                                 «  OK  »

                                                  <Cancel>


Fields: 5          Length: 56       Available: 3944
```

Fig. 1-57. Setup Modify Structure dialog box.

Choose the type of field by pressing the spacebar in that column and selecting the type from the pop-up. Type options are:

Type	Specifications	Width restrictions
Character	Any type of data	Up to 254.
Numeric	Numeric data only	Up to 20, including ± sign and decimal.
Date	Dates only	8.
Logical	Accepts T or F	1.
Memo	Any type of data	Expands to accept data entered; limited only by memory available.
Float	Scientific data	Up to 20, including ± sign and decimal place.

You can insert fields by placing the cursor on the field above which you want to insert a field and choosing the insert text button, or Insert from the Structure menu. A Newfield appears in the selected position, and you can type the field name you want, and choose the other specifications.

To delete a field, select that field and choose the Delete text button or the Delete option from the Structure menu.

To save your changes, choose OK. Answer Yes in the dialog box that appears if you want to make the changes permanent, or No to return to the Setup dialog box without saving them.

To exit the Structure dialog box without saving changes, choose Cancel.

Indexes   If there are any indexes currently open, they appear in the Indexes box in the middle of the Setup dialog box. An index orders your database according to specifications you choose. A database can have 25 indexes open at a time, but only one is active. There can be no more than 25 indexes open for all 25 work areas in the View window. When an index is open with a database, a bullet appears next to the database name in the work area.

Add...   To open an existing index, choose the Add... text button. This brings up an Open File dialog box, where you can select the index you want and choose Open. The index name appears in the Indexes list box.

You can continue to open indexes for the current database. The index with a bullet next to it controls the database order.

When you choose an index name in the Index list box, the index expression and filter appear in the text boxes below the list. The Index expression is the field name on which the database is indexed. The filter will be described in a later section.

The Add text button also lets you create a new index. After selecting Add..., select New in the Open File box. When the Index dialog box appears (Fig. 1-58), indicate the expression that will determine the order of the database by typing the field name in the Expr... text box, or by selecting the field from the scrollable list.

Fig. 1-58. New Index dialog box.

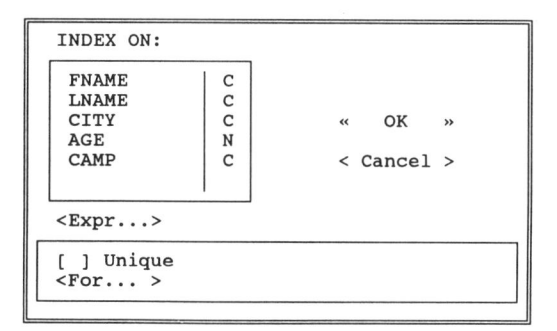

```
INDEX ON:

  FNAME      C
  LNAME      C
  CITY       C         «   OK    »
  AGE        N
  CAMP       C         < Cancel >

<Expr...>

[ ] Unique
<For... >
```

If you want the indexed database to include only one record for each index value, check the Unique check box. The database will then display the first record of each database type. For example, checking Unique in the Camp index would cause only one camper from each camp to appear on the list.

You can also limit the records shown in the indexed database by including a For clause in your index key expression. You can type the For clause in the For text box, or create the For clause in the Expression Builder. For example, if you wanted to see only campers over the age of 11, you could use the For clause Age 11.

When you have made your index selections, choose OK. The Save As dialog box appears. Type a new file name (FoxPro automatically assigns the .IDX extension to index files) and choose Save. The new index name now appears in the Indexes box of the Setup dialog box.

Modify... If you want to change the index key for an index, select that index in the Index box and then choose the Modify text button in the Index box. This calls up the Index dialog that you used when you created the index. Change the key expression by selecting a new field name from the list box, or create a new For clause as you did before. Choose OK when you have made the modifications you want, and answer Yes if you want to save the changes permanently.

Remove Open indexes appear in the Indexes box in the Setup dialog box. When you select an index in the list and choose Remove, the index name is removed from the list and closed.

Set Order If you have more than one index open for the current database, or a multiple index file is open the index (or tag) with the bullet next to its name in the Index box is the one determining the order of the records in the database. To use a different existing index to order your records, choose the index in the Index list and select Set Order.

If you choose the Index that is currently active, or if there is only one index open, the Set Order text button appears as No Order. If you choose No Order, none of the indexes is used to order the records in the database. They appear in the order they were originally entered.

[ ]**Set Fields...** The Set Fields dialog box shown in Fig. 1-59 lets you determine which fields will show when your database is displayed.

```
      Database Fields:                          Selected Fields:
    ┌─────────┬───┬────┬───┐
    │ FNAME   │ C │ 12 │ 0 │   < Move → >
    │ LNAME   │ C │ 12 │ 0 │
    │ CITY    │ C │ 12 │ 0 │   < All → >
    │ AGE     │ N │  2 │ 0 │
    │ CAMP    │ C │ 17 │ 0 │
    │         │   │    │   │   < Remove >
    │         │   │    │   │
    │         │   │    │   │   < Clear >
    └─────────┴───┴────┴───┘
           Database:                                  <Cancel>
          ┌─────────┐
          │ CAMPERS │                               «   OK   »
          └─────────┘
```

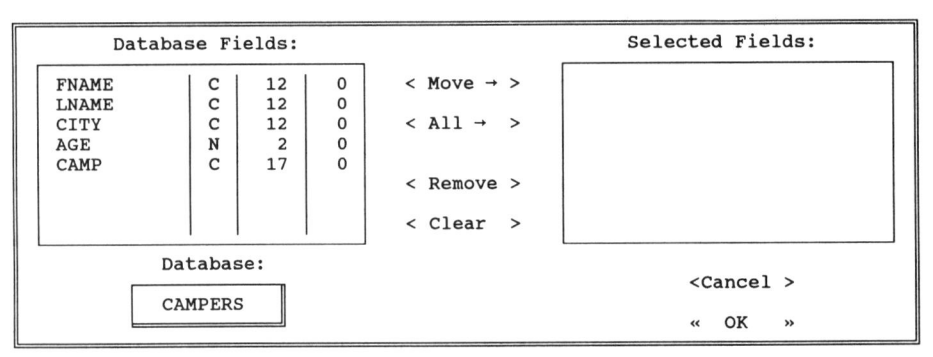

Fig. 1-59. Set Fields dialog box.

The current database is named in the Database box in the lower left corner of the Set Fields dialog box. You can change databases by selecting another from the pop-up menu. All the fields in the current database appear in the Database Fields list box. Initially the Selected Fields box is empty. This is where the fields you choose will be displayed. The four text buttons in the middle of the box determine the display of the database:

- Move When you select a database field from the Fields box and choose Move, that field appears in the Selected Fields box (if Move is disabled, it is because you have not selected a field yet).
- All If you want all the fields to be displayed, you can choose All (or exit the dialog box by choosing Cancel).
- Remove Use the Remove button after selecting a field in the Selected Fields box to remove it from the selected display. This button is only enabled if you have selected a field in the box.
- Clear Choose Clear to delete all fields from the Selected Fields box.

When you have selected the fields you want to display, choose OK. To exit the dialog without selecting new fields, choose Cancel.

In the Setup dialog box, you need to select the appropriate radio button to make your selected display work. To show only the fields specified in the Set Fields box, turn Set Fields on. To display all the fields in the database, turn Set Fields off.

[ ]**Filter...**   You can create a filter that allows only certain records to be available for processing in your database. Choose Filter and enter the condition that filters out records in the Expression Builder (see File New for details on the Expression Builder). For example, if you only want to process records on campers from the Bumblebee Brigade, the filter expression would be Camp = "Bumblebee Brigade".

When you display your database, only the records that meet the filter condition appear. The other records still exist, they are just not shown. To remove the filter, uncheck the Filter... check box.

[ ]**Format...**   If you have created a user-defined format file using the Program menu, you can assign a format to a database for data input. Choose the Format check box and select the form from the scrollable list in the Open File dialog box. Then choose Open.

When the Format... box is checked in the Setup dialog box, the new format appears whenever you select Append or Change from the Browse menu to add records to the database.

See also: File New p. 10

Database Browse

In the Browse window, you can view your database and edit records. The name of the database appears in the Browse window as shown in Fig. 1-60.

Fig. 1-60. Browse window.

Fname	Lname	CAMPERS City	Age	Camp
Axl	Rose	Dearborn	14	Woodpecker Wig
Sherry	Stone	Sorana Beach	12	Bumblebee Brig
Wally	Taylor	Provo	13	Lemur Lodge
Bo	Travis	New Orleans	11	Woodpecker Wig
Miles	Walker	Pahrump	12	Lemur Lodge

There are three ways to open a Browse window in the Interface:

- Choose Browse from the Database menu.
- Choose the Browse text button in the View window when a database is open.

- Double click on a work area in the View window that has an open database.

If you choose the Browse option from the Database menu when no database is open, an Open File dialog box appears. Select the database you want to browse and choose Open.

When you make changes to the database after browsing, those changes are saved, but when you subsequently choose Browse, the last version of the database is displayed. Notice that the Command window says Browse Last. To browse the new version of your database, you must activate the Command window (Ctrl – F2) and type Browse.

You can move around the records in your Browse window to view and edit particular fields. Press the Tab key to select successive fields to the right. When you Tab on the last field, the cursor moves to the first field in the database. The ↑ and ↓ move from row to row, and PgDn and PgUp move page by page. Press End to move to the end of your entry in a field, and press Home to move to the first character in the field. You can also use the scroll bars on the right and bottom of the Browse window.

To close a Browse window, choose Close from the File menu.

See also: Window Command p. 43
Window View p. 44

(The rest of the Database options follow the discussion about the submenu Browse.)

The Browse menu

Whenever a Browse window is active, the Browse menu is added to the menu bar (Fig. 1-61). The Browse menu also appears in the menu bar when you append records after creating a new file or choosing the Record Append option.

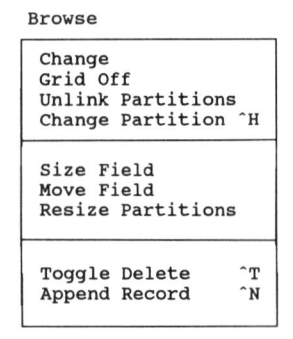

```
Browse
┌─────────────────────┐
│ Change              │
│ Grid Off            │
│ Unlink Partitions   │
│ Change Partition ^H │
├─────────────────────┤
│ Size Field          │
│ Move Field          │
│ Resize Partitions   │
├─────────────────────┤
│ Toggle Delete    ^T │
│ Append Record    ^N │
└─────────────────────┘
```

Fig. 1-61. The Browse menu.

Browse Append/Change

If you open the Browse menu just after opening your Browse window, the database is displayed in Browse mode. The Change option appears on the menu. When you choose Change, field names and contents are listed vertically, instead of horizontally. This is called the Append mode and is shown in Fig. 1-62.

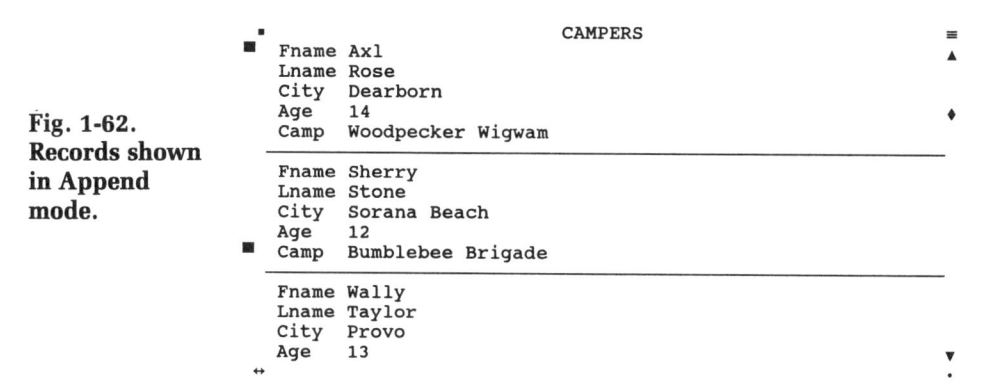

Fig. 1-62.
Records shown
in Append
mode.

```
                              CAMPERS
     Fname  Axl
     Lname  Rose
     City   Dearborn
     Age    14
     Camp   Woodpecker Wigwam

     Fname  Sherry
     Lname  Stone
     City   Sorana Beach
     Age    12
     Camp   Bumblebee Brigade

     Fname  Wally
     Lname  Taylor
     City   Provo
     Age    13
```

If you used the Append option from the Record menu to go to Append mode, the Change option is named Append when you are in Browse mode.

If you open the Browse menu while you are in Append mode, the option appears as Browse. Choosing Browse changes the format of your database so that fields are listed horizontally.

Browse Grid Off

In Browse mode, fields are displayed in a grid. To remove the vertical lines from the grid, choose Grid Off from the Browse menu. When you select this option, it changes to Grid On. Choose Grid On to replace the vertical lines.

Browse Unlink Partitions

If you have used Resize Partitions to create partitions in your Browse window you can choose Unlink Partitions to display a vertical scroll bar in both partitions. This allows you to scroll each partition independently of the other. When you choose this option, it changes to Link Partitions.

See also: Browse Resize Partitions p. 66

Browse Change Partition

When you have two partitions, choosing Change Partition lets you activate the currently inactive partition by moving the cursor into that partition.

Shortcut key: Ctrl – H

See also: Browse Resize Partitions p. 66

Browse Size Field

You can change the width of your fields with this option. In Browse mode, choose Size and use the Left or Right arrow to stretch or shrink the selected field. Press Enter to fix the size of the field.

Browse Move Field

You can relocate a field by selecting it and choosing Move Field from the Browse menu. Use the arrow keys to drag the field to its new position and press Enter. You can move a field in Browse or Append mode.

Browse Resize Partitions

You can partition the Browse window so you can scroll part of the database while the other portion stays in place. This is useful when you want to scroll through several fields but you want to keep the name field (usually at the left end of the database) in view.

When you choose Resize Partitions, a flashing window splitter appears, as shown in Fig. 1-63. Use the ← or → to move the splitter to the right of the fields you want to remain in view, and press Enter. The splitter stops flashing.

See also: Browse Change Partition p. 65
Browse Unlink Partitions p. 65

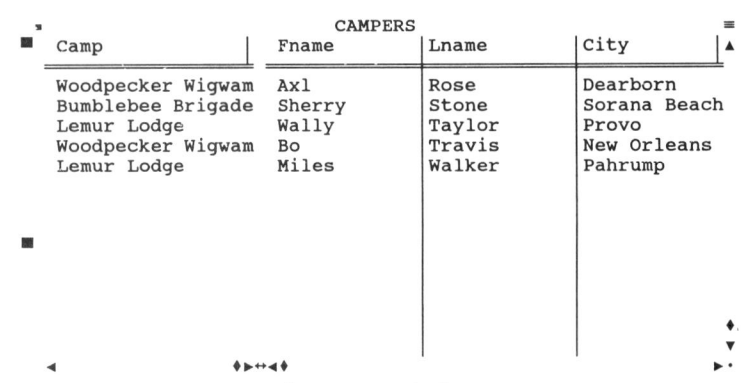

```
                    CAMPERS
 Camp              | Fname   | Lname   | City
 ------------------|---------|---------|-------------
 Woodpecker Wigwam | Axl     | Rose    | Dearborn
 Bumblebee Brigade | Sherry  | Stone   | Sorana Beach
 Lemur Lodge       | Wally   | Taylor  | Provo
 Woodpecker Wigwam | Bo      | Travis  | New Orleans
 Lemur Lodge       | Miles   | Walker  | Pahrump
```

Fig. 1-63. A partitioned Browse window.

Browse Toggle Delete

When you want to remove a record from the database, you must mark it for deletion. Select the record to be removed and choose Toggle Delete. You will see a bullet at the beginning of the record. The record is not actually removed until you pack the database using the Database Pack option.

Shortcut key: Ctrl – T

See also: Database Pack p. 81

Browse Append Record

Append Record adds a blank record to the end of the database. Because a blank record is automatically added when you complete entry of a record in a new database, Append Record is not available when you are browsing a file just created with the File New option.

Database Append From...

You can add records to the current database from another database with the Append From... option (Fig. 1-64).

Fig. 1-64. Append From dialog box.

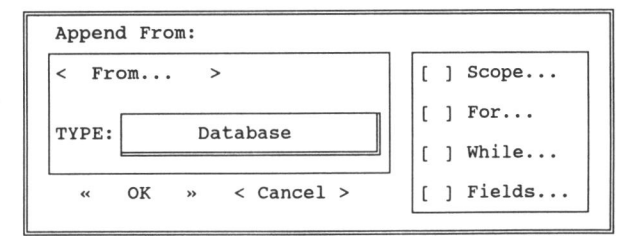

```
Append From:
<   From...   >            [ ] Scope...
                            [ ] For...
TYPE:  [  Database  ]       [ ] While...
   «   OK   »   < Cancel >  [ ] Fields...
```

From...   The Append From... dialog box has a From... text box in which you can type the name of the file you want to copy records from. If you select the From... text button a directory dialog appears and you can select the file from the scrollable list and choose OK to enter the file name in the From... text box.

The From... file does not have to be a database. You can select another file type from the Type pop-up. The pop-up contains:

Database	Standard FoxPro database with .DBF extension.
Delimited with Tabs	A text file in which each field is separated by Tabs.
Delimited with Commas	A text file in which each field is separated by commas.
Delimited with Spaces	A text file in which each field is separated by one space.
SDF	A text file in which the records have a fixed length and end with a carriage return and line feed.
DIF	Visicalc's Data Interchange Format.

FW2	Ashton Tate's Famework II.
MOD	Microsoft Multiplan version 4.01.
PDOX	Borland's Paradox version 3.5.
RPD	Ashton Tate's RapidFile version 1.2.
SYLK	Symbolic Link Interchange Format.
WK1	Lotus 1-2-3, version 2.x.
WK3	Lotus 1-2-3, version 3.x.
WKS	Lotus 1-2-3, version 1.x.
WR1	Lotus Symphony, version 1.1 or 1.2.
WRK	Lotus Symphony, version 1.0.
XLS	Microsoft Excel, version 2.0.

[ ]**Scope...** Four check boxes are to the right of the From... text box. The first calls the Scope... dialog box, which contains four radio buttons that determine which records will be included in the Append. Select the All button to append all records. It is only necessary to use the All button if you previously made some other selection. If you do not specify any scope, all records will automatically be appended.

Choose Next to append the next n number of records in the database. Next 1 appends just the current record.

When you choose Record, enter the record number that you want appended. If you want to append the current record and all the rest of the records in the database, choose Rest.

[ ]**For...** You can use a For clause to append records that meet certain criteria. For example, Lname > "B" would append only records with a last name entry that starts with C or higher. Choose fields and operators in the Expression Builder, or enter the For clause in the Expression Builder text box.

You will notice in the Expression Builder that the database shown in the pop-up is the name of the active database, and the fields listed are only the fields in that database. You cannot enter criteria that use field names that are in the database from which you are appending. For example, if you wanted to create a database of first and last names of campers, but you only want campers from the Lemur Lodge, you could not enter that criteria in the Expression Builder. You must add the field to the current database to include it in a For clause.

[ ]**While...** If you create a While clause in the Expression Builder, FoxPro appends records as long as the clause remains true. For example, campers were entered into the database by camp. You could create a While clause that would evaluate records according to the criterion Camp = "Bumblebee Brigade". As FoxPro moves down the list of records, as long as Bumblebee Brigade appears in the Camp field, records will be appended. When FoxPro reaches the first Lemur Lodge camper, it stops appending.

When you create the While clause in the Expression Builder, you must choose from fields in the active database. If you want to use a field from the closed database in your While clause, you must add it to the active database for the Append and delete afterward.

[ ]**Fields...**   The Fields... dialog box (Fig. 1-65) lets you pick the fields you want to be appended into the database. It is the same dialog box used in the Setup option on the Database menu. The Database pop-up displays the current database.

```
         Database Fields:                            Selected Fields:
    FNAME       C  | 12 | 0      < Move → >
    LNAME       C  | 12 | 0
    CITY        C  | 12 | 0      < All  → >
    AGE         N  |  2 | 0
    CAMP        C  | 17 | 0      < Remove >

                                  < Clear  >

              Database:
                                                       <Cancel >
              CAMPERS
                                                     «   OK   »
```

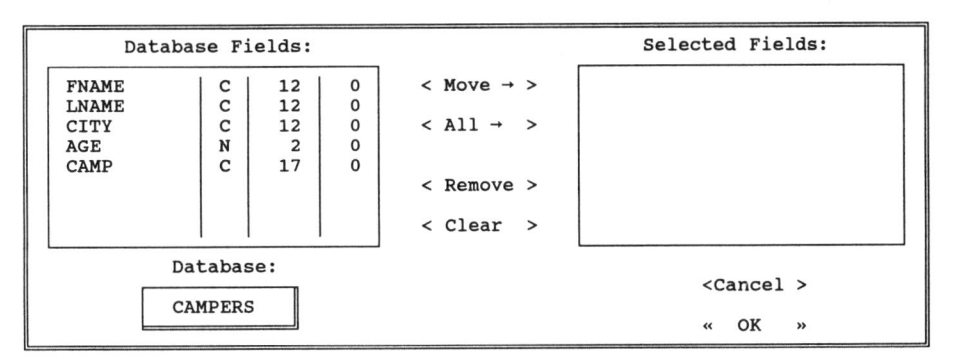

Fig. 1-65. Fields dialog box.

Select the desired field in the Field box and choose Move. It appears in the Selected Fields box.

Choose All to append all fields. It is only necessary to do this if you previously selected specific fields. If you do not specify any fields, all fields will automatically be appended.

To remove a field from the Selected Fields list, choose it in the list and select Remove. Choosing Clear removes all fields from the Selected Fields box.

When your selections are correct, choose OK to confirm them, or choose Cancel to exit the dialog box without specifying fields to be appended.

See also: Database Setup... p. 59

Database Copy To...

The Database Copy To... option lets you copy records from the active database into a new file (Fig. 1-66).

In the Copy To dialog box, type the new file name in the Save As text box. If you select the Save As... text button, the Save As dialog box appears and you can type the name there.

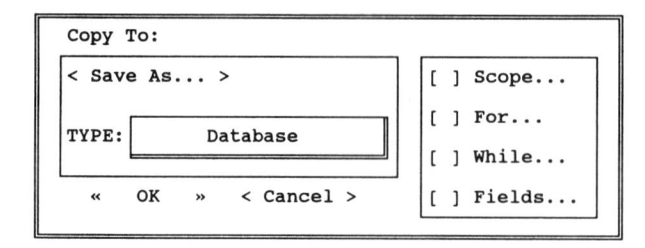

```
┌─────────────────────────────────────────────┐
│ Copy To:                                    │
│                                             │
│  < Save As... >        [ ] Scope...         │
│                                             │
│                        [ ] For...           │
│  TYPE: │  Database  │                       │
│                        [ ] While...         │
│                                             │
│    «  OK  »  < Cancel >  [ ] Fields...      │
│                                             │
└─────────────────────────────────────────────┘
```

Fig. 1-66. Copy To dialog box.

You can save the current file to a file other than a database. Choose one of the following from the Type pop-up:

Database	Standard FoxPro database with .DBF extension.
Delimited with Tabs	A text file in which each field is separated by Tabs.
Delimited with Commas	A text file in which each field is separated by commas.
Delimited with Spaces	A text file in which each field is separated by one space.
SDF	A text file in which the records have a fixed length and end with a carriage return and line feed.
DIF	Visicalc's Data Interchange Format.
FW2	Ashton Tate's Famework II.
MOD	Microsoft Multiplan version 4.01.
PDOX	Borland's Paradox version 3.5.
RPD	Ashton Tate's RapidFile version 1.2.
SYLK	Symbolic Link Interchange Format.
WK1	Lotus 1-2-3, version 2.x.
WK3	Lotus 1-2-3, version 3.x.
WKS	Lotus 1-2-3, version 1.x.
WR1	Lotus Symphony, version 1.1 or 1.2.
WRK	Lotus Symphony, version 1.0.
XLS	Microsoft Excel, version 2.0.

[ ]**Scope...** The four radio buttons in the Scope dialog box let you set conditions for the records to be copied. Choose All if you want all records copied (FoxPro copies all records automatically if no scope is indicated or choose All if you had previously made some other selection). If you select Next, type the number of records you want copied. Next starts with the current record. For the Record radio button, enter the number of a single record you want copied. Rest copies the current record and all the records following.

[ ]**For...** You can select records that meet certain criteria by creating a For clause in the Expression Builder. For example, if you wanted to copy records for

all campers whose first names were Wally or Sherry, your For clause would be Fname = "Wally" .or. Fname = "Sherry".

[ ]**While...** You can specify a While condition in the Expression Builder that will be tested against each record in the order that it is listed in the database. For example, if the While clause says Age < 12, FoxPro stops copying records when it reaches the first record in which the age is not less than 12.

[ ]**Fields...** The Fields dialog box lets you specify which fields you want copied. This is the same dialog box used in the Database Setup option.

The fields from the current database (shown in the Database pop-up) are listed in the Database Fields box. To copy a field, select it in the Fields box and choose Move. It appears in the Selected Fields list.

If you want to copy all fields, you can select All. This is not necessary if the Fields box is unchecked, because FoxPro automatically copies all fields unless other specifications are made.

To remove a fields from the Selected Fields box, select the field in the list and choose Remove. You can remove all fields from the Selected Fields list by choosing Clear.

When your selection is complete, choose OK to return to the Copy To dialog box with the selection confirmed, or choose Cancel to exit without saving the selection.

To copy records, choose OK in the Copy To box. Choose Cancel to exit without copying records.

Database Sort...

Sort... lets you create a new database sorted in the order you indicate in the Sort... dialog box, as shown in Fig. 1-67.

The current database is displayed in the Database pop-up. The pop-up lists only open databases and is disabled if only one database is open.

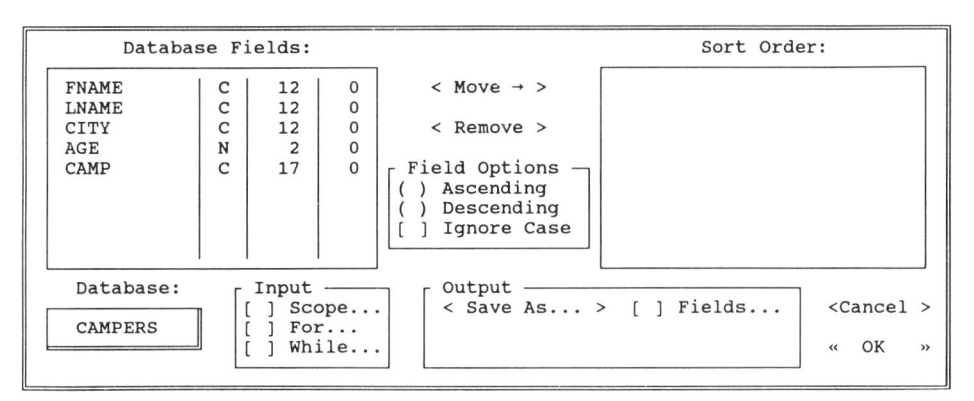

Fig. 1-67. Sort dialog box.

The fields in the current database are listed in the Database Fields list. Memo fields are disabled because you cannot sort on a memo field. The column to the right of the field name lists the first letter of the type of the field, and the next column shows the field length. The column on the right shows the number of decimal places used in the field.

Move   To determine the order of the new database, you must select fields from the Fields list, and press Enter or choose Move to move them into the Sort Order box. If, for example, you want campers to be listed in alphabetical order according to their last names, you would put the Lname field in the Sort Order box.

Field Options   To indicate that the order should go from A – Z rather than Z – A, turn on the Ascending radio button in the Field Options box. If some names are entered with initial capitals and others in lowercase, check the Ignore Case box. Otherwise, uppercase records will be sorted first. To see the exact order in which FoxPro sorts, choose ASCII Chart from the System menu.

You can continue choosing fields for the Sort Order box. You might want the secondary order to be first name, so you would move that into the second line of the Sort Order list. You must list fields in their order of importance: If you list the Fname field first, names will be in order alphabetically by first name first, then by last name.

To remove a field from the Sort Order list, choose the field and select Remove.

You can limit the records to be included in the new database by using the three Input check boxes.

[ ]Scope...   Turn on one of the four Scope radio buttons to select records for the new database based on their position in the current database.

- All selects all records.
- Next includes the next *n* records, starting with the current record. Type the number of records you want included.
- Record includes the record number you enter.
- Rest includes the current record and the rest of the records in the database.

Choose OK to save your selections, or Cancel to exit without saving them.

Indicate the new file name and the fields to be included in the new database in the Output box.

[ ]For...   If you want to limit the records in the new database to a certain condition, choose the For check box. In the Expression Builder, type a For clause or choose the items in the clause from the lists and pop-ups. For example, the new database might contain all campers except the Woodpecker Wigwam. In this case, the For clause would be Camp < > "Woodpecker Wigwam".

[ ]While... FoxPro tests a While condition against each record in the order that they are listed in the database and stops when the While condition is no longer true. For example, if the While clause says City = "Pahrump", FoxPro stops copying records when it reaches the first record in which the city is not Pahrump.

Save As... Type the name of the new database in the Save As text box, or choose Save As... and type the new name in the dialog box.

[ ]Fields... When the Fields... box is checked, only the fields you selected in the Set Fields dialog box appear as shown in Fig. 1-68 in the new database.

```
    Database Fields:                              Selected Fields:
    FNAME    C   12   0      < Move → >
    LNAME    C   12   0
    CITY     C   12   0      < All  → >
    AGE      N    2   0
    CAMP     C   17   0      < Remove >

                             < Clear  >

       Database:
                                                     <Cancel >
        CAMPERS
                                                  «   OK    »
```

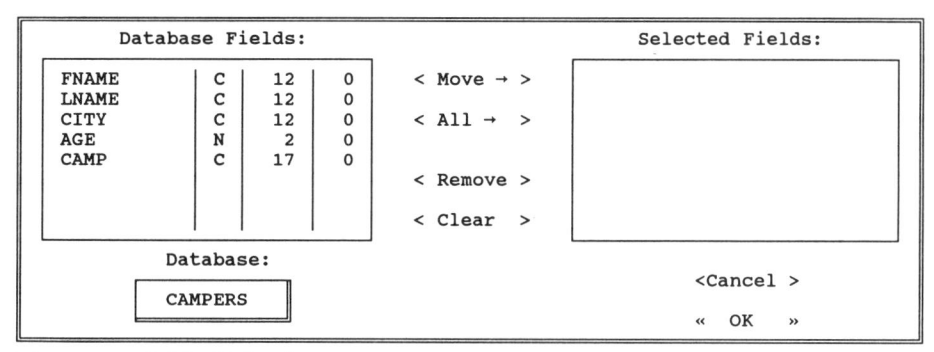

Fig. 1-68. Fields dialog box.

The Fields... dialog box contains a list of Database Fields from the current database (displayed in the Database pop-up). To select a field to be included in the new database, choose the field in the Database Fields list and press Enter or choose Move. The field name appears in the Selected Fields list.

You can put all the field names in the list by choosing All. Remove a field by selecting it in the Selected Fields box and choosing Remove.

Remove all the fields from the Selected Fields box by choosing Clear.

Choose OK when you are satisfied with your field selected, or Cancel to exit the dialog box without making a selection.

You can easily change the order of your fields in the Sort Order dialog. Position the cursor on the double-headed arrow next to a field and drag the field to the desired location in the list.

When your specifications are set, choose OK, and the new database is sorted. Choose Cancel to leave the dialog box without creating a new database.

Database Total

Total... (Fig. 1-69) sums numeric values for all records that satisfy the Expr... criterion you select.

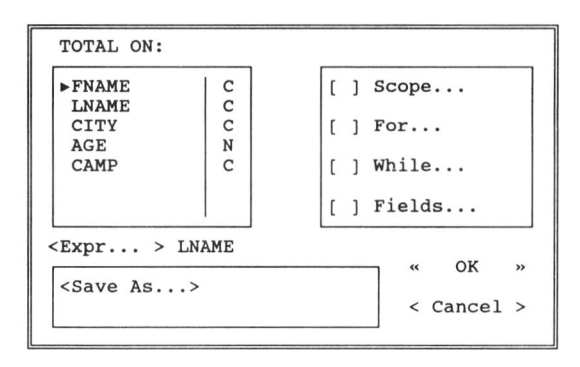

```
┌─────────────────────────────────────────────┐
│  TOTAL ON:                                  │
│  ┌─────────────────┐   [ ] Scope...         │
│  │ ►FNAME      C   │                        │
│  │  LNAME      C   │   [ ] For...           │
│  │  CITY       C   │                        │
│  │  AGE        N   │   [ ] While...         │
│  │  CAMP       C   │                        │
│  │                 │   [ ] Fields...        │
│  └─────────────────┘                        │
│  <Expr... > LNAME                           │
│  ┌─────────────────┐      «   OK   »        │
│  │ <Save As...>    │                        │
│  │                 │      < Cancel >        │
│  └─────────────────┘                        │
└─────────────────────────────────────────────┘
```

Fig. 1-69. Total On dialog box.

Expr... The Total On dialog box contains a scrollable list of the fields in the current database. You select one of these fields or type a field name in the Expr... text box. The field you total on should be the index key for the active index or the field you sorted on. When you execute Total without specifying Scope, For, While, or Fields, all numeric fields in the database that contain duplicate values in the Expr... field are totalled. For instance, in the Lname field is the index key, Total will sum the ages of campers who have the same last name.

The Expr... requirement in this option is so limiting that you will probably use Total... quite infrequently. In most cases, you will find Database Sum more useful.

Save As... You must enter a new file name in the Save As... text box. This is the file where the new database with totalled fields will be saved.

Other options to select records These options to limit or select records to be totalled are found in the box on the right side of the screen:

- [ ]Scope... You can further limit the records totalled by choosing the Scope... check box. Indicate whether you want all records totalled, the next n number of records, a particular record number, or the rest of the records in the database.
- [ ]For..., [ ]While... Use the For... or While... check boxes to create For and While clauses in the Expression Builder to set conditions that must be met by each record to be summed.
- [ ]Fields If you select Fields in the Fields... dialog box, only the selected fields will be totalled.

When your selections are complete, choose OK. Choose Cancel to exit without totalling.

See also: Database Sum p. 76

Database Average

You can use the Average option shown in Fig. 1-70 to average the numeric values in your database fields.

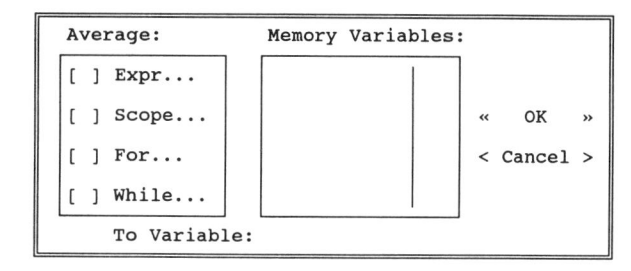

```
                    Average:        Memory Variables:
                    [ ] Expr...     ┌──────────┬─┐
                                    │          │ │        «  OK  »
Fig. 1-70. Average  [ ] Scope...    │          │ │
dialog box.                         │          │ │        < Cancel >
                    [ ] For...      │          │ │
                                    └──────────┴─┘
                    [ ] While...
                      To Variable:
```

Average The Average box in the Average... dialog box contains four check boxes:

- Expr... Choose Expr... if you want to specify the fields to be averaged. You can also build expressions that, for instance, add two fields together before Average is executed.
- [ ]Scope... Use the Scope... check box to choose from the four radio buttons listed. If you select All, all records will be averaged. Next lets you average the next n number of records, beginning with the current record. To specify a single record, choose Record and enter the record number. To average all records from the current record to the end of the database, choose Rest. When your selection is complete, choose OK.
- [ ]For... Use the For... Expression Builder to enter a condition that records must meet in order to be averaged. For example, if you want the average age of Woodpecker Wigwam campers, your For clause would be Camp = "Woodpecker Wigwam".
- [ ]While... A While clause specifies records to be averaged as long as the While condition exists as FoxPro reads down the database. If you enter Fname = "A" in the While Expression Builder, records will be averaged as long as first names start with A. When FoxPro reaches a first name that does not start with A, it finishes averaging.

Memory Variables If you have set Talk On in the On/Off panel of the View window, the average will show on screen when you execute the option. If you want to store the average value in a memory variable, enter the name of the variable in the To Variable text box.

After you perform Average, the variable will be in the Memory Variables list box. You can choose variables from the list for storage of averages in the future.

Choose OK to compute the average, or choose Esc or Cancel to exit without making the computation.

See also: Window View p. 44

Database Count...

The Count option (Fig. 1-71) lets you count the number of records that meet your criteria.

76   The FoxPro User Interface

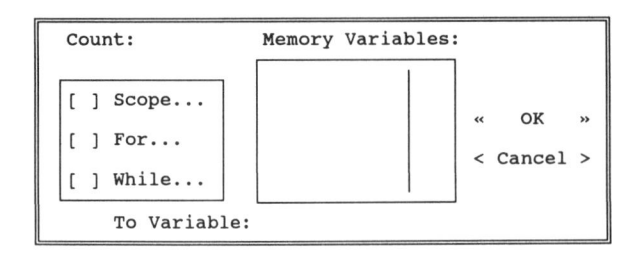

```
Count:         Memory Variables:

[ ] Scope...                          «   OK   »
[ ] For...                            < Cancel >
[ ] While...

   To Variable:
```

Fig. 1-71. Count dialog box.

Count   The Count... dialog box contains four check boxes:

- [ ]Scope...   Check the Scope... box if you want to indicate one of the four criteria indicated by the radio buttons. All counts all records in the database. Next counts the next *n* number of records, including the active record, when you enter a number after turning the button on. If you are wary of computer magic, choose Record and enter the record number you want to count. To count the rest of the records in the database, including the current record, choose the radio button Record.
- [ ]For...   If you want to count only the records that meet certain criteria, enter or build a For clause in the For... Expression Builder. If you want to know how many campers are staying at the Lemur Lodge, enter Camp = "Lemur Lodge".
- [ ]While...   FoxPro will count down the list of records until the While condition you enter in the While... Expression Builder is no longer true. If the Campers database is indexed by Camp, you could count all the campers in the Bumblebee Brigade by entering the While clause Camp = "Bumblebee Brigade" in the Expression Builder, and if positioned at the first record that matches the criteria.

Memory Variables   If you have set Talk On in the On/Off panel of the View window, the results of your count will show on screen. You can also store the results in a memory variable. Type the name of a new memory variable in the To Variable box, or select an existing variable from the Memory Variables list box. Once you use a variable, it shows in the list box.

When you are ready to count records, choose OK. Choose Cancel or press Esc to exit without counting.

See also: Window View p. 44

Database Sum...

The Sum option sums the values in numeric fields in your database (Fig. 1-72).

Sum   In the Sum... dialog box you can specify fields and records to be totalled:

- [ ]Expr...   Choose the Expr... check box if you want to sum on an expression. This means you will enter an expression, say, a field name, in the

Expression Builder, that limits the records to be summed to those with duplicate values. This is the same as using the Total option.
- [ ]Scope... You can use the four Scope radio buttons to specify records to be summed. Choose All to sum all records in the database. Choose Next to sum the next n records, starting with the active record. Choose the Record button if you want to verify that FoxPro is working. Enter the number of the single record you want to sum. Choosing Rest causes the rest of the records, starting with the current record, to be summed when you choose OK.
- [ ]For... You can create a For expression in the Expression Builder to limit the records to certain criteria. To find the total age of campers in the Lemur Lodge, enter the For clause Camp = "Lemur Lodge" in the Expression box.
- [ ]While... FoxPro will sum records as long as they meet the While criteria if you enter a While clause in the Expression Builder.

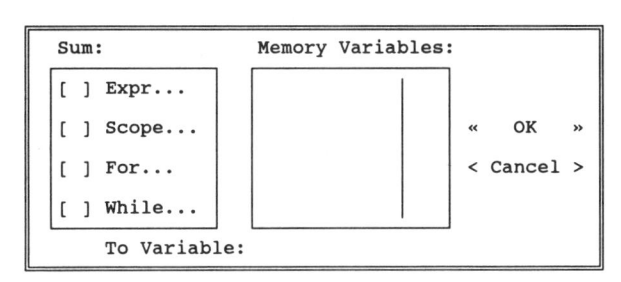

Fig. 1-72. Sum dialog box.

```
Sum:              Memory Variables:
[ ] Expr...
[ ] Scope...                         «   OK   »
[ ] For...                           < Cancel >
[ ] While...
    To Variable:
```

Memory Variables If you have set Talk On in the On/Off panel of the View window, the results of Sum will appear on screen. You can also store the results in a memory variable that you name by typing in the To Variable box. Once you have used a variable it appears in the Memory Variables box and can be chosen next time to store another calculation.

When you have set all your conditions, choose OK to sum records. To exit the dialog without summing, choose Cancel or press Esc.

See also: Database Total p. 73
Window View p. 44

Database Calculate

The Database Calculate option (Fig. 1-73) lets you use FoxPro commands and functions to help you perform financial and statistical operations on fields.

Calculate The four options in the Calculate dialog box follow. The Expression Builder accessed by the first option is not typical. You can use the other

```
 Calculate:        Memory Variables:
 [ ] Expr...      |              |
 [ ] Scope...     |              |   «   OK   »
 [ ] For...       |              |   < Cancel >
 [ ] While...     |              |
     To Variable:
```

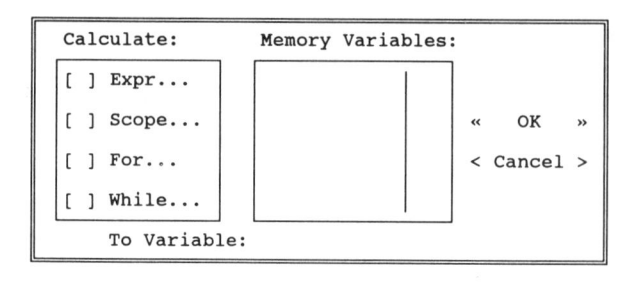

Fig. 1-73. Calculate dialog box.

three check boxes to determine which records will be included in the calculation:

- [ ]Expr...   In the Calculate dialog box, check the Expr... check box to build your expression. The Calculate Expression Builder is different from other Expression Builders: It has only one pop-up (Math), and there are fewer options here than usual. You can combine any of these options to create an expression string. See chapter 2 on commands and chapter 4 on functions for descriptions of how these expressions work.
- [ ]Scope...   The Scope dialog box has four radio buttons. Choose All to include all records in the calculation. If you choose Next and type a number, the next n records, including the current record, will be included. To calculate a single record, choose Record and enter the record number. Choosing Rest includes the current record and the rest of the records in the database.
- [ ]For...   You can further limit the records to be included in the calculation with a For clause. Build or enter the clause in the For Expression Builder.
- [ ]While...   If you want FoxPro to perform the calculation on successive records as long as they meet certain criteria, create a While expression in the Expression Builder using those criteria. FoxPro stops calculating as soon as it reaches a record that does not satisfy the criteria.

Memory Variables   You can save the results of the calculation in a memory variable. Type a name in the To Variable box, or select a variable from the Memory Variables list. If you strung several expressions together in the Expression Builder, you must string an equal number of variables in the To Variable text box.

Choose OK when you are ready to calculate. Press Esc or choose Cancel to exit with calculating. See also chapter 2 on FoxPro commands and chapter 4 on functions.

Database Report...

To create a report, you must use the File New option to access an empty report layout window. When you do so, the Report menu is added to the menu bar and you can add fields and other objects to the window.

Once the report exists, you can use the Report... option on the Database menu to specify settings and records to be included with the Report dialog box shown in Fig. 1-74.

```
Report:
<Form... >      [X] Environment      [ ] Scope...
[ ] Quick Report                     [ ] For...
                                     [ ] While...

[ ] Plain
[ ] No Eject
[ ] Summary
[ ] Heading

[ ] To Print                         «   OK   »
[ ] To File
( ) Console On  ( ) Console Off      < Cancel >
```

Fig. 1-74. Report dialog box.

Form... If a report form is already open, its name will appear in the Form... text box. To select a different report, or if the text box is blank, type the file name in the box or choose Form... and select the report file from the dialog box that appears.

[ ]Environment If you previously saved the report with the Save Environment box checked in the File Save As dialog box, you can restore the environment by checking the Environment box. The environment includes any databases, indexes, and view settings that were open when you saved the report. A report environment is saved with an .FRV extension rather than the .FRX report extension.

Scope... You can limit the scope of records included in the report by choosing one of the Scope... radio buttons. If All is turned on, all records are included in the report. If Next is on, the next n number of records, including the current record, are included. If you select Record, only the record number you enter appears in the report. Select Rest to include the rest of the records in the database, including the current record.

[ ]For... To set criteria that limit which records are included in the report, choose For.... Enter a For clause in the Expression Builder. For example, Lname < "L" will limit the records in the Camp Report to those campers whose last names start with a letter before L.

[ ]While... You can enter a While clause in the Expression Builder to cause FoxPro to add records to the report as long as the condition you set is true. If the While clause is Lname , "L", as long as the next record is a camper whose last name starts with a letter before L, the camper will be included in the report. The first time FoxPro reaches a record with a last name starting with L or greater, it stops adding records to the report, even if records following this camper have last names that start with a letter before L.

[ ]Plain If you check the Plain box, the report is printed with Page Headers on the first page only.

[ ]No Eject Check this box if you do not want to eject a blank page before the report prints.

[ ]Summary If you want to print only the Summary of the report, check this box.

[ ]Heading This box lets you add a heading line to each page of the report. Type the line in the text box.

[ ]To Print Check this box if you want to print the report.

[ ]To File Checking this box sends the report to an ASCII file.

[ ]Preview Check this box to get a preview of the report before printing it.

Console On/Off You can see the report on your screen while it is printing if you choose the Console On radio button. Because this slows down printing, choose Console Off if you do not need to see the report.

When you choose OK, the report is run. Choose Cancel or press Esc to exit the dialog box without running the report.

See also: File New p. 10
File Save As p. 35
Report Menu p. 16

Database Label

When you are ready to generate labels you created using the File New option and the Label menu, choose Label from the Database menu. The Label dialog box (Fig. 1-75) is just like the Report dialog box.

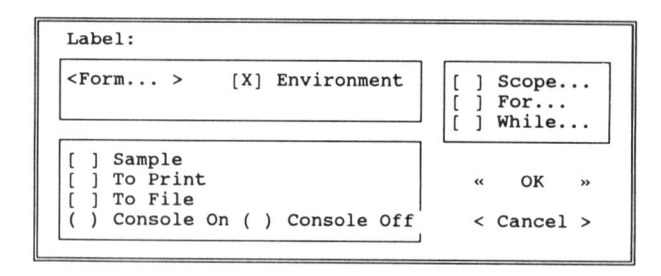

```
 Label:
 ┌─────────────────────────────┐   ┌──────────────┐
 │ <Form... >    [X] Environment│   │ [ ] Scope... │
 │                              │   │ [ ] For...   │
 │                              │   │ [ ] While... │
 └─────────────────────────────┘   └──────────────┘
 ┌─────────────────────────────┐
 │ [ ] Sample                  │      «   OK   »
 │ [ ] To Print                │
 │ [ ] To File                 │
 │ ( ) Console On ( ) Console Off│    <  Cancel  >
 └─────────────────────────────┘
```

Fig. 1-75. Label dialog box.

Form... If your label file is already open, its name appears in the Form... box. If not, you can type the name or select it from the Form... dialog box.

[ ]Environment If you previously saved your label file using the Save Environment check box in the File Save As dialog box, you can open the environment by checking the Environment box. The Environment includes the label layout file, its database, and any settings from the View window panels.

[ ]Scope If you want to limit the records that will be generated as labels according to their position in the database, you can use the four radio buttons in the Scope... dialog box. Choose All to generate all records. Choose Next and type the number of records, including the current record, that you want labels for. To generate a single label, choose Record and type the number of the record. Choose Rest to generate labels for the current record and the rest of the records following it in the database.

[ ]For... You can set other conditions to limit the records included in the label generation by entering a For clause in the For Expression Builder. You might, for example, send labels only to campers who live in California. The For expression that will do this is ST = "CA".

[ ]While... A While clause can be used to generate labels for records as long as a conditional statement is true. If you use the example above, ST = "CA" in the While Expression Builder, FoxPro generates labels for records as long as they include CA in the ST field. When it reaches the first record that does not have CA in the ST field, it stops generating labels, even if records below the current record do show CA in the ST field.

[ ]Sample If you check the Sample box, a single sample prints so you can check the alignment of your printer. The asterisks on the label show the size and placement of fields.

After you print a sample, FoxPro asks if you want more samples. You can continue choosing Yes and printing more samples until your printer alignment is correct. When you are ready to run all the labels, choose Do Labels. You can choose Cancel or press Esc to leave the dialog box without running labels.

[ ]To Print Check this box if you want the labels to print when you run them. If you do not check To Print, the labels will flash by on your screen.

[ ]To File You can store the labels in an ASCII file by checking this box.

Console On/Off Unless you specifically want to see the labels on your screen, you can choose the Console Off radio button. With the Console On, you see the labels as they are generated, but they also run more slowly.

When you have set your conditions, choose OK to run the labels. Choose Cancel or press Esc to leave the dialog box without taking action.

See also: File New *p. 10*
　　　　　　File Save As *p. 35*
　　　　　　Label Menu *p. 30*

Database Pack

After marking records for deletion using Toggle Delete from the Browse menu, or Delete from the Record menu, choose Pack to permanently delete them from the database.

Always make a backup before you pack your database.

See also: Browse Toggle Delete p. 66
Record Delete p. 95

Database Reindex

Occasionally index files become corrupted. If you notice that your open index file does not seem to be working properly, choose Reindex to reconstruct the index.

The Edit menu

With the options on the Edit menu shown in Fig. 1-76, you can edit all types of text in FoxPro. The Edit menu is available for editing in text files (.TXT extension), command (.PRG) files, memo fields in databases, and commands in the Command window. Some Edit options are available from the Browse window and the Color Picker dialog box.

Edit the Memo field in the CMPSCHD database shown in Fig. 1-77. Choose Database Browse to view the database in a Browse window.

```
Undo                        ^U
Redo                        ^R

Cut                         ^X
Copy                        ^C
Paste                       ^V
Clear

Select All                  ^A

Goto Line...
Find...                     ^F
Find Again                  ^G
Replace And Find Again      ^E
Replace All

Preferences...
```

Fig. 1-76. The Edit menu.

Day	Activity	Camp	Memo
1	Hike	Bumblebee Brigade	Memo
2	Swim	Bumblebee Brigade	memo
3	Bike	Bumblebee Brigade	memo
4	Canoe	Bumblebee Brigade	memo
5	Rocks	Bumblebee Brigade	memo
2	Hike	Lemur Lodge	Memo
3	Swim	Lemur Lodge	memo
4	Bike	Lemur Lodge	memo
5	Canoe	Lemur Lodge	memo
4	Swim	Woodpecker Wigwam	memo
5	Bike	Woodpecker Wigwam	memo
1	Canoe	Woodpecker Wigwam	memo
2	Rocks	Woodpecker Wigwam	memo
3	Hike	Woodpecker Wigwam	memo

Fig. 1-77. Cmpschd database.

You are going to put a hike description in the first hike record. First, open the memo field by placing the cursor on the memo field and press Ctrl – PgDn or double click with the mouse.

Now type the text shown in Fig. 1-78 into your memo window. Use normal typing methods. When you finish, place the cursor at the top of the memo window.

```
■                CMPSCHD->MEMO                    ≡
Sylvestri Vista Hike

Follow path behind Wigwam north half a mile; turn
45 degrees at split pine - point out flora and
give history of pine
```

Fig. 1-78. Text in a memo window.

Try using some of the options on the Edit menu. Suppose the hiking path really runs south from the Wigwam.

1. Choose Find... from the menu.
2. In the Look For box, type north.
3. In the Replace With box, type south.
4. Choose Find.
5. Choose Replace All from the Edit menu.

North becomes south. Now change it back:

1. Choose Undo from the menu.
2. Change south back to north again.
3. Choose Redo from the menu.

Now that you are absolutely sure you got the direction right, put the hike description in another hike record.

1. Choose Select All from the menu. All the text in the memo window becomes highlighted.
2. Choose Copy from the menu.
3. Close the window by pressing Ctrl - W.

In the Browse window, place the cursor on the memo field of the next hike record and open the window. Copy the text into the window. When you choose Paste from the menu, the text appears in the window. When you copied it from the original memo field, FoxPro stored it on a clipboard. When you selected Paste, FoxPro copied the clipboard into the window.

You can cut or copy and paste single characters, words, lines, paragraphs, or whatever you like. The keystrokes to use for selecting text are listed here:

Keystrokes	**Selects**
Shift – arrow (←/→)	One character at a time.
Shift – arrow (↑/↓)	One line at a time.
Shift – Ctrl – arrow (←/→)	From cursor to beginning/end of word.
Shift – Ctrl – End	From cursor to end of text.
Shift – Ctrl – Home	From cursor to beginning of text.
Ctrl – A	All text.

Press any cursor movement key to deselect.

With a mouse, you can select text by dragging through it. There are also a few shortcuts for selecting with a mouse:

To select	Action
A word	Point to the word and double click.
A line	Point to the line and triple click.
Word by word	Point to the first word, double click and drag.
Line by line	Point to the first line, triple click and drag.
Segment of text	Point to the beginning of the segment, then Shift – click at the end of the segment.

Deselect by dragging in the opposite direction before you release the mouse button. After you release the mouse button, you can deselect by Shift – clicking in the selected text at the point where you want the selection to end. Clicking in the window anywhere outside the selected area deselects the entire selection.

The Edit menu options are described in detail in the following sections.

Edit Undo

If you change your mind about an action you performed, you can choose Undo to reverse it. FoxPro remembers everything you have done since the beginning of your session, so you can choose Undo repeatedly to reverse successive actions all the way back to your first action. In Undo and Redo, actions are:

- Pressing Delete or Backspace.
- Selecting text and pressing Delete or Backspace.
- Selecting and starting to type replacement text.
- Moving the cursor and typing.
- Using any other keystrokes before pressing the spacebar and typing.
- Choosing any of these Edit menu options: Cut, Paste, Clear, or Replace All.

You can Undo actions after you have saved them, but if you close a file and reopen it, Undo is disabled until you perform new actions.

To undo an Undo, you must choose Redo from the Edit menu. If you choose Undo after undoing an action, the action immediately previous to the Undo is undone.

In a Browse window, Undo is available within fields. Each time you move to a new field, you start over; Undo is disabled until you make new changes in the field.

Shortcut key: Ctrl – U

See also: Edit Redo *p. 86*

Edit Redo

Redo undoes an Undo. In other words, if you perform an action and then choose Undo, the action is reversed. If you then choose Redo, the action is restored.

Redo only works on undone actions. You cannot, for example, cut and paste a line of text and then choose Redo to paste it again.

You can choose Redo repeatedly to undo Undo actions starting with the most recent and working back to the first.

If Undo has not been used, Redo is not available for selection.

Shortcut key: Ctrl – R

See also: Edit Undo p. 85

Edit Cut

Use Cut when you want to move text. When you select the text to be moved and choose this option, the cut text is stored on a clipboard in FoxPro.

To restore the text, move the cursor to the new position and choose Paste.

Shortcut key: Ctrl – X

See also: Edit Copy p. 86
          Edit Paste p. 86

Edit Copy

Copy copies the selected text and stores it in the FoxPro clipboard. The original text remains in place in the file and on screen.

Use Edit Paste to copy the text from the clipboard into the new cursor position.

Shortcut key: Ctrl – C

See also: Edit Cut p. 86
          Edit Paste p. 86

Edit Paste

Paste inserts text from the FoxPro clipboard into the new cursor position. Use this option after cutting or copying text with the Cut or Copy Edit menu options. When you use Cut or Copy, text is stored on a clipboard.

You can choose Paste repeatedly to paste the same clipboard text as many times as you like.

Shortcut key: Ctrl – V

See also: Edit Copy p. 86
          Edit Cut p. 86

Edit Clear

Choosing Clear after selecting text is the same as pressing Delete or Backspace. Text is erased without being saved to the clipboard.

If you choose Clear without selecting text, the entire window is erased.

Edit Select All

Select All selects all the text in the active editing window. In a Browse window, this option selects all the information in the current field.

Edit Goto Line...

Goto Line... is only enabled if you have unchecked the Wrap box in the Preferences... dialog box.

When you choose Goto Line..., a dialog box appears. Enter the line number you want to go to, and choose Goto. The cursor is moved to that line number.

See also: Edit Preferences p. 89

Edit Find...

You can find or replace specific text with this option. Open the file in which you want to find text, and choose Find.... The box in Fig. 1-79 appears.

Fig. 1-79. Find dialog box.

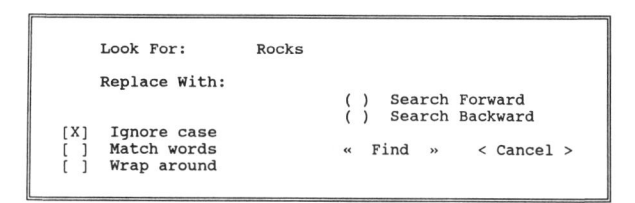

```
Look For:        Rocks
Replace With:
                                ( ) Search Forward
                                ( ) Search Backward
[X] Ignore case
[ ] Match words                 «  Find  »    < Cancel >
[ ] Wrap around
```

Look For   In the dialog box that appears, you can enter the text to be found in the Look For box. You can also find Enter, Tab, backslash, and line feed characters by typing:

Enter	\r
Tab	\t
Backslash	\\
Line feed	\n

Replace With   If you want to replace text, enter the replacement data in the Replace With box. While you can use Find in a Browse window, the dialog box does not contain a Replace With box. Use Record Replace to replace information in the Browse window.

When you choose Find, the Look For text is located, and the replacement is not performed until you choose Replace and Find Again.

There are three check boxes in the Find dialog box:

- [ ]Ignore Case   If you check this box and type Mad Max after Find, FoxPro finds mad max, too. When Ignore Case is unchecked, only Mad Max is located.
- [ ]Match Words   Check Match Words to find occurrences of the text that exist as complete words. For instance, with Match Words checked, only sham will be found if sham is the Look For text. With Match Words unchecked, sham will also find shambolic, shaman, unashamed, etc., if you have used them in your text.
- [ ]Wrap Around   If you do not like to put the cursor at the top of the page each time you do a search, check the Wrap Around box. This tells FoxPro to search for the Look For text from the cursor position to the end of the file, and then to go to the top of the file and search down to the cursor.

When you are ready to find your text, choose Find. The first occurrence of the text is highlighted for editing, or replaced if you entered replacement text.

Choose Cancel or press Esc to leave the dialog box without finding text.

See also: Edit Find Again p. 88
Edit Replace All p. 89
Edit Replace and Find Again p. 88
Record Replace p. 94

Edit Find Again

Find Again is only available if you have used the Find option to find the first occurrence of specified text.

To find the next occurrence, choose Find Again. FoxPro continues to search from the current cursor position. When there are no more occurrences of the text, a Not Found message appears.

See also: Edit Find p. 87

Edit Replace and Find Again

After you have found the first occurrence of text to be replaced using the Find option, you can choose Replace and Find Again to replace the text with the replacement text and find the next occurrence.

If you decide not to replace this occurrence of the text, you can choose Find Again to find the next occurrence without making the replacement.

See also: Edit Find p. 87
Edit Find Again p. 88

Edit Replace All

After you have used Find to find the first occurrence of text you want to replace, you can choose Replace All to replace every occurrence of that text in the active file.

See also: Edit Find p. 87
Edit Replace and Find Again p. 88

Edit Preferences...

The Preferences... dialog box shown in Fig. 1-80 contains a number of settings that you can select for the current session or all new files.

- [ ]Wrap words   Check Wrap words if you want text in the current window to wrap to the next line automatically when it reaches the right margin of the window.
- [ ]Auto indent   Auto indent automatically indents the current line by the same amount as the previous line.
- [ ]Make Backup   When you save an edited file or program, Make Backup stores a backup version (.BAK file) as well.
- [ ]Add Line Feeds   This check box causes a carriage return and line feed to be added to the end of all lines when the file is saved. Uncheck this box if you want to use your files on the Macintosh.
- [ ]Compile When Saved   For program files this check box compiles files after they are saved. If you do not check the box, programs are not compiled until they are executed.
- [ ]Ctrl – Z sensitive   If you want Ctrl – Z to be read as a mark for the logical end of a file, choose this check box. When this box is checked, FoxPro stops reading or writing a file when it encounters a Ctrl – Z. If you uncheck this box, FoxPro will read the whole file, even if it contains Ctrl – Z.
- [ ]Use these preferences   If you check this box, all settings become the default for new text, program, or memo windows.
- [ ]Save preferences   Check this box to store the preference settings in the resource file so they remain the same each time you open the file. Window size and position, and the cursor location are also stored when you check Save Preferences.

In a memo window, the Preferences... box contains Wrap words, Auto indent, and a text box for Tab Size. Enter the number of characters you want the Tab to move.

The Preferences... radio buttons let you determine whether text will be aligned with the left margin, the right margin, or the center of the editing window.

```
[X] Wrap words              Tab size:    4
[X] Auto indent
                            [ ] Use these preferences
                                as default for Memos
[ ] Ctrl-Z sensitive        [ ] Save preference

( ) Left justify
( ) Right justify
( ) Center justify             «  OK  »   <Cancel>
```

Fig. 1-80. Preferences dialog box.

The Record menu

Shown in Fig. 1-81, the Record menu allows you to work with individual records in your databases.

Fig. 1-81. The Record menu.

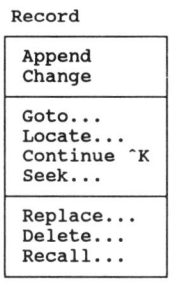

```
Record
Append
Change
Goto...
Locate...
Continue  ^K
Seek...
Replace...
Delete...
Recall...
```

Let's follow the mischievous Woodpecker Wigwam as they replace the CAMP field name information for their rivals, the Bumblebee Brigade.

With the Campers database open, Wigwam leader Axl Rose chooses Replace from the Record menu. In the dialog box, he unscrupulously enters the replacement information. He looks around, and then he:

1. Selects the field name in which information will be replaced: Camp.
2. Enters the replacement text, "Bumbling Brickheads," in the With box.
3. Checks the For check box and presses Enter to enter a For clause in the Expression Builder. The Woodpeckers enter: Camp = "Bumblebee Brigade". Without a For clause, all the Camp field information would be changed to Bumbling Brickheads.
4. Chooses OK to return to the Replace dialog box, and chooses Replace again. By typing Browse in the Command window, he and the other Woodpeckers get a good laugh seeing all the Bumblebees listed as Bumbling Brickheads.

This was so much fun the saboteurs decided to get rid of the Lemur Lodge altogether. To do this, they:

1. Choose Delete from the Record menu.
2. Check the For box and press Enter to call up the Expression Builder. To get rid of the Lemur Lodge, they build the expression Camp = "Lemur Lodge".
3. Choose OK to return to the Delete dialog, and choose Delete.

When the feckless leader of the Woodpeckers types Browse in the Command window to see the new version of the database, he goes crazy: The Lemurs are still there! The Delete option only marks the records for deletion; they are not actually erased until you choose Pack from the Database menu.

To save some poor unsuspecting Camp office worker from accidentally wiping out the Lemur Lodge records, you could choose Recall from the Record menu, choose a scope of All, and choose Recall from the dialog box. This unmarks all the records marked for deletion.

See if you can have this much fun with the rest of the Record menu.

Record Append

Append adds a blank record to the end of the active database in Append mode. Append mode lists fields and records vertically in the Append window.

In Browse mode, fields are listed horizontally. If you choose Record Append in Browse mode, the window changes to Append mode as it adds the blank record. To switch back to Browse mode, choose Browse from the Browse menu.

When you finish entering records, choose File Close or click the close box.

See also: Browse Browse p. 52
File Close p. 34

Record Change

Choose Change to display the active database vertically so you can edit records, as shown in Fig. 1-82.

When you choose Change, the Browse menu is added to the menu bar. Choose Browse to view records with the fields listed horizontally. You can also edit records in Browse mode.

You can choose Change from the Browse menu to return to Change mode, or choose Change from the Record menu.

When you finish editing, choose File Close or click the close box.

See also: Browse Browse p. 52
File Close p. 34

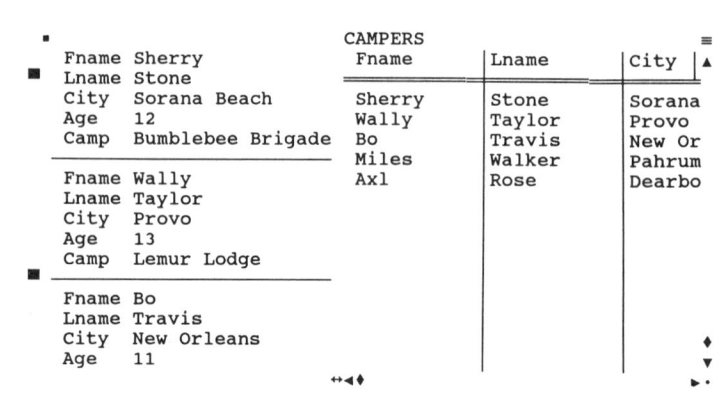

		CAMPERS		
Fname	Sherry	Fname	Lname	City
Lname	Stone			
City	Sorana Beach	Sherry	Stone	Sorana
Age	12	Wally	Taylor	Provo
Camp	Bumblebee Brigade	Bo	Travis	New Or
		Miles	Walker	Pahrum
Fname	Wally	Axl	Rose	Dearbo
Lname	Taylor			
City	Provo			
Age	13			
Camp	Lemur Lodge			
Fname	Bo			
Lname	Travis			
City	New Orleans			
Age	11			

Fig. 1-82. Append mode (left) and Browse mode (right).

Record Goto...

Choose Goto... to position the cursor on a record in the database. The Goto... dialog box has four radio buttons as shown in Fig. 1-83.

Fig. 1-83. Goto dialog box.

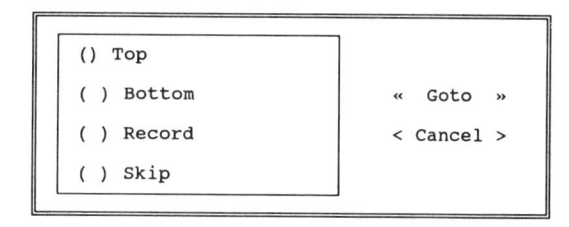

```
( ) Top
( ) Bottom          « Goto »
( ) Record          < Cancel >
( ) Skip
```

Turn on Top to put the cursor on the top record in the database. Choose Bottom to go to the bottom.

If you choose Record, type the number of the record you want to position on. You can skip the number of records you type when you choose the Skip button.

When you have selected the radio button you want, choose Goto.

Choose Cancel or press Esc to leave with moving the cursor.

Record Locate...

You can locate a record in the database that meets criteria specified in the Locate... dialog box (Fig. 1-84). Use one or a combination of the check boxes to define the records you want to find.

Fig. 1-84. Locate dialog box.

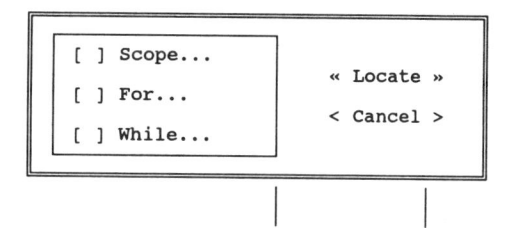

```
[ ] Scope...
[ ] For...           « Locate »
[ ] While...         < Cancel >
```

[ ]**Scope...** Scope finds records according to their position in the database. Choose All if you have not had your cup of coffee this morning and want time to go get a cup.

Choose Next to locate the next *n* number of records, including the current record. When you choose Locate, the cursor is positioned at the first record in this selection. To find the next record, choose Record Continue. Record finds the record number that you enter. Choose Rest to find the current record and the rest of the records in the database.

[ ]**For...** Checking the For... box opens the Expression Builder, where you can enter or build a For expression. You could locate all campers who live in

Pahrump by building the expression City = "Pahrump". Choose OK when your expression is complete.

When you choose Locate, the cursor moves to the first record that satisfies the criteria. Choose Record Continue to find the next record.

[ ]While... If you enter a While clause in the While... Expression Builder, FoxPro locates records as long as the condition of the clause is true. For City = "Pahrump", as soon as FoxPro reads a record that does not have Pahrump in the City field, it stops locating records.

Use the Continue option to continue locating records after the first one is found.

When all your conditions are set, choose Locate. The cursor moves to the first record that meet your conditions. To find the next record, choose Continue from the Record menu.

If no records match your conditions, the cursor moves to the end of the file or the last record in the specified Scope.

Choose Cancel or press Esc to leave the dialog box with locating records.

See also: Record Continue p. 94

Record Continue

Choose this option to find the next record that meets the criteria specified in Record Locate.

See also: Record Locate p. 93

Record Seek...

Seek... locates a record in the index of a database. When you select Seek..., the Expression Builder appears. The expression you enter or build must be based on the index key. For example, LNAME.IDX is the index for the Campers database. Its index key is Lname. To find a record in LNAME.IDX, your Seek expression must include the field Lname.

When you choose OK, FoxPro looks through the database and finds the first record that matches the expression. In a Browse window, the record is highlighted. If no records match the expression, the last record in the file is selected.

Record Replace

The Replace option (Fig. 1-85) lets you replace data in a field.

The Replace dialog box contains a list of the fields in the database shown in the Database pop-up. Select the appropriate database, and then select the field in which you want to replace data.

With... Type the replacement data in the With... text box, or choose With... to open the Expression Builder. Remember to enter text inside quotation marks.

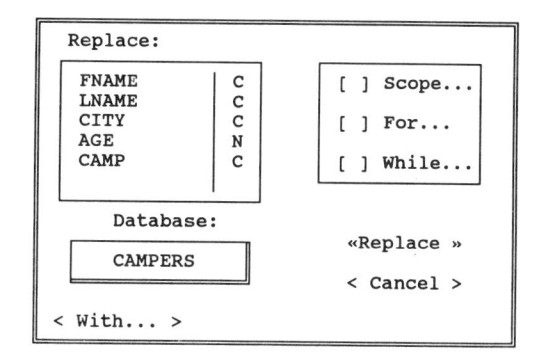

Fig. 1-85. Replace dialog box.

```
Replace:
  FNAME    C      [ ] Scope...
  LNAME    C
  CITY     C      [ ] For...
  AGE      N
  CAMP     C      [ ] While...

Database:
                     «Replace»
  CAMPERS
                     < Cancel >
< With... >
```

If you want to replace the information in particular records, use any combination of the check boxes to specify criteria.

[ ]**Scope...** The four Scope... radio buttons can be used to determine the location of the record in which field information is replaced. Choose All to replace the field input in all records in the database. Choose Next to perform Replace on the next n records, including the current record. Record lets you enter the number of the record in which you want the replacement. Choose Rest to replace data in the current record and the rest of the records in the database.

[ ]**For...** Choose For... to open the Expression Builder, where you can enter or create an expression to determine which records will be replaced. For example, the campers in the Woodpecker Wigwam were detected replacing the name Bumblebee Brigade with Bumbling Brickheads. The expression they used was Camp = "Bumblebee Brigade".

[ ]**While...** If you enter a While clause in the Expression Builder, FoxPro replaces data as long as the While condition is true. When the first Lemur Lodge record was reached, the Bumbling Brickhead replacement was over.

When you are ready to perform the replacement, choose Replace. To leave the dialog box without replacing data, choose Cancel or press Esc.

It is a good idea to make a backup before using the Replace option.

Record Delete...

This option lets you mark records for deletion. If you have already opened a Browse window with a database, the easiest way to mark single records is to use Browse Toggle Delete.

Marking records for deletion does not actually remove them from the database. To do this you must choose Pack from the Database menu.

When you choose Delete..., a dialog box opens. You can use one or more of the three check boxes shown in Fig. 1-86 to describe the records you want to mark.

[ ]**Scope...** The Scope... box has four radio buttons. To mark all records, turn on All. Choose Next and enter a number to mark the current record and the

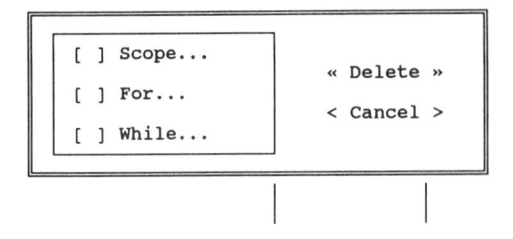

```
[ ] Scope...
                        « Delete »          Fig. 1-86. Delete
[ ] For...                                  dialog box.
                        < Cancel >
[ ] While...
```

next n records in the database. Next for 1 record is the Scope... default. Mark a single record by choosing Record and entering the record number. Choose Rest to mark the current record and the rest of the records in the database.

[ ]**For...**   To mark records that meet certain criteria, create a For clause in the Expression Builder. For instance, to mark all campers under age 14, enter Age < 14.

[ ]**While...**   You can specify a While condition in the Expression Builder that will be tested against each record in the order that it is listed in the database. For example, if the While clause says Age < 14, FoxPro stops copying records when it reaches the first record in which the age is not less than 14.

When you have completed your definitions, choose Delete. To exit the dialog box without deleting records, choose Cancel or press Esc.

See also: Browse Toggle Delete *p. 66*
              Database Pack *p. 81*

Record Recall...

Choose Recall... to unmark records marked for deletion with Record Delete or Browse Toggle Delete. The Recall... dialog box (Fig. 1-87) contains three check boxes with which you can identify the records to be unmarked. Keep in mind that, if you used these check boxes to mark the records, you need only specify All (the default) in the Scope... box to recall all the marked records.

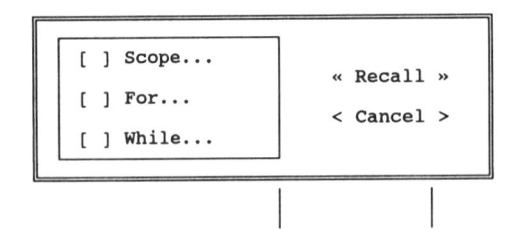

```
[ ] Scope...
                        « Recall »          Fig. 1-87. Recall
[ ] For...                                  dialog box.
                        < Cancel >
[ ] While...
```

[ ]**Scope...**   To recall all marked records, turn on the All radio button in the Scope box. Choose Next to recall the current record and the next n records that were marked. Next for 1 record is the Recall default. To unmark a single record, choose Record and enter the record number. Unmark the current record and the rest of the marked records in the database by choosing Rest.

Choose OK when your selections are correct, or choose Cancel to exit without changing the default selection.

[ ]**For...** You can unmark the marked records that satisfy a particular condition with this check box. Choose For... to open the Expression Builder, and enter or build the expression in the text box.

[ ]**While...** If you enter a While clause in the While... Expression Builder, FoxPro unmarks marked records until it reaches a record that does not match the While expression.

When you have set your recall conditions, choose Recall to unmark the records. To exit the dialog box without taking action, choose Cancel or press Esc.

See also: Browse Toggle Delete *p. 66*
Record Delete *p. 95*
Database Pack *p. 81*

The System menu

You can find out more about FoxPro or call additional desktop programs that you have installed with the options on the System menu (Fig. 1-88).

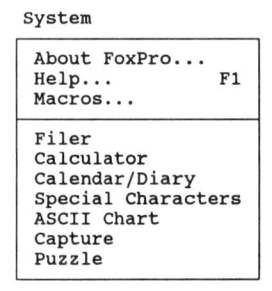

```
System
┌─────────────────────┐
│ About FoxPro...     │
│ Help...         F1  │
│ Macros...           │
├─────────────────────┤
│ Filer               │
│ Calculator          │
│ Calendar/Diary      │
│ Special Characters  │
│ ASCII Chart         │
│ Capture             │
│ Puzzle              │
└─────────────────────┘
```

Fig. 1-88. The System menu.

System About FoxPro...

The FoxPro dialog box contains revision information and the serial number of your copy of FoxPro. You will be asked for this information if you call Fox Software with questions. Click the mouse button or press Enter to remove About FoxPro from your screen.

System Help...

The Help window contains an alphabetical list of commands and keywords with descriptions. The Help window shown in Fig. 1-89 is a standard FoxPro window. You can scroll through the list or type a letter(s) to find the first topic that begins with that letter. To see help for a selected topic, press Enter or the spacebar, or double-click with the mouse.

```
            Help
┌──────────────────────────────┐
│ ▶ About FoxPro Help        ▲ │
│ ▶ (c) Fox Software 1984, 1989│
│ ▶ How to use Help...         │
│ ▶ What's New...              │
│ ▶     Interface...           │
│ ▶     Programming...         │
│ ▶ Compatibility...           │
│ ▶     FoxBASE+...            │
│ ▶     DB3 & DB4...         ▼ │
└──────────────────────────────┘
         « Help »
```

Fig. 1-89. The Help window.

To see the next topic, choose Next; to go back to the previous topic, choose Previous. To return to the list of topics, choose Topics.

If the help information does not fit in the window, you can use the arrow keys or PgUp/PgDn to see the rest.

You can copy and paste information from the Help window into other files in FoxPro. You can also paste information into the Help window, or make other editing changes, if you first SET HELP OFF in the On/Off panel of the View window.

Shortcut key: F1

See also: Edit Copy p. 86
             Window View p. 44

System Macros...

Macros are like FoxPro's hot keys. When you press a macro key combination, a predefined set of actions is automatically performed. You can create macros with the Macros... menu option.

The Macros dialog box (Fig. 1-90) contains a scrollable list of macros available for use. F2 through F9 are default macros. When you open this dialog, the Macro menu (Fig. 1-91) is added to the menu bar. This menu contains options that correspond to the text buttons in the dialog box.

New Macro   Choose this button or menu option to manually create a new macro. The Macro Definition dialog in Fig. 1-92 appears. You can also access this

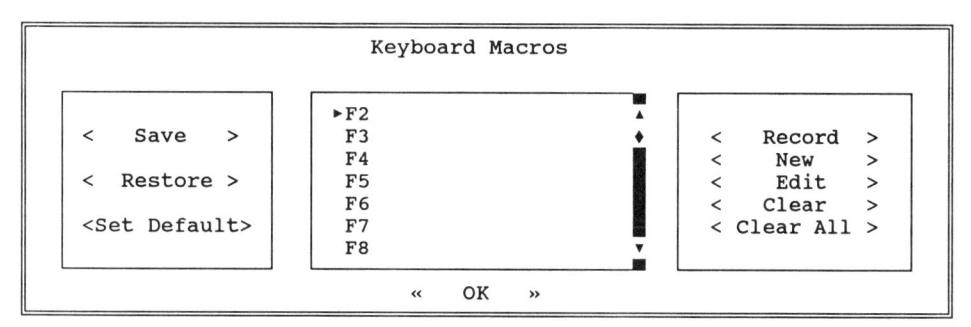

```
                          Keyboard Macros
  ┌──────────────┐   ┌──────────┐   ┌──────────────────┐
  │              │   │ ►F2      │   │ <    Record    > │
  │ <   Save   > │   │  F3      │   │ <    New       > │
  │              │   │  F4      │   │ <    Edit      > │
  │ < Restore  > │   │  F5      │   │ <    Clear     > │
  │              │   │  F6      │   │ < Clear All    > │
  │ <Set Default>│   │  F7      │   │                  │
  │              │   │  F8      │   │                  │
  └──────────────┘   └──────────┘   └──────────────────┘
                       «   OK   »
```

Fig. 1-90. Macros dialog box.

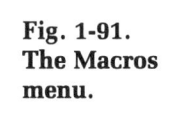

Fig. 1-91.
The Macros menu.

```
Record Macro     ^M
New Macro        ^N
Edit Macro       ^E
Clear            ^C
Clear All        ^A
Save Macros      ^S
Restore Macros   ^R
Set Default      ^D
```

Fig. 1-92.
New Macro dialog box.

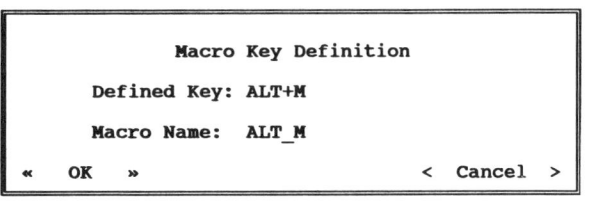

```
            Macro Key Definition
      Defined Key: ALT+M
      Macro Name:  ALT_M
   «  OK  »                       <  Cancel  >
```

dialog by pressing Shift – F10 in any area of FoxPro when you want to create a new macro.

You must press a key combination that will be the hot key for the macro. You can combine Ctrl, Alt, or Function with letter keys. Combinations that are allowed are listed below:

Key(s)	Can be combined with
Shift	F1 – F9
Ctrl	a – p, r, t – z, F1 – F9
Alt	a – z, F1 – F9
Shift – Ctrl	a – p, r, t – z, F1 – F10
Shift – Alt	a – z, F1 – F9
Alt – Ctrl	a – z, F1 – F9
Shift – Alt – Ctrl	a – z, F1 – F9
Alt – F10	a – z

In addition, F2 through F9 can be used alone. The first time you use FoxPro, F2 through F9 appear in your scrollable list of available macros. This is because they have been saved in a default file. You can change the default macros, and you can use F2 through F9 for other macros. How you can create defaults macros is described in the Set Default section.

You can create and save several macros using the same keystrokes, as long as you save them in different files. Of course, only one macro per keystroke set can be available for use at a time.

When you press the combination you want to use, it appears in the Defined Key text box. A macro name also appears in the Macro name box. You can accept this name or type a new one. Typically, you will use the macro keystrokes (with an underline replacing the hyphen) as the macro name. Macro names can be up to 20 characters long.

If you try to define a keystroke that already exists, a message box similar to the one in Fig. 1-93 asks if you want to overwrite the existing macro.

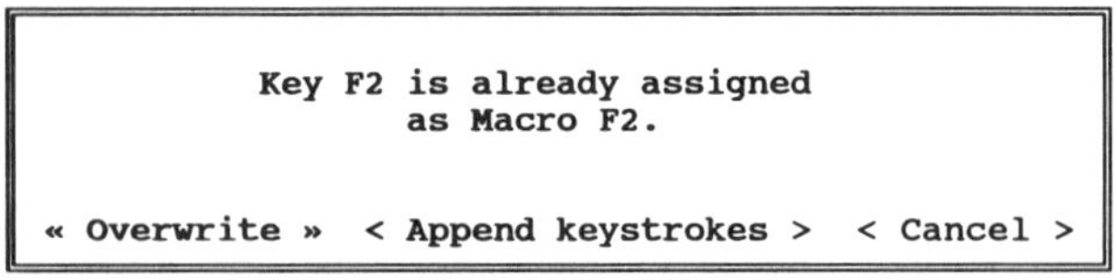

```
          Key F2 is already assigned
                as Macro F2.

 « Overwrite »   < Append keystrokes >   < Cancel >
```

Fig. 1-93. Overwrite message box.

You can choose Overwrite to replace the existing macro. You can add commands to the end of the existing macro if you choose Append keystrokes. Choose Cancel to exit without taking action.

When you are ready to create the new macro, choose OK from the Definition box, or Overwrite from the message box. A message appears showing the name of the macro you are defining. Type in the keystrokes that you want the macro to perform. A macro can contain up to 1024 keystrokes.

When you are done typing the keystrokes, choose OK.

Shortcut key: New Macro   Ctrl – N

Record   Choose this option to create a macro by recording the keystrokes as you run them. The Macro Definition dialog appears, just as it does with New Macro option, but once you have named the macro, you are then exited back to the previous window. Perform the actions that you want the macro to perform. FoxPro records all your actions.

When you are finished performing the macro actions, press Shift – F10. The Stop Recording dialog box appears. An example is shown in Fig. 1-94.

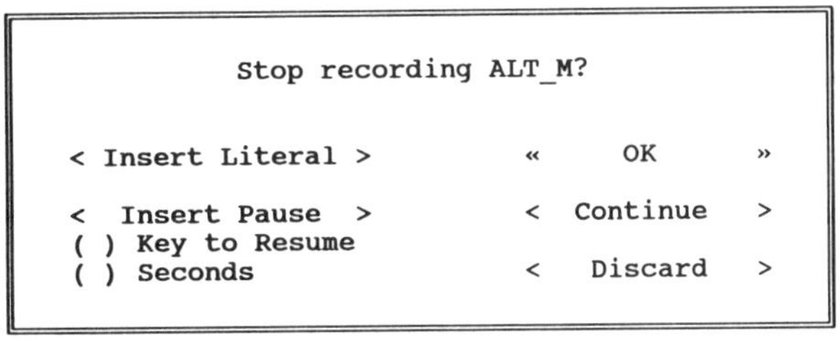

```
              Stop recording ALT_M?

   < Insert Literal >          «    OK    »

   < Insert Pause >          < Continue >
   ( ) Key to Resume
   ( ) Seconds              <  Discard  >
```

Fig. 1-94. Macro Stop Recording dialog box.

If you made an error and you want to erase what you have done, choose Discard. The Insert Literal button literally inserts the next keystroke you type into your macro. If you would like the macro to pause during execution, choose Insert Pause. When you run the macro, it will pause at this point. You can type keystrokes and choose menu options during this pause. When you are ready for the macro to continue, press Shift – F10.

If you decide you want to keep going with the macro you started, choose Continue, and you can continue recording the defined macro.

Choose OK if you are finished and you want the macro to be available for use.

Shortcut key: Record Macro   Ctrl – M

Clear and Clear All   When you create a macro, it appears in the scrollable list and you can use it to perform the actions you recorded. If you quit FoxPro after creating a new macro without saving it, the macro is erased.

Pressing Clear before the macro is saved also erases the macro. If you have saved the macro, however, pressing Clear simply clears it from the scrollable list. You can use the Restore text button, described below, to restore the file in which you saved the macro, and it will appear again on the scrollable list.

Clear clears the selected macro from the list. Clear All clears all the macros on the list.

Shortcut keys: Clear   Ctrl – C
                       Clear All   Ctrl – A

Save Macros   If you have created a macro that you will want to use again in other FoxPro sessions, use the Save text button to save it to a file. When you choose Save, a Save As dialog box appears. Choose the directory in which you want to save the macro, and type the file name in the text box. When you save a macro file, all the macros listed in the scrollable list are saved to that file with an .FKY file extension.

Choose OK when you are ready to save the macros, or choose Cancel to exit Save As without saving the file.

If you use Clear or Clear All after saving macros, you can create new macros with the same hot keys. You can save and clear these macros and restore the previously saved macros using the Restore text button.

Shortcut key: Save   Ctrl – S

Restore Macros   Restore is the equivalent of File Open for macro files. When you choose Restore, a Restore dialog box appears with a scrollable list of the macros in the current directory. Select the file that you want to restore and choose Open.

If you choose Restore when there is already a list of active macros in the Macro dialog box, the macros in the restored file are added to the list. If any of the restored macros use the same hot keys as the current list, the newly restored macro replaces the one listed previously. The original macro, however, is not deleted from the file or altered in any way.

Shortcut key: Restore   Ctrl – R

Set Default   You can create a macro file that restores automatically when you start FoxPro. Create or restore the macros that you want included in the file, and choose Set Default, or save them in a file called DEFAULT.FKY. FoxPro will save this file in the same directory where your FOXUSER file is stored, or in the current directory if there is no FOXUSER file. Choose OK to confirm your action.

To change the DEFAULT.FKY file, simply adjust the scrollable list to reflect the new macros you want in the file and choose Set Default again.

Shortcut key: Set Default   Ctrl – D

See also: Restore Macros p. 102

System Filer...

The FoxPro filer is a desk accessory that lets you manipulate all the files and directories on your hard disk without leaving FoxPro. Many of the filer's functions are similar to DOS commands you would execute from the DOS prompt.

When you choose Filer from the System menu, the Files panel appears on screen (Fig. 1-95) and the Filer menu (Fig. 1-96) is added to the menu bar. The Filer menu contains options that correspond to the text button in the Files and Tree panels.

```
System  File  Edit  Database  Record  Program  Window  Filer
                              Filer

   Name       Ext    Size   Last Modified    Attr
   [..]                     15-Jun-90  9:16a  ....    Drv.    [  D   ]
   AGE        .IDX   1024   19-Jun-90 11:21a  .a..
   BYCAMP     .IDX   1024   24-Jul-90  4:38p  .a..
   CAMP       .IDX   1024   19-Jun-90  1:38p  .a..    Dir.    [ BOOK ]
   CAMPADD    .DBF    501   22-Jun-90  7:39a  .a..
   CAMPADD    .LBV    179   20-Jun-90 12:21p  .a..
   CAMPADD    .LBX    131   20-Jun-90 12:21p  .a..    Files Like
   CAMPERS    .BAK    464   20-Jun-90 12:10p  .a..    *.*
   CAMPERS    .DBF    474   24-Jul-90  8:16a  .a..
   CAMPERS    .FRV    257   20-Jun-90  8:12a  .a..    <  Tag All  >
   CAMPERS    .FRX    623   20-Jun-90  8:12a  .a..    <  Tag None >
   CAMPREPO   .VUE    395   20-Jun-90 10:13a  .a..    <  Invert   >

   <  Find  >    <  Copy  >    <  Move  >    <  Delete >    <  Sort  >
   <  Edit  >    <  Attr  >    <  Rename >    <  Size   >    <  Tree  >
```

Fig. 1-95. The Files panel.

Fig. 1-96. The Filer menu.

```
Filer
┌──────────────────┐
│ Copy...       ^C │
│ Move...       ^O │
│ Delete...     ^D │
│ Rename...     ^R │
│ Edit...       ^E │
│ Attr...       ^T │
│ Size...       ^Z │
├──────────────────┤
│ Tag All       ^A │
│ Tag None      ^N │
│ Invert        ^V │
├──────────────────┤
│ Find...       ^F │
│ Mkdir...      ^K │
│ Chdir         ^H │
│ Sort...          │
├──────────────────┤
│ Tree Panel    ^L │
└──────────────────┘
```

Files panel   The scrollable list in the Files panel contains all the files in the current drive and directory. Use the Drv. and Dir. pop-ups to change the drive or directory and to display the appropriate files. You can also change directories by choosing the first file in the scrollable list. The [..] is the parent directory, so you move up the directory tree when you choose it in the list. If the current directory is the root directory, no parent directory is displayed in the list.

Files Like   You can limit which files appear in the scrollable list by using the Files Like box. You can type any portion of the file name and use the wildcard asterisk to display files with the characters you have typed, plus any other characters. For example, CAMP*.* would list all files that begin with CAMP, including

CAMPERS.DBF, CAMP.IDX, etc. If you want to indicate more than one specification, simply separate the phrases with a semicolon. For example, to list all .DBF and all .IDX files, you would enter *.DBF;*.IDX. Do not put spaces between the specifications. Press Enter to list the files you have specified.

Tag All and Tag None When you select a file on which you want to perform an operation, the file is *tagged*. A triangle appears in the scrollable list to the left of the file name.

You can tag individual files by Tabbing to the scrollable list and highlighting the desired file. Press the spacebar or click with the mouse.

To tag multiple files, highlight the first file, hold down the Shift key and use the ↑ or ↓, or point with the mouse to highlight and select the files you want. If you continue to hold down the Shift key and click on or arrow back to a tagged file, the file is untagged. The Shift key lets you toggle between tagged and untagged.

Tagged files remain tagged until you untag them, change drives, switch to the Tree panel, or exit the Filer. You have two tag options available:

- Tag All   Choose Tag All to tag all the files in the scrollable list. This is most useful when you have specified files using Files Like.
- Tag None   TagNone untags all the tagged files in the list. Unlike Tag All, Tag None untags all files in all directories, regardless of whether the files are shown in the scrollable list.

Invert Choose Invert to untag all tagged files and tag all untagged files in the current directory. This is handy when you want to tag all but a few files. Tag those files, then choose Invert to switch the tagging.

Find Use Find to tag files of a certain description in a number of different directories. In the Find dialog box, enter the file name or portion of the file name with asterisks that you want to find. This text box works the same way as the Files Like text box. Enter *.IDX as shown in Fig. 1-97 to find all index files, or *.IDX;*.PRG to find all index and program files. The Filer searches through the current directory.

[ ]Specify text to search for...   You can further specify which files will be found in this dialog box shown in Fig. 1-98. When you enter text strings of up to

```
Find and tag files which have names like
                *.idx
    [ ] Specify text to search for...
    [ ] Search subdirectories
    «  Find  »            < Cancel >
```

Fig. 1-97. Find dialog box.

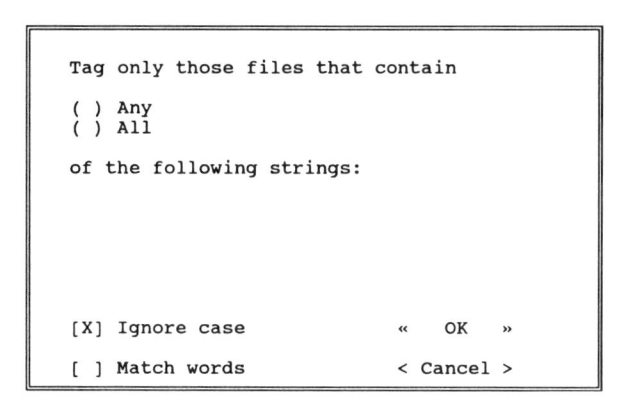

Fig. 1-98. Specify Text dialog box.

```
Tag only those files that contain
( ) Any
( ) All
of the following strings:




[X] Ignore case              «   OK   »

[ ] Match words              <  Cancel  >
```

256 characters in one or more of the text boxes, the Filer will tag files that contain those strings.

Choose the Any radio button to tag a file that has at least one of the strings you entered. If you want to tag only files that contain all three of the strings, turn on the All radio button.

The other options are:

- [ ]Ignore case   If you want the Filer to ignore case as it searches for strings, check this box. If one of your strings is Batter my heart three personed God, a file that contains batter my heart three personed god will also be tagged.
- [ ]Match words   If you have entered a short word, you can check Match words to ensure that only files with the exact words are tagged, and not files that contain your string within a word. For example, if your string is con, files with unconscious, connubial, or concentric will be tagged unless Match words is checked.

When you have entered your specifications, choose OK to return to the Find dialog box. Choose Cancel or press Esc to exit without making specifications.

[ ]Search subdirectories   If you want Find to search the current directory and all its subdirectories, check this box. If you want to search an entire drive, choose the root directory in the Dir. pop-up and check Search subdirectories.

When you are ready to tag files, choose Find. If you have specified a large number of files, this will take some time. When the search is complete, you are returned to the Files panel, and the tagged files are marked with an arrow in the scrollable list.

Copy   You can copy tagged files to a new location with this option. The original file is left intact, and you can rename the copy during the process. Figure 1-99 shows the dialog box.

```
Copy tagged files as   *.*

<Target directory...> D:\FOXPRO\BOOK\

            [ ] Replace existing files
            [ ] Preserve directories


         «  Copy  »           < Cancel >
```

Fig. 1-99. Copy dialog box.

Enter the new name or extension in the text box at the top of the Copy dialog box. The default, *.*, copies the files without changing the name. If you enter, for example, *.new, all the files will have the NEW extension in their new location.

Target Directory You can enter the target directory in this text box, or choose the text button or menu option, and select a directory in the dialog box that appears in Fig. 1-100.

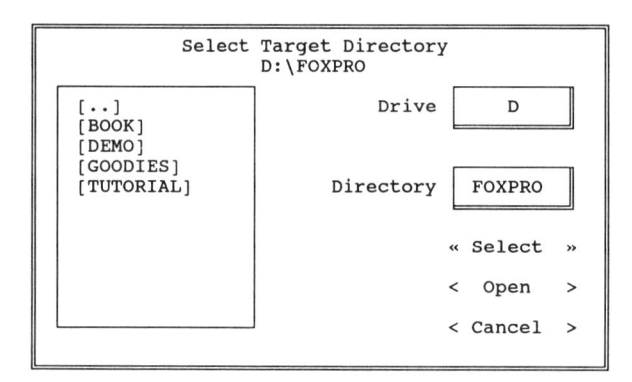

```
        Select Target Directory
              D:\FOXPRO
    [..]                Drive     D
    [BOOK]
    [DEMO]
    [GOODIES]
    [TUTORIAL]          Directory  FOXPRO


                        «  Select  »
                        <  Open    >
                        <  Cancel  >
```

Fig. 1-100. Target Directory dialog box.

Use the Drive and Directory pop-ups to indicate the desired location for the copied files. When you choose Select, you are returned to the Copy dialog box and the new drive and directory appear in the Target directory text box.

[ ]Replace existing files If you check this box, any files in the target directory with the same name as your entry in the Copy tagged files as text box will be overwritten. If you do not check this box and files exist with the same name as the copy name, a message box asks if you want to overwrite the existing files. Choose Yes to overwrite the files, or No to stop the operation and return to the Files panel.

When you are ready to copy the tagged files, choose Copy. Files that are currently open cannot be tagged or copied. After the operation is performed, the original files remain tagged, but the new files are not tagged.

Move Move works exactly the same way as Copy except that the tagged files are erased from their original location in the process. The Move dialog box contains the same options as the Copy dialog box, described in the preceding paragraphs.

Delete Delete removes tagged files from your hard disk. When you choose this option, a dialog box similar to Fig. 1-101 appears:

- Delete   The Delete dialog box asks if you are sure you want to delete the file named in the text box. Choose Delete to delete this file. This is the default button. If there are other tagged files, the next file name appears in the box.
- Skip   If you choose Skip, the file is not deleted, and the next tagged file appears.
- Delete All   Choose this option to delete the displayed file and all the others you have tagged without confirming deletions with the dialog box. It is a good idea to make a backup before you delete all tagged files, especially since Delete All erases tagged files in all directories, not just the directory displayed in the Files panel.

Fig. 1-101. Delete dialog box.

```
Are you sure you want to delete this file?
         D:\FOXPRO\BOOK\CAMPERS.DBF
« Delete »   < Skip >   < Delete All >   < Cancel >
```

You can stop the deletion by pressing Esc. Choose Cancel to return to the Files panel without deleting any files.

Edit   When you choose Edit, text editing windows open for all tagged files. You can tag as many files as your computer's memory and the DOS FILES = parameter allow. If an error message appears, you need to untag some files before you can continue.

Once the editing windows are open, you can use normal FoxPro editing techniques or options from the Edit menu to edit the windows.

Attr   The far right column of the scrollable list in the Files panel shows the DOS attributes of each file. You can change these attributes by selecting a file or a group of files and choosing the Attr text button or menu option.

The Attributes dialog box in Fig. 1-102 displays the name of the currently selected file and its current attributes. Use the four check boxes to change the attributes.

- [ ]Read Only   Read Only files can be viewed but not changed (even by the Filer). You can use the Filer to overwrite a Read Only file, but you are prompted for confirmation first.

- [ ]Archived Files that have been modified or newly created have the Archived attribute. Many backup programs only backup files that are archived. After the file is backed up, the Archived attribute is removed.
- [ ]Hidden You can hide files so that they do not appear in a DOS directory listing by checking this box. You cannot move, delete, rename, or overwrite hidden files.
- [ ]System DOS operating files should have the System attribute. This protects the file from being moved, deleted, renamed, or overwritten.
- Change and Change All You can apply the attributes you have selected to the file displayed in the dialog box, or to all the tagged files. Choose Change (the default) to change the current file. If you choose Change All, all the tagged files will be given the selected attributes. Keep in mind that Change All changes *all* tagged files in all directories, not just the current directory. Press Esc to stop a Change All execution.

```
   Do you want to change the attributes of

            D:\FOXPRO\BOOK\CAMPERS.DBF

    [ ] Read Only        [ ] Hidden File
    [X] Archived         [ ] System File

    « Change »    < Change All >    < Cancel >
```

Fig. 1-102. Attributes dialog box.

Choose Cancel before you begin an operation to return to the Files panel without changing any attributes.

Rename Choose this option to rename files that are tagged. The file name of the first tagged file appears twice in the Rename dialog box. You can edit the name in the To box, or type a new name as shown in Fig. 1-103. Choose Rename when you are ready to rename the file.

```
              Rename: CAMPADD.DBF

                  To: address

          «  Rename  »         < Cancel >
```

Fig. 1-103. Rename dialog box.

If a file already exists with the name you entered, a message box asks if you want to continue. If you choose Yes, the next tagged file appears in the Rename dialog, and this file name is left unchanged. Choose No to stop the operation and return to the Files panel.

Size When you are moving or deleting files on your disk, you want to know how much room you will be freeing. The Size dialog box (Fig. 1-104) gives you this information.

Fig. 1-104. Size dialog box.

```
Tagged File Statistics
    Files:              1
    Bytes:            501
Actual space occupied:
    Clusters:           1
    Bytes:          2,048
           «   OK   »
```

The top half of the box shows the number of tagged files in all directories (not just the current directory), and the number of bytes in those files.

The bottom half of the box displays the actual space occupied. Your DOS allocates disk space in units called *clusters*. The number of bytes in a cluster depends on the system. If your system allocates 2048 bytes per cluster, then the minimum amount of space reserved for a file is 2048, even if the file only uses 113 bytes. A file containing 2049 bytes will use two clusters for 4096 bytes.

The number of clusters used by your tagged files is multiplied by the cluster value to show the actual number of bytes occupied.

Sort You can sort files in a directory to change the order in which they appear in the scrollable list. If you use the Files Like box, only the specified files will be sorted. Otherwise, all files in the directory appear in the new order you select.

The Sort dialog box in Fig. 1-105 contains two sets of radio buttons.

Fig. 1-105. Sort dialog box.

```
         Select Sort Criteria
  ( ) Name
  ( ) Extension      ( ) Ascending
  ( ) Size
  ( ) Date           ( ) Descending
  ( ) Attributes
       «   OK   »        < Cancel >
```

The default selection is Name and Ascending. Choosing Name sorts the files in alphabetical order. Ascending sorts them from A – Z, Descending from Z – A.

Size sorts files according to the number of bytes they use. Choose Ascending to sort from smallest to largest, Descending for largest to smallest.

Sort files in date order by choosing the Date radio button. Ascending puts the files in order from the oldest to the newest, Descending from the newest to the oldest.

Attributes sorts files by attribute. Ascending attribute order is r, a, s, h. Descending order is h, s, a, r.

When you are ready to sort, choose OK. Files are displayed in the order you chose. Choose Cancel to leave the Sort box without changing the file order.

Tree Choose this option to bring up the Tree panel (Fig. 1-106). This panel lets you perform most of the same operations available in the Files panel, but it performs them on entire directories rather than specific files. Always make a backup before you do anything in the Trees panel.

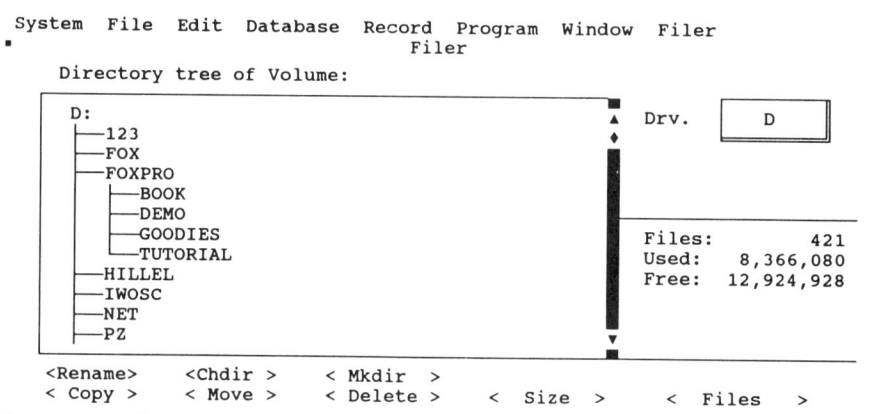

```
 System   File   Edit   Database   Record   Program   Window   Filer
                                            Filer
         Directory tree of Volume:
        ┌─────────────────────────────────────────┐    ▲  Drv.   ┌─────┐
        │ D:                                      │    │         │  D  │
        │  ├─123                                  │    ◆         └─────┘
        │  ├─FOX                                  │
        │  ├─FOXPRO                               │
        │  │   ├─BOOK                             │
        │  │   ├─DEMO                             │
        │  │   ├─GOODIES                          │       Files:          421
        │  │   └─TUTORIAL                         │       Used:     8,366,080
        │  ├─HILLEL                               │       Free:    12,924,928
        │  ├─IWOSC                                │
        │  ├─NET                                  │
        │  └─PZ                                   │
        │                                         │    ▼
        └─────────────────────────────────────────┘

   <Rename>    <Chdir >    < Mkdir  >
   < Copy >    < Move >    < Delete >    < Size >    < Files >
```

Fig. 1-106. The Tree panel.

To leave the Trees panel without taking action, press Esc or click the close control.

Drive The first time you choose Tree, the scrollable list displays the directories and subdirectories for the current drive. You can use the scroll bar or the ↑ or ↓ to see any directories that do not fit in the list window.

To change the drive, open the Drive pop-up and select the drive you want displayed in the list box. Beneath the Drive pop-up, you will see the number of files on that drive, the space they occupy, and the amount of free space.

Tagging directories Before you can perform operations on the files in directories, you must tag them, just as you do in the Files panel. When you execute an operation, it is performed only on the files in tagged directories.

To tag directories, Tab to the scrollable list. Use the ↑ or ↓ to highlight the directory you want, or point with the mouse. Then press the spacebar, or click.

To tag more than one directory at a time, hold down the Shift key and select the directories you want to tag. Dragging the mouse with the Shift key held down allows you to tag consecutive directories.

You can use the Shift key as a toggle to untag directories. When you press Shift and then press the spacebar or click, a tagged directory is untagged.

Use the following text buttons to perform operations on tagged directories.

Rename You can rename directories in the Rename dialog box (Fig. 1-107). When you choose this text button, the name of the first tagged directory appears in the dialog box. Type a new name in the text box and choose OK.

Fig. 1-107. Rename dialog box.

```
Rename: D:\FOXPRO\BOOK
    To: bestseller
          «  Rename  »              < Cancel >
```

Directory names must follow standard DOS conventions: maximum 8 characters with an extension of up to 3 characters.

If you have tagged more than one directory, directories appear one after the other in the dialog box to be renamed.

If you try to rename a directory with a name that already exists under the same parent directory, you will be denied access to the file.

When you rename a directory, none of the files in the directory is affected. The directory will move to the appropriate alphabetical position on the directory tree, under the same parent directory as the original name.

Change Directory   This is a convenient way to change the default working directory to avoid having to type the entire path when you want to work on a file in the directory.

To change directories, select the directory where you want FoxPro to look when no path is specified and choose ChDir. The bullet that marks the current directory moves to the directory you selected.

Make Directory   To make a new directory, select the directory that will be its parent directory and choose Mkdir. The Make Directory dialog box will appear (Fig. 1-108).

Fig. 1-108. Make Directory dialog box.

```
Make subdirectory in: D:\FOXPRO\BOOK
New Subdirectory name: Chapter1
          «  Mkdir  »              <Cancel >
```

Type the new directory name in the text box and choose Mkdir. If you try to use an existing name, a message box asks if you want to return to the Make Directory dialog to make a new directory in another tagged parent (Yes), or to the Tree panel (No).

Choose Cancel to leave the Make Directory dialog box without creating a new directory.

Copy   Use this text button to copy the tagged directory into another directory. Files that are currently open cannot be copied. In the Copy dialog box in Fig. 1-109, enter the name of the directory into which you want to copy the tagged directory.

If you choose the Target Directory text button, you can select the target directory from the Target dialog box. If files are in the target directory with the same names as files in the directory to be copied, checking the Replace existing files

```
<Target directory...> D:\FOXPRO\
                [ ] Replace existing files
                [ ] Preserve directories


        «  Copy  »              < Cancel >
```

Fig. 1-109. Copy dialog box.

box will overwrite the existing files in the target directory. If this box is not checked, an alert box asks if you want to overwrite files with the same name, and you can choose Yes to do so or No to skip the file and continue the operation.

With Preserve directories, if you tag more than one directory, you can simply copy all the files in all the tagged directories to a single target directory, or you actually copy the directory structure as well. When you choose Preserve directories, all the directories below the tagged directory farthest from the root directory will be preserved in the copy. For example, your C: directory might contain the subdirectories Metal, Classics, and Blues; and your directory tree, with additional subdirectories, would look like this:

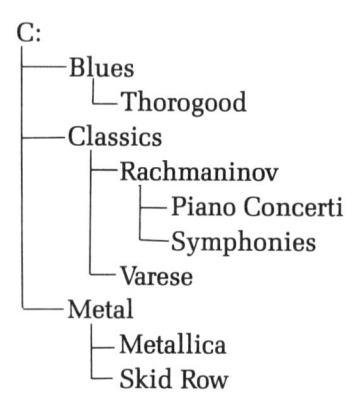

```
C:
├─Blues
│   └─Thorogood
├─Classics
│   ├─Rachmaninov
│   │   ├─Piano Concerti
│   │   └─Symphonies
│   └─Varese
└─Metal
    ├─Metallica
    └─Skid Row
```

If you tag the Classics directory and the Symphonies subdirectory, and copy them to D:\Favorites, the new D: drive tree looks like this:

```
D:
└─Favs
    └─Rachmaninov (empty)
        └─Symphonies
```

All files from tagged directories are copied, and the directory structure of directories above tagged directories is preserved. Because the Rachmaninov directory was not tagged, any files in that original directory were not copied. Because the Symphonies subdirectory was tagged, the Rachmaninov directory structure was copied intact.

Move Move works exactly the same way as Copy, except that the original tagged directories are deleted when you choose Move. You cannot move an open file.

If you tag a parent directory but you do not tag all its subdirectories, the tagged subdirectories will be moved, but the parent will be copied.

Delete Be careful with this option and do a backup before you choose it!

The tagged directory name appears at the top of the Delete dialog box shown in Fig. 1-110.

- [ ]Delete files only   If you check this box, only the files in the tagged directory will be deleted. The directory itself will remain intact.
- [ ]Remove all subdirectories   When you tag a parent directory and check this box, all subdirectories and their files will be deleted. If you want to delete only specific subdirectories, tag them individually and make sure this box is not checked.
- Delete   Choose Delete to remove the directory displayed in the dialog box. If you have tagged other directories, they will appear consecutively each time you choose Delete.
- Skip   If you want to go on to the next directory without deleting the directory displayed in the dialog box, choose Skip.
- Delete All   If you are brave enough to delete all the tagged directories without confirmation, choose Delete All. A message asks if you are sure you want to do this. If you choose Yes, all the tagged directories and their files are erased forever.

Fig. 1-110. Delete dialog box.

```
          Delete directory: D:\FOXPRO\BOOK

          [ ] Delete files only
          [X] Remove all sub-directories

       «Delete »    < Skip >    <Delete All >    <Cancel >
```

Choose Cancel before executing a Delete operation to leave the dialog box without taking action.

Size The Size dialog box (Fig. 1-111) is the same as the size dialog box in the Files panel. The top half of the box shows the number of files in the tagged directories and the number of bytes in those files. The bottom half of the box displays the actual space occupied. DOS allocates disk space in units called clusters. Depending on your system, DOS might allocate, say, 2048 bytes per cluster, in which case any file, no matter how small, uses at least 2048 bytes. A file containing 2049 bytes will use two clusters, or 4096 bytes.

Files Choose this option to return to the Files panel. (Refer to the beginning of this section for a description of the Files panel.)

114 *The FoxPro User Interface*

```
Tagged Directory Statistics
     Files:              25
     Bytes:          16,812
   Actual space occupied:
     Clusters:           25
     Bytes:          51,200
            «   OK   »
```

Fig. 1-111. Size dialog box.

System Calculator

The FoxPro Calculator is a desktop accessory that looks like a standard pocket calculator and is shown in Fig. 1-112.

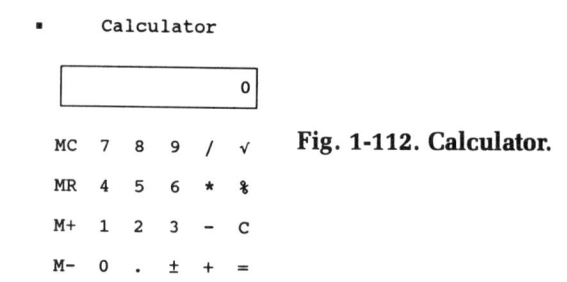

```
■    Calculator
     ┌──────────────┐
     │           0  │
     └──────────────┘
     MC  7  8  9  /  √
     MR  4  5  6  *  %
     M+  1  2  3  -  C
     M-  0  .  ±  +  =
```

Fig. 1-112. Calculator.

You can perform calculations by choosing the calculator buttons with the mouse. From the keyboard, type the equation as it would be written. All the keys have keyboard equivalents except:

Keystroke	**Calculator button**
Q	<RAD>
R	MR
N	±
A	M+
Z	MC
S	M-

To calculate, for example, to find the square root of 27 times 16 divided by 3, type

27*16/3Q=

The result is 12.

You can edit text in the display panel, and copy and paste into other documents. You can also copy numeric values from other documents into the display panel.

Calculator Preferences If you choose Preferences from the Edit menu, you can change preferences in the Calculator Preferences dialog box.

The three radio buttons determine whether NumLock on your keyboard is turned on or off. If the first radio button is on, NumLock simply remains the way it was when you choose Calculator from the System menu.

If you turn on Remember NumLock state, the Calculator reverts to whichever state NumLock was in last time you used it.

If you choose the third button, NumLock turns on automatically when you use the Calculator.

When you choose OK, your preferences takes effect. When you exit the Calculator, NumLock returns to the state it was in before you called the Calculator.

See also: Edit Preferences p. 89

System Calendar/Diary

The Calendar/Diary is a complete calendar and diary. When you choose this option, the Calendar/Diary dialog opens. The left half of the window in Fig. 1-113 displays the current month with today's date selected. The right half of window is the diary section, where you can enter text related to the selected date.

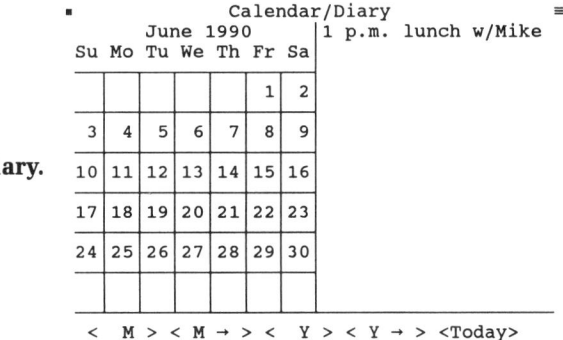

Fig. 1-113. Calendar/ Diary.

```
                   Calendar/Diary                ≡
         ■         June 1990       │1 p.m. lunch w/Mike
              Su Mo Tu We Th Fr Sa
                              1  2
              3  4  5  6  7  8  9
              10 11 12 13 14 15 16
              17 18 19 20 21 22 23
              24 25 26 27 28 29 30

              < M > < M → > < Y > < Y → > <Today>
```

When you open the calendar, a Diary menu appears at the right end of the menu bar. Keyboard users can use the menu to select options that correspond to the text buttons in the window.

To change the selected day in the calendar, use the arrow keys or click on the date you want to select. To change the month, choose PgUp to move backward and PgDn to move forward, or use the Month text buttons at the bottom of the window. To move backward and forward by year, use Shift – PgUp or Shift – PgDn, or choose the Year text buttons. Press T to return to today's date.

To make a diary entry, select the appropriate day and press Tab or click in the Diary panel. You can enter as much text as you like—there is no limit—and you can use standard FoxPro editing techniques to edit text (See the Edit menu description).

To return to the calendar, press Shift – Tab or click in the calendar with the mouse.

Eventually you will have enough old entries that valuable space on your disk is wasted. You can periodically delete entries by selecting a day on the calendar and choosing Delete... from the Diary menu. A message asks if you want to delete all entries prior to the day. Choose Yes to delete the entries, or No to return to the Calendar without making deletions.

You can close the Calendar window by choosing File Close, pressing Esc or clicking the close box.

See also: Edit menu p. 83

System Special Characters

FoxPro stores special characters like foreign punctuation marks, line drawing characters, and symbols in the Special Characters dialog box in Fig. 1-114.

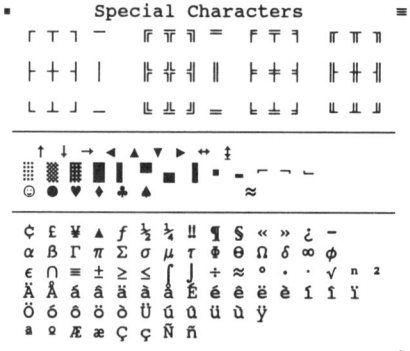

Fig. 1-114. Special characters.

To paste a special character into your current document, position the cursor where you want the character and choose Special Characters. Place the cursor on the character you want and choose it. You will find the character pasted into your file.

To close the Special Characters window, choose File Close, press Esc, or click the close box.

See also: Edit Copy p. 86
Edit Paste p. 86
File Close p. 34

System ASCII Chart

A complete ACSII Chart is stored in the ACSII Chart dialog box (Fig. 1-115).

To insert an ASCII character in your active file, position the cursor where

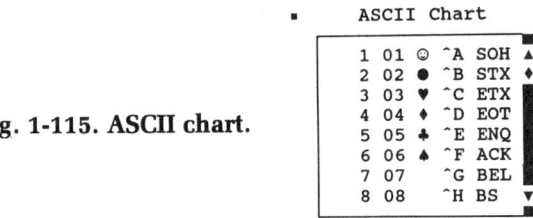

Fig. 1-115. ASCII chart.

```
            ASCII Chart
         ┌─────────────────┐
         │ 1  01 ☺  ^A SOH │
         │ 2  02 ●  ^B STX │
         │ 3  03 ♥  ^C ETX │
         │ 4  04 ♦  ^D EOT │
         │ 5  05 ♣  ^E ENQ │
         │ 6  06 ♠  ^F ACK │
         │ 7  07    ^G BEL │
         │ 8  08    ^H BS  │
         └─────────────────┘
```

you want the character and choose ACSII Chart. Scroll the chart to find the character you need, or, if you know the decimal equivalent, type the number to go directly to the character.

Select the character, and FoxPro pastes it at the cursor position in the window from which you opened the chart.

Close the chart by choosing File Close, pressing Esc, or clicking the close box.

See also: Edit Copy p. 86
              Edit Paste p. 86
              File Close p. 34

System Capture

Capture allows you to copy text from anywhere on the screen to the clipboard. This is just like Edit Copy except that the text you copy does not have to be inside a window.

When you choose Capture, a message tells you to select the top-left corner. Place the cursor at the top-left corner of the text you want to select, and press Enter or the mouse button.

The next message tells you to select the bottom-right corner. Move the cursor to the bottom-right of the text you want to select using the arrow keys or dragging with the mouse. Press Enter or release the mouse button to capture the text.

When the capture is complete, Captured and placed on clipboard appears on the screen.

Press Esc to cancel the capture.

See also: Edit Copy p. 86
              Edit Paste p. 86

System Puzzle

Have fun!

The Program menu

The Program menu shown in Fig. 1-116 lets you work with FoxPro program files.

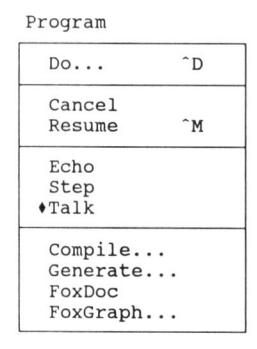

```
Program
 ┌─────────────────────┐
 │ Do...           ^D  │
 ├─────────────────────┤
 │ Cancel              │
 │ Resume          ^M  │
 ├─────────────────────┤
 │ Echo                │
 │ Step                │
 │ ♦Talk               │
 ├─────────────────────┤
 │ Compile...          │
 │ Generate...         │
 │ FoxDoc              │
 │ FoxGraph...         │
 └─────────────────────┘
```

Fig. 1-116. The Program menu.

Program Do...

Do... executes a program file. The Do... dialog box contains a list of .PRG files. Select the file you want to run and choose Do.

If you want to stop the program while it is running, press Esc. In the dialog box that appears, you can choose Cancel to stop running the program and close the file.

Choose Suspend to stop running the program but keep the file open so you can make changes. You can continue running the program if you choose Resume from the Program menu.

Choose Ignore to ignore the interruption and proceed with the program execution.

Shortcut key: Ctrl – D

See also: Program Resume p. 118

Program Cancel

Choose Cancel when you want to cancel execution of a program after choosing Suspend to interrupt running the program. This option is only available after you have chosen Suspend.

See also: Program Do... p. 118

Program Resume

The Resume option resumes execution of a suspended program. Resume is only available after you choose Suspend to interrupt the running of a program, or when you are using Step to step through a program.

Shortcut key: Ctrl – M

See also: Program Do... p. 118
Program Step p. 119

Program Echo

When you choose Echo, FoxPro displays the program file source code for you to monitor while a program is running. The program is displayed in the Trace window as it runs.

When you are finished using the Trace window, choose File Close, press Esc, or click the close box.

See also: Window Trace p. 44

Program Step

When you choose Step, the program pauses after each statement is executed. Choosing Step also activates Echo. If you set Echo off, Step is also set off.

After each step in the program you can choose Resume to continue stepping through the program.

Choose Cancel to abort program execution.

See also: Program Resume p. 118

Program Talk

When you choose Talk, the current status of processing is displayed in the current output window.

Program Compile...

In the Compile dialog box (Fig. 1-117) you can select one or more program (.PRG) or format (.FMT) files to be compiled. Compiled program files have an .FXP extension and compiled format files have a .PRX extension.

The scrollable list in the dialog box displays all the program and format files in the current directory. Change the drive or directory by making selections in the Drive and Directory pop-ups.

You can select more than one file from this list. From the keyboard, hold down Shift and press the spacebar to select each file name you want to compile. With the mouse, hold down Shift and click each file.

All   To select all the files in the list, choose All. To deselect multiple files, press Shift – spacebar or Shift – click on a selected file.

Clear   Choose Clear to deselect all the files.

Output To...   Type the directory path where your compiled files will be stored, or choose Output To... to display a Directory dialog.

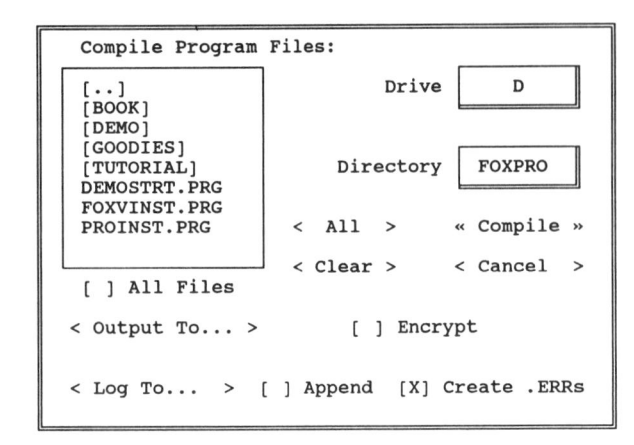

```
┌─────────────────────────────────────────────┐
│ Compile Program Files:                      │
│ ┌─────────────────┐                         │
│ │ [..]            │      Drive    ┌───┐    │
│ │ [BOOK]          │               │ D │    │
│ │ [DEMO]          │               └───┘    │
│ │ [GOODIES]       │                         │
│ │ [TUTORIAL]      │    Directory  ┌──────┐ │
│ │ DEMOSTRT.PRG    │               │FOXPRO│ │
│ │ FOXVINST.PRG    │               └──────┘ │
│ │ PROINST.PRG     │   <  All  >  « Compile »│
│ │                 │                         │
│ └─────────────────┘   < Clear >  < Cancel > │
│ [ ] All Files                               │
│                                             │
│ < Output To... >     [ ] Encrypt            │
│                                             │
│ < Log To... >  [ ] Append  [X] Create .ERRs │
└─────────────────────────────────────────────┘
```

Fig. 1-117. **Compile dialog box.**

In the Directory dialog, select the drive, directory and/or subdirectory where you want the compiled files stored and choose Select. The path appears in the Output To... text box.

[ ]Encrypt Choose Encrypt if you want your compiled file(s) to be scrambled for security.

[ ]Create.ERRs FoxPro keeps track of any errors it finds when it compiles files. You can store these errors in a log file or an .ERR file. If you check Create.ERRs, the error messages for each selected file will be stored in a separate file with the same base name with an .ERR extension.

Log To... If you want to store error messages found for all the files selected to be compiled in one log file, type a name for the file in the text box, or choose Log To... to display a Save As dialog box where you can type the name. Then choose Save and the file name appears in the Log To... text box.

[ ]Append You can add the errors for the selected files to an existing log file by checking the Append box and entering the name of the log file in the Log To... text box.

Compile When your selections are complete, choose Compile.

Program Compile

When a program (.PRG) file is open in a window, the Compile... option displays as Compile. Choosing Compile simply compiles the open .PRG file.

If FoxPro finds errors as the program is compiling, the line with the error is highlighted in the editing window and a dialog box tells you your error. Choose Ignore to ignore the error and continue compiling. If you choose Ignore All, FoxPro ignores this error and any that follow. Choose Cancel to stop compilation.

If you SET LOGERROR ON before you choose Compile, FoxPro stores the errors messages it finds in an .ERR file with the same name as the program file.

Program Generate

The Generate option is used with the Screen Builder. Refer to chapter 7 for more information on how to use this option.

Program FoxDoc

FoxDoc is an application system documenter. Chapter 6 on FoxDoc contains a full description of how to use FoxDoc.

Program FoxGraph...

The FoxGraph option is disabled unless you have installed FoxGraph on your hard disk. This is a graphics application that you can purchase separately.

The FoxGraph dialog box is similar to a File Open dialog box. Unless you check All Files, only files with .GR3, .GRF, and .GR4 extensions will appear in the scrollable list.

To load a file containing a graph description, choose one of the .GR* files from the list and select Load. The graph description appears in the Graph Setup dialog box.

To create a new graph, choose New and specify the graph description in the dialog box.

To work with existing graphs, choose FoxGraph. This bypasses the Setup dialog box.

Choose Cancel or press Esc to exit the dialog box.

For more details on FoxGraph, refer to your *FoxGraph Reference Manual*.

2

FoxPro commands

FoxPro commands can be issued from the command window or from within programs. Each option from the Control Center has a corresponding command that can be issued outside of the Control Center. However, many additional commands cannot be issued from the Control Center. Many of these commands (such as DO WHILE and IF) are used only within programs.

In this chapter, the commands are listed in alphabetical order. Each command is followed by a short description, and then details for using it. In situations where variable information must be provided, the argument is placed in italic. In cases where optional clauses can be used, examples show the command with and without the clause.

\ and \ \

Description The \ and \ \ commands output lines of text to the screen or to a file.

Operational rules If SET TEXTMERGE has been set to a file name, the text is sent to a file, otherwise it appears on the screen. This command is similar to the TEXT ... ENDTEXT command in that text does not have to be enclosed in quotes. You can embed an expression in the text by enclosing it in the text merge delimiters, < < > >. The delimiters can be changed with the SET TEXTMERGE DELIMITERS command.

The \ command issues a carriage return before printing the line of text, so it is one line below the previous item displayed. The \ \ command prints at the current screen or file position. The \ command by itself displays a blank line.

Use the NOSHOW keyword to suppress screen output.

Examples The following program sends the displayed message to a file named INVITE.TXT.

```
** Mailing.PRG
** program that creates a form letter to each name in the database
USE Maillist INDEX Mzip
SET TEXTMERGE TO Invite
DO WHILE .NOT. EOF( )
   \ Dear <<fname>>,
   \
   \ Please come to our party Saturday night at 8:00 pm.
   \ Yours, Corky
   SKIP
ENDDO
SET TEXTMERGE TO
```

When run, the program displays:

Dear Harry,

Please come to our party Saturday night at 8:00 pm.
Yours, Corky

See also: TEXT ... ENDTEXT p. 238
            SET TEXTMERGE p. 263

? *and* ?? *expression list*

Description   The ? and ?? commands display the contents of the *expression list*.

Operational rules   The ? command issues a carriage return before printing the expression list, so it is positioned one line below the previous item displayed. The ?? command prints at the current screen or printer position. The ? command by itself displays a blank line.

You can use the PICTURE and FUNCTION clauses to define the display of the expressions. See the @...SAY...GET section for a list of valid PICTURE and FUNCTION codes. Use the AT function to define the column where the expression will display.

Examples

? Fname FUNCTION "@T", Lname PICTURE "@!"
John SMITH
? Fname FUNCTION "@T", Lname AT 50
John   Smith

See also: @ p. 125

??? *expression*

Description The ??? sends an expression to the printer without changing the position of the printer head.

Operational rules This command is helpful to use when you need to send printer control codes at the beginning of a printout. The ? and ?? commands can be used to perform the same function, but they might move the printer head, disturbing the layout of the printout. Control codes can be designated in several ways, namely:

1. The CHR( ) function. For example: CHR(27) + "E"
2. The ASCII number: "{27}{69}"
3. The character, such as: "{ESC}{69}"
4. A combination. For example: "{27}E"

See also: @ SAY...GET p. 125
            CHR( ) p. 287

@ *row, col* SAY *expression* GET *expression*

Description This command displays and receives information formatted on the screen.

Operational rules The @ command allows you to designate the row and column where the expressions will be displayed. The SAY argument is used for displaying an expression, while the GET argument allows editing of the expression. GET expressions may be fields or memory variables. The READ command must follow the list of @... GETs for a screen.

The following optional functions can be used with the FUNCTION clause or preceded with a @ in the PICTURE clause to display output in these various ways. To combine functions, place them together with the @ sign (i.e: @T!).

- A   Alphabetic characters only.
- B   Left align numeric data.
- C   A CR (credit) shows after a positive number (use with SAY only).
- D   Uses the format from the SET DATE command for editing dates.
- E   Edits as a European date (MM/DD/YY)
- I   Output is centered in the field.
- J   Right justifies output.
- K   Entire field is selected for editing.
- L   Leading zeros display in numbers.
- M   Precedes a list of items which the user can choose from. Items must be separated with commas. When editing, the user can press the spacebar to scroll the choices of items.
- R   Precedes a format string that will display but not be saved.

S   Precedes a number that defines how long the display will be. If the field is longer, it will horizontally scroll when edited.
T   Trims leading and trailing blanks from the field.
X   A DB (debit) shows after a negative number (use with SAY only).
Z   Values of zero display as blanks.
(Negative number display surrounded by parentheses (SAY only).
!   Alphabetical characters converted to uppercase.
^   Displays numbers in scientific notation.
$ Displays numbers in currency format.

Use the PICTURE option to change displays such as uppercase conversion, and comma mode. Below is a list of picture template symbols. If your template is not as long as the GET variable, or the variable will be truncated to the length of the template then:

A   Allows only letters.
L   Allows logical data only.
N   Allows letters or digits.
X   Allows any character.
Y   Allows only Y or N.
!   Converts to uppercase.
9   Allows only digits and signs.
Allows only digits, blanks and + or −.
$ Displays a dollar sign, $, in place of leading zeros.
*   Displays an asterisk, *, in place of leading zeros.
,   Displays commas between thousands.
.   Decimal point position.

The $, COL( ), and ROW( ) functions allow you to use relative row and column referencing. Each represents the current position of the cursor.

Several clauses can be used to test validity with the GET command. They are:

RANGE *exp, exp*

The RANGE clause verifies that the entry is between the range of two expressions. If it is not, an error message appears which alerts the user to the valid range of entries.

VALID *expL / expN*

The VALID clause checks whether *expL* is true (.T.) before allowing the user to move on to the next field. This clause is particularly useful when *expL* is a user-defined function. A custom error message can be added to the end of the VALID statement using the ERROR clause.

If the VALID clause is followed by a numeric expression (most often a user-defined field that evaluates as a numeric), the return value determines how the verification will behave. If the value is 0, the cursor remains in the field and an error message is displayed. If the value is a positive number, the cursor advances that number of fields (GET statements) for the next input field. If the value is negative, the cursor moves back that number of fields.

WHEN *expL*

The cursor will only go to this field for editing if *expL* evaluates as true (.T.).

DEFAULT *exp*

When appending records, the expression *exp* becomes the default for this field.

MESSAGE *expC*

The message, *expC*, is displayed on the last line of the screen when the cursor moves to this GET statement. If SET STATUS is off, the message does not display.

WINDOW name

This function is used for editing memos. The *name* function must be the name of a predefined window. Precede this clause with the word OPEN, and the window will be open by default. The user must still press Ctrl – Home to edit the memo even if the window is open.

SIZE *expN1, expN2*

This clause allows you to change the size of the GET display. The default size is one row with the width of the expression that is being edited. The height, *expN1*, is in rows. The width, *expN2*, is in characters.

COLOR standard / enhanced
COLOR SCHEME expn

This function allows you to change colors for the SAY and GET fields. When using the COLOR clause, the first expression sets the colors for the SAY statement and the second sets the colors for the GET statement. To use the COLOR SCHEME clause, simply enter the number of the scheme that has been defined with the SET COLOR SCHEME command.

DISABLE | ENABLE

When GET fields are disabled, they appear in the Disabled colors and the cursors skip over the field. The default is ENABLE.

Examples

@ 3,1 SAY "Database of California Clients"
@ 5,1 SAY "Enter Last Name" GET Lname PICTURE " !XXXXXXXXXXXXXXX"

    @ 5,50 SAY "First Name" GET Fname PICTURE "!XXXXXXXXXXXXXXX"
    @ $+2,1 SAY "Address:" GET Address
    @ $+1,1 SAY "   City:" GET City
    @ $,$+1 SAY "   State:" GET State PICTURE "@!" DEFAULT "CA"
    @ $,$+1 SAY "Zip:" GET Zip PICTURE "#####" RANGE "90000","97000"
    @ $+2,1 SAY "Phone:" GET Phone PICTURE "(###)###-####"
    @ $+2,1 SAY "Cust. Code:" GET Code VALID LEFT(Code,1) $ "A,D,L";
       ERROR "Code must begin with A, D or L"
    @ $+2,1 SAY "Taxable? " GET Tax PICTURE "Y" VALID IIF(TAX="Y",1,2)
    @ $+1,1 SAY "Tax ID # " GET Tax_id PICTURE "###-###-####"
    @ $+2,1 SAY "Year-to-Date Sales $ " GET Sales
    READ

See also: READ p. 216

@ row1, col1, row2, col2 BOX

Description   The @...BOX command creates a box on the screen.

Operational rules   This command draws a box in the rectangular area made up of corner *row1, col1* through the opposite corner or *row2, col2*.

The optional character argument *expC* defines the characters to be used in drawing the box. The string can be up to 9 characters, each character defining each corner, each side, and the fill character. The default is a single line.

Examples   The example draws a single line box at the bottom half of the screen:

    @ 10, 1 TO 15, 75 BOX

See also: @SAY...GET p. 125

@ row1, col1 CLEAR
@ row1, col1 CLEAR TO row2, col2

Description   The @...CLEAR command clears a rectangular area of the screen.

Operational rules   This command erases the rectangular area made up of corner *row1, col1* through the bottom right corner of the screen. Use the CLEAR TO option to clear through the bottom right corner *row2, col2*.

See also: @SAY...Get p. 125

@ row1, col1 FILL TO row2, col2

Description   The @...FILL TO command colors in a rectangular area of the screen.

Operational rules This command colors in a rectangular area made up of corner *row1, col1* through the opposite corner or *row2, col2*.

The optional argument COLOR*attribute* defines the color of the box. The attribute codes are listed under the SET COLOR TO command. The argument COLORSCHEME *expN* defines the color according to a predefined color scheme.

Examples

@ 1, 1 FILL TO 5, 30 COLOR r/b

See also: @SAY...GET p. 125

@ *row, col* GET Check Boxes

Description This command creates a check box.

Operational rules Check boxes allow a field to be marked True or False (Yes or No). The box is displayed at *row* and *col* on the screen. The GET variable may be a field or memory variable. If it is a logical expression, it will be .T. when the check box is marked, .F. otherwise. If it is numeric, it will be 1 when marked, 0 otherwise.

To create a check box, you must use the FUNCTION and/or PICTURE clauses. The FUNCTION clause is *C and then the prompt for the box. The PICTURE clause is @*C and the prompt. To use both, the FUNCTION clause must contain *C and the PICTURE clause must contain the prompt.

The T and N options set whether a box should terminate the READ. To terminate the READ if the box is checked, place a T directly after the C in clause. The N option is the default. It sets a box to not terminate the READ.

A *hot key* is a highlighted letter that allows the status of the check box to be changed from anywhere on the editing screen. To assign a hot key, place \< in front of the desired letter in the prompt.

See also: @ SAY...GET p. 125
            READ p. 216

@ *row, col* GET Invisible Buttons

Description This command creates invisible buttons.

Operational rules *Invisible buttons* are much like *push buttons* in that the user selects a particular button, excluding the rest. The main difference is that invisible buttons do not have prompts like push buttons do. Instead, they are just rectangular regions of the screen. They are often used for displaying over text.

The area is displayed at *row* and *col* on the screen. The GET variable may be a numeric field or memory variable. Its value will correspond to the button chosen. The first button is 1, the next 2, etc.

To create invisible buttons, you must use the FUNCTION and/or PICTURE clauses. The FUNCTION clause is *I, and the PICTURE clause is @*I. If more than one button is to be created, a semicolon must be specified for each button. To use both clauses, the FUNCTION clause must contain *I and the PICTURE clause contains the number of semicolons.

The T and N options set whether a button should terminate the READ. To terminate the READ if the button is chosen, place a T directly after the C in clause. The N option is the default. It sets a button to not terminate the READ.

The H and V options set whether the buttons are in a horizontal or vertical row. The default is vertical.

The SIZE, ENABLE, MESSAGE, VALID, WHEN, DEFAULT, COLOR and COLOR SCHEME clauses are all available with this command. See the @...SAY...GET section for descriptions of these clauses. The DEFAULT clause is used for defining the variable type of the GET memory variable. If the variable is already defined or it is a field, DEFAULT is ignored. The default height and width of an invisible button is 0, with one space between each button. Use the SIZE *height*, *width*, *spaces* clause to change the size of the invisible button area.

See also: READ p. 216
            @ SAY...GET p. 125

@ *row, col* GET Lists

Description   This command creates a list.

Operational rules   Lists allow the user to pick an option from a box that they can scroll within. The box is displayed at *row* and *col* on the screen.

The GET expression can be a field or memory variable. If it is a number, it becomes the number of the item chosen. If it is a character, it becomes the character equivalent of the list item.

To define the elements of a list you may use a predefined pop-up using the POPUP clause, or call elements of an array by using the FROM clause. Pop-ups are defined with the DEFINE POPUP command.

The SIZE, ENABLE, MESSAGE, VALID, WHEN, DEFAULT, COLOR, and COLOR SCHEME clauses are all available with this command. See the @...SAY...GET section for descriptions of these clauses. The DEFAULT clause is used for defining the variable type of the GET memory variable. If the variable is already defined or it is a field, DEFAULT is ignored.

The default size of the list is determined by the widest item in the list, and the number of rows below the list. Use the SIZE *length*, *width* clause to change the size of the list area. The length expression is by number of rows, and width is number of characters.

The colors are derived from the current window or screen. To change the default list color scheme, set the scheme according to the following table:

Color pair
1. Not used
2. Not used
3. Not used
4. Not used
5. Message
6. Selected item
7. Not used
8. Not used
9. Enabled list
10. Disabled list

The first half of the color pair specifies the prompt color, the second half the background.

Examples The first example is a list that was defined using the POPUP clause. The program sets up a list of all available data files. The user chooses the file, and the program opens it. The SCROLL option in the DEFINE POPUP command creates a scroll bar on the right of the list that can be used by a mouse.

```
** DATAFILES.PRG
** program that allows the user to pick a database
CLEAR
memfile = " "
DEFINE POPUP datafiles PROMPT FILES LIKE *.DBF SCROLL
@ 5,1 GET memfile POPUP datafiles SIZE 15,20
READ
USE &memfile
```

When run, the program displays a list of all data files on the default directory. The size of the list area is 15 rows by 20 characters.

The second example is a list that was defined by an array. The program is a list of three predetermined data files. The user chooses the file, and the program opens it.

```
** DATA2.PRG
** program that allows the user to pick a database
CLEAR
DIMENSION datafile(3)
memfile = " "
datfile(1) = "STUDENTS.DBF"
datfile(2) = "TEACHERS.DBF"
```

```
        datfile(3) = "PARENTS.DBF"
        @ 5,1 GET memfile FROM datafile SIZE 5,15
        READ
        USE &memfile
```

See also: DEFINE POPUP p. 168
            @ SAY...GET p. 125

@ *row, col* GET Pop-ups

Description   This command creates a pop-up.

Operational rules   Pop-ups display a list of options which the user can choose from. The list of options is only displayed when the cursor is at that particular field on the screen. When the cursor is elsewhere, the pop-up displays as a rectangle with double right and bottom lines. The pop-up is displayed at *row* and *col* on the screen.

The GET variable can be a memory variable or field. If it is a number, it becomes the number of the item chosen. If it is a character, it becomes the character equivalent of the list item.

To create a pop-up, you must use the FUNCTION and/or PICTURE clauses. The FUNCTION clause is ^, followed by the list of items separated with semicolons. The PICTURE clause is @^ followed by the list. To use both clauses, the FUNCTION clause must contain ^ while the PICTURE clause contains the list of items.

The T and N options set whether the pop-up should terminate the READ. To terminate the READ, place a T directly after the ^ in clause. The N option is the default. It sets a pop-up to not terminate the READ.

A hot key, as you know, is a highlighted letter that allows an option to be chosen from anywhere in the pop-up list. To assign a hot key, place \ in front of the desired letter in the prompt. The FROM clause can be used to define the items in the list from an array.

The SIZE, ENABLE, MESSAGE, VALID, WHEN, DEFAULT, COLOR, and COLOR SCHEME clauses are all available with this command. See the @...SAY...GET section for descriptions of these clauses. The DEFAULT clause is used for defining the variable type of the GET memory variable. If the variable is already defined or it is a field, DEFAULT is ignored.

The default size of the pop-up box is determined by the widest item in the list, and the number items. Use the SIZE *length, width* clause to change the size. Because the length is always determined by the number of items, it will ignore the number placed in *length*.

The colors are derived from the current window or screen. To change the default pop-up color scheme, set the scheme according to the following table:

Color pair
1. Not used
2. Not used
3. Not used
4. Not used
5. Message
6. Selected item
7. Hot keys
8. Not used
9. Enabled option
10. Disabled option

The first half of the color pair specifies the prompt color, the second half, the background.

Examples The first example is a screen with two pop-ups used in editing a student's record. The first pop-up determines the Sex field (Male, Female, Unknown). The second determines the grade of the student. Hot keys are set for the options in the first pop-up:

```
** STUDENT.PRG
** program fills out a student's personal information

choices = 'Freshman;Sophomore;Junior;Senior'
@ 3,1 SAY 'Student Database — Personal Information '
@ 5,1 SAY TRIM(fname)+' '+lname
@ 7,1 SAY "Sex:" GET sex FUNCTION '^ \<Male;\<Female;\Unknown'
@ 7,40 say "Class:" GET class FUNCTION '^' PICTURE choices
READ
```

The second example is the same program for editing the class field, the only difference being that the items in the list are defined by an array.

```
** DATA2.PRG
** program that allows the user to pick a database
CLEAR
DIMENSION mclass(4)
mclass(1) = 'Freshman'
mclass(2) = 'Sophomore'
mclass(3) = 'Junior'
mclass(4) = 'Senior'
@ 3,1 SAY 'Student Database — Personal Information '
```

```
@ 5,1 SAY TRIM(fname)+' '+lname
@ 7,40 SAY "Class:" GET class FROM mclass FUNCTION
READ
```

See also: DEFINE POPUP p. 168
               @ SAY...GET p. 125

@ *row, col* GET Push Buttons

Description   This command creates push buttons.

Operational rules   Push buttons are most often used to determine an action. For instance, many FoxPro dialog boxes terminate with the push buttons <Cancel> and <<OK>>.

The GET variable may be a memory variable or field. If it is a number, it becomes the number of the item chosen. If it is a character, it becomes the character equivalent of the list item.

To create a push button, you must use the FUNCTION and/or PICTURE clauses. The FUNCTION clause is *, followed by the list of push button prompts, separated with semicolons. The PICTURE clause is @* followed by the list. To use both clauses, the FUNCTION clause must contain * while the PICTURE clause contains the list of items.

The T and N options set whether the push button should terminate the READ. To terminate the READ, place a T directly after the * clause. The N option is the default. It sets a button to not terminate the READ. The H and V options set whether the buttons are in a horizontal or vertical row. The default is vertical.

A hot key, as previously mentioned, is a highlighted letter that allows an option to be chosen from anywhere in the push button area. To assign a hot key, place \ < in front of the desired letter in the prompt. The default button is the one that displays within << >> brackets instead of < >. To set a default, place \! before the prompt. To assign a button that is chosen when Esc is hit, precede the prompt with \?.

The SIZE, ENABLE, MESSAGE, VALID, WHEN, DEFAULT, COLOR, and COLOR SCHEME clauses are all available with this command. See the @...SAY...GET section for descriptions of these clauses. The DEFAULT clause is used for defining the variable type of the GET memory variable. If the variable is already defined or it is a field, DEFAULT is ignored.

The default size of a button is determined by the width of the prompt, with one space between each button. Use the SIZE *height, width, spaces* clause to change the size. Because the height is always one, it will ignore the number placed in *height*.

The colors are derived from the current window or screen. To change the default push button color scheme, set the scheme according to the following table:

Color pair
1. Not used
2. Not used
3. Not used
4. Not used
5. Message
6. Selected button prompt
7. Hot keys
8. Not used
9. Enabled button prompt
10. Disabled button prompt

The first half of the color pair specifies the prompt color, the second half the background.

Examples The example is a screen with push buttons that will determine the order that a report will be printed in—*Alpha*, *Zip*, or *Class*. Hot keys are set for the first letter of each option, with the Zip option being the default push button. The buttons are set in a horizontal layout instead of the vertical default.

```
** STUDENT.PRG
** program that asks the desired order for the printout.
** program assumes indexes Alpha.IDX, Zip.IDX and Class.IDX

@ 3,1 SAY 'Student Roster'
mindex = ' '
@ 15,1 SAY 'Choose the sort order for the listing:'
@ 17,1 GET mindex FUNCTION '*H \<Alpha;\!\<Zip;\<Class'
READ
SET INDEX TO &mindex
```

When run, the program would display:

Choose the sort order for the listing:

<Alpha> < <Zip> > <Class>

See also: @ SAY...GET p. 125

@ *row, col* GET Radio Buttons

Description   This command creates radio buttons.

Operational rules   *Radio buttons* are much like push buttons, in that they determine one choice out of a list. A period is placed next to the chosen option.

The GET variable may be a memory variable or field. If it is a number, it becomes the number of the item chosen. If it is a character, it becomes the character equivalent of the list item.

To create a radio button, you must use the FUNCTION and/or PICTURE clauses. The FUNCTION clause is *R, followed by the list of radio button prompts, separated with semicolons. The PICTURE clause is @*R followed by the list. To use both clauses, the FUNCTION clause must contain *R while the PICTURE clause contains the list of prompts.

The T and N options set whether the radio button area should terminate the READ. To terminate the READ, place a T directly after the *R clause. The N option is the default. It sets a button area to not terminate the READ. The H and V options set whether the buttons are in a horizontal or vertical row. The default is vertical.

A hot key is a highlighted letter that allows an option to be chosen from anywhere in the radio button area. To assign a hot key, place \ in front of the desired letter in the prompt.

The SIZE, ENABLE, MESSAGE, VALID, WHEN, DEFAULT, COLOR and COLOR SCHEME clauses are all available with this command. See the @...SAY...GET section for descriptions of these clauses. The DEFAULT clause is used for defining the variable type of the GET memory variable. If the variable is already defined or it is a field, DEFAULT is ignored.

The default size of a button is determined by the width of the prompt, with one space between each button. Use the SIZE *height*, *width*, *spaces* clause to change the size. Because the height is always one, it will ignore the number placed in *height*.

The colors are derived from the current window or screen. To change the default pop-up color scheme, set the scheme according to the following table:

Color pair
1. Not used
2. Not used
3. Not used
4. Not used
5. Message
6. Selected radio prompt
7. Hot keys
8. Not used
9. Enabled radio prompt
10. Disabled radio prompt

The first half of the color pair specifies the prompt color, the second half the background.

Examples The example is a screen with radio buttons that will determine the order that a report will be printed in—*Alpha, Zip* or *Class*). Hot keys are set for the first letter of each option. The buttons are set in a horizontal layout instead of the vertical default. They are four spaces apart from each other instead of the one space default.

```
** STUDENT.PRG
** program that asks the desired order for the printout

@ 3,1 SAY 'Student Roster'
mindex = ' '
@ 15,1 SAY 'Choose the sort order for the listing:'
@ 17,1 GET mindex FUNCTION '*RH \<Alpha;\!<Zip;\<Class';
SIZE 1,6,4
READ
SET INDEX TO &mindex
```

When run, the program will display:

Choose the sort order for the listing:

( ) Alpha   ( ) Zip   ( ) Class

See also: @ SAY...GET p. 125

@ *row, col* EDIT Text Edit Region

Description   This command creates a text editing region.

Operational rules   Text editing regions are used with memo fields and long character expressions. A rectangular box is displayed where the entire field can be edited. All of the commands available in the FoxPro editor can be used in a text editing region. The GET variable can be a memory variable or field.

To create a text editing region, you must use the SIZE *height, width* clause. An optional third number can be entered in the clause to determine the number of characters that can be edited. If the height is set to one, a special text editing region is created that scrolls horizontally. Otherwise, the text will word wrap and scroll down as it is typed into the area.

The I and J functions determine special alignment. Use FUNCTION 'J' to right justify text, FUNCTION 'I' to center text.

The ENABLE, MESSAGE, VALID, WHEN, DEFAULT, COLOR, and COLOR SCHEME clauses are all available with this command. See the @...SAY...GET section for descriptions of these clauses. The DEFAULT clause is only valid if the memory variable has not been defined. If the variable is already defined or it is a field, DEFAULT is ignored.

The SCROLL clause creates a scroll bar on the right of the area that can be used by a mouse. The scroll bar is only displayed if the text is too large to fit in the region.

Text editing regions are exited by pressing Tab or Ctrl – Tab. The TAB clause causes the Tab key to insert a tab instead of exiting the region. When the clause is active, Ctrl – Tab is the only key that exits the region. The NOTAB clause is the default.

The colors are derived from the current window or screen. To change the default pop-up color scheme, set the scheme according to the following table:

Color pair
1. Not used
2. Not used
3. Not used
4. Not used
5. Message
6. Selected text editing region
7. Not used
8. Not used
9. Enabled text editing region
10. Disabled text editing region

The first half of the color pair specifies the foreground, the second half the background.

Examples The example is a screen with a text editing region that allows for editing of a memo field. The region is 5 rows high by 60 characters across. A scroll bar is created for getting to text that has scrolled off of the screen.

```
** STUDENT.PRG ** program fills out a student's narrative information

@ 3,1 SAY 'Student Database — Narrative Information '
@ 5,1 SAY TRIM(fname)+' '+lname
@ 7,1 SAY 'Enter Narrative:'
@ 8,1 EDIT narr SIZE 5,60 SCROLL
READ
```

See also: @ SAY...GET p. 125

@ row, col MENU array expN

Description The @...MENU creates a pop-up menu.

Operational rules This command displays a pop-up menu that the user can choose options from. The top left corner of the menu will be at *row, col*. The options in the menu are contained in *array*. The number of options to display are defined with *expN*.

Use the TITLE *expC* to display a title at the top of the menu.

Examples

DIMENSION SORTS(3)
Sorts(1) = "Alpha"
Sorts(2) = "Zip"
Sorts(3) = "Other"

@ 3,3 MENU Sorts, 3 TITLE "Choose an order to sort by"
READ MENU TO Choice

DO CASE
  CASE Choice = 1
    SET INDEX TO MAILALPH
  CASE Choice = 2
    SET INDEX TO MAILZIP
  CASE Choice = 3
    ACCEPT "Enter Expression to Sort By " TO Other
    INDEX ON &Other TO Temp
    GO TOP
ENDCASE

See also: DEFINE POPUP *p. 168*

@ *row, col* PROMPT *expC*

Description The @...PROMPT creates a light bar menu.

Operational rules This command displays a light bar menu that the user can choose options from. The left corner of the menu will be at *row, col* and *expC* is the option. Each option in the menu is defined with a @...PROMPT command. Use the MESSAGE *expC* to display a message at the location specified with the SET MESSAGE TO command.

Examples

@ 3,1 PROMPT "Alpha" MESSAGE "Sort in Alphabetical Order"
@ 3,10 PROMPT "Zip" MESSAGE "Sort by Zip Code"
@ 3,20 PROMPT "Order" MESSAGE "Sort in User-Defined Order"
SET MESSAGE TO 22
MENU TO Choice

DO CASE
  CASE Choice = 1
    SET INDEX TO MAILALPH

```
        CASE Choice = 2
           SET INDEX TO MAILZIP
        CASE Choice = 3
           ACCEPT "Enter Expression to Sort By " TO Other
           INDEX ON &Other TO Temp
           GO TOP
     ENDCASE
```
See also: MENU TO p. 195

@ row1, col1 TO row2, col2

Description   The @...TO command creates a box on the screen allowing more options than the @...BOX command.

Operational rules   This command draws a box in the rectangular area made up of corner *row1, col1* through the opposite corner or *row2, col2*.

The optional arguments DOUBLE, PANEL, or *character string* define the character to be used in drawing the box. The default is a single line.

The optional clause COLOR *attribute* defines the color of the box. The attribute codes are listed under the SET COLOR TO command. You can also use the COLOR SCHEME *expN* to use a predefined color scheme.

Examples   The first example draws a single line box at the bottom half of the screen. The second example draws a colored double line box.

```
@ 10, 1 TO 15, 75
@ 1, 1 TO 5, 30 DOUBLE COLOR b/r
```

See also: @SAY...GET p. 125

= expr

Description   The = command evaluates the expression.

Operational rules   This command is particularly useful with functions that perform an operation, such as the CAPSLOCK(.T.) function, which turns on the CapsLock mode. Many user-defined functions also perform operations. This command is the most efficient way to run such a function because you do not have to store the expression to a memory variable or use the ? command, which displays the expression.

Examples

```
= CAPSLOCK(.T.)
```

ACCEPT *prompt* TO *mem variable*

Description The ACCEPT command displays the prompt and pauses until the user enters something.

Operational rules This command is most often used in programs where few questions are to be prompted on the screen. Each ACCEPT command halts the program until the user types in an answer and presses Enter. The ACCEPT command is easier to use than full-screen editing commands such as @...GET, because:

1. The memory variable does not have to be initialized before issuing the command.
2. Screen coordinates do not have to be set. (ACCEPT displays the prompt in the same manner as the ? command).

However, the ACCEPT command is not as powerful as the full-screen editing commands, especially because the entry cannot be formatted. Memory variables created by the ACCEPT command are always of the character type. The variable becomes the length of the entry typed in.

If the optional *prompt* is not used, the ACCEPT command simply pauses and waits for the user to enter something.

Examples The following program prompts the user to enter their name. The memory variable Mname becomes the length of the entry:

ACCEPT "Enter Your Name " TO MNAME
? "Hi there ", MNAME

See also: @SAY...GET p. 125

ACTIVATE MENU *menu name*

Description ACTIVATE MENU displays a bounce-bar menu on the screen.

Operational rules Bounce-bar menus are menus that show a list of options. The user can navigate through the options with the arrow keys. To choose an option, the user highlights it with the cursor, and presses Enter.

Menus are designed with the DEFINE MENU and DEFINE PAD commands. The ON PAD and ON SELECTION PAD commands define the operations to be performed when a pad is selected. Once the definitions are set, you can use ACTIVATE MENU to call it up. Use DEACTIVATE MENU to erase a menu from the screen.

Use the optional PAD *pad name* clause to define which menu item should be highlighted first. The default is the first pad.

The NOWAIT option causes the menu to be displayed, but the program does not wait for an option to be selected. See DEFINE MENU for a program that creates a bounce-bar menu.

See also: DEFINE MENU p. 166

ACTIVATE POPUP *pop-up name*

Description   ACTIVATE POPUP displays a pop-up menu on the screen.

Operational rules   Pop-up menus are menus that appear on the screen, often as a "menu within a menu" that displays as bounce-bar options are highlighted. Pop-up menus can have their own options listed, and the user can navigate through these options with the up and down arrow keys. To choose an option, the user highlights it with the cursor, and presses Enter.

Although bounce-bar menus can be vertically or horizontally oriented, pop-up menus are always vertical.

The NOWAIT option causes the pop-up to be displayed, but the program does not wait for an option to be selected. Use the AT *row, col* option to define where on the screen the pop-up is to be activated. This position takes precedence over that of the DEFINE POPUP setting. Use BAR *expN* to automatically select a particular bar of the pop-up menu. The command ACTIVATE POPUP BAR 3 automatically selects the third bar.

Pop-up menus are designed with the DEFINE POPUP and DEFINE BAR commands. The ON SELECTION POPUP command defines the operations to be performed when a bar from the pop-up menu is selected. Once the definitions are set, you can use ACTIVATE POPUP to call it up. Use DEACTIVATE POPUP to erase a pop-up menu from the screen. See DEFINE BAR for a program that creates a pop-up menu within a bounce-bar menu.

See also: DEFINE BAR p. 163

ACTIVATE SCREEN

Description   ACTIVATE SCREEN "zooms" into a window, displaying it on the entire screen.

Operational rules   Windows are designed with the DEFINE WINDOW command. Use ACTIVATE WINDOW to then display it. The window must be displayed on the screen before ACTIVATE SCREEN is issued.

Example   The following program displays a window on the screen, and then expands it to the entire screen:

```
DEFINE WINDOW Wind1 FROM 3,3 TO 10,30
ACTIVATE WINDOW Wind1
```

```
? "This is Window 1"
ACTIVATE SCREEN
```

See also: DEFINE WINDOW p. 170

ACTIVATE WINDOW

Description   ACTIVATE WINDOW displays a window.

Operational rules   Windows are designed with the DEFINE WINDOW command. Use ACTIVATE WINDOW to then display it.

Use the optional keyword ALL to activate all defined windows. Use the BOTTOM and TOP keywords to place them behind (BOTTOM) or in front (TOP) of other windows. The SAME option places a window where it was before being hidden. The NOSHOW option does not show the window, although output is still directed there.

See also: DEFINE WINDOW p. 170

APPEND

Description   The APPEND command allows the user to add new records to the database.

Operational rules   This command brings up the editing screen. Each new record is added on to the bottom of the file. If a format screen has been set, that format is used instead of the basic edit screen format.

See also: EDIT p. 176

APPEND BLANK

Description   The APPEND BLANK command adds one more record to the database without going into the full-screen edit mode.

Operational rules   The new record added with the APPEND BLANK command has no entries in any of the fields, hence the BLANK argument.

Example

```
USE Maillist
APPEND BLANK
SET FORMAT TO Mailedit
READ
CLOSE FORMAT
```

The program adds a record to the file using APPEND BLANK. This method is advantageous to the full-screen APPEND command because the user cannot scroll to any other records, and the program regains control after the entry of this one record.

See also: APPEND p. 143

APPEND FROM *data file*

Description   The APPEND FROM command adds records from a database into the current file.

Operational rules   When appending from a file, the optional file types are:

Type	Description
DELIMITED	Variable length fields separated with commas.
DELIMITED WITH *expC*	Variable length fields separated with *expC*.
DELIMITED WITH BLANK	Variable length fields separated with a space.
DELIMITED WITH TAB	Variable length fields separated with Tab.
DIF	Visicalc's Data Interchange Format.
FW2	Ashton Tate's Framework II.
MOD	Microsoft Multiplan version 4.01.
PDOX	Borland's Paradox version 3.5.
RPD	Ashton Tate's RapidFile version 1.2.
SDF	Fixed length field ASCII file.
SYLK	Symbolic Link interchange format.
WK1	Lotus 1-2-3, version 2.x.
WK3	Lotus 1-2-3, version 3.x.
WKS	Lotus 1-2-3, version 1.x.
WR1	Lotus Symphony, version 1.1 or 1.2.
WRK	Lotus Symphony, version 1.0.
XLS	Microsoft Excel, version 2.0.

The optional FOR *conditional* argument appends only the records that match a certain criteria. Use the FIELDS *fieldlist* clause to select the fields that will be appended. Use APPEND FROM ? to pull up the Open File dialog and choose a file.

When data from a worksheet is read in (DIF, WKS, XLS, etc.), each row becomes a record, and each column a field. If one of the optional file types is used, FoxPro assumes the default extension of the file name. For example, Lotus version 1.0 files are assumed to end with a .WKS extension, ASCII files assume a .TXT extension. Enter the extension if it is not the default. If the file name does not have an extension, be sure to use a period (.) after the file name.

Example

USE Maillist

APPEND FROM Mail	(add records from another FoxPro file)
APPEND FROM Mail FOR State = "CA"	(add records that match criteria)
APPEND FROM Mail SDF	(add records from fixed ASCII file)
APPEND FROM Mail DELIM	(add records from comma delim file)
APPEND FROM Mail DELIM WITH /	(add records with fields separated with /)
APPEND FROM Mail FIELDS Fname,Lname,City	

See also: APPEND p. 143

APPEND FROM ARRAY *array*

Description The APPEND FROM command adds records from an array into the current file.

Operational rules When appending from a single dimension array, each array element represents a field. When appending from a two-dimensional array, each column represents a field, and each row represents a record.

Use the FOR *condition* clause to select records to be appended. The condition statement must be based on the field names that the array variables will be read into, and not the array name.

Example

USE Maillist
APPEND FROM ARRAY Data

See also: APPEND p. 143

APPEND MEMO *memo field* FROM *file name*

Description The APPEND MEMO command reads the *memo field* from *file name* into the specified memo field of the current file.

Operational rules The optional OVERWRITE argument replaces the value of the memo field. If this option is not used, the command simply appends the memo data to the end of the current memo.

You can read memos from a text file when running this command from the Control Center.

Example

USE Maillist	
APPEND MEMO Comments FROM Mail.txt	(adds memos from Mail.txt)

AVERAGE

Description   AVERAGE provides the arithmetic mean of the numeric fields of a data file.

Operational rules   If no arguments are provided, FoxPro displays the average of each numeric field in the database. You can provide a field list to specify the field(s) to be summed.

To create memory variables whose values are the averages, use the TO *memory variable list* or TO ARRAY *array*. When calculating to an array, the array must be declared as single dimension, and each field in the field list updates the next row of the array.

You can use the optional FOR *condition*, WHILE *condition*, and *scope* arguments to include only a subset of the records in the calculation.

Examples

AVERAGE
AVERAGE Wage, Bonus to Awage, Abon
AVERAGE Wage TO Awage FOR State = "CA"
AVERAGE Wage, Bonus, Commsion TO ARRAY Mamount

The last example assumes that Mamount has been declared as a one-dimensional array. After the AVERAGE, Mamount(1) is equal to the average of the Wage field.

See also: DECLARE p. 162

BROWSE

Description   The Browse mode allows the user to add/edit records in the current file.

Operational rules   When browsing a file the records appear in list format, one record per row. Full screen editing is in effect with the addition of the following keys:

Ctrl – ←   Horizontally scroll left.
Ctrl – →   Horizontally scroll right.

Many of the optional arguments place restrictions on the capabilities of the BROWSE command:

- NOAPPEND   Prevents records from being appended.
- NOCLEAR   Does not clear the screen when the Browse mode is exited.
- NODELETE   Prevents records from being deleted.
- NOEDIT   Prevents records from being edited (may only be viewed).
- NOFOLLOW   When editing indexed records, NOFOLLOW stays at the cur-

rent records position even if a change causes the record to move its place in the indexed database.
- NOLGRID   When the window is split, turns off the vertical field separators in the left window (like choosing Grid Off from the BROWSE menu).
- NOLINK   When the window is split, as one partition is scrolled, do not scroll the other (the default is for partitions to scroll in tandem).
- NOMENU   Prevents access to the BROWSE menu pop-up.
- NOOPTIMIZE   Disables Rushmore (the default is for Rushmore to be enabled).
- NORGRID   When the window is split, turns off the vertical field separators in the right window.
- NOWAIT   When called from a program, the program continues executing while the BROWSE screen is in use.

The optional FIELDS *fieldname list* arguments restrict the fields or field order displayed in the BROWSE command. The SET FIELDS TO command can also set the order. To create a calculated field, use this clause and the equation that defines the calculated field.

Within the FIELDS clause several optional switches may be used. Precede the switch with slash (/) or colon (:). The switches are:

/*expN*	Field is displayed as width of *expN*.
/B = *expr1, expr2*	Field falls between the range (boundaries) of *expr1* and *expr2*.
/H	Specifies the field heading over the field (the default is the name of the field).
/R	Field is read only.
/V = *expr*	If expression is not true (.T.), error message is displayed and field not exited.
/V = *expr*:E = *expC*	*expC* is displayed as the error message.
/V = *expr*:F	Validation check is run whether or not the field is changed (forced valuation). The default is for validation only if the field is edited.
/W = *expL*	Field can only be edited when *expL* is evaluated as true (.T.).
/P	Specifies a picture option for each field. See the @...SAY command for a list of picture and function codes. Example: BROWSE FIELDS Names /P = '@!', Income /P = '#,###,###'

Use multiple verification switches by entering the /V only once. For example, /V = *exp1*:F:W*exp*/ only allows verification if the field has been edited, and only allows editing when *exp2* is true (.T.).

The FORMAT clause allows you to use a format file from the Browse mode. The fields from the format file will be chosen for the BROWSE screen, and all PICTURE, RANGE, WHEN, and VALID clauses from the file are in effect. The other optional arguments are:

- COLOR *attribute*   Defines the color of the Browse window.
- COLOR SCHEME *expN*   Chooses a predefined color scheme for the Browse window.
- FOR *expL*   Displays only records that match logical clause *expL*. If *expL* is not an optimizable clause, the BROWSE command will run slowly.
- FREEZE *field name*   Only allows *field* to be edited although other fields can be viewed.
- KEY *expr1*   Specifies a key value (or range of values *expr1, expr2* for records that are to be displayed in the Browse window. The database must be indexed on the key.
- LAST   Retrieves the settings of the last Browse option, so they do not have to be set again.
- LEDIT   When the window is split, set the left partition into Change mode. Much like choosing Change from the Browse menu pop-up.
- LPARTITION *expN*   When used in conjunction with the PARTITION option, it splits the Browse window and places the cursor in the left partition. (The default is for the cursor to be placed in the right partition) .
- NORMAL   Ignores user-defined window characteristics which would effect the display of the Browse screen.
- PARTITION *expN*   Splits the Browse window at column *expN*. This is the same as using the window splitter with the mouse, or choosing Resize Partitions from the Browse menu.
- PREFERENCE *name*   Uses the Browse screen setting saved last time with the PREFERENCE name.
- REDIT   When the window is split, set the right partition into Change mode.
- SAVE   Leaves the Browse window on the screen after it has been exited. This option is available only within programs. The default is to remove all windows from the screen.
- TIMEOUT *expN*   Waits *expN* seconds for input. If that time has elapsed, it closes the Browse window. This option is available only within programs.
- VALID *expL*   After editing a record, if logical clause *expL* is false, the cursor will not move off the record.
- WHEN *expL*   When you move to a record and logical clause *expL* is false, the record becomes read-only.
- WIDTH *expN*   Limits the maximum width of all fields.

- WINDOW *window name*   Allows the Browse window to be opened within another window.

Multiple databases can be browsed together when the relation has been set using SET RELATION TO. Include the command SET SKIP to define a one-to-many relationship and see all records from the child database. For instance, suppose there is a data file of students related to a file of classes and there are 30 students per class. If the class file is the parent database, the student file is the child database. When fields from both files are displayed in Browse mode, and SET SKIP has been activated, it shows one record for the parent database and multiple records for the child.

If both files are displayed in the Browse mode, press Ctrl – ↓ to move to the next parent record. Press Ctrl – ↑ to move to the previous parent record.

Example

BROWSE
BROWSE NOAPPEND NODELETE
BROWSE FIELDS Lname,Fname,City,Zip
BROWSE FIELDS Name /R,Sex /P = "!"/V = Sex$"MF":E = "Must be M or F"

See *also*:   APPEND p. 143
             EDIT p. 176

BUILD APP *.fxp file* FROM *project*

Description   Uses information from a project file to create a .FXP file.

Operational rules   The project file must contain all of the files needed in the application.

See *also*:   CREATE PROJECT p. 159

BUILD PROJECT *project file* FROM *file list*

Description   Creates a project database (.PJX) that contains information regarding all files in the *file list*.

Operational rules   A project file is a database that contains information regarding all files that are used in an application. Project files are used with the BUILD APP command for building a .FXP file and for building .EXE files.

The file types that may be used in the *file list* are programs, menus, reports, labels, screen, and library files. The project database may be opened with the USE command and manipulated. If changes have been made to any of the files in the file list, use BUILD PROJECT *project file* without the FROM clause to update the .PJX file.

See *also*:   CREATE PROJECT p. 159

CALCULATE *option list*

Description The CALCULATE command performs a calculation of all or a subset of records in the current database.

Operational rules The command displays the answer to the calculations. Valid calculations for the *option list* are: AVG( ), CNT( ), MAX( ), MIN( ), NPV( ), STD( ), SUM( ), and VAR( ).

Keep in mind that if the talk is set OFF, the calculation will not display on the screen. The optional TO *memory variable* initializes a memory variable that is equal to the calculation. Use a *memory variable list* or *array name* if more than one calculation is in the *option list*. The array must already be declared, and must be a one-dimensional array.

The optional FOR *condition*, WHILE *condition*, and *scope* arguments are used to calculate only records that match a specified criteria.

Example

CALCULATE MAX(Grade)
CALCULATE MIN(Sales) FOR Salesman = "JONES"
CALCULATE STD(Grade) TO Stdgrad
CALCULATE MAX(Grade), MIN(Grade), STD(Grade) to Mxgrad, Mngrad, Sdgrad
CALCULATE MAX(Grade), MIN(Grade), STD(Grade) to Mxgrad

The last example assumes that Mxgrad is a one-dimensional array that has been declared.

See also: RECCOUNT( ) p. 357

CALL *module name*

Description The CALL command runs a binary program loaded into memory.

Operational rules FoxPro can run binary (assembly language and machine language) programs. To do this you must:

1. Load the program into memory with the LOAD command.
2. Run the program with the CALL command.
3. Release it from memory with the RELEASE MODULE command.

Binary programs are useful in instances where a function must be performed that FoxPro cannot do. For instance, certain screen graphics manipulation and file maintenance on non-FoxPro files can be done only through binary programs.

You can pass variables to the program using the WITH *expression list* option. You can pass up to seven expressions.

See also: LOAD p. 192

CANCEL

Description The CANCEL command halts a program and returns to the command window.

Operational rules This command stops a program without exiting the FoxPro system. The user is exited to the command window. All data files remain open, while all private memory variables are released. If the command is issued from the runtime version, the user is exited to DOS.

This command is equivalent to choosing the Cancel option from the prompt Cancel, Suspend, Ignore that is displayed when an error is encountered in a program, or when the user presses Esc while running a program.

CHANGE

The CHANGE command is equivalent to EDIT.

See: EDIT p. 176

CLEAR

Description The CLEAR command is used to clear the screen, the memory, the open databases, or other elements from FoxPro.

Operational rules The CLEAR command without any arguments clears the screen.

The optional argument MEMORY clears all memory variables. The arguments MENUS, POPUPS, and WINDOWS clear those on-screen options. GETS removes the ability to move into fields currently displayed with the @...GET command. TYPEAHEAD clears the keyboard buffer. PROGRAM clears the program file from memory so it can be edited.

The CLEAR ALL command removes everything currently in memory, although it does not close files and indexes.

Example

```
CLEAR      (clears the screen)
CLEAR MEMORY      (clears all memory variables)
CLEAR MENUS, POPUPS      (clears all menus and pop-up menus)
CLEAR TYPEAHEAD      (clears the keyboard buffer)
```

See also: CLOSE p. 152

CLEAR READ

Description The CLEAR READ command clears the READ, the current level and returns control to the previous READ.

Operational rules FoxPro supports multiple READ's. This is most often needed when a GET statement calls a user-defined-function (UDF) through the VALID or WHEN clause. The UDF may have a READ in it, but once the function is through processing, the control goes back to the initial READ. FoxPro supports up to four levels of READ's.

See also: CLEAR p. 151

CLOSE

Description The CLOSE command is used to close any file currently open.

Operational rules The CLOSE command ensures that the contents of a currently open file have been saved. To close one database file, issue the USE command while in that SELECT area.

The optional arguments ALTERNATE, DATABASES, FORMAT, INDEX, and PROCEDURE close only files of each particular type. The argument ALL closes files of all types.

Use the MEMO *memo field* or MEMO ALL clause to close a memo window or windows opened with the MODIFY MEMO command.

Example

```
CLOSE DATABASES    (close all databases)
CLOSE INDEX        (closes all index files)
CLOSE ALL          (closes all files)
```

See also: CLEAR p. 151

COMPILE *file name*

Description The COMPILE command is used to compile a source code program file to a .FPX object code file.

Operational rules FoxPro requires that program files are compiled into object code before running. Object code files allow the programs to run much faster. These files, unlike source code files, cannot be edited with MODIFY COMMAND.

FoxPro automatically compiles programs when DO *program name* is issued if the .PRG file but no .FPX file exists. The program (.PRG) file is compared to the object code (.FPX) file. If the two are different, then it recompiles the object code. Use SET DEVELOPMENT OFF to turn off automatic compiling.

The COMPILE command checks for errors in the source code. If an error is found, the command displays the line number of the error and aborts the compile.

See also: SET DEVELOPMENT p. 252

CONTINUE

Description   The CONTINUE command is used to locate the next record that matches the criteria used in the LOCATE command.

Operational rules   The LOCATE command is used to find the first record that matches a specified criteria. If the criteria is based on a field that is indexed, the SEEK command will find the record much faster than the LOCATE command.

To find the next record that matches the criteria, use the CONTINUE command. If no other records match the criteria, the record pointer moves to the end of file, and EOF( ) is true (.T.).

Example

```
. USE Maillist
. LOCATE FOR Lname = "SMITH"
. ? Lname, Fname
SMITH JOHN
. CONTINUE
. ? Lname, Fname
SMITHSON ANDY
```

See also: LOCATE p. 192

COPY FILE *file name* TO *file name*

Description   The COPY FILE command makes a duplicate copy of any type of file.

Operational rules   This command is equivalent to the COPY command from DOS. The DOS command is actually faster than COPY FILE, and it can be accessed from FoxPro through the RUN command. However, some users cannot access the RUN command because they do not have enough memory. In this case, COPY FILE can be substituted.

Example

```
COPY FILE Mail.Frm TO Mail2.Frm
```

See also: RUN p. 224

COPY INDEXES *index file list* TO *.cdx file*

Description   The COPY INDEXES command copies a list of index files into a new or existing multiple index (.CDX) file.

Operational rules   Multiple indexes contain index "tags" allowing for many indexes to be maintained through one file.

If the multiple index file does not exist, it is created. If it does exist, the new index tag is simply added to the current list of tags. If the optional TO *.cdx file* is not used, FoxPro automatically creates a file with the same name as the .DBF file but with a .CDX extension.

Use the optional to ALL option instead of the *index file list* and it will add all open index files to the .CDX file.

Examples

COPY INDEX Mailzip   (adds Mailzip.idx to Maillist.cdx)
COPY INDEX Mailzip TO Mail2   (adds Mailzip.idx to Mail2.cdx)

See also: COPY TAG p. 155

COPY MEMO *memo field* TO *file name*

Description   The COPY MEMO command copies the text from a memo file to another file.

Operational rules   If *file name* does not exist, FoxPro creates it with a .TXT default extension. If the file does exist, it is overwritten unless the optional ADDITIVE argument is used. This appends the memo field text to the bottom of *file name*.

Example

COPY MEMO Comment TO Narrative
COPY MEMO Comment TO Narrative ADDITIVE

See also: APPEND MEMO p. 145

COPY STRUCTURE TO *file name*

Description   The COPY STRUCTURE command copies only the structure of the current file to *file name*.

Operational rules   The new file is a FoxPro database with a .DBF extension. It will not contain any records.

The optional FIELDS *field list* argument copies only the specified fields to the new database. If the original file has a structural index file, the WITH CDX and WITH PRODUCTION options create a structural index for the new database.

Examples

COPY STRUCTURE TO Mail2
COPY STRUCTURE TO Mail2 FIELDS Lname,Fname,City

See also: APPEND p. 143

COPY TAG *tag name* TO *.IDX file*

Description   The COPY TAG command copies a tag from a multiple index file to an index (.IDX) file.

Operational rules   Multiple indexes contain index "tags" allowing for many indexes to be maintained through one file. The multiple index file must be open when this command is issued.

If the optional OF *.cdx file* is not used, FoxPro automatically copies from a file with the same name as the .DBF file but with a .CDX extension. If that file isn't found, it then searches other open .CDX files for the corresponding tag name.

Use the optional to ALL option instead of the *index file list* and it will add all open index files to the .CDX file.

Example

COPY TAG Zip TO Mailzip   (creates Mailzip.idx)
COPY TAG Zip OF Mail2 TO Mzip   (creates Mzip.idx from Mail2.cdx)

See also: DELETE TAG p. 172

COPY TO *file name*

Description   The COPY TO command copies the records from the current file to *file name*.

Operational rules   Unless a type is specified, the new file is a dbase database with a .DBF extension. When copying to a file, the optional file types are:

Type	Description
SDF	Fixed length fields ASCII file.
DELIMITED	Variable length fields separated with commas.
DELIMITED WITH *expC*	Variable length fields separated with *expC*.
DELIMITED WITH BLANK	Variable length fields separated with a space.
DELIMITED WITH TAB	Variable length fields separated with Tab.
DIF	Visicalc's Data Interchange Format.
MOD	Microsoft Multiplan version 4.01.
SDF	Fixed length field ASCII file.
SYLK	Symbolic Link interchange format.
WK1	Lotus 1-2-3, version 2.x.
WK3	Lotus 1-2-3, version 3.x.
WKS	Lotus 1-2-3, version 1.x
WR1	Lotus Symphony, version 1.1 or 1.2.
WRK	Lotus Symphony, version 1.0.
XLS	Microsoft Excel, version 2.0.

FOXPLUS   Only needed if the file contains a memo field, as FoxPro memo fields are structured differently.

The optional FOR *condition* and WHILE *condition* and scope arguments are used to copy only records that match a specified criteria.

The optional FIELDS *field list* argument copies only the specified fields to the new database. If the original file has a structural index file, the WITH CDX and WITH PRODUCTION options create a structural index for the new database.

Use the NOOPTIMIZE option to disable Rushmore. An alternate method is to globally disable Rushmore by using the SET OPTIMIZE command.

Example

COPY TO Mail2 FOR LNAME = "S"   (copies for specified criteria)
COPY TO Mail2 NEXT 100   (copies next 100 records)
COPY TO Mail2 SDF   (copies to a fixed ASCII file)
COPY TO Mail2 DELIMITED   (copies to a variable length file)
COPY TO Mail2 Lname, Fname, City (copies to a three-field file)

See also: APPEND p. 143
              EXPORT TO p. 178

COPY TO *file name* STRUCTURE EXTENDED

Description   The COPY TO STRUCTURE EXTENDED command copies the structure of the current file to a special type of file that contains the structure in its records.

Operational rules   The new file is made up of five fields: FIELD_NAME, FIELD_TYPE, FIELD_LEN, and FIELD_DEC. There is one record in this database for each field in the current file.

This command can be used to create structures of new files within programs. The program can make decisions on the structure (such as adding or deleting fields, or changing names and lengths) through editing the extended file, and then issuing the CREATE FROM command. This allows the user to create or modify a structure without using the full-screen CREATE or MODIFY STRUCTURE commands.

See also: MODIFY STRUCTURE p. 198

COPY TO ARRAY *array name*

Description   The COPY TO ARRAY command copies the records from the current file an array.

Operational rules The array must be declared before running this command. If the array is two-dimensional, each record is given a row in the array. If the array is one-dimensional, then FoxPro simply adds in each field from each record. The copying stops at the last field and record, or when all dimensions are filled, whichever comes first.

The optional FOR *condition*, WHILE *condition*, and *scope* arguments are used to copy only records that match a specified criteria. The optional FIELDS *field list* argument copies only the specified fields to the array.

Example

```
. USE Maillist
. DECLARE Mail[5,6]
. COPY TO ARRAY Mail FOR ZIP = "92111"
  5 records copied
. ? Mail[1,1] + Mail[1,2]
John  Smith
. ? Mail[2,1] + Mail[2,2]
Joe  Schmo
```

See also: APPEND FROM ARRAY *p. 145*

COUNT

Description The COUNT command counts the number of records in the current database.

Operational rules The command displays the number of records counted. Keep in mind that if the talk is set OFF, the count does not display on the screen. The optional TO *memory variable* initializes a memory variable that is equal to the number of records counted.

The optional FOR *condition*, WHILE *condition*, and *scope* arguments are used to count only records that match a specified criteria.

Example

```
COUNT FOR Zip = "92111"
COUNT TO Zcount WHILE Lname = "SMITH"
```

See also: RECCOUNT( ) *p. 357*

CREATE

Description The CREATE command creates the layout for a FoxPro database file.

Operational rules A FoxPro database file is defined by its field names, the type of each field, the length of each field, and whether the field is to be indexed. The default extension for a database file is .DBF. A database can have up to 255 fields. Field names can be from 1 to 10 characters, and can contain letters, numbers, and the underline character (_). Field names must begin with a letter. Each field must be one of the following types: Character, numeric, floating point number, logical, date, or memo.

Character field widths can be from 1 to 254 in length. Numeric fields can be up to 20 digits. Date fields are automatically 8, memo fields are 10, and logical fields are 1. Data entered in a memo field is not stored in the .DBF file, but is a second file with the extension .DBT.

See also: MODIFY STRUCTURE p. 198

CREATE *file name* FROM *structure extended file*

Description   The CREATE FROM command creates a database file from a special type of file that contains the structure in its records.

Operational rules   The structured file is made up of four fields: FIELD_NAME, FIELD_TYPE, FIELD_LEN, and FIELD_DEC. This database has one record for each field in the current file. These files can be created from the COPY TO STRUCTURE EXTENDED command.

Structure extended files can be used to create structures of new files within programs. The program can make decisions on the structure (such as adding or deleting fields, or changing names and lengths) through editing the extended file, and then creating the file with CREATE FROM. This allows the user to create or modify a structure without using the full-screen CREATE or MODIFY STRUCTURE commands.

See also: COPY TO STRUCTURE EXTENDED p. 156

CREATE LABEL *file name*

Description   The CREATE LABEL command uses the FoxPro label generator to create format for mailing labels.

Operational rules   When in the label generator, you set the dimensions of the label, the number of labels to print across the page, and then the contents of each label (fields and templates).

If you use the optional ? argument, in place of *file name*, FoxPro then brings up the dialog box that allows you to enter a name. If *file name* already exists, the CREATE LABEL command does not overwrite it. Instead, it allows you to modify the file. The default extension of label format files is .LBX.

Use LABEL FORM to print the labels. Labels printed with this command automatically omit blank lines for records that have no contents in particular fields.

See also: LABEL FORM p. 189

CREATE MENU

Description   Activates the FoxPro menu builder which helps you build menus and pop-ups.

Operational rules   The menu builder creates a menu (.MNX) file that contains information regarding the menu created in the menu builder. The file may be opened with the USE command and manipulated. This command is equivalent to choosing New... from the File menu, and specifying a Menu file.

If the file name is not included, the menu file is temporarily named UNTITLED and must be named when saved. The optional ? argument can be used to get the Open File dialog box where you can choose from a list of .MNX files or enter a new name.

Use the WINDOW *window name* clause to place the menu layout within a window. It will take on all characteristics of the window. Use IN WINDOW *window name* to open the menu layout in the parent window. The menu layout must be smaller than the parent, and stay within the parent window's boundaries. The IN SCREEN option is the default. This causes the menu builder to be placed on the screen instead of within a window.

See also: DEFINE MENU p. 166
MENU p. 193

CREATE PROJECT

Description   Activates the Project window which helps you build a project file.

Operational rules   A project database (.PJX) contains info regarding a group of files that are all used in one application.

The .PJX file is a database that contains information regarding all the files in the project. Project files are used with the BUILD APP command for building a .FXP file and for building .EXE files. The file can be opened with the USE command and manipulated.

CREATE PROJECT is equivalent to choosing New... from the File menu, and specifying a Project file.

If the file name is not included, the menu file is temporarily named UNTITLED and must be named when saved. The optional ? argument can be used to get the Open File dialog where you can choose from a list of .PJX files or enter a new name.

Use the WINDOW *window name* clause to place the Project window within another window. It will then take on all of the characteristics of that window. Use IN WINDOW *window name* to open the Project window inside a parent window. The Project window must be smaller than the parent, and stay within the parent window's boundaries.

The IN SCREEN option is the default. This causes the Project window to be placed on the screen instead of within a window.

See also: BUILD PROJECT p. 149

CREATE QUERY

Description Activates the RQBE window, which helps you create a query.

Operational rules When in the RQBE window, you define the field to select by, the comparison operator (Like, Exactly Like, More Than, Less Than, etc.) and the comparison. You can select multiple criteria by connecting them with AND (the default) or OR. You can also select the method to output the query (Browse, Report, Label, Cursor, etc.)

The RQBE window builds an SQL SELECT command. The SELECT command allows you to specify the query and then FoxPro determines the most optimal way to retrieve the information.

CREATE QUERY is equivalent to choosing New... from the File menu, and specifying a Query file. The query is stored in a program file with a .QRY extension. The file can be opened with the MODIFY COMMAND command and manipulated. To run a query, use DO *query file name*.

If the file name is not included, the query file is temporarily named UNTITLED and must be named when saved. The optional ? argument can be used to get the Open File dialog where you can choose from a list of .QRY files or enter a new name.

See also: FoxPro SQL/RQBE Chapter 9

CREATE REPORT *file name*

Description The CREATE REPORT command uses the FoxPro Report generator to create a report format (.FRX) file.

Operational rules When in the report generator, you set the dimensions of the report, headings, contents of the body of the report, and subtotal groupings.

If you omit *file name*, FoxPro asks for the name when you save the file. If you use the optional ? argument in place of *file name*, FoxPro then brings up the dialog box that allows you to enter a name. If *file name* already exists, the CREATE REPORT command does not overwrite it. Instead, it allows you to modify the file.

Print reports using the REPORT FORM command.

See also: REPORT FORM p. 220

CREATE SCREEN

Description This command activates the FoxPro screen builder which helps you create screen formats.

Operational rules The Screen builder allows you to create screen layouts and easily define pop-ups, radio buttons, and other objects.

CREATE SCREEN is equivalent to choosing New... from the File menu, and specifying a Screen file. The screen's information is stored in a fill with a .SCX extension. The file can be opened with the USE *file name* command and manipulated. If the file name is not included, the screen file is temporarily named UNTITLED and must be named when saved. The optional ? argument can be used to get the Open File dialog where you can choose from a list of .SCX files or enter a new name.

Use the WINDOW *window name* clause to place the Screen builder window within another window. It will take on all characteristics of that window. Use IN WINDOW *window name* to open the screen builder inside a parent window. The Screen Builder window must be smaller than the parent, and stay within the parent window's boundaries. The IN SCREEN option is the default. This causes the screen builder to be placed on the screen instead of within a window.

See also: FoxPro Screen Builder *Chapter 7*

CREATE VIEW *.vue file name*

Description The CREATE VIEW command creates a view (.VUE) file from the current settings.

Operational rules A *view file* saves information regarding the following settings:

- Open data and index files and their work areas.
- Current selected work area.
- Relationships set between files.
- Open format files.
- Current filter conditions.
- Current help and resource files.

To quickly restore all these settings with one command, use SET VIEW TO *.vue file name*. The CREATE VIEW command creates the .VUE file from the current settings.

See also: SET VIEW TO p. 264

DEACTIVATE MENU

Description DEACTIVATE MENU erases a bounce-bar menu from the screen.

Operational rules Menus are designed with the DEFINE MENU and DEFINE PAD commands. Use ACTIVATE MENU to then display them. DEACTIVATE MENU erases the current menu from the screen, but does not clear it from memory.

See DEFINE MENU for a program that creates a user-defined menu.

See also: DEFINE MENU p. 166

DEACTIVATE POPUP

Description DEACTIVATE POPUP erases a pop-up menu from the screen.

Operational rules Pop-up menus are designed with the DEFINE POPUP and DEFINE BAR commands. Use ACTIVATE POPUP to display. DEACTIVATE POPUP erases the current pop-up menu from the screen, but does not clear it from memory.

See DEFINE BAR for a program that creates a user-defined pop-up menu.

See also: DEFINE BAR p. 163

DEACTIVATE WINDOW

Description DEACTIVATE WINDOW erases a window from the screen.

Operational rules Windows designed with the DEFINE WINDOW command. Use ACTIVATE WINDOW to then display it. DEACTIVATE WINDOW erases the window from the screen, but does not clear it from memory.

See also: DEFINE WINDOW p. 170

DECLARE *array name* [*number of rows,number of columns*]

Description Use DECLARE to establish an array.

Operational rules You must declare arrays before using them. *Arrays are special memory variables that have multiple values.* An array is setup like a table. When storing values to an array, you define which number of the table you are storing to. The DECLARE statement declares the maximum number of values to be stored in each dimension of the array.

An array can be single- or multi-dimensional. The first number is called the *row number*. If the array is two dimensional, there is a second number which is called the *column number*. You may declare more than one array at a time. Arrays dimensions may be entered in square brackets ([ ]) or parentheses.

To define an array element use the STORE or = command, just like defining any other memory variable. All data in an array is initially equal to .F.

To change the size of an array, use the DECLARE command again. With Fox-Pro 1.0, this caused data already defined in the array to lost, but with FoxPro version 2.0, the data remains.

The DECLARE command is identical to DIMENSION.

Example

. DECLARE Subtotal[5,2]   && declare an array named Subtotal
. Subtotal[1,1] = 100
. STORE 200 TO Subtotal(1,2)
. DECLARE Marray(3,3), Marray2(4,2), Marray3(6,6)

See also: STORE p. 236

DEFINE BAR *line number* OF *pop-up name* PROMPT *expC*

Description DEFINE BAR sets the contents of a pop-up menu.

Operational rules Each option in a FoxPro-designed menu is called a *bar*. It is possible to design a pop-up menu that is displayed whenever one of the bars in the main menu is highlighted with the cursor.

DEFINE BAR allows you to define the options that exist within the pop-up menu. Once the pop-up menu is displayed, the user can move the cursor to any of the options in the pop-up, creating a "menu within a menu."

Each pop-up option is given a *line number* starting with one. The *pop-up name* is defined with the DEFINE POPUP command. The actual option is defined as *expC*.

To define a menu where each option has a pop-up menu that contains additional options, issue the following commands:

1. DEFINE MENU to name the menu.
2. DEFINE PAD to name and position each option in the menu.
3. ON PAD to activate each pop-up for each pad.
4. DEFINE POPUP to name and position each pop-up menu .
5. DEFINE BAR to position each option within the pop-up menu.

To run the menu, the following commands must be issued. ON SELECTION to call the procedure that runs each bar option from the pop-up menu, then the ACTIVATE MENU calls the menu (with pop-ups) to screen.

To define a hot key, place \ before the appropriate letter in the prompt. A separating bar may be placed between options defining a bar using a prompt of

\-. You may also use the option KEY *key label* to define a hot key. When the KEY option is used, the *key label* is displayed as text next to the bar. The key label must be a valid key label name (see the ON KEY LABEL command). You can define the text to be displayed by using the KEY *key label text* command.

Use the MARK option to display a character before an option. The diamond is the default mark. Use MARK *expC* to define the character to be used as the mark.

Use the optional MESSAGE *expC* clause to display a message at the bottom of the screen when this particular option is highlighted. Use the optional SKIP clause if you want the option displayed, but unable to be chosen (the option display in half intensity). Use the SKIP FOR *expL* to skip the option only when *expl* is True (.T.).

The COLOR and COLOR SCHEME clauses allow you to set your own colors in the pop-up menu.

Use the options BEFORE *expN* and AFTER *expN* to determine where the bar will be displayed in the pop-up. These must be used in conjunction with the RELATIVE keyword in the DEFINE POPUP command. The BEFORE clause causes the pop-up to appear before pop-up *expN*, and AFTER causes the pop-up to appear after pop-up *expN*. You can also use the functions _MFIRST and MLAST to reference the first and last pop-up options. When the RELATIVE keyword is not used, undefined bar numbers are reserved blank bars within the pop-up.

For instance, the following pop-up would have Guests as the top pop-up, and no blank bar is reserved for bar 2.

```
DEFINE POPUP Whch RELATIVE FROM 3,2
DEFINE BAR 1 OF Whch PROMPT "Members"
DEFINE BAR 3 OF Whch PROMPT "Guests" BEFORE _MFIRST
```

The following pop-up Whch2 would have Prospects as the middle pop-up, before Guests. Again, no blank bar is reserved for bar 3 because the RELATIVE keyword is used.

```
DEFINE POPUP Whch RELATIVE FROM 3,2
DEFINE BAR 1 OF Whch PROMPT "Members"
DEFINE BAR 2 OF Whch PROMPT "Guests" BEFORE _MFIRST
DEFINE BAR 4 OF Whch PROMPT "Prospect" BEFORE 2
```

Example The following program creates the menu and pop-up options displayed in Fig. 2-1. This program only sets up the pop-up for the leftmost option, Add.

```
DEFINE MENU Mail
DEFINE PAD Adit OF Mail PROMPT "Add " AT 2,2
DEFINE PAD Edit OF Mail PROMPT "Edit" AT 2,20
```

```
DEFINE PAD List OF Mail PROMPT "List" AT 2,38
DEFINE PAD Exit OF Mail PROMPT "Exit" AT 2,56

ON PAD Adit OF Mail ACTIVATE POPUP Wch_fil

DEFINE POPUP Wch_fil FROM 3,2
DEFINE BAR 1 OF Wch_fil PROMPT "\Members"      && M is the hot key
DEFINE BAR 2 OF Wch_fil PROMPT "Guests"
DEFINE BAR 3 OF Wch_fil PROMPT "\-"       && separating line
DEFINE BAR 4 OF Wch_fil PROMPT "Prospect" KEY "Alt-F2"
ON SELECTION POPUP Wch_fil DO Chooser WITH BAR( )

ACTIVATE MENU Mail

PROCEDURE Chooser
PARAMETER Barchoice
DO CASE
   CASE Barchoice = 1
      USE MEMBERS
   CASE Barchoice = 2
      USE GUESTS
   CASE Barchoice = 4
      USE PROSPECT
ENDCASE
APPEND
RETURN
```

See also: DEFINE POPUP p. 168
            ON KEY LABEL p. 204

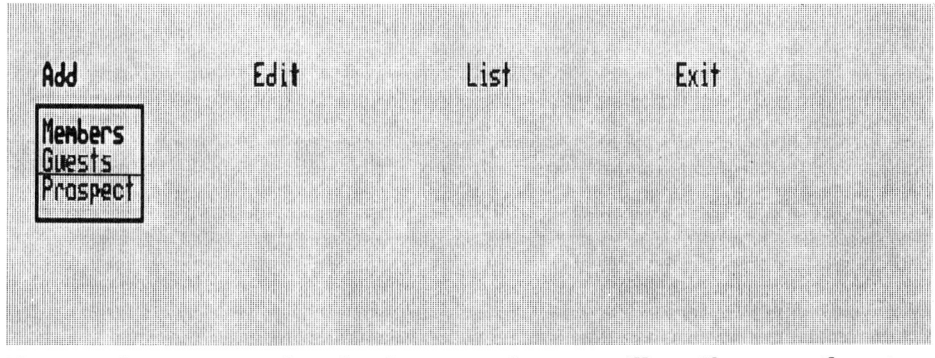

Fig. 2-1. The pop-up options for the screen that you will see if you run the set-up program in the text.

DEFINE BOX FROM *print col1* TO *print col2* HEIGHT *expN*

Description DEFINE BOX sets coordinates and borders of a box to be printed.

Operational rules The default border of the box is a single line box. The optional DOUBLE, and *border definition string* allow you to change the border characters. See SET BORDER regarding the layout of the *border definition string*. Use the AT LINE *expN* to specify the line to begin the box.

To print the box, the system variable _box must be set to true (.T.).

Examples

DEFINE BOX FROM 2 TO 60 HEIGHT 10

See *also*:   SET BORDER p. 247

DEFINE MENU *menu name*

Description DEFINE MENU assigns the name of a bounce-bar menu.

Operational rules Before a menu can be designed, it must be named. DEFINE MENU simply allows you to name the menu. Use DEFINE PAD to set each of the options and their coordinates.

To define and run a bounce-bar menu, the following commands must be issued:

1. DEFINE MENU to name the menu.
2. DEFINE PAD to name and position each option in the menu.
3. ON SELECTION PAD to assign the commands that will be run when a pad is selected.
4. ACTIVATE MENU to run the menu.

Use the optional KEY *key label* clause to define a key that activates the menu. The key label must be a valid key label name (see the ON KEY LABEL command). Use the optional MESSAGE *expC* to display a message at the bottom of the screen when the menu is displayed.

Use the IN *window name* or IN WINDOW *window name* clause to place the menu bar within a window. It will take on all characteristics of that window. Use BAR to create a bar menu that scrolls through the options if the number of pads exceeds the size of the defined menu screen or window. You may specify the screen or window row in which a menu bar is placed with the BAR AT LINE *expN* clause.

Use the MARK option to display a character before an option. The diamond is the default mark. Use MARK *expC* to define the character to be used as the mark. This option defines the mark for all pads in the menu bar. Check marks defined in DEFINE PAD take precedence over those in DEFINE MENU.

Use NOMARGIN to eliminate the extra space placed to the left of each menu pad. The COLOR and COLOR SCHEME clauses allow you to set your own colors in the pop-up menu.

Example The following program creates the menu and activates the options displayed in Fig. 2-2.

```
DEFINE MENU Mail
DEFINE PAD Adit OF Mail PROMPT "Add" AT 2,2
DEFINE PAD Edit OF Mail PROMPT "Edit" AT 2,20
DEFINE PAD List OF Mail PROMPT "List" AT 2,38
DEFINE PAD Exit OF Mail PROMPT "Exit" AT 2,56

ON SELECTION PAD Adit OF Mail APPEND
ON SELECTION PAD Edit OF Mail EDIT
ON SELECTION PAD List OF Mail DO Lister
ON SELECTION PAD Exit OF Mail QUIT
ACTIVATE MENU Mail
```

See also: DEFINE PAD p. 167

Fig. 2-2. The options activated by this program.

DEFINE PAD *pad name* OF *menu name* PROMPT *expC* AT *row, col*

Description DEFINE PAD sets the options that will display in a bounce-bar menu.

Operational rules Use DEFINE PAD to set each of the options and their coordinates of a menu that has been named with DEFINE MENU. The AT clause and coordinates are optional. If you do not include them, FoxPro will place the first option in the left corner of row one. Each subsequent option will be one space to the right.

There is no limit to the pads that may be defined, other than the computer's memory limits.

Use the optional MESSAGE *expC* to display a message at the bottom of the screen when the menu is displayed. Use the optional SKIP clause if you want the option displayed, but unable to be chosen (the option display in half intensity). Use the SKIP FOR *expL* to skip the option only when *expl* is true (.T.).

Use the MARK option to display a character before an option. The diamond is the default mark. Use MARK *expC* to define the character to be used as the mark.

To define a hot key, place \ before the appropriate letter in prompt. You can also use the option KEY *key label* to define a hot key. When the KEY option is used, the key label is displayed as text next to the bar. The key label must be a valid key label name (see the ON KEY LABEL command). You can define the text to be displayed by using the KEY *key label text* command.

The COLOR *color pair list* and COLOR SCHEME *expN* clauses allow you to set your own colors for an individual pad.

Use the options BEFORE *pad name* and AFTER *pad name* to determine where the pad will be displayed in the menu. The BEFORE clause causes the pad to appear before *pad name*, and AFTER causes the pad to appear after *pad name*. When these clauses are used in conjunction with the BAR keyword in the DEFINE MENU command, they determine the physical placement of a pad in the menu. When the BAR keyword is not used, they determine the activation order, but the physical placement of the pads is determined by the order they were created.

For instance, the following menu would have the List option displayed before Edit:

```
DEFINE MENU Mail
DEFINE PAD Adit OF Mail PROMPT "Add "
DEFINE PAD Edit OF Mail PROMPT "Edit"
DEFINE PAD List OF Mail PROMPT "List" BEFORE Edit
```

See DEFINE MENU for a program that creates a bounce-bar menu.

Examples

```
DEFINE PAD Adit OF Mail PROMPT "Add " AT 2,2
DEFINE PAD Adit OF Mail PROMPT " \ >Add "     && A is hot key
DEFINE PAD Adit OF Mail PROMPT "Add " MESSAGE "Add Records To Mail.dbf"
```

See also: DEFINE MENU p. 166

DEFINE POPUP *pop-up name* FROM *row, col*

Description DEFINE POPUP sets the placement and name of a pop-up menu.

Operational rules DEFINE POPUP designs a pop-up menu that is displayed vertically. You can call pop-up menus that display whenever an option from a bounce-bar menu is highlighted. This creates a "menu within a menu." The coordinates *row* and *col* define the placement of the top left corner of the pop-up.

See DEFINE BAR for a complete program that displays a bounce bar menu with pop-up menus.

Use the optional MESSAGE *expC* to display a message at the bottom of the screen when the pop-up is displayed. Use the FOOTER *expC* to display a footer that displays centered at the bottom border of the pop-up. Use the TITLE *expC* to display a title that displays centered at the top border of the pop-up.

You do not need to provide the optional TO *row2, col2* for the bottom corner coordinates of the menu. FoxPro will choose a best fit determined by the number and width of bars within the pop-up menu, set with the DEFINE BAR command.

The PROMPT FIELD *field name*, PROMPT FILES, and PROMPT STRUCTURE clauses are used when you want the options of the pop-up to be files or fields. You might not use DEFINE BAR if you are going to use any of the PROMPT options. PROMPT FIELD displays the contents of *field* in each record of the file in the pop-up window. PROMPT FILES displays a list of the files (you can use the optional LIKE *skeleton* clause) contained in the current catalog. PROMPT STRUCTURE displays all fields in the active database.

Use the IN WINDOW *window name* or IN *window name* clause to place the pop-up window within a window. It takes on all characteristics of that window. Use the option KEY *key label* to define a hot key that activates the pop-up. The *key label* must be a valid key label name (see the ON KEY LABEL command). Use the option MARK to display a character before an option. The diamond is the default mark. Use MARK *expC* to define the character to be used as the mark for all options in the pop-up. A check mark specified in DEFINE BAR takes precedence over one defined in DEFINE POPUP.

The COLOR *color pair list* and COLOR SCHEME *expN* clauses allow you to set your own colors in the pop-up menu. The SHADOW option places a shadow behind the pop-up.

Use MARGIN to place an extra space to the left and right of each option. If this option is used in conjunction with check marks, the marks are displayed one space left of the option. Without the MARGIN clause, the check marks overwrite the first character of the prompt.

The MOVER clause allows the options in the pop-up to be rearranged by the user. To do this, a double-headed arrow is placed to the left of each option. The options can be rearranged by using the mouse (click on the arrow and drag the option up or down) or the keyboard (select the option and press Ctrl – ↑ or Ctrl – ↓.

The MULTI clause allows multiple options to be chosen from a pop-up. When an option is chosen from this type of pop-up, a check mark is placed to the left of the option. Multiple options can be selected by the mouse (hold down Shift and click the options) or the keyboard (hold down Shift and press Enter or the spacebar). See the MARGIN clause regarding placement of the check marks.

The RELATIVE clause allows you to control where options in the pop-up are placed. When the RELATIVE keyword is not used, undefined bar numbers are reserved blank bars within the pop-up. See the DEFINE BAR command for examples of how the BEFORE and AFTER keywords can change the placement of bars in the pop-up when used in conjunction with RELATIVE.

The SCROLL keyword places a scroll bar to the right of the pop-up. Scroll bars allow you to use a mouse to move quickly through the pop-up. The scroll bar is only displayed when the pop-up is too long to fit in the screen or active window.

Examples

DEFINE POPUP Whch_file FROM 3,2
DEFINE POPUP Whch_file FROM 3,2 TO 8,12
DEFINE POPUP Whch_file SCROLL FROM 3,2 PROMPT FILES LIKE M*
DEFINE POPUP State_pop FROM 3,2 PROMPT FIELD States

See also: DEFINE BAR p. 163

DEFINE WINDOW *window name* FROM *row1, col1* TO *row2, col2*

Description   DEFINE WINDOW sets coordinates, borders, and colors of a user-defined window.

Operational rules   The default border of the window is a single line box. The optional DOUBLE, NONE, and *border definition string* allow you to change the border characters. PANEL draws a wider border. See SET BORDER regarding the layout of the *border definition string*. SYSTEM emulates the look of system windows (size control and zoom control appear in the border). When SYSTEM is included, you cannot specify a border.

To display a defined window, use the ACTIVATE WINDOW command. You can define multiple windows, but output is directed to the most recently activated one.

The COLOR option allows you to define two sets of foreground/background color combinations, one for *standard*, one for *enhanced*. You can include a different color for *frame*. The COLOR SCHEME *expN* option allows you to call a predefined color scheme. Use FILL *expC* to define a character that fills the window.

The CLOSE clause allows you to close the window using the mouse. NOCLOSE is the default. The FLOAT clause allows you to move the window around the screen. NOFLOAT is the default. The GROW clause allows you to change the size of the window. NOGROW is the default. The SHADOW clause creates a darkened area behind the window. NOSHADOW is the default.

The ZOOM clause allows the user to zoom into the window so that it covers the entire screen. To do this, choose the Zoom ↑ option from the Window menu pop-up or press Ctrl – F10. The mouse can also be used (click on the upper right corner of the window). NOZOOM is the default.

Use IN WINDOW *window name* or IN *window name* to open a window inside a parent window. The screen builder window must be smaller than the parent, and stay within the parent window's boundaries. The IN SCREEN option is the default. This causes the window to be placed on the screen instead of within a window.

Use the FOOTER *expC* to display a footer that displays centered at the bottom border of the window. Use the TITLE *expC* to display a title that displays centered at the top border of the window. The SHADOW clause creates a darkened area behind the window.

The GROW option allows the user to resize the window. To do this, choose the Size option from the Window menu pop-up or press Ctrl – F8. The mouse can also be used (click on the lower right corner of the window, hold down the mouse button and adjust).

NOGROW is the default. This prevents the window from being resized.

The MINIMIZE option allows the window to reduce to a minimum size. To do this, choose the Zoom↓ from the window menu pop-up. The mouse can also be used (hold down Shift and double click on the top border of the window).

Examples

DEFINE WINDOW Wind1 FROM 3,2 TO 10,78 TITLE "Data Entry Window"
DEFINE WINDOW Wind1 FROM 3,2 TO 10,78 COLOR GR/B, B/GR, W
DEFINE WINDOW Wind1 FROM 3,2 TO 10,78 "#","#","#","#","$","$","$","$"

See also: SET BORDER p. 247

DELETE

Description   The DELETE command marks a record for deletion from the current database file.

Operational rules   To delete a record from the database file, mark all records to be deleted with the DELETE command or through the Edit or Browse screens. Then issue the PACK command.

The PACK command actually removes the records. It makes a copy of the data file without the records marked for deletion, so it can take a while to run. The PACK command renumbers the records.

The DELETE command is equivalent to pressing Ctrl – T or choosing Toggle Delete while editing or browsing. Records marked for deletion display an asterisk when listed and a bullet when in Browse mode. The SET DELETED ON command tells FoxPro to ignore deleted records when displaying, editing, and listing. This allows deleted records to appear removed without having to PACK.

You can make global deletions with the optional FOR *condition*, WHILE *condition*, and *scope*.

Example

```
DELETE
DELETE FOR State = "NY"
DELETE NEXT 5
```

See also: PACK p. 209

DELETE FILE *file name*

Description   DELETE FILE removes an entire file from the disk.

Operational rules   This command is equivalent to the ERASE command. You cannot erase a file that is currently open. The DELETE FILE command does not allow wildcards (? and *) to delete multiple files at one time, so you might prefer to use the DEL command from DOS. To run a DOS command while at the command window, use ! or RUN.

The optional ? argument can be used to get a listing of files from which you can choose.

Example

```
DELETE FILE Maillist.dbf
ERASE Maillist.dbf
DELETE FILE ?
! DEL Maillist.*
```

See also: RUN/! p. 224

DELETE TAG *tag name*

Description   The DELETE TAG command removes a tag from a multiple index (.CDX) file.

Operational rules   Multiple indexes contain index "tags" allowing for many indexes to be maintained through one file. The multiple index file must be open when this command is issued.

If the optional OF *.cdx file* is not used, FoxPro automatically looks for a file with the same name as the .DBF file but with a .CDX extension. If that file isn't found, it then searches other open .CDX files for the corresponding tag name.

Use the optional to ALL clause to delete all tags. If the currently selected database has a structural index file, all tags are removed, the .CDX file is deleted from the disk, and the database is no longer flagged as having such a file. Use ALL OF *.cdx file* to remove all tags from a multiple index other than the structural one.

Example

DELETE TAG Zip OF Mailzip   (deletes Zip from Maillist.cdx)

See also: COPY TAG p. 155

DIMENSION

The DIMENSION command is the same as the DECLARE command.

See: DECLARE p. 162

DIR *or* DIRECTORY

Description   DIRECTORY lists the names of a group of files.

Operational rules   This command works very much like the DOS directory command. However, if no clause is included, it only shows database (.DBF) files. Otherwise, it allows use of the DOS wildcards (? and *).

Use the TO PRINT or TO FILE *file name* clauses to send the output to the printer or to a text file (default extension .TXT).

Example

```
DIR            && shows all .DBF files
DIR A:*.*      && shows all files from the A drive
DIR *.FRX      && shows all .FRX files
DIR TO PRINT   && prints the directory of .DBF files
```

See also: RUN/! p. 224

DISPLAY *commands*

Each DISPLAY command is equivalent to a LIST command. The only difference is that when DISPLAY is issued, only one screen is displayed at a time, and the user is requested to Press a key to continue .... The LIST commands list the entire contents without pausing between screens. For information about each DISPLAY command, see its LIST companion. The commands are:

```
LIST            DISPLAY
LIST FILES      DISPLAY FILES
```

LIST MEMORY   DISPLAY MEMORY
LIST STATUS   DISPLAY STATUS
LIST STRUCTURE   DISPLAY STRUCTURE

See also: LIST p. 189

DO *program or procedure name*

Description   The DO command calls a program or procedure.

Operational rules   From the command window, call the master module of the program. Use DO *program* within a command file to call other programs. Each program that is called extends one level lower. Use the RETURN command to return to the calling program. The program then continues processing at the line below the DO command.

Use DO *procedure* to call a procedure, which is a subroutine placed within the program file or in a procedure file. See the PROCEDURE command regarding details of procedures. Use the IN *program file* clause to call a procedure which is not in the current program or procedure file.

Lower level programs can access memory variables initialized in upper level programs. However, memory variables initialized in lower level programs are local to that program, and cannot be accessed from higher levels.

To change a variable's value in a lower level program (or procedure) and pass that value back to the calling program, set the variable as a parameter. Include the WITH *parameter list* clause in your DO statement.

Examples

DO Mainmenu
DO Heading WITH Title, Pageno

See also: PARAMETERS p. 209
            PROCEDURE p. 213

DO CASE
   CASE *condition*
      commands
   CASE *condition*
      commands

·

·

·

OTHERWISE
commands
ENDCASE

Description   The DO CASE command is used within programs to provide conditional processing.

Operational rules   If the *condition* is true (.T.), then the program processes all commands between the CASE and next CASE statement. The program only processes the first condition that is true. The DO CASE command must end with an ENDCASE statement. It is good programming technique to indent all commands within the CASE statements. For example:

```
DO CASE
   CASE Choice = "1"
      DO Addit
   CASE Choice = "2"
      DO Print
   CASE Choice = "3"
      QUIT
   OTHERWISE
      CANCEL
ENDCASE
```

The DO CASE command must be used in situations where each case is mutually exclusive. In other words, instances where only one of the CASE statements can be true. This CASE statement is an example.

You can use the OTHERWISE command as the last case to handle situations when none of the cases are true.

See also: IF p. 184

DO WHILE *condition*
   commands
ENDDO

Description   The DO WHILE command is used within programs to provide a looping capability with conditional processing.

Operational rules   If the *condition* is true (.T.), then the program will continue processing all commands between the DO and ENDDO statement until *condition* is not true. It is good programming technique to indent all commands within the DO and ENDDO statements. For example:

```
DO WHILE Mem < 10
   ? Mem
   Mem = Mem + 1
ENDDO
```

The LOOP command can be used within a DO WHILE to return to the beginning of the loop. Use the EXIT command to exit the loop and continue processing the program at the command line below ENDDO.

Example The following command skips through the Maillist database, and displays one record at a time. If a record has N in the Active field, the record is not displayed. Although this is a valid program, a simpler program could be written that performs the same function with the SCAN FOR command:

```
USE Maillist
DO WHILE .NOT. EOF( )
   IF Active = "N"
      SKIP
      LOOP
   ENDIF
   CLEAR
   ? Fname, Lname, Phone
   ACCEPT "Display another? " TO Cont
   IF Cont = "N"
      EXIT
   ENDIF
   SKIP
ENDDO
```

See also: DO CASE p. *174*

EDIT

Description The Edit mode allows the user to add or edit records in the current file.

Operational rules When editing a file, the records appear one record at a time on the screen. The full-screen editing commands are in effect. If a custom format (.FMX) file is active, the screen will display using its definitions.

Many of the optional arguments place restrictions on the capabilities of the EDIT command:

- NOAPPEND   Prevents records from being appended.
- NOCLEAR   Does not clear the screen when EDIT is exited.
- NODELETE   Prevents records from being deleted.
- NOEDIT   Prevents records from being edited (may only be viewed).
- NOFOLLOW   When editing indexed records, NOFOLLOW stays at the current records position even if a change causes the record to move its place in the indexed database.
- NOMENU   Prevents access to the BROWSE menu pop-up.

The optional FIELDS *fieldname list* arguments restrict the fields that are displayed in the Edit screen. The default is all fields. Use this command to also change the order that fields are displayed on the Edit screen.

The optional FOR *condition* and WHILE *condition* and *scope* arguments are used to edit only records that match a specified criteria.

You can supply a *record number*, otherwise EDIT will edit the current record. The scope RECORD causes EDIT to edit only one record, otherwise you can move to other records in the file with PgDn and PgUp.

Example

```
EDIT
EDIT 5
EDIT RECORD 5
EDIT FOR State = "CA"
EDIT NOAPPEND NODELETE
EDIT FIELDS Lname,Fname,City,Zip
```

See also: APPEND p. 143
BROWSE p. 146

EJECT

Description EJECT advances the paper to the next page.

Operational rules The EJECT command will send a form feed (ASCII character 12) to advance the paper to the top of the next page. However, if the system memory variable _padvance has been set to LINEFEEDS, the correct number of linefeeds to advance the page will be sent instead.

EJECT will reset PROW( ) and PCOL( ) to zero. EJECT PAGE, unlike the EJECT command, affects the _pageno and _plineno system variables. Use EJECT PAGE when the ON PAGE handler is in effect.

See also: EJECT PAGE p. 177

EJECT PAGE

Description EJECT PAGE advances the paper to the next page, and takes in consideration printer system variables.

Operational rules The EJECT PAGE command will send a form feed unless the system variable _padvance has been set to LINEFEEDS, in which case the correct number of linefeeds will be sent to advance the paper to the top of the next page.

EJECT PAGE, unlike the EJECT command, affects the _pageno and _plineno system variables. Use EJECT PAGE when the ON PAGE handler is in effect.

See also: ON PAGE p. 206

ERASE

See the DELETE FILE command on *p. 172*

EXIT

Description EXIT is used within the DO...ENDDO, FOR...ENDFOR, and SCAN...ENDSCAN commands to leave the loop.

Operational rules This command must be used within one of the three commands mentioned in the description. EXIT causes the program to go to the bottom of the loop and precede with the next command.

Example

```
USE Maillist
SCAN
   CLEAR
   ? Fname, Lname, Phone
   ACCEPT "Display another? " TO Cont
   IF UPPER(Cont) = "N"
      EXIT
   ENDIF
ENDSCAN
```

EXPORT TO *file name*

Description The COPY TO command copies the records from the current file to a file other than a FoxPro file.

Operational rules A type must be specified, although the keyword TYPE is optional. If you do not include an extension on *file name*, it will choose the default extension for that file type. When exporting to a file, the types are:

Type	Description
DIF	Visicalc's Data Interchange Format
MOD	Microsoft Multiplan version 4.01
SYLK	Symbolic Link interchange format
WK1	Lotus 1-2-3, version 2.x
WK3	Lotus 1-2-3, version 3.x
WKS	Lotus 1-2-3, version 1.x
WR1	Lotus Symphony, version 1.1 or 1.2
WRK	Lotus Symphony, version 1.0
XLS	Microsoft Excel, version 2.0

The optional FOR *condition* and WHILE *condition* and *scope* arguments are used to copy only records that match a specified criteria.

The optional FIELDS *field list* argument copies only the specified fields to the new database. Use the NOOPTIMIZE option to disable Rushmore. An alternate method is to globally disable Rushmore by using the SET OPTIMIZE command.

The EXPORT command is equivalent to the COPY TO command used with one of the optional file types.

Example

EXPORT TO Mail2 MOD FOR LNAME = "S"   (copies for specified criteria)
EXPORT TO Mail2 WK1 NEXT 100   (copies next 100 records)
EXPORT TO Mail2 DIF Lname, Fname, City (copies to a three-field file)

See also: COPY TO p. 155

EXTERNAL

Description   Tells the FoxPro project manager where undefined references in the project can be found.

Operational rules   A project database (.PJX) contains information regarding a group of files that are all used in one application.

Project files are used with the BUILD APP command for building a .FXP file and for building .EXE files.

Sometimes the group of files include undefined references to other files. This is most common when name expressions and macro substitution are used in program. Use the EXTERNAL command to alert the project manager of these files. The command must include one of the following keywords and the corresponding file name. The file name extension default is based on that of the keyword:

Keyword	**File**
LABEL	Label definition file
LIBRARY	Library file
MENU	Menu definition file
PROCEDURE	Procedure file
REPORT	Report definition file
SCREEN	Screen definition file

The ARRAY *array name* clause is needed when an array is passed to a UDF or procedure.

Example

EXTERNAL REPORT Budget
mreport = "Budget"
REPORT FORM &mreport TO PRINT

FIND *literal*

Description The FIND command moves to the first record in the index that matches *literal*.

Operational rules FIND searches the master index for *literal*. This command is very much like the SEEK command, except that SEEK searches for an expression instead of a literal. When the argument is a literal, you do not place quotes around it. Therefore, if it is a character memory variable, it should be preceded with an ampersand (&). There is no way to use FIND with a numeric memory variable.

If a match is found, the record pointer moves to that record. Use SKIP to find the next record that matches. If no records match, FOUND( ) will be set to false, and the record pointer will be moved to the end of the file (EOF( ) is true). However, if SET NEAR is ON, the pointer will go to the nearest record in the index.

Example

. USE Maillist index Mlname
. Find Smith
Record 2
. Mname = "Brown"
. Find &Mname
Record 7

See also: SEEK p. 228

FLUSH

Description FLUSH all buffers to the disk.

Operational rules The FLUSH command sends all data in RAM to the disk so that if the program is exited incorrectly (the power goes off or the computer gets reset before exiting FoxPro) no data will be lost. The CLOSE FILES command also flushes the buffers, but the FLUSH command is more efficient if you wish to continue using the files.

See also: CLOSE p. 152

FOR *memvar* = *expN1* TO *expN2*
commands
ENDFOR

Description The FOR command is used within programs to run a looping process a specified number of times.

Operational rules All commands between the FOR and ENDFOR statements are run the number of times between *expN1* and *expN2*.

The *memvar* does not need to be defined before issuing the command. It evaluates to *expN1* the first time through the loop, and it automatically increases by one when it hits the ENDFOR and loops back to the FOR. The loop continues until *memvar* reaches *expN2*.

The optional clause STEP *expN* causes the counter to increment by *expN* instead of by 1. The incrementer can be either a positive or negative number.

It is good programming technique to indent all commands within the FOR and ENDFOR statements. For example:

```
FOR Mem = 1 TO 10
   ? Mem
ENDFOR
```

The LOOP command can be used within a FOR command to return to the beginning of the loop. Use the EXIT command to exit the loop and continue processing the program at the command line below ENDFOR.

Example The following command skips through ten records of the Maillist database, displaying each record on the screen. If a record has N in the Active field, the record is not displayed. Although this is a valid program, a simpler program could be written that performs the same function with the SCAN FOR command:

```
USE Maillist
FOR Mem = 1 TO 10
   IF Active = "N"
      SKIP
      LOOP
   ENDIF
   CLEAR
   ? Recno( ), Fname, Lname, Phone
   SKIP
ENDFOR
?
INPUT "Enter Number to Edit" GET Memrec
EDIT Memrec
```

See also: DO WHILE p. 175

FUNCTION *procedure name*

Description FUNCTION allows you to create user-defined functions that perform like FoxPro's built-in functions.

Operational rules If a certain function must be performed more than once in a program, it is easier to create a user-defined function with the FUNCTION command. User-defined functions are created just like procedures, except that they are called from within commands, instead of being called in a separate command.

Functions begin with the FUNCTION command, and end with RETURN( ). A user-defined function can have multiple arguments.

Example In the following program, the heading program calls a user-defined function that prints the heading centered on the page, depending on the width of the paper:

```
Mhead = "Income Analysis"
? CENTERIT(Mhead,75)
    .
    .
    .
FUNCTION CENTERIT( )
  PARAMETERS Heading, Width
  MCENTER = SPACE(Width/2 - LEN(Heading)/2)) + Heading
  RETURN(MCENTER)
```

See also: PARAMETERS p. 209

GATHER FROM *array* or GATHER FROM *memvar*

Description The GATHER FROM command replaces the fields in the current records with the values of the array or memory variable.

Operational rules When gathering from an array, each array element represents a field. To gather from a memory variable, it must have been created with the SCATTER command. This is very useful in programs that edit a record in a data file. Before the edit session, SCATTER the record to a memory variable. Then, if the user exits with a key defined as the "abort" key, use the GATHER FROM command to set all fields back to their previous values.

Use the FIELDS *field list* option to define the fields to be gathered.

Example

```
USE Maillist
SCATTER TO Save_it
@ 3,1 SAY "Database of Clients"
@ $,60 SAY "Press ESC to Abort"
@ 5,1 SAY "Enter Last Name" GET Lname PICTURE "!XXXXXXXXXXXXXX"
@ 5,50 SAY "First Name" GET Fname PICTURE "!XXXXXXXXXXXXXX"
```

```
@ $+2,1 SAY "Address:" GET Address
@ $+1,1 SAY " City:" GET City
@ $,$+1 SAY " State:" GET State PICTURE "@!"
@ $,$+1 SAY "Zip:" GET Zip PICTURE "#####"
READ
IF LASTKEY( ) = 27
   GATHER FROM Save_it
ENDIF
```

See also: SCATTER TO *p. 227*

GETEXPR *prompt* TO *memvar*

Description   The GETEXPR command calls up the FoxPro Expression Builder to help you create a memory variable.

Operational rules   This command is especially useful for setting user-defined criterion within programs. The expression builder walks the user through the steps of setting up the criteria. GETEXPR can be used to create any type of memory variable, although it always returns in string form. To designate the type of variable, use the TYPE *expC* clause where type can be C, N, L, or D.

Place an optional error message after the TYPE clause with the syntax TYPE *expC ; expC2* where *expC2* is the error message. Set a default variable with the DEFAULT *expC* clause.

Example

```
USE Maillist
GETEXPR "Enter selection criteria" TO Crit TYPE "L"
SET FILTER TO &Crit
LIST OFF Fname, Lname, City
```

See also: SCATTER TO *p. 227*

GOTO *record number* or GO *record number*

Description   The GOTO command moves to the specified record.

Operational rules   The alternate arguments are BOTTOM and TOP. GOTO TOP moves to the top record, which is record number 1 in a nonindexed file, or the first record in an indexed file. GOTO BOTTOM moves to the bottom record, which is the last record number in a nonindexed file, or the last record in an indexed file. To reach the end of the file (where EOF( ) is true), issue GOTO BOTTOM, and then SKIP. The record number will display as one more than REC-COUNT( ).

The optional argument IN alias allows you to move the record pointer in a file other than the current file.

Example

GOTO BOTTOM
GO 5
GO 5 IN Maillist

See also: SEEK p. 228

HELP

Description   The HELP command brings up the FoxPro help screens.

Operational rules   When in the help screens, you will get a screen full of help regarding a particular subject. You can then highlight additional keywords, and press Enter to get screens of information regarding other topics.

The optional argument *keyword* allows you to get a screen of information regarding a particular topic.

Example

HELP
HELP INDEX

HIDE WINDOW

Description   HIDE WINDOW erases a window from the screen but allows you to still use it.

Operational rules   Windows are designed with the DEFINE WINDOW command. Use ACTIVATE WINDOW to then display it. Both HIDE and DEACTIVATE erase the window from the screen. When you use HIDE, you can still direct output to it, although the output is not displayed.

See also: DEFINE WINDOW p. 171

IF *condition*
commands
ENDIF

Description   The IF command is used within programs to provide conditional processing.

Operational rules   If *condition* is true (.T.), then the program will process all commands between the IF and ENDIF statement. If *condition* is false (.F.), then the program continues processing after the ENDIF statement. It is good programming technique to indent all commands within the IF and ENDIF statements. For example:

```
IF Mprn = "P"
  SET PRINT ON
  EJECT
ENDIF
```

An alternate IF structure is IF...ELSE...ENDIF. This is useful in situations where one procedure should be performed if the condition is true, with a different procedure if the condition is false. Although IF statements can be nested (just remember each IF must have a companion ENDIF), it is often better to use the DO CASE command if many conditions are to be tested.

Example

```
ACCEPT "Display to Screen, Printer, or File? (S/P/F)" TO Mprn
IF Mprn = "P"
  SET PRINT ON
  EJECT
ELSE
  IF Mprn = "F"
    SET ALTERNATE TO Prnfile
    SET ALTERNATE ON
  ELSE
    SET CONSOLE ON
  ENDIF
ENDIF
```

See also: DO CASE p. 175

INDEX ON *key expression* TO *index file name*

Description   This command puts the data in order by key expression.

Operational rules   The INDEX ON command sorts the current data file, but is different than the SORT command in the following areas:

- An index (.IDX) file is smaller than the data file.
- The index file does not affect the .DBF file, so the record numbers remain intact.
- As long as the index file is opened along with the data file, new records will maintain the sorted order.

You can index a file on one field, multiple fields, or by fields within functions. If you are combining character fields and numeric fields, you must convert the numeric field to a string with the STR function. The following are examples of each:

INDEX ON Lname TO Mname	(sorts by Lname field)
INDEX ON UPPER(Lname) TO Mname	(sorts ignoring case)
INDEX ON Lname+Fname TO Mname	(sorts by Fname within Lname)
INDEX ON STR(Dept,2)+Lname TO Mname	

The UNIQUE argument causes it to include only the first records that contain a particular key. For instance, if the file is indexed on City, the index only takes the first entry for each city. This is helpful when getting lists of all unique entries for a certain field.

To sort a numeric field in descending order, use the key of −1**numeric field*. To sort a date field in descending order, use the key of {12/13/2199} − *expD*. Both of these expressions evaluate to numbers.

The FOR *criteria* filters out records that do match the criteria. Keep in mind that with that index open, you cannot access records if they are not in the filter. This is a very good clause to use if you are making a temporary index for any situation that filters out records because it makes access much faster.

To keep an index correctly updated, it must be open at all times that data is appended or edited. You can open the index when you open the data file with the USE *file* INDEX *file* command, or with the SET INDEX TO command. If you do change data when the index is not open, you will need to open it and REINDEX the file.

Examples

```
INDEX ON Amount TO Mamt
INDEX ON Amount TO Mamt FOR City = "San Diego"
INDEX ON Date TO Mdate UNIQUE     && only puts in the first record of each date
INDEX ON {12/31/2199}-Date TO Mdate    && dates in descending order
```

See also: USE p. 240

INPUT prompt TO mem variable

Description   The INPUT command displays the prompt and pauses until the user enters something.

Operational rules   This command is most often used in programs where few questions are to be prompted on the screen. Each INPUT command halts the program until the user types in an answer and presses Enter. The INPUT command is easier to use than full-screen editing commands such as @...GET, because:

- The memory variable does not have to be initialized before issuing the command.

- Screen coordinates do not have to be set. (INPUT displays the prompt in the same manner as the ? command).

However, the INPUT command is not as powerful as the full-screen editing commands, especially because the entry cannot be formatted. Memory variables created by the INPUT command are numeric if a number is entered, otherwise they are of the character type. The variable becomes the length of the entry typed in.

The ACCEPT command is just like INPUT, except the memory variable will always be a character.

Examples The following program prompts the user to enter their name and age. The memory variable Mname becomes the length of the entry. It is a character variable because the user typed in a string. The memory variable Mage becomes numeric as long as the user types in a number.

```
INPUT "Enter Your Name: " TO Mname
? "Hi there ", Mname
INPUT "Enter Your Age: " TO Mage
? "Are you really ", Mage, "?"
```

See also: ACCEPT p. 141

INSERT

Description The INSERT command allows the user to add new records to the database at the position of the current record.

Operational rules The INSERT command brings up the full-screen edit mode, just like the APPEND command. The record is added one below the current record. For instance, if the pointer is at record 10, the new record is inserted as record 11, and the numbers of all records following are increased by one.

Use the BEFORE clause to insert records at the current record number instead of one record after. Use BLANK to insert a record without going into the full-screen edit mode. When inserting a blank record, all fields of the record will be blank.

See also: EDIT p. 176

JOIN WITH *alias* TO *new file name* FOR *condition*

Description The JOIN command makes a new file out of two files.

Operational rules The new file will be made up of all of the fields in the active file, plus all of the names in the joined file. For every time a record in the active file matches a record in the second file, you have one record in the new file. The JOIN command can take a very long time to run if both files are large.

The field order of the new file is all of the fields from the first file plus all of the fields from the second file, up to the 255 field limit. To change the field order, or restrict the fields in the new file, use the optional argument FIELDS *field list*.

Example In this example, a new file named Salename is made up of each sales record which includes the sales information from Sales and the name of the client from Maillist.

```
. USE Maillist IN 1
. USE Sales IN 2
. SELECT 1
. JOIN WITH Sales TO Salename FOR A - > Clicode = B - > Clicode FIELDS;
   A - > Clicode, A - > Name, B - > Date, B - > Amount
```

See also: SELECT p. 229

KEYBOARD expC

Description The KEYBOARD allows you to put characters into the keyboard buffer, which is then played out at the next input command.

Operational rules This command is very useful in creating demonstration programs because you can make the keyboard type things automatically. The characters to be played, *expC*, stay in the buffer until a command that looks for input is issued.

Example In the example given here, if the user answers Y to the first question, the program types in the name and address onto the screen.

```
ACCEPT "Do you want the program to enter the data? " TO Demo
IF UPPER(Demo) = "Y"
   KEYBOARD "George Jetson" + CHR(13) + "Los Gatos" + CHR(13)
      + "CA92111"
ENDIF
@ 5,1 SAY "Enter Name" GET Name
@ $+1,1 SAY " City:" GET City
@ $,$+1 SAY " State:" GET State PICT "!!"
@ $,$+1 SAY "Zip:" GET Zip
READ
```

See also: EDIT p. 176

LABEL FORM *label file name*

Description The LABEL FORM command prints labels for a data file. The label format must already be created with the CREATE LABEL command.

Operational rules The CREATE LABEL command allows you to set the label dimensions, number of labels across, and contents of the label within a label definition (.LBX) file. To run the labels, make sure the data file is your current file, and issue the LABEL FORM command.

The argument ? can be used in place of the *label file name*. FoxPro displays a list of .LBX files to choose from. Use the optional FOR *condition*, WHILE *condition*, and *scope* arguments to print labels for a subset of the data file. Labels default to printing on the screen. Use the TO PRINTER option to print to the printer, or the TO FILE *file name* to print to an ASCII file.

The SAMPLE option prints a sample label, allowing you to set up the printer just right. After it prints the sample, it asks Do you want more samples?. It continues this process until you enter N.

The PREVIEW option displays a group of labels (one screenful) on the screen letting you verify that the label definition is set up correctly. After exiting the preview screen, the LABEL FORM command must be issued again (without PREVIEW) to actually begin printing the labels.

Use the NOOPTIMIZE option to disable Rushmore. This is only relevant when the FOR clause is being used. An alternate method is to globally disable Rushmore by using the SET OPTIMIZE command.

Example

```
LABEL FORM Mlabel
LABEL FORM Mlabel TO PRINT
LABEL FORM Mlabel FOR State = "CA"
LABEL FORM Mlabel NEXT 100 TO FILE Labels && creates Labels.Txt
```

See also: CREATE LABEL p. 158

LIST

Description LIST displays a list of the records in a file.

Operational rules The list is not formatted. It simply displays a row of field names and then lists the records. If the fields are wider than the screen, each record wraps on the screen and uses multiple rows.

The optional FIELDS *field list* argument allows you to specify which fields and the order in which they display. The default order is file structure order.

You can actually omit the word FIELDS and simply enter *field list*. The optional OFF argument does not display the field names.

Use the optional FOR *condition*, WHILE *condition*, and *scope* arguments to list records for a subset of the data file. Lists default to printing on the screen. Use the TO PRINTER option to print to the printer, or the TO FILE *file name* to print to an ASCII file.

The DISPLAY command is much like the LIST command, except that the DISPLAY command pauses the screen at each screenful of information. To pause the LIST command, you must press the Pause key (or Ctrl – S) as it is scrolling.

Examples

```
LIST
LIST OFF FOR State = "CA"
LIST NEXT 100 TO PRINT
LIST Lname, Fname, City
LIST Lname, Fname WHILE Zip = "9"
```

See also: DISPLAY p. 173

LIST FILES

Description   LIST FILES lists all files from a directory that match a parameter.

Operational rules   The default list is a list of .DBF files, along with their size, number of records, and last update date. Use LIKE *skeleton* to get a list of files other than the *.DBF default. Skeletons follow the wildcard conventions of DOS:

- An asterisk (*) represents any combination of characters.
- A question mark (?) represents any one character.

The file list defaults to printing on the screen. Use the TO PRINTER option to print to the printer, or the TO FILE *file name* to print to an ASCII file.

Examples

```
LIST FILES
LIST FILES LIKE *.prg
LIST FILES LIKE *.* TO PRINTER
```

See also: DISPLAY FILES p. 173

LIST HISTORY

Description   This command lists the last set of commands issued at the dot prompt.

Operational rules FoxPro keeps a history of the commands last entered at the dot prompt. Press the ↑ to move back through the commands, and the ↓ to move forward. This is useful when you want to repeat a command already given, or to make slight changes in a command. It is also handy if you have entered a command with a syntax error in it. Instead of typing the command over again, use the ↑ to retrieve it, and then edit it.

The optional LAST *expN* allows you to specify the number of commands you wish to print. The list defaults to printing on the screen. Use the TO PRINTER option to print to the printer, or the TO FILE *file name* to print to an ASCII file.

Examples

LIST HISTORY
LIST HISTORY LAST 5
LIST HISTORY TO FILE Histfile

See also: DISPLAY HISTORY p. 174

LIST STATUS

Description This command lists the status of the current work environment.

Operational rules LIST STATUS will display a list of all open files, indexes, format files, and their respective work areas. If index files are open, their keys are displayed. If multiple index files are open, their tags are displayed also. It also displays all filter conditions, file relationships, and other information such as settings for the printer, function keys, and other SET commands.

If FoxPro/LAN is being used, shared attribute status on each file, locked records, and other lock settings are also displayed.

The status list defaults to printing on the screen. Use the TO PRINTER option to print to the printer, or the TO FILE *file name* to print to an ASCII file.

See also: DISPLAY STATUS p. 174

LIST STRUCTURE

Description This command lists the structure of the current database file.

Operational rules LIST STRUCTURE will display a list of all field names, their lengths, and types. This command also lists the name of the file, last date updated, total number of records, and total bytes in a record.

See also: DISPLAY STRUCTURE p. 174

LOAD *binary file name*

Description The LOAD command loads a binary program into memory.

Operational rules FoxPro can run binary (assembly language and machine language) programs. To do this you must:

1. Load the program into memory with the LOAD command.
2. Run the program with the CALL command.
3. Release it from memory with the RELEASE MODULE command.

Binary programs are useful in applications where a function must be performed that FoxPro cannot do. For instance, certain screen graphics manipulation and file maintenance on non-FoxPro files can be done only through binary programs.

You should always release the program from memory once it is no longer needed, otherwise you might get memory error messages.

See also: CALL p. 150

LOCATE FOR *condition*

Description The LOCATE command moves to the first record in the data file where *condition* is true (.T.).

Operational rules LOCATE searches the file sequentially, starting from the top. This command is very much like the SEEK command, except that SEEK searches on an indexed file, so it is much faster, especially with large files.

Use the alternative WHILE *condition*, and *scope* in place of FOR *condition*.

If a match is found, the record pointer moves to that record. Use CONTINUE to find the next record that matches. If no records match, FOUND( ) is set to false, and the record pointer is moved to the end of the file (EOF( ) is true).

Example

```
. USE Maillist
. LOCATE FOR Lname = "Smith"
Record =    5
. LOCATE FOR Lname = "Smith" .AND. State = "CA"
Record =    7
. CONTINUE
End of LOCATE scope
. ? EOF( )
.T.
```

See also: SEEK p. 228

MENU BAR *array, expN*

Description MENU BAR creates a bounce-bar menu.
Operational rules The three FoxPro MENU creation commands are:

- MENU BAR, which defines the bounce-bar menu.
- MENU, which defines the pop-up menus within the bounce-bar options.
- READ MENU, which activates the menu.

See the next section, MENU, for an example which shows how it is more efficient to create a menu system using these commands than the DEFINE MENU commands.

The main menu, defined by MENU BAR is a *horizontal bounce-bar menu*. Each option in a FoxPro-designed menu is called a *bar*. It is possible to design a vertical pop-up menu that is displayed whenever one of the bars in the main menu is highlighted with the cursor. Once the bounce-bar menu is displayed, the user can move the cursor to any of the options in the bar pop-up, creating a "menu within a menu."

To define a bounce-bar menu where each option has a pop-up menu that contains additional options, the following commands must be issued:

1. Set array variables as each bounce-bar option.
2. Set a different array for each pop-up menu option.
3. MENU BAR installs the bounce bar using the array values.
4. MENU installs the pop-up using the pop-up array values.
5. READ MENU activates the entire menu system.

The MENU BAR *array* is a two-dimensional character string array. Each menu option is defined with the second dimension of 1. Define a message for each option with the second dimension of 2. The number of menu options is defined with *expN*.

See the MENU BAR and READ MENU BAR sections for details regarding those commands.

See also: MENU p. 193
            READ MENU p. 217

MENU *expN1, array, expN2*

Description MENU creates a pop-up menu.
Operational rules The three FoxPro menu creation commands are:

- MENU BAR, which defines the bounce-bar menu.
- MENU, which defines the pop-up menus within the bounce-bar options.
- READ MENU, which activates the menu.

These three commands together create the same type of menu system created with DEFINE MENU and DEFINE POPUP commands, but are much more efficient. Compare the program example following, which creates the same menu system displayed in the DEFINE MENU section, with the program from that section. As you will see, the MENU creation uses many less commands.

Each menu defined by the MENU command is a vertical pop-up. The pop-ups are used in conjunction with a horizontal bar menu (defined with MENU BAR) where a certain pop-up menu is displayed whenever the corresponding bar of the main menu is highlighted.

To define a bounce-bar menu where each option has a pop-up menu that contains additional options, the following commands must be issued:

1. Set array variables as each bounce-bar option.
2. Set a different array for each pop-up menu option.
3. MENU BAR installs the bounce bar using the array values.
4. MENU installs the pop-up using the pop-up array values.
5. READ MENU activates the entire menu system.

The first parameter of MENU, *expN1*, is the position on the bar menu where the pop-up will be displayed. The *array* is a one-dimensional character string array. Each menu option is defined as a number of the array. The number of options within the pop-up is defined with *expN2*.

A fourth optional parameter, *expN4* defines the number of options to display on the screen at one time. In cases where there are many options, you might not want them all to show in the menu. FoxPro allows the user to scroll to options not displayed.

See the MENU BAR and READ MENU BAR sections for details regarding those commands.

Example The following program creates the menu and pop-up options displayed in Fig. 2-1 of the DEFINE BAR command. This program only sets up the pop-up for the leftmost option, Add.

```
DIMENSION OPTIONTOP(4,2)

OPTIONTOP(1,1) = "Add "
OPTIONTOP(2,1) = "List"
OPTIONTOP(3,1) = "Exit"
OPTIONTOP(1,2) = "Append Records into Database "
OPTIONTOP(2,2) = "List Records "
OPTIONTOP(3,2) = "Exit to DOS"

DIMENSION POPS(4)

POPS(1) = "Members"
POPS(2) = "Guests"
POPS(3) = "Prospect"
```

```
    ROW = 1
    COL = 1

    MENU BAR OPTIONTOP, 3
    MENU 1,POPS, 3
    READ MENU BAR TO ROW,COL
```

MENU TO *memvar*

Description   MENU TO activates a light bar menu created with the @ ...PROMPT command.

Operational rules   This command displays a light bar menu that the user can choose options from. Define the options and positions of the menu using the @...PROMPT command. If the *memvar* is one of the menu options, the cursor begins by highlighting that option. If it is not a valid option, the cursor defaults to the first option. The menu option selected is returned to *memvar*.

Examples

```
@ 3,1 PROMPT "Alpha" MESSAGE "Sort in Alphabetical Order"
@ 3,10 PROMPT "Zip" MESSAGE "Sort by Zip Code"
@ 3,20 PROMPT "Order" MESSAGE "Sort in User-Defined Order"
SET MESSAGE TO 22
MENU TO Choice

DO CASE
   CASE Choice = 1
      SET INDEX TO MAILALPH
   CASE Choice = 2
      SET INDEX TO MAILZIP
   CASE Choice = 3
      ACCEPT "Enter Expression to Sort By " TO Other
      INDEX ON &Other TO Temp
      GO TOP
ENDCASE
```

See also: @...PROMPT *p. 139*

MODIFY COMMAND *file name*

Description   MODIFY COMMAND invokes the FoxPro text editor.

Operational rules   Program (.PRG) files can be edited with this command. Omit the COMMAND clause, and use text editor to edit files other than those with .PRG extensions.

The FoxPro editor is invoked unless an alternative one has been set in the Config.db file. Use the command TEDIT = *program* to call an alternate editor. For example, TEDIT = WS would call up WordStar (WS.EXE) as the editor.

MODIFY LABEL *file name*

Description   MODIFY LABEL command changes the setting of a label format (.LBX) file.

Operational rules   For more details, see CREATE LABEL. Use the NOENVIRONMENT option to prevent the environment originally saved with the CREATE LABEL command from being restored.

Use the SAVE option to leave the label format window on the screen after exiting the window. This command can only be used by programs.

See *also*:   CREATE LABEL p. 158

MODIFY MEMO *memo field*

Description   MODIFY MEMO edits the contents of the *memo field*.

Operational rules   This command is equivalent to editing a record and pressing Ctrl – PgDn when at the memo field. MODIFY MEMO is very useful in programs because the program can control how the user will get into the memo editor—they are not forced to use the Ctrl – PgDn method.

Multiple memo fields can be edited by listing more than one memo field in the statement. The NOWAIT clause allows the program to continue processing while the memo is open. Otherwise, the program halts execution until the memo window is closed.

Example

MODIFY MEMO Narrative
MODIFY MEMO Narrative, History
MODIFY MEMO Narrative NOWAIT

MODIFY MENU *file name*

Description   The MODIFY MENU command brings up the FoxPro menu builder for editing a menu file.

Operational rules   For more details, see CREATE MENU.

Use the SAVE option to leave the menu builder on the screen after exiting the window. This command can only be used by programs.

See *also*:   CREATE MENU p. 159

MODIFY PROJECT *file name*

Description The MODIFY PROJECT command brings up the FoxPro project window for editing a project file.
Operational rules For more details, see CREATE PROJECT.
Use the SAVE option to leave the project window on the screen after exiting the window. This command can only be used by programs.

See also: CREATE PROJECT p. 159

MODIFY QUERY *file name*

Description The MODIFY QUERY command brings up the RQBE window for editing a query.
Operational rules For more details, see CREATE QUERY.

See also: CREATE QUERY p. 160

MODIFY REPORT *file name*

Description MODIFY REPORT is used for editing the settings in a report format (.FRX) file.
Operational rules For more details, see CREATE REPORT.
Use the NOENVIRONMENT option to prevent the environment originally saved with the CREATE REPORT command from being restored.
Use the SAVE option to leave the report generator window on the screen after exiting the window. This command can only be used by programs.

See also: CREATE REPORT p. 160

MODIFY SCREEN *file name*

Description MODIFY SCREEN is used for editing the settings in a screen format (.SCX) file.
Operational rules For more details, see CREATE SCREEN.
Use the NOENVIRONMENT option to prevent the environment originally saved with the CREATE SCREEN command from being restored.
Use the SAVE option to leave the screen builder window on the screen after exiting the window. This command can only be used by programs.

See also: CREATE SCREEN p. 161

MODIFY STRUCTURE

Description   MODIFY STRUCTURE allows you to change the layout of a FoxPro database file.

Operational rules   This command is the same as CREATE, except it is used on existing file structures. Make sure that there is enough room on your disk for the new file plus the space used by the old file (roughly double the .DBF file space).

For more details, of file structures, see CREATE.

See: CREATE p. 157

MOVE POPUP *pop-up name* TO *row, column*

Description   Use MOVE POPUP to move a pop-up to a new location on the screen.

Operational rules   You can issue the new coordinates of the pop-up with *row, column*. An alternate method is to move the pop-up relative to its current position. To do this, replace TO *row, column* with BY *change in row, change in column*.

You can move the pop-ups of the system menu by using the name of the system menu pop-up (_msystem, _mfile, _medit, _mdata, _mrecord, _mprog or _mwindow). To return them to their original locations, use SET SYSMENU TO DEFAULT.

Example   The first example moves the pop-up to row 5, column 20. The second example moves the File pop-up (from the system menu) down 5 rows and over 10 columns from its current position.

    MOVE POPUP Mpop TO 5, 20
    MOVE POPUP _mfile BY 5,10

See also: DEFINE WINDOW p. 170

MOVE WINDOW *window name* TO *row, column*

Description   Use MOVE WINDOW to move a window to a new location on the screen.

Operational rules   Use this command to reposition a window on the screen. You can issue the new coordinates of the window with *row, column*. An alternate method is to move the window relative to its current position. To do this, replace TO *row, column* with BY *change in row, change in column*.

The first example moves the window to row 5, column 20; the second example moves the window up two rows from its current position:

MOVE WINDOW Mwind TO 5, 20
MOVE WINDOW Mwind BY 1, 0

See also: DEFINE WINDOW p. 170

NOTE
&&
*

Description NOTE allows the user to type lines of comment in a program file.

Operational rules It is always a good practice to place notes and comments in program files. This documents the program and makes it easier to understand if you must go back to it to make changes, or for someone else who looks at it.

When FoxPro encounters the NOTE command, it ignores the rest of the text on that line. The asterisk (*) can be used in place of NOTE. To make your note extend past one line, place a semicolon at the end.

The other comment command is two ampersands (&&). These can be placed after a command, on the same line. Enter the text after the ampersands.

Example

```
*************  ************************
* Maillist.prg — Mailing List Program
* Last Updated: 5/1/89
NOTE — Maillist.prg prints selected records in a name & phone format
USE Maillist INDEX Mzip      && open file and index, etc.
```

ON BAR *expN* OF *pop-up name*

Description ON BAR activates a pop-up or menu when a bar *expN* or *pop-up name* is chosen.

Operational rules This command is used in conjunction with a pop-up, creating a "menu within a menu," or "submenuing" system. When the user selects a particular option from the pop-up menu, ON BAR defines the next pop-up or menu that is to be called. To call commands or procedures from a pop-up, use ON SELECTION POPUP.

The ON BAR command must be followed by either ACTIVATE POPUP *pop-up name* or ACTIVATE MENU *menu name*, depending on whether a sub-pop-up or submenu is being defined.

When a pop-up option has a submenu or sub-pop-up attached to it, an arrow is placed to the right of the option. The MARGIN keyword should be used in defining the pop-up options, otherwise the arrow might overwrite the last character of the option's prompt.

Example The example creates a pop-up that allows the user to pick a printer brand off of a menu of available printers. The first pop-up provides the choices of dot matrix or laser. If the user chooses dot matrix, another pop-up appears, listing a choice of three dot matrix printers. If the user chooses laser, a pop-up with two choices appears.

```
DEFINE POPUP Mprint FROM 2,20 MARGIN MESSAGE "Choose your type of printer"
DEFINE BAR 1 OF Mprint PROMPT " \ <Dot Matrix"
DEFINE BAR 2 OF Mprint PROMPT " \ <Laser"
ON BAR 1 OF Mprint ACTIVATE POPUP Dotty
ON BAR 2 OF Mprint ACTIVATE POPUP Laser

DEFINE POPUP Dotty FROM 2,20 MESSAGE "Choose your dot matrix printer"
DEFINE BAR 1 OF Dotty PROMPT " \ <Epsex"
DEFINE BAR 2 OF Dotty PROMPT " \ <Okidrata"
DEFINE BAR 3 OF Dotty PROMPT " \ <Toshiga"

DEFINE POPUP Laser FROM 2,20 MESSAGE "Choose your laser printer"
DEFINE BAR 1 OF Laser PROMPT " \ <Hewlett Packard"
DEFINE BAR 2 OF Laser PROMPT " \ <Canyawn"
ON SELECTION POPUP ALL DO Prnchoice
ACTIVATE POPUP Mprint

PROCEDURE Prnchoice
? "The printer you chose was the " + PROMPT( )
WAIT "Is that Correct? " TO Mchk
```

See also: DEFINE WINDOW p. 170

ON ERROR *command*

Description ON ERROR calls *command* if an error occurs within a program.

Operational rules Use this command to trap errors so that the program does not fall out with the FoxPro error message. This command should be placed at the beginning of the program, and it remains effective until an error or another ON ERROR command is encountered. Disable the trap by issuing ON ERROR without the *command* argument.

Several functions can be useful in conjunction with this command. ERROR( ) returns the number of the error. MESSAGE( ) returns the description of the error.

Example   The following program calls the procedure Errmess if an error occurs.

```
SET PROCEDURE TO Mailpro
ON ERROR DO Errmess
USE Maillist INDEX Mzip
   etc.
**    ERRMESS.PRG
DO CASE
  SET PRINTOFF
  CASE ERROR( ) = 126 .OR. ERROR( ) = 125
    ? "Please put your printer on line"
    WAIT
    SET PRINT ON
    RETRY
  OTHERWISE
    ? "The following error has occurred", MESSAGE( )
    ? "Number ", ERROR( )
    WAIT
    RETURN TO MASTER
ENDCASE
```

See also: ERROR( ) p. 300

ON ESCAPE *command*

Description   ON ESCAPE calls *command* if the Escape key is pressed within a program.

Operational rules   Use this command to detect when the user presses the Esc key so that the program does not fall out with the FoxPro abort message. This command has precedence over any ON KEY traps that have been set. SET ESCAPE OFF disables this command. You can also disable the trap by issuing ON ESCAPE without the *command* argument.

Example   The following program calls the program Escmess if the Esc key is pressed:

```
ON ESCAPE DO Escmess
USE Maillist INDEX Mzip
```

```
        SET PRINT ON
           etc.
        **    ESCMESS.PRG
        SET PRINT OFF
        ? "Program aborted, press any key to return to the main menu"
        ?
        WAIT ""
        RETURN TO MASTER
```

See also: ON KEY p. 202

ON KEY *command*

Description   ON KEY calls *command* if any key is pressed within a program.

Operational rules   You may only have one ON KEY in effect. If ON ESCAPE is in effect, pressing Esc triggers that command instead of the ON KEY command. If it is not in effect, the Esc key triggers the ON KEY command. Disable the trap by issuing ON KEY without the *command* argument.

Example

```
? "Press any key to abort printing"
ON KEY DO Keyabort
USE Maillist INDEX Mzip
   etc.

PROCEDURE Keyabort
   SET PRINT OFF
   ? "Printing has been aborted"
   WAIT
   RETURN TO MASTER
```

See also: ON ERROR p. 200

ON KEY = *expN command*

Description   ON KEY calls *command* if the specified key is pressed within a program.

Operational rules   ON KEY allows you to set a particular command for the specified key. Only one ON KEY = can be set at a time. This command only works when used in conjunction with the READ command. This command can be used for pulling up help screens and setting *macros* (automatic keystrokes) for entry screens.

The *expN* is the ASCII character of the key. The following table shows the *expN* to be used for nonprintable characters:

Key code	Keys
272 – 281	Alt – Q,W,E,R,T,Y,U,I,O,P
286 – 294	Alt – A,S,D,F,G,H,J,K,L
300 – 306	Alt – Z, X,C,V,B,N,M
315 – 324	F1 to F10 function keys
327	Home
328	↑
329	PgUp
331	←
333	→
335	End
336	↓
337	PgDn
338	Ins
339	Del
340 – 349	Shift F1 to Shift F10
350 – 359	Ctrl – F1 to Ctrl – F10
360 – 369	Alt – F1 to Alt – F10
370	Ctrl – Print Screen
371	Ctrl – ←
372	Ctrl – →
373	Ctrl – End
374	Ctrl – PgDn
375	Ctrl – Home
376 – 385	Alt – 1 to Alt – 10
386	Alt – -
387	Alt – =
388	Ctrl – PgUp

Example In this example, the ON KEY command is used for bringing up a context sensitive help screen. The VARREAD( ) function displays the name of the GET expression where the F1 key was pressed. Before the help screen is retrieved, the current screen is saved to a memory variable, so it can be refreshed once the help box is exited:

```
USE Maillist
ON KEY = 315 DO Helpit
@ 1,1 SAY "Press F1 to get help for a particular field"
@ 3,1 GET Code
@ 4,1 GET Desc
```

```
    READ
    etc.

*** Helpit.Prg
SAVE SCREEN TO Mscreen
@ 12,0 CLEAR
@ 12,1, 21,78 BOX
DO CASE
   CASE VARREAD( ) = "CODE"
      @ 15, 5 SAY "Help for Code Field . . . "
   CASE VARREAD( ) = "DESC"
      @ 15,5 SAY "Help for Desc Field . . . "
ENDCASE
WAIT ""
RESTORE SCREEN FROM Mscreen
RETURN
```

See also: VARREAD( ) p. 384

ON KEY LABEL *key label command*

Description   ON KEY LABEL calls *command* if the specified key is pressed within a program.

Operational rules   ON KEY allows you to set a particular command for each specified key. Multiple ON KEY LABEL commands may be set at a time. This command can be used for pulling up help screens and setting "macros" (automatic keystrokes) for entry screens.

Disable the trap by issuing ON KEY LABEL *keylabel* without the *command* argument.

The *key label* is the letter of the key. The following table shows the key label to be used for nonprintable characters:

Key label	Keys
ALT-A to ALT-Z	Alt – A to Alt – Z
ALT-0 to ALT-9	Alt – 0 to Alt – 9
CTRL-A to CTRL-Z	Ctrl – A to Ctrl – Z
F1 to F10	F1 to F10 function keys
HOME	Home
UPARROW	↑
PGUP	PgUp
LEFTARROW	←
RIGHTARROW	→
END	End

DNARROW	↓
PGDN	PgDn
INS	Ins
DEL	Del
SHIFT-F1 to SHIFT-F9	Shift – F1 to Shift – F9
CTRL-F1 to CTRL-F10	Ctrl – F1 to Ctrl – F10
ALT-F1 to ALT-F10	Alt – F1 to Alt – F10
CTRL-LEFTARROW	Ctrl – ←
CTRL-RIGHTARROW	Ctrl – →
CTRL-END	Ctrl – End
CTRL-PGDN	Ctrl – PgDn
CTRL-HOME	Ctrl – Home
CTRL-PGUP	Ctrl – PgUp
RIGHTMOUSE	Right mouse
LEFTMOUSE	Left mouse
MOUSE	Mouse

Example In this example, the ON KEY LABEL command is used for bringing up two types of help screen. If the user presses F1 they get a context-sensitive help screen. If they press Alt – F1 they get a general help screen. Before either help screen is retrieved, the current screen is saved to a memory variable with SAVE SCREEN, so it can be refreshed once the help box is exited (using RESTORE SCREEN).

```
USE Maillist
ON KEY LABEL F1 DO Helpit ON KEY LABEL ALT-F1 DO Genhelp
@ 1,1 SAY "Press F1 to get help for a field, ALT-F1 for general help"
@ 3,1 GET Code
@ 4,1 GET Desc
READ
   etc.

*** Helpit.Prg

SAVE SCREEN TO Mscreen
@ 12,0 CLEAR
@ 12,1, 21,78 BOX
DO CASE
   CASE VARREAD( ) = "CODE"
      @ 15, 5 SAY "Help for Code Field . . . "
   CASE VARREAD( ) = "DESC"
      @ 15,5 SAY "Help for Desc Field . . . "
ENDCASE
WAIT " "
```

```
RESTORE SCREEN FROM Mscreen
RETURN

*** Genhelp.Prg

SAVE SCREEN TO Mscreen
@ 12,0 CLEAR
@ 12,1, 21,78 BOX
@ 15,5 SAY "General help for screen editing . . . "
WAIT
RESTORE SCREEN FROM Mscreen
RETURN
```

See also: VARREAD( ) p. 384

ON PAD *pad name* OF *menu name*

Description ON PAD displays a pop-up or menu bar when the user is highlighting *pad name*.

Operational rules This command is used in conjunction with a menu created with the DEFINE MENU and *DEFINE PAD* commands. When the user highlights a particular option, the ON PAD command calls a submenu (pop-up or menu bar) to appear.

The optional ACTIVATE POPUP *pop-up name* argument allows the user to then use the arrow keys to move among the bars of the pop-up menu, creating a sub-pop-up menu. Use ACTIVATE MENU *menu name* to activate another menu bar.

See the DEFINE POPUP command for an example of a menu program.

See also: DEFINE POPUP p. 168

ON PAGE AT LINE *expN command*

Description ON PAGE calls *command* when line *expN* is reached on a printed page.

Operational rules This command can be used to print page breaks and headers after every *expN* number of lines. Previous versions of FoxPro did not have this command, and users were forced to check for line numbers using memory variables. If the routine is to eject the page, use the EJECT PAGE command (not the EJECT command).

Set ON PAGE before turning on the printer with SET PRINT ON or SET DEVICE TO PRINT. To disable the ON PAGE trap, issue the ON PAGE command without an argument.

Example

```
USE MaillistINDEX Mzip
SET PRINT ON
ON PAGE AT LINE 58 DO Header
DO Header
DO WHILE .NOT. EOF( )
   ? Lname,Fname
   SKIP
ENDDO
ON PAGE

PROCEDURE Header
EJECT PAGE
? "Mailing List by Zip Code"
? REPLICATE("- ",35)
RETURN
```

See also: SET PRINTER p. 259
         EJECT PAGE p. 177

ON READERROR *command*

Description   ON READERROR calls *command* if an error occurs on an entry screen.

Operational rules   The errors that occur on edit screens are invalid data entries, entries outside of the RANGE specification, and entries that do not meet the VALID conditions. FoxPro automatically provides an error message for these instances, but ON READERROR allows you to run your own error handling routines.

This command should be placed at the beginning of the program, and it remains effective until an error or another ON READERROR command is encountered. Disable the trap by issuing ON READERROR without the *command* argument.

See also: ON KEY p. 202

ON SELECTION BAR *expN* OF *pop-up name command*

Description   ON SELECTION BAR calls *command* when the user has selected bar *expN* from pop-up menu *pop-up name*.

Operational rules   This command is used in conjunction with a menu created with the DEFINE POPUP command. If the user chooses bar number *expN*, ON SELECTION BAR defines the command or procedure that will then be performed.

Disable the branching by issuing ON SELECTION BAR without the *command* argument.

This command is similar to ON SELECTION POPUP which assigns a command to an entire pop-up menu. To assign a submenu (pop-up or menu) to appear when a particular option is chosen, use ON BAR.

See also: ON BAR p. 199
ON SELECTION POPUP p. 209

ON SELECTION MENU *menu name command*

Description   ON SELECTION MENU calls *command* when the user has selected any pad from the bounce-bar menu *menu name*.

Operational rules   This command is used in conjunction with a menu created with the DEFINE MENU command. When the user exits the menu, ON SELECTION MENU defines the command or procedure that will then be performed.

You can use ALL in place of *menu name* to select the same command for all menus. Disable the branching by issuing ON SELECTION MENU without the *command* argument.

See also: DEFINE MENU p. 166

ON SELECTION PAD *pad name*
OF *menu name command*

Description   ON SELECTION PAD calls *command* when the user has selected *pad name*.

Operational rules   This command is used in conjunction with a menu created with the DEFINE MENU and DEFINE PAD commands. When the user selects a particular option from the pad, ON SELECTION defines the command or procedure that will then be performed.

The *command* can utilize the MENU( ) or PAD( ) functions which determine the last selected option. Disable the branching by issuing ON SELECTION PAD without the *command* argument.

See the DEFINE MENU section for an example of a menu that utilizes ON SELECTION PAD.

See also: DEFINE MENU p. 166

ON SELECTION POPUP pop-up name command

Description ON SELECTION POPUP calls *command* when the user has selected *popup name* from a pop-up menu.

Operational rules This command is used in conjunction with a menu created with the DEFINE POPUP command. When the user selects a particular option from the pop-up menu, ON SELECTION POPUP defines the command or procedure that is then performed.

You can use ALL in place of *popup name* to select the same command for all pop-ups. Disable the branching by issuing ON SELECTION POPUP without the *command* argument.

See the DEFINE POPUP section for an example of a menu that utilizes ON SELECTION POPUP.

See also: DEFINE POPUP p. 168

PACK

Description The PACK command permanently deletes all records marked for deletion from the current database file.

Operational rules To delete a record from the database file:

1. Mark all records to be deleted.
2. Issue the PACK command.

PACK makes a copy of the data file without the old records, so it may take a while to run. PACK will renumber the records as deleted records are removed. Make sure that there is enough room on your disk for the new file plus the space used by the old file (roughly double the .DBF file space).

The SET DELETED ON command tells FoxPro to ignore deleted records when displaying, editing, and listing. This allows deleted records to appear as if they have already been removed without having to PACK.

With the advent of FoxPro version 2.0, two optional clauses were added to this command. The keyword MEMO causes the memo (.FPT) file to be packed—all unused space is deleted and the file is reduced in size. The keyword DBF causes the database to be packed, but the memo file is not packed. When now keyword is used, both data file and memo file (if there is one) are packed.

See also: DELETE p. 171

PARAMETERS *parameter list*

Description PARAMETERS is used to pass memory variables to a subprogram, procedure, or user-defined function, where those variables can be changed and passed back.

Operational rules If a program calls a procedure or function without the PARAMETERS command, any variables changed will not retain their new values after returning back to the calling program.

When using PARAMETERS, call the procedure, program or function by defining the parameter list using WITH *parameter list*. The variables in the calling parameter list must match the number of items in the PARAMETERS parameter list. The names of the variables do not need to match.

The way an array is passed in the PARAMETER statement is determined by UDFPARMS. If it is set to REFERENCE, the entire array is passed. If it is set to VALUE, the first element of the array is passed.

Example

```
USE Maillist INDEX Mzip
SET PRINT ON
Line = 99
DO WHILE .NOT. EOF( )
    IF Line > 60
    DO Header with Line, "Mailing List by Zip Code"
    ENDIF
    ? Lname,Fname
    Line = Line + 1
    SKIP
ENDDO

PROCEDURE Header
PARAMETERS Lineno, Title
EJECT PAGE
? "Page #",Lineno
?
? Title
?
? REPLICATE("-",75)
Line = 5
RETURN
```

See also: PROCEDURE p. 213

POP MENU *menu name*

Description POP MENU pulls a menu from the stack.

Operational rules Menus can be placed on a stack using the PUSH MENU command. This command allows you to make changes to the menu and use it temporarily in its changed state. POP MENU is then used to pull the menu from the stack, restoring it back to its original state.

Menus are designed with the DEFINE MENU command. Once the definitions are set, you can use ACTIVATE MENU to call it up. Use DEACTIVATE MENU to erase a menu from the screen. See DEFINE MENU for a program that creates a bounce-bar menu.

See also: DEFINE MENU p. 166
PUSH MENU p. 215

POP POPUP *pop-up name*

Description   POP POPUP pulls a pop-up from the stack.

Operational rules   Pop-up menus can be placed on a stack using the PUSH POPUP command. This command allows you to make changes to the pop-up and use it temporarily in its changed state. POP POPUP is then used to pull the pop-up from the stack, restoring it back to its original state.

Pop-up menus are designed with the DEFINE POPUP and DEFINE BAR commands. Once the definitions are set, you can use ACTIVATE POPUP to call it up. Use DEACTIVATE POPUP to erase a pop-up menu from the screen. See DEFINE BAR for a program that creates a pop-up menu within a bounce-bar menu.

See also: DEFINE BAR p. 163
PUSH POPUP p. 215

PLAY MACRO *macro name*

Description   PLAY MACRO performs a macro.

Operational rules   Macros are sets of keystrokes that FoxPro automatically performs for you. Run a macro by pressing the keystroke that you specified for calling the macro. Macros are created using the SAVE MACROS command.

To call a macro from a program, use PLAY MACRO. This causes the keystrokes to perform as if someone had pressed the key combination that runs the macro. The macro is then played the first time that input is requested in the program (for instance at an ACCEPT, @...GET, or EDIT command).

If multiple PLAY MACRO commands are pending, it performs them in reverse order. In other words, the most recent PLAY MACRO is performed first.

You can keep separate sets of macros in a macro library file. To make a macro library current, use the RESTORE MACROS command.

See also: RESTORE MACROS p. *222*

PRINTJOB commands
ENDPRINTJOB

Description PRINT JOB utilizes FoxPro system memory variables while printing.

Operational rules Examples of some of the system memory variables are printer setup codes (_psetup), number of copies (_pcopies), page eject controls (_peject) and beginning page number (_pbpage). These variables can only be utilized with FoxPro built-in reporting capabilities (such as the REPORT FORM), or within programs that call PRINTJOB.

System variables should be defined before the PRINTJOB command is issued. Print jobs can work in conjunction with reports printed through SET PRINT ON or SET FORMAT TO PRINT. At the end of the reporting commands, finish with ENDPRINTJOB.

Examples

```
USE MaillistINDEX Mzip
SET PRINT ON
_pcopies = 3
_peject = "both"
PRINTJOB
ON PAGE AT LINE 58 DO Header
DO WHILE .NOT. EOF( )
   ? Lname,Fname
   SKIP
ENDDO
ENDPRINTJOB
SET PRINT OFF
PROCEDURE Header
? "Page #",-pageno
? REPLICATE ("-",75)
RETURN
```

PRIVATE *memvar list*

Description PRIVATE is used to declare a private memory variable in a lower level program. This command prevents changes from being passed back to the calling program.

Operational rules Private memory variables allow two variables with the same name. One memory variable can be in a lower level program, and the other can be in the program that called it. If the value of the variable in the lower level program is changed, it will not affect the value of the variable in the calling program. Memory variables created in programs default to being private variables.

The keywords ALL or LIKE *skeleton* can be used in place of *memvar list*.

Examples

PRIVATE Date, Amount, Time
PRIVATE ALL
PRIVATE LIKE D*

See also: PUBLIC p. *214*

PROCEDURE

Description The PROCEDURE command must be at the beginning of each subroutine.

Operational rules A program calls a procedure with the DO *procedure name* command. Procedures are best utilized for parts of a program that are called more than once. Procedures run faster than if they were their own separate command (.PRG) files.

Procedures can be placed in the program file (usually at the bottom), in a procedure file, in any program file that called the current file, or in a file (.FPX or .PRG) with the procedure name. Procedure names can be up to eight characters (no spaces allowed).

A procedure file can hold up to 1170 procedures. Use SET PROCEDURE TO *procedure file* at the top of your main program to open the procedure file. Procedures that are called from more than one program should be placed in the procedure file. Procedures that are only called from one program should be placed at the bottom of that file.

Procedures must begin with PROCEDURE and end with a RETURN. Memory variables that are changed within the procedure do not retain the changes in the calling program unless they have been declared public or have been passed through the PARAMETER keyword.

Examples

```
USE Maillist INDEX Mzip
Line = 99
DO WHILE .NOT. EOF( )
   IF Line > 60
      DO Header
   ENDIF
```

```
    ? Lname,Fname
    Line = Line + 1
    SKIP
ENDDO

PROCEDURE Header
EJECT
? "MAILING LIST PRINTOUT FOR",DATE( )
?
? REPLICATE("-",75)
Line = 5
RETURN
```

See also: PARAMETERS p. 209

PUBLIC memvar list

Description   PUBLIC is used to declare a public memory variable in a lower level program. This allows changes to the variable to be passed back to the calling program.

Operational rules   Public memory variables allow you to make changes to a memory variable in a lower level program or subroutine and pass those changes back to the calling program. Variables created at the dot prompt are automatically PUBLIC variables, while variables created in programs default to PRIVATE variables.

Public memory variables are logicals until they are initialized to some other type. It is important that you do not declare a memory variable PUBLIC after it has been initialized. Therefore, it is a good idea to include the PUBLIC command for all variables at the beginning of the master program so it is given before any of the variables have been set.

The argument ARRAY *array list* can be used in place of *memvar list* if you are declaring array memory variables.

Examples

```
** Main.Prg
PUBLIC Mem
Mem = 5
Mem2 = 5
DO Subprog
? Mem, Mem2     && Mem is 10, but Mem2 is still 5

PROCEDURE Subprog
Mem = 10     && Mem is public; it equals 10 in both programs
```

```
    Mem2 = 10      && Mem2 is private; it stays 5 in Main.Prg
    RETURN
```

See also: PRIVATE p. 212

PUSH MENU *menu name*

Description   PUSH MENU places a menu on the stack.

Operational rules   Placing menus on a "stack" allows you to make changes to the menu and use it temporarily in its changed state. POP MENU is then used to pull the menu from the stack, restoring it back to its original state. Menus are placed on and removed from the stack in a "last in, first out" order.

Menus are designed with the DEFINE MENU command. Once the definitions are set, you can use ACTIVATE MENU to call it up. Use DEACTIVATE MENU to erase a menu from the screen. See DEFINE MENU for a program that creates a bounce-bar menu.

See also: DEFINE MENU p. 166
              POP MENU p. 210

PUSH POPUP *pop-up name*

Description   PUSH POPUP places a pop-up on the stack.

Operational rules   Placing pop-up menus on a "stack" allows you to make changes to the pop-up and use it temporarily in its changed state. POP POPUP is then used to pull it from the stack, restoring it back to its original state. Pop-ups are placed on and removed from the stack in a "last in, first out" order.

Example   In the following example, the pop-up menu has three bars: Add, Edit, and Browse. The pop-up is pushed to the stack, and the second bar is removed with the RELEASE BAR command. The pop-up is then restored to its original state with the POP POPUP command.

```
    DEFINE POPUP editor

    DEFINE BAR 1 OF editor PROMPT 'Add'
    DEFINE BAR 2 OF editor PROMPT 'Edit'
    DEFINE BAR 3 OF editor PROMPT
'Browse'
    ACTIVATE POPUP editor NOWAIT

    PUSH POPUP editor
    RELEASE BAR 2 OF editor
```

WAIT
POP POPUP editor

See also: DEFINE POPUP p. 168
POP POPUP p. 211

QUIT

Description   QUIT ends the current FoxPro session.

Operational rules   QUIT closes all files before exiting. FoxPro files can be damaged or destroyed if the computer is turned off or reset without quitting. To help prevent this from happening, close files with the CLOSE commands once you no longer need them during a FoxPro session. You can also call the FLUSH command periodically to dump memory buffers without closing files.

See also: CLOSE p. 152

READ

Description   The READ command allows you to edit variables designated with the @...GET command.

Operational rules   The @...GET command allows you to display more than one variable or field on the screen for editing. Use the @...GET and @...SAY command to "paint" the screen. The READ command must follow the list of @...GET's for a screen. The user can then move back and forth while editing the GET variables.

READ will allow editing of all @...GET statements made since the last READ, CLEAR GETS, or CLEAR command. The optional SAVE argument prevents GETS from being cleared after the last READ command. When you use READ SAVE, make sure that you CLEAR GETS when you do want to remove them.

When a READ command is issued, Enter, Tab, or ↓ moves forward from object to object. To exit a READ, press Esc, Ctrl – W, or press Enter after the last object, GET.

Format files hold a group of @...GET statements, so the READ command can be used in conjunction with SET FORMAT TO when using custom screen layouts.

Multiple READ levels occur when UDF's are used in the WHEN or VALID clauses of the GET statement. If the UDF contains a READ, there are multiple READs. FoxPro supports up to four nested READs.

The optional CYCLE keyword prevents the READ from terminating after passing through the last GET. To terminate, Esc, Ctrl – W must be pressed, or the CLEAR READ or TIMEOUT clause must be given.

The optional ACTIVATE *expL* clause is executed when READ is issued, and each time the current READ window changes. DEACTIVATE *expL* is executed when another READ window is activated. The optional SHOW *expL* clause is executed whenever SHOW GETS is issued.

FoxPro version 2.0 added many new optional clauses to the READ command. Many of these clauses are also found in the @...GET command. For more detailed information on any of the clauses, see the @...GET section. The clauses are:

- VALID *expL*   If *expL* is true, the READ is terminated, otherwise the cursor remains in the same GET field. If VALID returns a number, the cursor moves to the corresponding object.
- WHEN *expL*   The READ is only executed when *expL* is true.
- OBJECT *expN*   Determines which object is initially selected.
- TIMEOUT *expN*   Determines how many seconds can elapse without user input before the READ is terminated.
- NOMOUSE   Prevents objects from being selected with the mouse.
- COLOR *color pair list*   Specifies color of the current GET object.
- COLOR SCHEME *expN*   Color pair 2 determines color of the current GET object.

Examples

Use Maillist
@ 5,1 SAY "Enter Last Name" Lname
@ 5,50 SAY "First Name" GET Fname
READ

See also: *@SAY...GET p. 125*

READ MENU TO *memvar*

Description   READ MENU TO activates a pop-up menu defined with the @...MENU command.

Operational rules   This command activates a pop-up menu that the user can choose options from. See the @...MENU command regarding the setup of the menu.

Examples

DIMENSION SORTS(3)
Sorts(1) = "Alpha"
Sorts(2) = "Zip"
Sorts(3) = "Other"

@ 3,3 MENU Sorts, 3 TITLE "Choose an order to sort by"
READ MENU TO Choice
DO CASE
   CASE Choice = 1

```
            SET INDEX TO MAILALPH
        CASE Choice = 2
            SET INDEX TO MAILZIP
        CASE Choice = 3
            ACCEPT "Enter Expression to Sort By " TO Other
            INDEX ON &Other TO Temp
            GO TOP
    ENDCASE
```

See also: @...MENU p. 138

RECALL

Description   The RECALL command "unmarks" records marked for deletion.

Operational rules   To delete a record from the database file, mark all records to be deleted and then issue the PACK command.

The RECALL command reinstates the current record. Use the optional FOR *condition*, WHILE *condition*, and *scope* arguments to recall records for a subset of the data file. To reinstate all records, use the ALL argument.

Examples

```
RECALL
RECALL FOR State = "CA"
RECALL NEXT 100
RECALL ALL
```

See also: DELETE p. 171

REINDEX

Description   REINDEX recreates all open index (.IDX and .CDX) files.

Operational rules   Index files usually must be reindexed if they were not closed properly. This occurs when the computer is turned off or reset without using the QUIT command. Index files will also need to be reindexed if they were not open when records were added or edited in the database.

The optional COMPACT keyword creates compact indexes even if the originals were not compact. Compact indexing causes the files to be smaller, and for index operations (such as SEEK) to run faster. The only reason not to use compact index files is if you are trying to maintain compatibility with FoxPlus or Mac/Fox.

See also: INDEX p. 185

RELEASE *memory variable list*
or **RELEASE BAR** *bar number* **OF** *pop-up name*
  RELEASE BAR ALL OF *pop-up name*
  RELEASE MODULE *module name list*
  RELEASE MENUS *menu name list*
  RELEASE PAD *pad number* **OF** *menu name*
  RELEASE PAD ALL OF *menu name*
  RELEASE POPUPS *pop-up name list*
  RELEASE WINDOWS *window name list*

Description The RELEASE command erases certain variables from memory, opening up space for new variables.

Operational rules To delete select memory variables use RELEASE with the memory variable list, or with the ALL, ALL LIKE *skeleton*, or ALL EXCEPT *skeleton* argument.

RELEASE MODULE erases a binary file that has been loaded with the LOAD command. You cannot erase menus, pop-ups, or windows unless they are no longer in use. When menus, pop-ups, windows, and pads are released, they are removed from memory and erased from the screen.

The EXTENDED keyword is used with RELEASE MENUS and RELEASE POPUPS to release all subordinate pads, pop-ups, bars, and ON routines.

Examples

RELEASE ALL
RELEASE ALL LIKE S*
RELEASE MENUS Main, Edit
RELEASE PAD 1 OF Editor
RELEASE BAR ALL OF mpop

See also: CLEAR MEMORY *p. 151*

RENAME *old name* TO *new name*

Description RENAME changes the name of a file.

Operational rules You cannot erase a file that is currently open. The RENAME command does not allow wildcards (? and *) to rename multiple files at one time, so you might prefer to use the REN command from DOS. To run a DOS command while at the dot prompt, use ! or RUN.

Example

RENAME Maillist.dbf TO Mail.dbf
RENAME C:\ DATA \ Maillist.dbf TO C:\ DATA \ Mail.dbf

See also: RUN/! *p. 224*

REPLACE *field* WITH *expression*

Description The REPLACE command performs a "global find and replace" routine in the current database.

Operational rules Use the optional FOR *condition*, WHILE *condition*, and *scope* arguments to perform the operation in a subset of the data file. To replace a field in all records, use the ALL argument. Without one of these clauses, REPLACE only replaces the contents in the current record.

You can provide a list of fields to be replaced in one command. Replacing several fields at one time is faster than issuing separate REPLACE commands.

The ADDITIVE clause is for replacing memo fields with an expression. ADDITIVE causes the *expression* to be appended to the memo. If you do not use this clause, using this command with memo fields will replace the current memo entry with *expression*.

Do not perform a global replace on the key field of the current index. All the records may not become replaced because each record is reindexed as its key changes. It is better to close the index, run the REPLACE command, and then reindex.

Examples

```
REPLACE ALL Wages WITH Wages * 1.1
REPLACE City WITH "San Jose", State WITH "CA" FOR City = "SJ"
REPLACE NEXT 100 City WITH UPPER(City)
REPLACE Narrative WITH Comment1 + Comment2 ADDITIVE
```

REPORT FORM *report form file name*

Description The REPORT FORM command prints a formatted report for a data file. The report format must already be created with the CREATE REPORT command.

Operational rules The CREATE REPORT command allows you to set the report dimensions, headings, groupings, and contents of the report within a report (.FRG) file. To run the report, make sure the data file (or multiple files) is your current file, and issue the REPORT FORM command.

The argument ? can be used in place of the *report file name*. FoxPro will display a list of .FRX files to choose from.

Use the optional FOR *condition*, WHILE *condition*, and *scope* arguments to print the report for a subset of records from the data file.

Reports default to printing on the screen. Use the TO PRINTER option to print to the printer, or the TO FILE *file name* to print to an ASCII file.

The PLAIN clause prevents the headers to print on pages other than the first. HEADING *expC* causes an additional line of text, *expC*, to print on the top of each page. NOEJECT prevents the initial form feed even if it has been set to Yes in the CREATE REPORT generator. SUMMARY prints a summary report (subtotals only) even if has been set to No in the CREATE REPORT generator.

If the report has groupings, the primary file should be indexed by the field(s) to be grouped on. If a report view (.FRV) file has been created with the same name as the report definition (.FRX) file, you can use the ENVIRONMENT clause. This calls the view file and restores all of its settings (opens files and indexes in correct work areas, sets relationships and filters, etc).

The PREVIEW displays the first page of the report (one screenful) on the screen letting you verify that the report definition is set up correctly. After exiting the preview screen, the REPORT FORM command must be issued again (without PREVIEW) to actually begin printing the report.

Use the NOOPTIMIZE option to disable Rushmore. This is only relevant when the FOR clause is being used. An alternate method is to globally disable Rushmore by using the SET OPTIMIZE command.

Examples

```
REPORT FORM Mlist
REPORT FORM Mlist PREVIEW
REPORT FORM Mlist TO PRINT
REPORT FORM Mlist TO PRINT HEADING "Rotary Club Mailing"
REPORT FORM Mlist FOR State = "CA" PLAIN NOEJECT
REPORT FORM Mlist NEXT 100 TO FILE Mreport   && creates Mreport.Txt
REPORT FORM Mlist ENVIRONMENT TO PRINT
```

See also: CREATE REPORT *p. 161*

RESTORE FROM *file name*

Description   The RESTORE command reads a memory (.MEM) file and loads all variables into memory.

Operational rules   Memory files are created with the SAVE TO command, which saves all or a subset of current variables to a file.

RESTORE causes all current variables to be deleted unless the ADDITIVE option is included. If any current memory variables have the same name, they are overwritten with the new values. When variables are restored from within a program, they automatically become PRIVATE unless they were previously declared PUBLIC in the program.

Examples

```
RESTORE FROM Memfile
RESTORE FROM Memfile ADDITIVE
```

See also: SAVE TO *p. 226*

RESTORE MACROS FROM *macro file*

Description The RESTORE MACROS command reads a macro (.FKY) file and loads all macros into memory.

Operational rules Macro files are created with the SAVE MACROS command, which saves all macros to a file. You can also save macros from the System menu pop-up. If current macros have the same name, they are overwritten with the new values.

See also: SAVE MACROS p. 225

RESTORE SCREEN FROM *memory variable*

Description The RESTORE SCREEN command displays a screen layout or window that has been saved with SAVE SCREEN command.

Operational rules This command is useful in situations where you are overlaying the current screen with information, such as a help window. To erase the information and restore the screen to its previous display, use the following sequence of commands:

1. Issue the command SAVE SCREEN TO *memvar* to save the screen settings to *memvar*.
2. Display the information, and when you are done . . .
3. RESTORE SCREEN FROM *memvar* to restore the screen settings.

Example The following program displays a help box when the user presses the F1 key. Before the help is displayed, the screen layout is saved to the memory variable Mscreen. To return from the help screen, the program calls RESTORE SCREEN to restore it to its previous settings:

```
USE Maillist
ON KEY LABEL F1 DO Helpit
@ 1,1 SAY "Press F1 to get help "
@ 3,1 GET Code
@ 4,1 GET Desc
READ
   etc.

*** Helpit.Prg
SAVE SCREEN TO Mscreen
@ 12,0 CLEAR
@ 12,1, 21,78 BOX
@ 15,5 SAY "General help for screen editing . . . "
WAIT
```

RESTORE SCREEN FROM Mscreen
RETURN

See also: SAVE SCREEN p. 225

RESTORE WINDOW
window name list FROM *file name*

Description   The RESTORE WINDOW command reads a window (.WIN) file and loads the window into memory.

Operational rules   Window files are created with the SAVE WINDOWS command, which saves the currently defined window to a file. Enter all names of windows to be restored in the *window name list*. You can use the ALL keyword in place of the list.

See also: SAVE WINDOW p. 226

RESUME

Description   The RESUME command causes a program to resume processing after it has been suspended.

Operational rules   When a program encounters an error, it asks the user whether they want to Cancel, Suspend, or Ignore. If the user chooses Suspend, the program drops out to the command window. All memory variables still exist, as does the file status. At this point, files and variables can be manipulated. If the user then chooses RESUME, the program resumes processing at the next command line.

If the user chooses Cancel, memory variables are erased, and the program cannot resume processing. SUSPEND can also be placed within a program to make it return to the command line leaving memory variables intact.

See also: SUSPEND p. 237

RETRY

Description   The RETRY command causes a program to resume processing, rerunning the line from which it exited.

Operational rules   This command is particularly useful in error handling routines. After the error has been encountered, the routine can fix it. By using RETRY, it can then go back and retry the command where the error occurred.

SET PROCEDURE TO Mailpro
ON ERROR DO Errmess

```
    USE Maillist INDEX Mzip
    SET PRINT ON
      etc.
    PROCEDURE ERRMESS
    DO CASE
      SET PRINT OFF
      CASE ERROR( ) = 126 .OR. ERROR( ) =
        ? "Please put your printer on line"
        WAIT
        SET PRINT ON
        RETRY
      OTHERWISE
        ? "The following error has occurred", MESSAGE( )
        WAIT
        RETURN TO MASTER
    ENDCASE
    RETURN
```

See also: ON ERROR p. 200

RETURN

Description   The RETURN command causes a program or subroutine to return to the calling program.

Operational rules   If the RETURN command is placed in the master program, it drops out to the command window. When placed in any other program, RETURN returns to the calling program, one line below the line that made the call.

The TO MASTER clause causes a return to the highest level calling program (usually the main menu in menu-based systems). The TO *procedure* clause allows you to choose the program to return to. You may issue RETURN *expr* to return a value to the calling program.

You are not required to place RETURN at the end of a program or procedure, because there is an implicit RETURN at the end.

See also: DO p. 174

RUN *DOS commands*

Description   The RUN command calls any program available from the DOS prompt.

Operational rules RUN calls any program that can be run from the DOS prompt. Some programs use up too much memory to be called from FoxPro, however. The ! command is equivalent to the RUN command.

FoxPro comes with a program named FoxSwap that swaps out memory so you should be able to even run programs that run out of memory with the RUN command. To use FoxSwap, use the following syntax:

RUN FOXSWAP *program*

Examples

RUN DATE
! CHKDSK

SAVE MACROS TO *macro file*

Description The SAVE MACROS command saves currently defined macros to a macro (.FKY) file.

Operational rules Macro files are created with the SAVE MACROS command, which saves all macros to a file. Load these macros with the RESTORE MACROS command.

See also: RESTORE MACROS p. 222

SAVE SCREEN TO *memory variable*

Description The SAVE SCREEN command saves the settings of the current screen layout or window so that it can be restored with the RESTORE SCREEN command.

Operational rules This command is useful in situations where you are overlaying the current screen with information, such as a help window. To erase the information and restore the screen to its previous display, use the following sequence of commands:

1. Issue the command SAVE SCREEN TO *memvar* to save the screen settings to *memvar*.
2. Display the information, and when you are done, . . .
3. RESTORE SCREEN FROM *memvar* to restore the screen settings.

See the RESTORE SCREEN sections for an example of a program that uses these commands.

See also: RESTORE SCREEN p. 222

SAVE TO *file name*

Description   The SAVE command creates a memory (.MEM) file of current memory variables and their values.

Operational rules   Memory files are created with the SAVE TO command, which saves all or a subset of current variables to a file. Use the ALL LIKE *skeleton* or ALL EXCEPT *skeleton* clauses to save a subset of current memory variables.

Use the RESTORE command to load the variables into memory.

Examples

SAVE TO Memfile
SAVE TO Memfile ALL LIKE S*

See also: RESTORE FROM p. 221

SAVE WINDOW *window name list* TO *file name*

Description   The SAVE WINDOW command saves the current window settings to a window (.WIN) file.

Operational rules   Window files are created with the SAVE WINDOWS command, which saves the currently defined window to a file. You can substitute ALL in place of *window name list*.

See also: RESTORE WINDOW p. 223

SCAN
commands
ENDSCAN

Description   SCAN processes all or selected records of a database.

Operational rules   SCAN is much like the DO WHILE command when processing a database. However SCAN, unlike DO WHILE, automatically advances the record pointer with each loop, eliminating the need for the SKIP command.

You can use the optional FOR *condition*, WHILE *condition*, and *scope* arguments to process only a subset of the data file.

As with the DO WHILE command, you can use the LOOP to loop back to SCAN and begin processing the next record. You can use the EXIT command to end the SCAN process.

Example

USE Maillist
SCAN FOR State = "CA"
   IF Active = "N"   && skip records where Active = "N"

```
        LOOP
    ENDIF
    ? Lname, Fname
    REPLACE Printed WITH "Y"
ENDSCAN      && automatically go to next record
```

See also: DO WHILE p. 175

SCATTER TO *array*

Description   The SCATTER TO command stores the values of the fields in the current record to an array or group of memory variables.

Operational rules   When scattering to an array, each array element represents a field. When scattering to a memory variable, FoxPro takes care of making sure each field gets saved. This command is very useful in programs for editing records in a data file. Before the edit session, SCATTER the record to a memory variable. Then, if the user exits with a key defined as the "abort" key, use the GATHER FROM command to set all fields back to their previous values.

Use the FIELDS *field list* option to limit the fields to be scattered. Use the BLANK option to create a set of memory variables that do not contain the entries from the record, but instead are the same type and length of each field in the record. The value of each of these variables will be "blank." In other words, numeric variables will be zero, character variables will be spaces, logicals will be .F., and dates will be { / / }.

Example

```
USE Maillist
SCATTER TO Save_it
@ 3,1 SAY "Database of Clients"
@ $,60 SAY "Press ESC to Abort"
@ 5,1 SAY "Enter Last Name" GET Lname PICTURE "!XXXXXXXXXXXXXX"
@ 5,50 SAY "First Name" GET Fname PICTURE "!XXXXXXXXXXXXXX"
@ $+2,1 SAY "Address:" GET Address
@ $+1,1 SAY " City:" GET City
@ $,$+1 SAY " State:" GET State PICTURE "@!"
@ $,$+1 SAY "Zip:" GET Zip PICTURE "#####"
READ
IF LASTKEY( ) = 27
   GATHER FROM Save_it
ENDIF
```

See also: GATHER FROM p. 182

SCROLL *row1, col1, row2, col2, expN*

Description   The SCROLL command scrolls the output in the specified area to be scrolled vertically or horizontally.

Operational rules   The coordinates *row1, col1* define the upper left corner of the region, and *row2, col2* is the bottom right corner. *expN* defines how many lines are to be scrolled. If this parameter is positive, the region scrolls up. If it is negative, the region scrolls down.

SCROLL defaults to scrolling vertically. To scroll horizontally, include a second numeric expression, *expN2*. If this parameter is positive, the region scrolls *expN2* characters right. If it is negative, the region scrolls *expN2* characters left.

Example

SCROLL 1,0, 10, 50, 3

SEEK *expression*

Description   The SEEK command moves to the first record in the index that matches *expression*.

Operational rules   SEEK searches the master index for *expression*. The expression must be of the same type as the key expression of the master index.

If a match is found, the record pointer moves to that record. Use SKIP to find the next record that matches. If no records match, FOUND( ) is set to false, and the record pointer is moved to the end of the file (EOF( ) is true).

If SET EXACT is OFF, the expression does not have to be complete. For instance, the command SEEK "S" will find the first record in the index that begins with S. If SET EXACT is ON, the expression must match exactly. If SET NEAR is ON and no match is found, the record pointer is placed at the first record whose key follows *expression*.

Example

. USE Maillist INDEX Mlname
. SEEK "Smith"
Record 2
. Mname = "Brown"
. SEEK Mname
Record 7

See also: FIND p. 181

SELECT *select item* FROM *database*

Description The SQL SELECT command opens files, sets relations, filters records, selects fields for output, sorts, and more. In short, this one command can take the place of a group of five or six normal commands.

Operational rules The SELECT command is FoxPro first foray into SQL (Standard Query Language). There are many clauses to this command, and it is very complex. Because of SELECT's complexity, FoxPro has the RQBE window, which helps you put together the pieces of the command. See chapter 9 for more information on the RQBE window.

The SELECT command begins with either SELECT ALL or SELECT *item list*. This selects the fields and items which are to be output. The item list can include fields, constants, formulas, or one of the column functions (AVG(field), COUNT(field), SUM(field), etc.). If items are coming from more than one file, it is a good idea to prefix them with their *alias* and a period (.). Use the DISTINCT keyword to exclude duplicates of any rows from the query.

FROM *database list* This clause lists the database(s) to be used in the selections. If a file isn't open, SELECT opens it in a work area. The file remains open when the SELECT command is complete. You can place an alias name in front of the database file name to open the file with an alias.

INTO *destination* This clause determines where the result will be stored. When INTO is used, the output is not displayed. The choices are:

- ARRAY *arrayname*   Memory variable array.
- CURSOR *database*   A temporary database named *database*. The temporary database remains open and can be used and manipulated, but it is erased when it is closed.
- DBF *database* or TABLE *database*   Creates a .DBF file named *database*.

TO *textfile* or TO PRINTER   This clause sends the output to an ASCII text file named *textfile* or to the printer. When sending to a file, use the keyword ADDITIVE if appending the output to an existing text file.

WHERE *joincondition* This clause sets the relationship between two files. The *joincondition* specifies the linking fields from each database. For instance, if Mail.dbf is linked to Statenam.dbf by the fields Mail−>Statecod and Statenam−>State, the *joincondition* would be Mail.Statecod = Statenam.State. You can set more than one relationship by separating join conditions with the word AND. If multiple files are used and there is no join condition, every field in the first database is joined with every field in the second database. This could result in a very large output.

WHERE *filtercondition*   The WHERE clause also specifies the filter conditions. Filter conditions can use the normal comparison operators (=, <, >, < >, !, etc.). But they can also use the following operators:

ALL (*subquery*)
ANY (*subquery*) or SOME (*subquery*)
BETWEEN *startrange* AND *endrange*
EXISTS (*subquery*)
IN (*valueset*)
IN (*subquery*)
LIKE *subquery*

The last five selections can be preceded with NOT to negate the criteria. Set more than one relationship by separating conditions with either AND or OR. You can also use HAVING in place of the WHERE keyword.

A subquery is a SELECT within a SELECT. When the word ALL is used, the field must meet the query for all values generated by the subquery. When the word ANY or SOME is used, the field just has to match one of the values generated by the subquery. The word EXISTS evaluates as True unless the subquery is the null set. The word IN is true if the field is found within the value set (values separated with commas) or subquery. LIKE can use the wildcard characters % (single unknown character) and _ (group of unknown characters) in the comparison.

GROUP BY *grouping field*   This clause is much like the grouping that is used when creating a report. The database should be sorted on the *grouping field*.

ORDER BY *order item*   This clause sorts the output by *order item*.

The other optional clauses are NOCONSOLE (prevents the results from printing to screen), PLAIN (prevents field headings from appearing in the screen output), and NOWAIT (does not pause between screens if the output is so long that it scrolls off the screen).

Examples

```
SELECT company.name, company.city;
   FROM company;
   HAVING company.state = "CA"
```

Displays all Californian companies and their cities from the COMPANY database.

```
SELECT company.name, company.city;
   FROM company;
   INTO calcomp
```

Creates a database named calcomp.dbf of all Californian companies and their cities.

```
SELECT name, city;
  FROM company;
  ORDER BY city, company;
  WHERE state = "CA"
```

Displays all Californian companies sorted alphabetically within city.

```
SELECT company.name, taxes.rate;
  FROM company,taxes;
  WHERE company.city = taxes.city;
  AND company.state = "CA"
```

Displays all Californian companies and their tax rate by looking up their city's tax rate in taxes.dbf.

```
SELECT company.name ;
  FROM company ;
  WHERE company.type IN("FINANCE","REAL ESTATE","LAW FIRM")
```

Displays all companies that have a type field of FINANCE, REAL ESTATE, or LAW FIRM.

```
SELECT company.name, taxes.rate ;
  FROM company,taxes ;
  WHERE company.city = taxes.city;
    AND taxes.rate BETWEEN .06 AND .065
```

Displays all companies and their tax rates for cities with rates between .06 and .065.

```
SELECT company.name ;
  FROM company ;
  WHERE company.city IN (SELECT company.city FROM company
  WHERE company.type = "LAW FIRM")
```

Displays all companies that are in a city where there is a LAW FIRM.

SELECT *work area*

Description The SELECT command specifies the current work area to open files in.

Operational rules Up to 10 work areas can be opened at a time. Each area may have only one data (.DBF) file, but multiple index (.IDX) files open in it. Work areas can be identified by numbers (1 through 10) or letters (A through J).

The usual process for working with multiple files is to SELECT each area and open the files in it with the USE command. Then, to change the current work area, simply call the SELECT command. When selecting the current work area, you can use the alias name in place of the number or letter.

To access fields from a file not in the current work area, precede the field name with the work area letter or alias name and an arrow (– >).

Example

```
. SELECT A
. USE Maillist
. SELECT B
. USE States
. ? A – >Lname, A – >Fname, State
```
Smith   Joe   California
```
. SELECT A
. SKIP
. ? Lname, Fname, B – >State
```
Brown   Sue   California

See also: USE p. 240

SET

See the next chapter for details regarding all of the FoxPro SET commands.

SHOW GETS

Description   SHOW GETS redisplays all GET fields.

Operational rules   GET objects (memory variables, field names, push buttons, pop-ups, etc.) often need to be redisplayed when UDFs are used.

Multiple READ levels occur when UDFs are used in the WHEN or VALID clauses of a GET statement. If the UDF contains a READ, there are now multiple READs. Use the LEVEL *expN* clause to redisplay the objects in a different READ level than the current one. FoxPro supports up to four nested READs.

The COLOR *color pair list* and COLOR SCHEME *expN* clauses allow you to set your own colors for the redisplayed objects. Including ENABLE allows the redisplayed objects to be chosen. DISABLE prevents any of them from being chosen, and the objects are displayed in the disabled colors.

Use the WINDOW *window name* clause to redisplay the objects in a different window. Use the SHOW GET *var* or SHOW OBJECT *expN* commands to redisplay a particular GET object.

Example   In the example below, a user-defined function disables all fields when a person's record is marked Inactive.

```
@ 1,30 SAY "Student's Individual Record"
@ 3,1 SAY "Name: " GET Name
```

```
    @ 5,1 SAY "Inactive? " GET Activ PICTURE "Y" VALID CHKACT( )
    @ 7,1 SAY "Grade: " GET Grade
    READ

    FUNCTION CHKACT
      IF Activ = "N"
        SHOW GETS DISABLE
      ENDIF
      RETURN
```

See also: @SAY...GET p. 125

SHOW MENU *menu name*

Description   SHOW MENU displays the currently defined menu without activating it.

Operational rules   The menu displays on the screen, but you cannot move the cursor through it or make selections. The optional PAD *pad name* defines the pad that is highlighted.

See the DEFINE MENU section for an example of a program that sets up the menu.

See also: DEFINE MENU p. 166

SHOW OBJECT *expN*

Description   SHOW OBJECT redisplays a GET object *expN*.

Operational rules   GET objects (memory variables, field names, push buttons, pop-ups, etc.) often need to be redisplayed when UDFs are used. SHOW GET can also be used to redisplay an individual button within a set of invisible, radio, or push buttons. GET objects are numbered in the order that the cursor passes through them in a READ statement. *expN* must match the GET object's number.

The optional PROMPT *expC* is used with push buttons, radio buttons, or check boxes to replace the current prompt.

Multiple READ levels occur when UDFs are used in the WHEN or VALID clauses of the GET statement. If the UDF contains a READ, there are now multiple READs. Use the LEVEL *expN* clause to redisplay the object in a different READ level. FoxPro supports up to four nested READs.

The COLOR *color pair list* and COLOR SCHEME *expN* clauses allow you to set your own colors for the redisplayed object. Including ENABLE allows the redisplayed object to be chosen. DISABLE prevents it from being chosen, and the object is displayed in the disabled colors.

Use the SHOW GETS command to redisplay all GET objects. Use SHOW GET *var* to refer to a GET object by the object's name.

Example   In the example below, a user-defined function disables the field after the user has passed through it:

```
@ 2,1 SAY "Taxable? " GET Mtax VALID DISTAX( )
@ 3,1 SAY "Rate" GET Mrate
READ

FUNCTION DISTAX( )
IF Mtax = "N"
   SHOW OBJECT 2 DISABLE
ENDIF
RETURN
```

See also: @SAY...GET p. 125

SHOW POPUP *pop-up name*

Description   SHOW POPUP displays the currently defined pop-up menu without activating it.

Operational rules   The menu displays on the screen, but you cannot move the cursor through it or make selections. This command is most often used when designing menus so you can test the appearance of your pop-up menu.

See the DEFINE POPUP section for an example of a program that sets up the pop-up menu.

See also: DEFINE POPUP p. 168

SHOW WINDOW *window name*

Description   SHOW WINDOW displays the currently defined window without activating it.

Operational rules   The window displays on the screen, but you cannot direct output to it. This command is most often used when designing windows so you can test the appearance of them.

You can also use this command to rearrange how the windows lay over each other. The TOP (over all others), BOTTOM (behind all others), and SAME (at previous position) clauses to define which layer the window should be on.

You can place a list of window names in the parameter *window name*, or use the keyword ALL to display all defined windows.

See also: DEFINE WINDOW p. 170

SIZE POPUP *pop-up name* TO *height, width*

Description SIZE POPUP resizes a previously defined pop-up.

Operational rules This command allows you to change the size of the pop-up without having to issue the DEFINE POPUP command again. The height is measured in rows and the width in columns.

The TO *height, width* clause can be replaced with BY *height, width*. This changes the pop-up relative to its current size. If the argument(s) is positive, the pop-up size increases, if it is negative, the pop-up size decreases.

See the DEFINE POPUP section for an example of a program that sets up a pop-up menu.

See also: DEFINE POPUP p. 168

SKIP

Description SKIP is used to move to the next record in a database.

Operational rules If the database is not indexed, SKIP simply moves to the next record number. If the database is indexed, this is the next record in the index.

The optional *expN* causes the pointer to skip *expN* records. The number can be either positive, which causes it to move forward, or negative, which causes it to move backwards.

If the pointer is at the bottom record and a SKIP is issued, the record pointer will move to the end of file, and EOF( ) will be true (.T.). If the pointer is at the top record and a SKIP − 1 is issued, the record pointer moves to the beginning of file, and BOF( ) will be true (.T.).

The SET FILTER and SET DELETED ON commands are honored by SKIP. Use the IN *alias* option to skip in a work area other than the current one.

Example

```
. USE Maillist
. SKIP
Record 2
. SKIP 2
Record 4
. SKIP −1
Record 3
```

See also: CONTINUE p. 153

SORT TO *file name* ON *field*

Description SORT creates a new database file with the records in order by *field*.

Operational rules The SORT command copies the data file, so it uses up the same amount of space. If records are added to the new sorted file, they are not maintained in the sorted order.

You can sort a file on multiple fields by providing a field list in place of *field*. Fields may be followed by the following arguments:

/A   Sort in ascending order.
/D   Sort in descending order.
/C   Ignore differences between upper and lowercase.

To combine these arguments, use only one slash (for example, /DC). The arguments ASCENDING and DESCENDING are then used for all fields that do not have a slash argument.

Use the optional FOR *condition*, WHILE *condition*, and *scope* arguments to process only a subset of the data file.

Examples The following commands each create a file named Mname.dbf which is a sorted version of the current file:

```
SORT TO Mname ON Lname
SORT TO Mname ON Lname, Fname /C
SORT TO Mname ON Zip /A, Amount /D
SORT TO Mname ON Lname FOR State = "CA"
```

See also: INDEX p. 185

STORE *expression* TO *memory variable* or *memory variable* = *expression*

Description STORE creates and/or changes the value of a memory variable.

Operational rules Memory variables are most often used in programs, although they can be used from the command window. Memory variables are much like fields, in that they can be character, numeric, logical, or data type. The data type of a memory variable is established by its value. A variable's name can be from 1 to 10 characters. However, memory variables are not stored in a file, so they are lost when the FoxPro session is over.

The = command is equivalent to the STORE command, except you can only store a value to one memory variable at a time with =. STORE accepts either a memory variable or memory variable list.

These commands can also be used to set the values of array elements; however, the array must already have been initialized with the DECLARE or DIMENSION command.

Examples

```
Mtot = 0
Mtot = Mtot + 1
STORE "Smith" TO Mname
STORE Lname TO Mname
STORE 0 TO Gtot, Mtot, Ltot
STORE 500 TO Marray(1,2)
```

See also: DECLARE p. 162

SUM

Description   SUM provides the totals of the numeric fields of a data file.

Operational rules   If no arguments are provided, FoxPro displays the sum total of each numeric field in the database. You can provide a field list to specify the field(s) to be summed.

To create memory variables whose values are the sums, use the TO *memory variable list* or TO ARRAY. When summing to an array, the array must be declared as single dimension, and each field in the field list updates the next row.

You can use the optional FOR *condition*, WHILE *condition*, and *scope* arguments to include only a subset of the records in the calculation.

Examples

```
SUM
SUM Wage, Bonus to Mwage, Mbon
SUM Wage TO Mwage FOR State = "CA"
SUM Wage, Bonus, Commsion TO ARRAY Mamount
```

The last example assumes that Mamount has been declared as a one-dimensional array. After the SUM, Mamount(1) is equal to the total of the Wage field, Mamount(2) is equal to the total of Bonus, etc.

See also: DECLARE p. 162

SUSPEND

Description   The SUSPEND command drops the current program out to the command window.

Operational rules   When a program encounters an error, it will ask the user whether they want to Cancel, Suspend, or Ignore. Using the SUSPEND command in programs is equivalent to when the user chooses Suspend at the error message. All memory variables still exist, as does the file status. At this point, files and variables can be manipulated. If the user then chooses RESUME, the program resumes processing at the next command line.

SUSPEND can be placed within a program to make it return to the command window. The CANCEL command also halts the program, but memory variables will be erased, and the program cannot resume processing.

See also: RESUME p. 223

TEXT
text characters
ENDTEXT

Description   This displays all text entered between the TEXT and ENDTEXT commands.

Operational rules   TEXT is the easiest command for printing text on the screen or to a printer. Simply enter the text as you want it displayed. You do not need to surround character strings with quote marks, as you do with the ? command.

Memory variables, expressions, and functions are only evaluated if SET TEXTMERGE is ON, otherwise all entries are interpreted literally. When SET TEXTMERGE is ON, the delimiters defined with SET TEXTMERGE DELIMITERS must be used to surround expressions. The default delimiters are << >>.

This is information that will display just as it looks. Notice that there are no quote marks around the strings or commands such as ? or ??.

Examples

TEXT
Today's date is << DATE( ) >>
ENDTEXT

See also: ? p. 124

TOTAL *field* TO *file name*

Description   TOTAL copies a database to a second file that contains subtotals of each numeric field.

Operational rules   Unless the optional FIELDS *fields list* clause is included, the new file will have the same structure as the active file. For each unique *key field* record in the active file, you will have one record in the new file . The active file must be indexed by *key field* before issuing the command.

The numeric fields in the new file contain the sum totals for each particular key. Character, date, and logical fields contain the information of the first record that matches the unique key. Memo fields are not copied to the new file.

You can use the optional FOR *condition*, WHILE *condition*, and *scope* arguments to include only a subset of the records in the new file.

Examples

```
. USE Dues INDEX Member
. ? RECCOUNT( )
    20
. TOTAL ON Membcode TO Totdues
. USE Totdues
. LIST Membcode, Dues
```

Record #	MEMBCODE	DUES
1	A01	200.00
2	A02	150.00
3	A12	50.00
4	B03	100.00
5	B05	150.00

See also: SUM p. 237

TYPE *file name*

Description   TYPE displays the contents of *file name*.

Operational rules   The TYPE command works just like the TYPE command from DOS. It is most often used when displaying the contents of a program (.PRG) or format (.FMX) file. Files that are not standard ASCII do not display clearly with the TYPE command.

The output defaults to printing on the screen. Use the TO PRINTER option to print to the printer, or the TO FILE *file name* to print to an ASCII file.

The NUMBER clause numbers each line in the program. Page numbers, the current date, and the name of the program display at the top unless SET HEADING is off.

Examples

```
TYPE Maillist.prg
TYPE Maillist.prg TO PRINTER
TYPE Maillist.prg TO PRINTER NUMBER
```

See also: LIST FILES p. 190

UPDATE ON *key field* FROM *alias*
REPLACE *field name* WITH *expression*

Description The UPDATE command performs a global find and replace on *field name* while relating two files.

Operational rules The UPDATE command sets a relationship between the active file, where the replace will occur, and *alias*. The two files must each have *key field*, and *alias* must be indexed on that field. The current file must also be indexed on the field unless the RANDOM clause is included.

If there are multiple records with the same key in the active file, then only the first record that matches is updated.

Example

```
. SELECT 1
. USE Dues INDEX Member
. LIST
```

Record #	MEMBCODE	DUES
1	A01	40.00
4	A01	60.00
2	A02	50.00
3	A12	50.00
5	A12	50.00

```
. SELECT 2
. USE Members INDEX Membcode
. UPDATE ON Membcode FROM Dues REPLACE Totdues WITH totdues + Dues
. LIST
```

Record #	MEMBCODE	DUES
1	A01	100.00
4	A02	50.00
2	A12	100.00

See also: SET RELATION p. 232

USE *file name*

Description The USE command opens a database (.DBF) file in a work area.

Operational rules The file is opened in the current work unless the IN *work area* option is included. If a file is already open in that area, it is closed so that the new one can be opened. To close a file in a work area without opening a new file, issue USE without a *file name*.

The optional ? argument can be used in place of *file name*. FoxPro then provides a list of all .DBF files, which you can choose from.

The INDEX *index file list* clause allows you to open index (.IDX and .CDX) files with the database file. The optional ? argument can be used in place of *index file list*. FoxPro then provides a list of all single and multiple index files that you can choose from. Index files are numbered in the order that they are listed in *index file list*, tags in the order they were created. The first is the master. The master is the key order used for listings and with the SEEK command.

The ORDER *expN* clause designates the index file or tag that is to be the master. This is most often used with multiple index files when you do not want the first tag to be master. You can also use ORDER *.idx file name* to designate the .IDX file that is to be master. ORDER TAG *tag name* designates the tag name which is to be master. ORDER TAG *tag name* OF *.cdx file name* designates the master tag name when there is more than one open multiple index.

The ASCENDING and DESCENDING clauses change the way the database is normally accessed. For instance, if the master index was created in ascending order, the DESCENDING keyword can be used to access it as if it was created in descending order. This is preferable to recreating the index in the opposite order.

The NOUPDATE clause prevents any changes to the file, although it can be displayed. The EXCLUSIVE clause is only used on multi-user systems. It places a file lock on the file. You must use the AGAIN clause to open an already opened file in another work area.

Use ALIAS *aliasname* to change the name of the file's alias. The default alias name is the file's name. Files are also given alias letters (work area A through J, W11 through W25) and alias numbers (1 through 25). The alias is used for accessing fields from the database when the file is not in the current work area. An alias name can consist of up to 10 characters.

Example

```
. USE Maillist INDEX Mailname
. USE Maillist INDEX Mailname DESCENDING
. USE Maillist INDEX Mailname,Mailzip, Memcode
. USE Maillist INDEX Mailname,Mailzip ORDER Mailzip
. USE Maillist INDEX Maillist ORDER TAG Zip
. USE Maillist IN 3
. USE Maillist IN 3 EXCLUSIVE
. USE Maillist ALIAS Mail
```

See also: INDEX p. 185

WAIT

Description   WAIT pauses the processing until a key is pressed.

Operational rules   WAIT halts the program until the user presses a key. Use the TO *memory variable name* clause to create a character memory variable which stores the keyboard entry. If the optional *prompt* is not used, FoxPro displays Press any key to continue as the default message. To display no prompt, use the character string " " as the prompt.

Use the WINDOW keyword to display the message in a window in the upper right corner of the screen. Use WINDOW NOWAIT to display the message in a window that behaves like the FoxPro system messages. Pressing any key removes the window from the screen. NOWAIT does not discard the keystroke.

TIMEOUT *expN* determines how many seconds can elapse without user input before the WAIT is terminated. TIMEOUT must be the last clause in the WAIT statement.

Examples

WAIT
WAIT "Do you want to print (Y/N)" TO PRN
WAIT " "
WAIT "Invalid Option Choice" WINDOW TIMEOUT 10

See also: ACCEPT p. 141

ZAP

Description   ZAP erases all records from the database file.

Operational rules   Use ZAP in place of the commands DELETE ALL and PACK. ZAP is much faster and provides the verification question Zap?.

See also: DELETE p. 171
            PACK p. 209

ZOOM WINDOW *window name size*

Description   ZOOM WINDOW resizes a system or user-defined window.

Operational rules   This command allows you to change the size of a system window (command, browse, text editing, etc.) or a window that you have created with DEFINE WINDOW.

It is possible to place a window within another window. The inside window will take on all characteristics of the outer window. The larger window is called the parent, the smaller window the child. The child window must be smaller than the parent, and stay within the parent window's boundaries.

The *size* can be one of a variety of size keywords. The keywords are:

- MIN Reduces to the minimum size, leaving just the name of the window and its title on the screen. This is the same as moving to the top border and pressing Ctrl – F9 or choosing Zoom↓ from the Window menu.
- MAX Expands to the full screen, (or if a child window, the full size of the parent). This is the same as moving to the top border and pressing Ctrl – F10 or choosing Zoom↑ from the Window menu. User-defined windows can only be sized if the ZOOM keyword was used in their definition.
- NORM Returns a window to its normal size.
- SIZE *height,width* Sizes the window to *height* measured in rows, and *width* measured in columns.

The optional AT *row,col* and FROM *row,col* clauses allow you to move the window's location at the same time you change the size. The *row, col* represents the placement of the window's upper left corner. This clause performs the same operation as the MOVE WINDOW command.

The clause TO *row, col* represents the placement of the window's bottom right corner. This clause is most often used in conjunction with the AT or FROM clauses.

Examples

ZOOM WINDOW Mwind MAX
ZOOM WINDOW Mwind SIZE 5,70 AT 0,0

3

FoxPro SET commands

THE SET COMMANDS ARE A SPECIAL GROUP OF COMMANDS THAT CHANGE MANY of the default settings of FoxPro. The SET commands can be issued from the command window or from a program. In addition, the command SET by itself provides a window for changing many of the settings such as screen colors, function keys, default disk drives, and many other options. This command also brings up the View window, which allows you to open up a group of data and index files with relationships and filters already set.

In this chapter, the commands are listed in alphabetical order. Each command displays the possible options. The option in capital letters is the default FoxPro setting. For instance,

SET PRINT on/OFF

shows that the default setting for this command is OFF. Variable options are in italic, such as,

SET MARGIN TO *expN*

which shows that a numeric expression must be used as the option. Any optional clauses are placed in square brackets.

SET ALTERNATE on/OFF
SET ALTERNATE TO [*file name* [ADDITIVE]]

Description SET ALTERNATE stores all output except full-screen commands to a text file.

Operational rules The SET ALTERNATE command is a two-step process. First, create a text file using SET ALTERNATE TO *file name* followed by SET ALTER-

NATE ON. This output overwrites any data previously in the file of that name; however, this can be avoided by following SET ALTERNATE TO *file name* with ADDITIVE, and then hitting Return.

Through the command SET ALTERNATE OFF, the text file can remain open, although no output is saved to it. The command CLOSE ALTERNATE closes the text file. Be sure to close the text file before using the file. The text file is a standard ASCII file that can be modified via MODIFY COMMAND or a word processor.

SET ANSI ON/off

Description SET ANSI ON pads the shorter string with blanks when comparing strings in SQL searches.

Operational rules When SQL makes comparisons between strings, it compares character by character until the shorter of the two strings is exhausted. However, if ANSI is set ON, the shorter string is padded with blanks for the comparison. The = = operator performs the same function as SET ANSI ON.

For example, if SET ANSI is ON, the following is false because it pads the left expression with blanks:

'San' = 'San Diego'

If SET ANSI is OFF, the following is true, because it stops the comparison at the third character:

'San' = 'San Diego'

SET AUTO SAVE on/OFF

Description The SET AUTOSAVE command saves each record to the disk after alterations have been made, thus reducing possibility of lost data. When AUTOSAVE is OFF, records are saved to the disk as the buffer is filled.

Operational rules AUTOSAVE can be activated (or deactivated) by the command SET AUTOSAVE ON (OFF) from the command window or the SET menu.

SET BELL ON/off
SET BELL TO *frequency,duration*

Description The SET BELL command controls the audible tone that is heard when an error is made or when a field is filled.

Operational rules From the command window, enter SET BELL OFF, or from SET menu, select OFF. When SET BELL is OFF, no tone is heard.

The *frequency* adjustment changes the pitch of the bell. It might be any number between 19 and 10,000 hertz. The default is 512 hertz. The *duration* adjustment changes the length of the bell. It can be any number between 1 and 19. The default is 2.

SET BLINK ON/off

Description   SET BLINK allows screen elements to be set to blink. It can only be used with EGA and VGA monitors.

Operational rules   When this is on, screen attributes (borders, shadows, etc.) can be set to blink when setting their colors. The SET BLINK OFF command allows more colors to be available, as background colors can be brightened.

SET BORDER TO
[SINGLE/DOUBLE/PANEL/NONE/border definition string]

Description   SET BORDER changes the border of windows, menus, and @...SAY commands from a single line box to a variety of styles via user-defined options.

Operational rules   The available border choices are single line or double line, and reverse video display. By using SET BORDER in conjunction with the @...SAY and @...TO commands, borders can vary in size and combine double lines and single lines. DOUBLE changes the border to double line, and PANEL displays the border in reverse video format. You can set your own border character using *border definition string*. To return to the single-lined box, use the command SET BORDER TO followed by Enter.

A second, optional border definition string can be set for the border that appears when the window is not active.

SET CARRY on/OFF
SET CARRY TO [*field list* [ADDITIVE]]

Description   SET CARRY carries forward all changes made in a record to proceeding records when using APPEND, INSERT, or BROWSE. SET CARRY TO brings the contents specified fields forward to the next record when using the aforementioned commands.

Operational rules   SET CARRY TO *field list* specifies fields to be updated, while SET CARRY ON updates all fields. The use of ADDITIVE adds the field list to the existing list that have already been specified. SET CARRY TO without an argument restores the default condition where all fields are updated. If SET CARRY is OFF, the SET CARRY TO automatically sets CARRY ON as well as defines the field list.

SET CENTURY on/OFF

Description   This command allows for the input and display of the century prefixes in the year portion of dates.

SET CLEAR ON/off

Description This command controls whether the screen is cleared after quitting FoxPro and setting a format screen.

Operational rules The two commands this setting affects are QUIT and SET FORMAT TO. If it is off, the format screen superimposes on the current screen instead of clearing it.

SET CLOCK on/OFF
SET CLOCK TO [row,column]

Description The CLOCK command determines if the clock will be displayed, and its position on the screen.

Operational rules Select SET CLOCK ON for the clock's display on the screen. To align its position, use the SET CLOCK TO command with the appropriate coordinates. SET CLOCK TO without any coordinates following reverts the clock back to its default position.

SET COLOR ON/OFF
SET COLOR TO [standard],[enhanced],[perimeter],[background]
SET COLOR OF NORMAL/MESSAGES/TITLES/BOX/HIGHLIGHT/ INFORMATION/FIELDS TO [color attribute]

Description The COLOR command changes the colors and other attributes of the screen.

Operational rules SET COLOR ON/OFF is used to select between color and monochrome display. The default is dependent upon the particular system FoxPro is run on. You can choose the color setup through the SET COLOR TO command or the Color... dialog box from the Window pop-up.

SET COLOR TO allows the color of the standard text, highlighted areas, borders, and backgrounds to be changed. SET COLOR TO not followed by an argument resets the display to default setting in the Config.fx file.

Standard denotes the color of the background and the standard text. *Enhanced* is the color of the text and background of the highlighted areas. *Perimeter* is the color of the border. The colors are represented by:

Color	Symbol	Color	Symbol
Black	N or blank	Red	R
Blue	B	Magenta	RB
Green	G	Brown	GR
Cyan	BG	Yellow	GR+
Blank	X	White	W
Gray	N+		

Example.

SET COLOR TO B/G, GR + /R, R

This command produces blue text on a green background; the highlighted areas are yellow text with a red background, and a red border.

SET COLOR OF...TO enables the colors of particular screen area groupings to be changed while the rest of the screen remains in its assigned colors.

NORMAL refers to unselected items of menus, layout editor design surface, calculated field expressions, and output from @...SAY commands. MESSAGES is the interior of error, help, and prompt boxes; unavailable or unselected menu or list choices; field window contents; and message lines. TITLES included headings and underlined text, and BOXES encompasses borders. HIGHLIGHT is all highlighted material; INFORMATION refers to the clock, status line, and the selected button in the Help and Error box. Finally, FIELDS comprises data entry areas and all highlighted field areas.

SET COLOR OF SCHEME *expN* TO *color pair list*

Description The COLOR OF SCHEME command changes the color pairs that make up a particular color scheme.

Operational rules Each color scheme is 10 pairs of colors. You can define up to 11 schemes. The order of the pairs is dependent on the scheme being used. See Appendix B for a table of what each pair of numbers represents in each scheme. The numbers of the schemes are:

1. User window.
2. User menu.
3. Menu bar.
4. Menu pop-ups.
5. Dialogs.
6. Dialog pop-ups.
7. Alert.
8. Windows.
9. Window pop-ups.
10. Browse.
11. Report.

For example, in scheme 1 (user window), the 10 color pairs represent:

1. SAY fields.
2. GET fields.
3. Border.
4. Title, active.

5. Title, idle.
6. Selected item.
7. Clock.
8. Shadow.
9. Enabled control.
10. Disabled control.

You can place a comma to represent color pairs that you want to remain the same.

SET COLOR OF SCHEME *expN1* TO *expN2*

Description This command takes the color pairs from one scheme and copies them into another scheme.

Operational rules The scheme to copy from is *expN1*, and the scheme you are copying it to is *expN2*.

SET COLOR SET TO *color set name*

Description This command loads colors from a color set.

Operational rules Color sets are saved using the SET COLOR OF SCHEME command or through the Color Picker dialog box.

SET COMPATIBLE OFF/on

Description This command allows FoxBASE+ programs to run without any changes.

Operational rules Certain commands and functions have changed between the two versions. When COMPATIBLE is set ON, FoxPro runs the program as FoxBASE+ would.

SET CONFIRM on/OFF

Description CONFIRM, when activated, holds the cursor at a field that has been filled until Return is pressed.

Operational rules CONFIRM is activated from the command menu or the SET menu. When CONFIRM is set OFF, then the cursor automatically advances to the next field when a field is filled.

SET CONSOLE ON/off

Description The SET CONSOLE command can be used within a program to turn the screen display on and off.

Operational rules Working only within a program, SET CONSOLE is used to prevent display of output to the screen: It cannot be used from the dot prompt. Input is accepted through such commands as WAIT and ACCEPT, but neither the prompts nor what is being typed will display to the screen.

An @...SAY...GET overrides the console setting as well as all error messages and safety prompts.

SET CURRENCY TO [exp]
SET CURRENCY LEFT/right

Description This command changes the character symbolizing currency, and positions the currency symbol on either the left or right.

Operational rules SET CURRENCY TO accepts a currency symbol of up to nine characters in length. The SET CURRENCY TO command allows FoxPro to work with currencies with right-side conventions like the French franc.

SET DATE [TO]
AMERICAN/ansi/british/german/italian/japan/usa/mdy/dmy/dmy/ymd

Description SET DATE determines the convention for date display.

Operational rules This date allows you to change date conventions quickly to aid in date output and date input. The date conventions available are:

AMERICAN	MM/DD/YY
ANSI	YY.MM.DD
BRITISH/FRENCH	DD/MM/YY
GERMAN	DD.MM.YY
ITALIAN	DD-MM-YY
JAPAN	MM/DD/YY
USA	MM-DD-YY
MDY	MM/DD/YY
DMY	DD/MM/ YY
YMD	YY/MM/DD

SET DECIMALS TO *expN*

Description The number of significant digits to the right of the decimal point in the display of numeric functions and calculations is determined by the *expN* of the SET DECIMALS TO command.

Operational rules The maximum number of decimal places that can be displayed is 18. The default is two decimal places.

SET DEFAULT TO *drive* [:] [*directory*]

Description SET DEFAULT specifies the drive and/or directory where all FoxPro operations take place and files are stored.

Operational rules The default drive is the drive that FoxPro was started on. FoxPro does not check if the specified drive exists and does not return to the previous drive after quitting out of FoxPro.

Some examples of valid defaults are:

```
SET DEFAULT TO D:\DATA
SET DEFAULT TO D
SET DEFAULT TO \FOX\DATA    && subdirectory is in current drive
SET DEFAULT TO \            && change to root directory
```

SET DELETED on/OFF

Description SET DELETED mandates whether deleted files are recognized by other FoxPro commands.

Operational rules This command affects commands such as BROWSE, LOCATE, LIST, REPORT, and EDIT. If SET DELETED is on, all records marked for deletion are not displayed, as if they have been removed. However, you can GOTO a deleted record, or display it within a scope even if SET DELETED is ON.

SET DEVELOPMENT ON/off

Description This command runs a checking program that updates the compiled object file (.FPX) every time a program (.PRG) is modified.

Operational rules The *object file* is a file containing an "execute only" form of FoxPro commands. Object files cannot be modified. Every time a FoxPro program is modified, an updated version of this executable object replaces the previous object file. If SET DEVELOPMENT is OFF, an updated object file is not created; moreover, the modifications of the program do not register until the program has been compiled.

SET DEVICE TO SCREEN/*printer*/*file file name*

Description The SET DEVICE command determines the destination of output from @...SAY commands to the screen, a printer, or a file.

Operational rules When SET DEVICE is set to the PRINTER, the output from @...SAY commands goes directly to the printer, and all @...GET commands are ignored.

SET DISPLAY TO MONO/COLOR/EGA25/EGA43/MONO43

Description SET DISPLAY specifies either monochrome or color display, and determines the number of lines displayed.

Operational rules This command can only be used if the operating hardware can support monochrome and/or color display and an equivalent graphics card that can support a 43-line display. If these requirements are not met and the command is used, an error message is given.

SET DOHISTORY on/OFF

Description This command shows commands from the program file in the command window.

Default As a program is running, each command line displays in the command window when DOHISTORY is ON

SET ECHO on/OFF

Description SET ECHO is used in debugging programs by displaying commands as they are executed.

Operational rules SET ECHO is used only during debugging and can be used in conjunction with the three other debugging commands SET DEBUG, SET STEP, and SET TALK.

SET ESCAPE ON/off

Description SET ESCAPE ON allows the execution of a program to be stopped via the Esc key.

Operational rules With SET ESCAPE OFF, the Esc key no longer operates. SET ESCAPE OFF should only be used with tested programs, for the only other way to halt execution is rebooting computer. This can result in loss of data.

SET EXACT on/OFF

Description SET EXACT ON requires an exact match in length and contents when comparing strings in searches.

Operational rules When SET EXACT is OFF, a character string matches another as long as the comparison string is the same length or longer and contains the same characters as the model string. With EXACT ON, the comparison string must match the model string character for character. For instance, if SET EXACT is OFF, the command

    LIST FOR Lname = "S"

lists all records with an Lname that begins with S. If SET EXACT is ON, the comparison part of the criteria would have to have the same length as Lname, for instance:

    LIST FOR Lname = "Smith   "   && Lname has a length of 8

SET FIELDS on/OFF
SET FIELDS TO *field list*
SET FIELDS TO ALL

Description Use SET FIELDS to define a list of fields that might be accessed by one or more files. The defined field list is used by all commands that have a *field list* option available in their use.

Operational rules A field list must be identified before SET FIELDS is activated. SET FIELD TO strikes all fields from the active database from the field list, and SET FIELDS TO ALL includes all fields from the active database.

SET FILTER TO [*condition*]

Description SET FILTER TO processes and displays only those records that meet a specified condition.

Operational rules SET FILTER TO deactivates the filter for the active database file. SET FILTER TO <condition> specifies a condition for displaying records. The condition can be any valid FoxPro expression like CITY = "Los Angeles" or BDAY = {09/12/68}. Filters are activated when the record pointer is moved. SKIP or GOTO must be used to begin the use of a filter.

SET FIXED on/OFF

Description This command determines whether a fixed number of decimal places are displayed for numbers.

Operational rules This command only affects the display of numeric memory variables and values of calculations. It does not affect the display of numeric fields, as they each have their own designated number of decimal places.

SET FORMAT TO [*format file/?*]

Description SET FORMAT TO selects the format file (.FMT) to be used with the APPEND, BROWSE, CHANGE, EDIT, INSERT, or READ commands.

Operational rules Format files are created with FoxView, the screen creation utility, or through MODIFY COMMAND, the editor. If SET FORMAT TO is not activated, then the standard display and entry form is used. SET FORMAT TO ? displays a menu of format files. CLOSE FORMAT or SET FORMAT TO (followed by an Enter) closes the format file.

SET FULLPATH ON/off

Description The SET FULLPATH command displays the path names in the functions NDX( ) and DBF( ).

SET FUNCTION *expN/expC/key label* TO *expC*

Description SET FUNCTION allows the function keys to be programmed with up to 238 characters per function key to be used in data entry operations.
Default The default key assignments are as follows:

Key	Assignment	Key	Assignment
F1	HELP	F6	DISPLAY STATUS
F2	SET	F7	DISPLAY MEMORY
F3	LIST	F8	DISPLAY
F4	DIR	F9	APPEND
F5	DISPLAY STRUCTURE	F10	Alt – S

Operational rules The function keys can be set from the command window or the Config.db file. Shift – F1 through Shift – F9, and Ctrl – F1 through Ctrl – F10 can be programmed with functions as well. The Alt keys, Shift – F10, and the F11 and F12 keys cannot be programmed. When programming function keys, a semi-colon(;) denotes <enter> (for hitting the Enter key) causing Fox-Pro to execute the command. Quotes can be used to denote text strings.

SET HEADING ON/off

Description With SET HEADING ON, the column titles of the fields are displayed using the commands DISPLAY, LIST, SUM, and AVERAGE.

SET HELPFILTER TO *expL*

Description SET HELPFILTER displays a subset of help topics that match the condition in *expL*. The *expL* should refer to fields in the help database.
Operational rules The help database, Foxhelp.DBF contains the following structure:

Field name	Description
Topic	List of topics this help screen includes.
Details	Memo field of the help window itself.
Class	Character field that classifies the topic.

To remove the HELPFILTER, use the keyword AUTOMATIC.
Examples

SET HELPFILTER TO Topic = 'INDEX'
SET HELPFILTER TO 'WINDOW' $ Topic
SET HELPFILTER TO 'WINDOW' $ Details

SET HELP ON/off SET HELP TO *file*

Description   SET HELP ON summons a pop-up window listing FoxPro help options when a command is entered incorrectly at the dot prompt.

Operational rules   When an error is made and help window appears, the options of canceling or editing the command, or using the help system to find appropriate command usage are offered.

You can set your own help screens using SET HELP TO *file*. The default help file is Foxhelp.dbf.

SET HOURS TO [12/24]

Description   This command determines the time format of the clock to either a 12-hour or a 24-hour cycle.

Default   The default is set to 12.

SET INDEX TO [?/*file name list*]

Description   Use SET INDEX TO to open index files.

Operational rules   SET INDEX TO ? will display a catalog of index files. If the ? is replaced by a list of file names, those files are opened to be used with the active database file. The first index becomes the master index. To deactivate all open indexes, issue the command SET INDEX TO with no parameters.

The ASCENDING and DESCENDING clause selects the order for the index. ASCENDING is the default.

The ORDER clause allows you to choose a master index other than the first file (or first tag of a multiple index file). The following are all valid uses of the ORDER clause:

ORDER *expN*   The variable *expN* refers to the index file as it appears in the index file list, or a tag in the order the tag was created.

ORDER *.idx index file*   Refers to the name of the index file.

ORDER TAG *tag name* OF *.cdx file*   Refers to the name of the tag within multiple index file *.cdx file*.

SET INTENSITY ON/off

Description   SET INTENSITY determines whether the field widths of input areas when using APPEND or EDIT, or @...SAY...GET commands are highlighted. Input areas are highlighted with SET INTENSITY ON.

SET LIBRARY TO [*file name*]

Description   SET LIBRARY specifies an external library, used with External Routine API.

Operational rules External Routine API allows a user to write routines in C or 80 × 86 assembly. API functions can only be used if an external routine library is open. FoxPro assumes an extension of .PLB for this type of file. Use the keyword ADDITIVE to open additional libraries.

SET LOGERRORS ON/off

Description SET LOGERRORS saves compilation errors to a file.

Operational rules The error file is given the same name as the program, with an .ERR extension.

SET MARGIN TO *expN*

Description Use SET MARGIN to adjust the left margin of the printer; it does not affect the screen.

Default The left margin default setting is 0.

SET MARK OF MENU *menu name* TO *expC*
SET MARK OF PAD *pad name* OF *menu name* TO *expC*
SET MARK OF POPUP *pop-up name* TO *expC*
SET MARK OF BAR *expN* OF *pop-up name* TO *expC*

Description SET MARK OF sets the check mark character placed next to each option in a menu or pop-up.

Operational rules A *check mark* is a single character placed to the left of the option in a pop-up or menu. Replace *expC* with the logical statement *expL* to toggle on and off check marks. When *expL* is false, the check mark is not displayed.

SET MARK TO *[expC]*

Description SET MARK changes the delimiter of date displays.

Operational rules A new delimiter can be set by enclosing the desired character in quotes. For example, SET MARK TO " - " will separate the month, day, and year by dashes. The default is the slash (/).

SET MEMOWIDTH TO *expN*

Description SET MEMOWIDTH allows for the alteration in the widths of memo field output.

SET MESSAGE TO [*expC*] SET MESSAGE TO *expN*

Description A string defined by the user via SET MESSAGE is displayed on the bottom line of the screen.

Operational rules The MESSAGE length can be a maximum of 79 characters consisting of a phrase surrounded by quotes or the contents of a field denoted by a field name. The MESSAGE appears centered on line 23 of the screen.

You can change the placement of the message with the SET MESSAGE TO *expN* command. The row number for the message is *expN*, where a row of 0 will display no message. Use the keywords LEFT, CENTER, or RIGHT to set the alignment of the message in this command.

SET MOUSE TO *expN*

Description The sensitivity of the mouse is adjusted with the SET MOUSE TO command.

Operational rules The sensitivity is set between 1 and 10. A setting of 1 is the least sensitive, and 10 is the most sensitive. The default value is 5.

SET NEAR OFF/on

Description SET NEAR positions the database record pointer to the record following that which is most similar to the search criteria in database file searches that fail to find an exact match. The default setting is OFF.

SET ODOMETER TO *expN*

Description For commands that display a record count, SET ODOMETER determines the interval that the record count is updated.

Operational rules The update interval can be in the range of 1 through 200. The default is set to 100.

SET OPTIMIZE ON/off

Description When OFF, Rushmore is disabled.

Operational rules FoxPro 2.0 introduced the Rushmore technology, which greatly speeds up commands that use the FOR clause. Sometimes, however, Rushmore must be disabled. This is in instances when the command is modifying fields that the query has generated as keys. SET OPTIMIZE OFF globally disables Rushmore, although most commands that take advantage of it also have NOOPTIMIZE clauses of their own.

SET ORDER TO

Description Use SET ORDER TO to change the controlling index without closing any index files.

Operational rules The argument determines the order of index files in a list. This order is important when using the SET INDEX TO and USE commands because the master (first) index is the one used in the SEEK, LIST, and REPORT commands. SET ORDER TO with no argument or with an argument of 0 restores the database file to its natural order with no index file as master.

The ASCENDING and DESCENDING clauses select the order for the index. ASCENDING is the default. Use IN *work area* or IN *alias* to change the order in a selection area other than the current one.

The following are all valid uses of the SET ORDER command:

SET ORDER TO *expN*   The *expN* refers to the index file as it appears in the index file list, or a tag in the order the tag was created.

SET ORDER TO *.idx index file*   Refers to the name of the index file.

SET ORDER TAG *tag name* [OF *.cdx file*]   Refers to the name of the tag within multiple index file *.cdx file*. The *.cdx file* is not needed unless more than one multiple index file with the same *tag name* is open.

SET PATH TO [*path list*]

Description   FoxPro does not use the DOS path command; the SET PATH command establishes a path for FoxPro to use when searching for files that are not in the current directory. The default is the current directory.

SET POINT TO [*expC*]

Description   SET POINT specifies the character denoting the decimal point.

Operational rules   Any single alphanumeric character can be specified for the decimal point. A space cannot be used for the decimal. The default can be restored by entering SET POINT TO without an argument. The default character is a period (.).

SET PRINTER on/OFF
SET PRINTER TO *dos device*
SET PRINTER TO FILE *file name*

Description   SET PRINTER ON routes all output except output specified by the @...SAY command to the printer or a file. Output can be redirected via the SET PRINTER TO commands to a file or other printer.

Operational rules   With SET PRINTER ON, output previously mentioned is routed to the printer. Another printer can be specified via the SET PRINTER TO command. The parallel ports (LPT1, LPT2, LPT3) or the serial ports (COM1 and COM2) represent alternate destinations for printer output. SET PRINTER TO FILE *file name* directs the printer output to a file.

SET PROCEDURE TO [*procedure file name*]

Description Use this command to open procedure files.

Operational rules A *procedure file* is a small program that performs a basic task and can be called from any program or another procedure. Procedures are used widely in programming for this reason. Only one procedure file can be open at a time. A procedure file can hold up to 1700 procedures.

If a file extension is not specified, FoxPro searches for and compiles, if necessary, the desired file with the .PRG extension.

To close the current procedure file, issue the command with no *file name* argument.

SET RELATION TO *expN* INTO *alias*

Description SET RELATION allows use of two database files by linking them via a key expression that occurs in both files.

Operational rules An active database file is linked to an open database file in another work area via a common field. The *alias* database must be indexed on the common field. SET RELATION TO without an argument removes the relation in use. Use the DISPLAY STATUS command to see all relationships currently set.

The following program sets a relationship between two files. The common field is Clicode:

```
. SELECT 1
. USE Sales
. SELECT 2
. Use Clients INDEX Code
. SELECT 1
. SET RELATION TO Clicode INTO Clients
. LIST OFF Clicode, Amount, Date, B- >Name
```

CLICODE	AMOUNT	B- >NAME
A01	50.00	JIM JONES
A02	150.00	RUTH DOE
A01	200.00	JIM JONES
A03	100.00	HARRY CAREY
A02	50.00	RUTH DOE

SET RESOURCE ON/off
SET RESOURCE TO *file*

Description SET RESOURCE allows you to specify a resource file.

Operational rules FoxPro resource files contain information about user-defined settings such as colors, window locations, sizes, etc.

If the setting is set ON, then any changes made to the FoxPro environment are saved in the resource file.

SET SAFETY ON/off

Description SET SAFETY prevents accidental overwriting of files by requiring a verification that the file is to be overwritten.

Operational rules With SAFETY ON, if a file of same name as the file being created exists or if the ZAP command is used, the message:

File already exists

Overwrite Cancel

appears on the screen. Note that an acknowledgment is necessary to overwrite the file. When SET SAFETY is OFF, files can be overwritten without a warning message.

SET SEPARATOR TO [expC]

Description SET SEPARATOR allows the numeric separating conventions of other countries to be used in the display of numbers.

Operational rules The separator character can be only one character long. The default setting is the comma (,).

SET SHADOWS ON/off

Description The shadowing behind windows can be turned off and on using SET SHADOWS.

Operational rules This command only affects the FoxPro windows; it does not affect user-defined ones. Use the SHADOW option when defining windows to affect their shadowing.

SET SKIP TO *alias*

Description Skips through each record in the child database when a one-to-many relationship is set.

Operational rules When two data files are linked with the SET RELATION command, there will be a one-to-many relationship if the child database has more than one record that corresponds to a record in the parent database. Use SET SKIP TO *alias* where *alias* is the child database, so that when the SKIP command is issued, each corresponding record in the child database is skipped to before the next record in the parent database. If there is more than one child database, *alias* can be a list of child databases.

To remove SET SKIP, issue the command without the *alias* argument.

The following program sets a one-to-many relationship between two files. The common field is Clicode.

```
SELECT 1
Use Clients INDEX Code
SELECT 2
USE Sales
SELECT 1
SET RELATION TO Clicode INTO Sales
SET SKIP TO Sales
LIST Clicode, Name, B->Amount
```

Record #	CLICODE	NAME	B->AMOUNT
1	A01	JIM JONES	50.00
1	A01	JIM JONES	200.00
2	A02	RUTH DOE	150.00
2	A02	RUTH DOE	50.00
3	A03	HARRY CAREY	100.00

SET SPACE ON/off

Description   SET SPACE ON causes a space to be printed between expressions when using the ? or ?? commands.

Operational rules   The SPACE command prints a space between expressions separated by a comma in the ? or ?? command.

SET STATUS ON/off

Description   SET STATUS ON specifies that the status bar displays at the bottom of the screen using full-screen commands and within programs.

Operational rules   The status bar displays the command name, active file, and the record number in fraction form with the number of records. This is only displayed when SET STATUS is ON.

SET STEP OFF/on

Description   This command is a debugging tool that executes a program line by line, pausing after each task.

Operational rules   The Step mode opens the Trace window. Use the buttons at the bottom of the window to step line by line through the program. At each point you can Cancel or Resume processing.

SET SYSMENU ON/off/AUTOMATIC
SET SYSMENU TO *System menu pop-up list*

Description This command changes the System menu bar.

Operational rules To disable access to the System menu, set SYSMENU OFF. Set SYSMENU AUTOMATIC to display the menu during a program and allow it to be accessible as appropriate.

Use the TO *System menu pop-up list* to choose a subset of options to be displayed in the System menu. The names of the options are _MSYSTEM, _MFILE, _MWINDOW, etc.

SET TALK ON/off

Description SET TALK ON displays the responses of FoxPro commands

Operational rules Memory variables, record number, and output from commands like APPEND FROM, COPY, PACK, STORE, and SUM are displayed with TALK ON. It is recommended that SET TALK be ON when working from the command window. In programs, many times this information is not desired output, so in programs you will probably want to SET TALK OFF.

Use SET TALK WINDOW to direct talk to a particular window.

SET TEXTMERGE OFF/on
SET TEXTMERGE TO *file*

Description This command sets the ability of the \ and TEXT...ENDTEXT commands to evaluate fields and memory variables.

Operational rules The \ and TEXT...ENDTEXT command output text to the screen, printer, or file. To display the contents of a memory variable or field, the expression should be surrounded with the text merge delimiters, which are < > by default. If TEXTMERGE is set OFF, the delimiters are ignored, and the variables are output literally.

Use SET TEXTMERGE TO *file name* to direct \ and TEXT...ENDTEXT output to a file. Use the keyword ADDITIVE to append the data to the end of a file.

Use the WINDOW *window name* clause to direct the output to a named window. Use the NOSHOW clause to suppress screen output. To return to displaying output on the screen, use the SHOW clause.

SET TEXTMERGE DELIMITERS TO *expC, expC2*

Description This command sets the delimiters used with the \ and TEXT...ENDTEXT commands to evaluate fields and memory variables.

Operational RULES The \ and TEXT...ENDTEXT command output text to the screen, printer or file. To display the contents of a memory variable or field, the expression should be surrounded with the text merge delimiters, which are < > by default. To change the delimiter characters, use SET TEXTMERGE DELIMITERS TO *expC*, *expC2*, where *expC2* is the right delimiter. If *expC2* is omitted, *expC* is used for both delimiters. To restore the default delimiters, issue the command without *expC*.

SET TYPEAHEAD TO *exp*

Description SET TYPEAHEAD determines the number of keystrokes FoxPro saves in its buffer. It is useful for fast typists who type faster than a program executes commands.

Operational rules The numeric expression can be within the range of 0 to 128. The default setting is 20 characters. SET TYPEAHEAD works only when SET ESCAPE is ON. Set the typeahead buffer to 0 to deactivate INKEY( ) and ON KEY.

SET UNIQUE on/OFF

Description When SET UNIQUE is ON, only the first record of those with the same key value is included in index files created.

Operational rules An index file created while SET UNIQUE was ON retains its UNIQUE form when reindexed whether SET UNIQUE is ON or OFF. Furthermore, records added to the database file are not added to the index file if they include a key value already residing in the index file. A UNIQUE index file can be changed to a standard index file by the commands SET UNIQUE OFF, INDEX ON, and to restore the duplicate records, REINDEX.

SET VIEW on/OFF

Description SET VIEW ON opens up the View window.

Operational rules The View window is where you can retrieve a View, which opens up a group of data and index files with relationships and filters already set. From this window you can also change the setting of the SET commands and other parameters.

SET VIEW TO *file*

Description SET VIEW TO retrieves a View file.

Operational rules When a view file is retrieved, it automatically opens up a group of data and index files with relationships and filters already set. Save current setting to a view file with the SAVE VIEW TO command.

SET WINDOW OF MEMO TO *window name*

Description SET WINDOW allows the use of windows to edit memos when using the commands APPEND, BROWSE, CHANGE, EDIT, and READ.

Operational rules The window name is defined prior to using SET WINDOW via the DEFINE command.

4

FoxPro functions

FUNCTIONS ARE USED WITHIN COMMANDS AND WITHIN THE INTERFACE AS EXPRESsions. Each function returns a value, in the same way that a formula returns a value. There are many functions of many types, but in general they fall into one of the following categories:

   string functions
   arithmetic functions
   date functions
   screen handling functions
   file handling functions

In this chapter, the functions are listed in alphabetical order. Each function is followed by a short description. Most functions have at least one argument within the parentheses. Variable options are in lowercase italic. For instance,

   ABS(*expN*)

shows that a numeric expression must be used as the argument.

&

Description & is called the macro substitution function. Include it any time that you are using a string memory variable with a command that does not require quotes around the string. Examples of these commands are FIND, USE, and other commands that expect a file name.

This function can also be used for referencing fields or memory variables, because field and variable names do not have quotes around them.

Operational rules The macro substitution can be used with a character memory variable, or as a prefix or a suffix to a literal string. When the macro is used as a prefix, it must be followed by a period (.) to show where the macro ends and the literal begins.

The first example shows a macro being used with a memory variable to open a file. The macro must be used because otherwise the command would be given as USE Mfile, and FoxPro would look for a file named Mfile instead of Maillist. The second example shows the function used for referencing fields in a database. The third example shows the function used as a prefix and a suffix to a literal.

Examples

. Mfile = "MAILLIST"
. USE &Mfile

Beginning with FoxPro is another way you can open a file with a memory variable that is faster than macro substitution. If you begin the file name with the character string of the drive and/or the directory, you can simply use the memory variable. The following command is valid:

. USE "C:\" + Mfile

. ACCEPT "Enter the field to list: " TO Mfield
Enter the field to list: LNAME
. LIST &Mfield
Smith
Jones
Miller
. Wch = "STR"
. Mstr = "Hi There"
. Str1 = "Bye Now"
. ? M&WCH
Hi There
. ? &WCH.1
Bye Now

See also: USE p. 240

expN1 % expN2

Description This operator returns the remainder of *expN1/expN2* (modulo). For instance, the MOD(5,2) is 1 because 5 divided by 2 equals 2 with 1 left over.

Operational rules The % operator can be helpful in finding every nth occurrence of a number. For instance, in the sequence 1, 6, 11, 16, etc., each of the numbers has a modulo of 1 when *expN2* is 5.

expN2 cannot be a 0 because a denominator of zero is an infinite number. If y is negative, then the MOD( ) returns a negative answer.

Examples

```
. ? 5 % 2
1
. ? 11 % −3
−1
```

See also: MOD( ) *p. 337*

ABS(*expN*)

Description ABS displays the positive value of X, whether X is a positive or negative number.

Operational rules This function can be used to circumvent an ERR from occurring when taking the square root of a negative number, showing the number of days between two dates, or to display a negative number as positive, as in an outstanding balance on a bill.

Examples

```
. Mem = −64
. ? SQRT(ABS(Mem))
8
. ? ABS({9/9/89} − {12/25/89})
```

See also: SQRT( ) *p. 369*

ACCESS( )

Description The ACCESS( ) functions show the access level of the user. Access levels are only used in networked systems. A user's access level is anywhere between 1 and 8. The lower the access level, the more privileges the user has. You set each user's access level with the PROTECT command.

PROTECT is also the command you use to set the privilege schemes that define what each access level can do. The two types of privileges are *file* and *field*.

File privileges assign which access level can delete, append, read, and edit a file. For instance, suppose your application has two files, Journal.dbf and Accounts.dbf. You can set Journal to have all four privileges at access level 4, but set Accounts to read/only at that level. This way, users that are level 4 can change the Journal file, but only look at the Accounts file. Of course, level 1 is given all privileges on all files.

All levels less than the specified one have the privilege, and all levels greater do not. For instance, if 4 is the UPDATE privilege for the Journal file, 1 through 3 automatically have that privilege, and 5 through 8 do not.

The three types of field privileges are *full*, *read-only*, and *none*. This allows you to restrict access to certain fields in a database. For instance, even though the file Customer might have complete file privileges at access level 3, you can set the field named Comments to read-only at that same level.

Operational rules There are three cases where the ACCESS function returns 0:

1. The system is a single-user system.
2. The user entered the system without using the log-in screen.
3. The file Dbsystem.db was not found by FoxPro during start-up.

When writing programs on network systems, it is a good idea to check the access level of the current user in the beginning of the program.

Examples The following program informs users what file privileges they have, and keeps out any users with access level 0:

```
DO CASE
  CASE ACCESS( ) = 0
    ? "Sorry, can't continue. Please enter through the log-in screen."
    QUIT
  CASE ACCESS( ) > 4
    ? "You will be able to look at the fields, but not edit them."
  OTHERWISE
    ? "You will be able to add, update and delete records. "
    ? "Do not abuse this privilege!"
ENDCASE
WAIT
DO Mailedit
```

ACOPY(array1,array2)

Optional ACOPY(*array1,array2,expN1,expN2,expN3*)

Description ACOPY copies the contents of *array1* into a second array, *array2*.

Operational rules The second array must be large enough to hold the number of elements from the first array. The function returns the number of elements copied, otherwise it returns −1.

The optional expression *expN1* specifies the element number where copying is to start. The expression *expN2* specifies the number of elements to be copied. If *expN2* is 1, all elements starting with element *expN1* are copied. *expN3* specifies the element number of the destination array where copying is to begin.

If the arrays are two dimensional, the AELEMENT( ) function returns the element number of a particular row and column. This can be helpful when using *expN1* or *expN2*.

See also: AELEMENT( ) p. 273

ACOS(*expN*)

Description ACOS(x) returns the arccosine (the inverse cosine) of an angle. This trigonometric function is used in calculating the degrees of an angle when the lengths of two of the sides are known. The RTOD function converts the answer, which is given in radians, to degrees. Therefore, the RTOD(ACOS(x)) is equal to ACOS(x)*180/PI.

Operational rules Figure 4-1 shows a circle with points marked in radians (0 to pi) to illustrate the limits of the ACOS and other trigonometric functions. The argument x, must be between −1 and 1. Keeping in mind that the cosine represents the x-axis value at any point, the ACOS function always returns a value between 0 and pi (approximately 3.1416).

If you use memory variables as the argument, the function then uses 20-place numeric accuracy. You can change the number of decimal points displayed in the answer with the SET DECIMALS command.

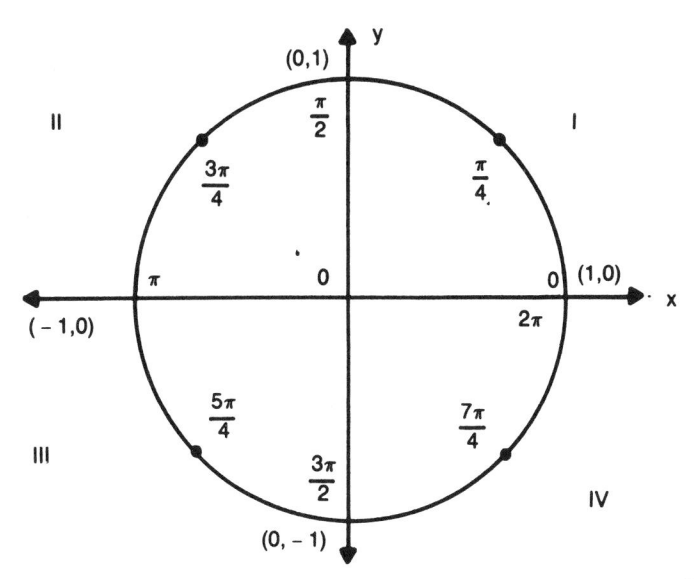

Fig. 4-1. **This circle with points marked in radians shows the limits of the ACOS and other trigonometric functions.**

Examples

```
. ? ACOS(1)
    0
. ? RTOD(ACOS(0))
    90
```

See also: ASIN( ) p. 277
            COS( ) p. 290
            PI( ) p. 345
            SET DECIMALS p. 251
            SIN( ) p. 367

ADEL(*array,expN*)

Optional   ADEL(*array,expN*,2)

Description   ADEL deletes element *expN* from an array.

Operational rules   When an element is deleted from *array*, all elements below it are moved back. The function returns 1 if the deletion is successful, otherwise it returns −1.

If the arrays are two dimensional, the function defaults to deleting row *expN*. Use the optional argument ,2 to delete a column.

Example   The example displays a four-element array of team names where the second element is deleted.

```
. ? team(1), team(2), team(3), team(4)
Cubs  Giants  Dodgers  Braves

. mm = ADEL(team,2)
    1
. ? team(1), team(2), team(3), team(4)
Cubs  Dodgers  Braves
.F.
```

See also AELEMENT( ) p. 273

ADIR(*array*)

Optional   ADIR(<array>,<expC1>,<expC2>)

Description   ADIR copies information about files into *array*.

Operational rules   The array size is increased automatically to hold the file information of all files that match the skeleton. The function returns the number of files that match the skeleton.

ADIR( ) is best used with two-dimensional arrays, as the column returns five pieces of information about a file. If the array is one dimensional, use AELE-

MENT( ) to find the corresponding number for a particular row and column pair. The information copied is:

Column #	Information
1	File name
2	File size
3	File date
4	File time
5	File attributes (Archive, Hidden, Read only, System)

The optional expression *expC1* specifies a file skeleton such as *.DBF or BUDGET.*. If *expC1* is omitted, the skeleton *.* is used.

The optional expression *expC2* specifies additional information that can be returned. The letter D in the expression returns information about subdirectories. The letter H returns information about hidden files, and S returns information about system files.

Example

```
. mm = ADIR(mfiles,'*.frx')
3
. ? mfiles(1,1), mfiles(1,2), mfiles(1,3), mfiles(1,4), mfiles(1,5)
STUDENT.FRX      3916      07/12/91      10:50:12      .A...
. ? mfiles(2,1), mfiles(2,2), mfiles(2,3), mfiles(2,4), mfiles(2,5)
CLASSES.FRX      5114      09/01/91      12:20:44      .A..R.
```

See also: AELEMENT( ) p. 273
    AINS( ) p. 275

AELEMENT(*array,expN1*)

Optional AELEMENT(*array,expN1,expN2*)

Description AELEMENT returns an element number from its row and column subscripts.

Operational rules Several FoxPro functions (such as ACOPY( ) and ASORT( )) require that elements of two-dimensional arrays are defined by their element number instead of their row and column number subscripts. AELEMENT( ) converts the row and column number to this number.

If the array is one dimensional, only the argument *expN1* is needed. In that case the function simply returns *expN1*, as long as *expN1* is not greater than the arrays dimension.

The expression *expN2* is required for two-dimensional arrays.

Example When DISPLAY MEMORY shows the contents of an array, the array is listed in element number order.

. DIMENSION TEAMS(2,2)
. DISPLAY MEMORY LIKE TEAMS
TEAMS   Pub   A
(1, 1)   L   .F.   (element number 1)
(1, 2)   L   .F.   (element number 2)
(2, 1)   L   .F.   (element number 3)
(2, 2)   L   .F.   (element number 4)

See also: AELEMENT( ) p. 273
            DIMENSION p. 173
            DISPLAY MEMORY p. 173

AFIELDS(*array*)

Description   AFIELDS copies information about a database's structure into *array*.

Operational rules   The array size is increased automatically to hold the information. The copy is always a copy of the currently selected database. The function returns the number of fields in the database.

AFIELDS( ) is best used with two-dimensional arrays, as the column returns four pieces of information about a file. If the array is one dimensional, use AELEMENT( ) to find the corresponding number for a particular row and column pair. The information copied is:

Column #	Information
1	Field name
2	Field type
3	Field length
4	Number of decimal places

Example
. USE Students
. mm = AFIELDS(mstruc)
8
. ? mstruc(1,1), mstruc(1,2), mstruc(1,3), mstruc(1,4)
NAME   C   25   0
. ? mstruc(2,1), mstruc(2,2), mstruc(2,3), mstruc(2,4)
GPA   N   5   2

See also: AELEMENT( ) p. 273

AINS(*array,expN*)

Optional AINS(*array, expN*,2)
Description AINS inserts an element *expN* into an array.
Operational rules When an element is inserted into *array*, all elements below it are moved down. The function returns 1 if the insertion is successful, otherwise it returns – 1.

If the arrays are two dimensional, the function defaults to inserting row *expN*. Use the optional argument ,2 to insert a column.

Example The example displays an array of team names where a third element is inserted.

```
. ? team(1), team(2), team(3), team(4)
Cubs  Giants  Dodgers  Braves
. mm = AINS(team,2)
1
. ? team(1), team(2), team(3), team(4)
Cubs     .F.      Giants     Dodgers
```

See also: AELEMENT( ) p. 273
          ADEL( ) p. 272

ALIAS(*expN*)

Description ALIAS returns the alias name of a specified work area.
Operational rules Use the IN keyword with the USE command to choose the work area before opening a file. The valid work areas are 1 through 10, or A through J. The file name is the default alias, although you can provide a different one by using the ALIAS keyword with the USE command.

If you do not specify an area when using the ALIAS function, it returns the name of the current work area.

Examples

```
. USE Journal IN 1
. USE Account IN 2 ALIAS Coa
. ? ALIAS(1)
Journal
. ? ALIAS(2)
COA
```

See also: SELECT p. 229
          USE p. 240

ALEN(*array*)

Optional   ALEN(*array,expN*)
Description   ALEN returns the number of elements in an array.
Operational rules   If the *array* is the only argument, the total number of elements is returned. If *expN* is 1, the function returns the number of rows. If *expN* is 2, it returns the number of columns. An *expN* of 0 is equivalent to not using the argument.
Example

```
. DIMENSION aa(2,3)
. ? ALEN(aa)
6
```

See also: AELEMENT( ) p. 273
DIMENSION p. 173

ALLTRIM(*expC*)

Description   Given the string *expC*, ALLTRIM returns that same string with leading and trailing spaces removed.
Operational rules   This function is useful when comparing strings. Also use it to eliminate leading and trailing spaces for printing purposes.
Examples

```
.One = " Hello"
.Two = " Hello "
.? One = Two
.F.

.? ALLTRIM(one) = ALLTRIM(two)
.T.

.? ALLTRIM(one) + ", John"
Hello, John
```

ASCAN(*array,expr*)

Optional   ASCAN(*array,expr,expN1,ex pN2*)
Description   ASCAN searches an array for *expr*.
Operational rules   The function returns the matching element number. If no match is found, the function returns 0.
  If SET EXACT IS ON, *expr* must be the same length as the matching array expression. Otherwise, matches are made based on the number of characters of *expr*.

Use the optional argument *expN1* to define the place to start searching in the array. Use *expN2* to define the number of elements to be searched.

Example

```
. ? team(1), team(2), team(3), team(4)
```
Cubs Giants Dodgers Braves"
```
. ? ASCAN(team,"G")
2
. SET EXACT ON
. ? ASCAN(team,"G")
0
```

See also: AELEMENT( ) p. 273
          ADEL( ) p. 272

ASC(*expC*)

Description The ASC function is used to show the ASCII number of a character. If the argument is a string of more than one character, the function returns the number of the first character of the string.

Each key on a computer keyboard has a number that corresponds to it. These numbers are called ASCII codes (pronounced as-kee), which stands for American Standard Code for Information Interchange. Almost all microcomputers use the ASCII codes when storing information.

Operational rules See the CHR( ) section for a table of ASCII codes. Following this chart, "A" is number 65, while "a" is number 97. The first 32 numbers represent characters such as the backspace (BS) and escape (ESC) which cannot be entered as a character expression.

Examples

```
. ? ASC("a")
    97
. Mem = "A"
. ? ASC(Mem)
65
```

See also: CHR( ) p. 287

ASIN(*expN*)

Description ASIN( ) returns the arcsine (the inverse sine) of an angle. This trigonometric function is used in calculating the degrees of an angle when the lengths of two of the sides are known. The RTOD function converts the answer, which is given in radians, to degrees. Therefore, the RTOD(ASIN(x)) is equal to ASIN(x)*180/PI.

Operational rules The ACOS( ) section shows a circle with points marked in radians. This illustrates the limits of the ASIN function. The argument *x* must be between − 1 and 1. Keeping in mind that the sine represents the y-axis value at any point, the ASIN function always returns a value between − PI/2 to PI/2.

If you use memory variables as the argument, the function then uses 20-place numeric accuracy. You can change the number of decimal points displayed in the answer with the SET DECIMALS command.

Examples

? ASIN(PI( ))
   0
? RTOD(ASIN(PI( )))
   90

See also: ACOS( ) p. 271
              PI( ) p. 345
              SET DECIMALS p. 251
              SIN( ) p. 367

ASORT(*array*)

Optional ASORT(*array,expN1,expN2 , expN3*)
Description ASORT sorts an array.
Operational rules The array can be sorted in ascending or descending order. If it is a two-dimensional array, it is sorted by the rows so that the row number changes, but the column number remains the same. The function returns 1 if the sort is successful, otherwise, it returns − 1.

Use the optional argument *expN1* to define the place to start sorting. The default is 1. If the array is two dimensional, *expN1* represents the column number that gets sorted (the default is column 1).

Use *expN2* to define the number of elements to be sorted. If the array is two dimensional, *expN2* represents the row number to start sorting at. If *expN2* is − 1 or omitted, the function sorts all elements from the starting position through to the end.

The default order is ascending. To sort in descending order, use any non-zero number for *expN3*.

Example

. ? mcharm(1,1), mcharm(2,1), mcharm(3,1)
Heart Moon Clover
. ? mcharm(1,2), mcharm(2,2), mcharm(3,2)
Pink Yellow Green
. ? ASORT(mcharm)

```
. ? mcharm(1,1), mcharm(2,1), mcharm(3,1)
Clover  Heart  Moon
. ? mcharm(1,2), mcharm(2,2), mcharm(3,2)
Green  Pink  Yellow
```

In the example above, the two-dimensional array, mcharm, is sorted with ASORT. The array was originally defined as:

Row, column:	1	2
1	Heart	Pink
2	Moon	Yellow
3	Clover	Green

When sorted with the ASORT function, the array becomes sorted by column 1, the name of the symbol:

Row, column:	1	2
1	Clover	Green
2	Heart	Pink
3	Moon	Yellow

To sort alphabetically by color, use the optional argument *expN1*. The function ASORT(mcharm,2) would result in the following sort:

Row, column:	1	2
1	Clover	Green
2	Heart	Pink
3	Moon	Yellow

See also: ASCAN( ) p. 276

ASUBSCRIPT(*array,expN1,expN2*)

Description   ASUBSCRIPT returns a row or column subscript given an element number.

Operational rules   FoxPro functions such as ASCAN( ) return an element number. To convert that number to the corresponding row and/or column, use ASUBSCRIPT( ). This function is the opposite of the AELEMENT( ) function, which returns the element number given the row and column subscript.

If the array is one dimensional, use a 1 in *expN2*. In that case the function simply returns *expN1*, as long as *expN1* is not greater than the array's dimension.

Place a 1 in expression *expN2* to return the row subscript. When *expN2* is 2, it returns the column subscript.

Example When DISPLAY MEMORY shows the contents of an array, the array is listed in element number order.

```
. DIMENSION teams(2,2)
. DISPLAY MEMORY LIKE TEAMS
TEAMS   Pub  A
( 1, 1)    L    .F.    (element number 1)
( 1, 2)    L    .F.    (element number 2)
( 2, 1)    L    .F.    (element number 3)
( 2, 2)    L    .F.    (element number 4)
. ? ASUBSCRIPT(teams,3,1)
   2
```

See also: AELEMENT( ) p. 273
DIMENSION p. 173
DISPLAY MEMORY p. 174

AT(expC,expC)

Optionals   AT(expC,expC or memofield name)
AT(expC,expC,expN)

Description   The AT function returns the position where one string appears within another.

Operational rules   The arguments are entered as:

AT("substring","string to search")

The function is very useful for finding key words within comments or addresses, or for finding the first space in a full name or address. If the substring does not exist in the string, the function returns 0.

The optional third argument *expN* searches for the *expN*th occurrence of substring in the string to search.

Example

```
. ? AT("Street","5 Main Street")
   8
. ? AT(" ","5 Main Street",2)
   7
```

The following example shows how the AT can be used in conjunction with the SUBSTR function to extract last names from fields that contain both the first and last names. The arguments of the SUBSTR are SUBSTR(*string,start number,n*).

Therefore, the function in D1 states, "extract part of the Name field, starting at the position of the space, and going until the field ends:"

```
. USE CLIENTS
. LIST OFF NAME
```
NAME
John Smith
Bonnie Miller
Tom Jones

```
. LIST SUBSTR(NAME, AT(" ",NAME))
```
Smith
Miller
Jones

See also: SUBSTR( ) p. 372

ATAN(expN)

Description   ATAN( ) returns the arc tangent (the inverse tangent) of an angle.

Operational rules   This trigonometric function is used in calculating the degrees of an angle when the lengths of two of the sides are known. The RTOD function converts the answer, which is given in radians, to degrees. Therefore, the RTOD(ATAN(x)) is equal to ATAN(x)*180/PI( ).

The tangent represents the sine/cosine value at any point on a circle. Therefore, the ATAN function always returns a value between – pi/2 to pi/2, representing a quadrant I or IV angle.

Examples

```
? ATAN(0)
     0    (radians)
?ATAN(1)*180/PI( )
    45    (degrees)
```

See also: COS( ) p. 290
           SIN( ) p. 367

ATC(expC,expC)

Optionals   ATC(expC,expC or *memofield name*)
ATC(expC,expC,expN)

Description The ATC function returns the position where one string appears within another without case sensitivity.

Operational rules The arguments are entered as:

ATC("substring","string to search")

The function is very useful for finding key words within comments or addresses, or for finding the first space in a full name or address. If the substring does not exist in the string, the function returns 0.

The optional third argument *expN* searches for the *expN*th occurrence of substring in the string to search.

The ATC function is equivalent to the following function:

AT(UPPER(expC), UPPER(expC))

Example.

. ? ATC("street","5 Main Street")
      8

See also: AT( ) p. 280

ATCLINE(expC,expC)

Description The ATCLINE function returns the line number in a memo field where the substring appears with no case sensitivity.

Operational rules The arguments are entered as:

ATCLINE("substring","memofield")

The function is used for finding key words within narrative entries. If the substring does not exist in the memo, the function returns 0.

The ATCLINE function is equivalent to the following function:

ATLINE(UPPER(expC), UPPER(expC))

ATLINE(expC,expC)

Description The ATLINE function returns the line number in a memo field where the substring appears.

Operational rules The arguments are entered as:

ATLINE("substring","memofield")

The function is used for finding key words within narrative entries. If the substring does not exist in the memo, the function returns 0.

Use this function in conjunction with the MLINE( ) function, which returns any line from the memo as a character string.

Example The following example assumes that the database has a memo field named Notes:

. STORE ATLINE("12/15/90",NOTES) TO MEMOLN
   8
. ? MLINE(NOTES,MEMOLN)
Phone call 12/15/90: discussed lease option

See also: MLINE( ) p. 336

ATN2(*expN,expN*)

Description   ATN2(X,Y) returns the arc tangent (the inverse tangent) of an angle whose tangent is y/x.

Operational rules   Because both y and x are given, the quadrant can be calculated. Therefore, unlike the ATAN( ) function, the result will be between – pi and pi.

Examples

?ATN2(1,0)
   0   (radians)
? RTOD(ATN2(1, – 1))
   – 45   (degrees)

See also: ATAN( ) p. 281
         RTOD( ) p. 363

BAR( )

Description   BAR( ) returns the bar number of the most recent selection from a pop-up menu.

Operational rules   Each bar in a pop-up menu is numbered using the DEFINE BAR command. BAR( ) returns zero if no pop-up menu is active.

See also: ACTIVATE POPUP p. 142
         DEFINE POPUP p. 168

BETWEEN(*expr1,expr2,expr3*)

Description   BETWEEN returns .T. if *expr1* is greater than or equal to *expr2* and *expr1* is less than or equal to *expr3*.

Operational rules All expressions in the arguments must be of the same type (numeric, character, or date).

The BETWEEN function is equivalent to the following criteria selection:

expr1 > = expr2 .AND. expr1 < = expr3

Examples

```
. ? BETWEEN(5,2,9)
.T.

. USE CLIENTS
. LIST FOR BETWEEN(AMT, 100,500)
NUMBER    CLIENT    AMT
   4      Smith     300
   6      Miller    450
   7      Jones     100
```

BOF( )

Optional BOF(*alias* or *expN*)

Description BOF returns a logical true (.T.) when the record pointer is at the top of a file and is then moved one record back. This function is useful in programs where the database is being read in reverse order.

Operational rules The SKIP command moves the record pointer forward one record, and SKIP − 1 moves the pointer backward one record. The top record in a nonindexed file is record number one. The top record in an indexed file is the first record in the index.

The two situations where the BOF( ) returns .T. are:

1. When the pointer is at the top record, and SKIP − 1 is issued.
2. When the top record is being edited, and the user presses PgUp.

If no file is opened in the current work area, BOF( ) returns a logical false (.F.).

The optional *alias* can be either the alias name, or work area. Work areas are designated from 1 to 25, or A through J.

Examples

```
. USE MAILLIST
. GOTO TOP
. SKIP − 1
. ? BOF( )
.T.

GOTO BOTTOM
DO WHILE .NOT. BOF( )
```

```
    ? LNAME,FNAME
    SKIP - 1
ENDDO
```

See also: EOF( ) p. 299
              SKIP p. 235

CAPSLOCK( )

Optional   CAPSLOCK(*expL*)

Description   This function automatically turns on and off the CapsLock key (to all uppercase or back to normal).

Operational rules   CAPSLOCK(.T.) switches the CapsLock on, and CAPSLOCK(.F.)switches the CapsLock off. If the parameter is given, CAPSLOCK( ) returns the mode before the change. If the optional parameter is left out, CAPSLOCK( ) returns the state of the CapsLock key without changing mode.

Examples

```
.?CAPSLOCK(.T.)
.T.    CapsLock Turns on.

.?CAPSLOCK( )
.T.    If the CapsLock is still on.
```

See also: NUMLOCK( ) p. 340

CDOW(*expD*)

Description   CDOW returns the name of the day, given a date expression.

Operational rules   The three ways to enter a date as an argument are:

1. Enclose the date in curly brackets: {12/5/89}
2. Use the CTOD function: CTOD("12/5/2010")
3. Use a field name or memory variable.

The date is assumed to be in the 1900s when two digits are used for the year.

An invalid date as the argument generates an error message.

Examples

```
. CDOW({9/6/60})
Tuesday
. CDOW(CTOD("12/25/89"))
Monday
```

See also: CTOD( ) p. 291
              DTOC( ) p. 296

CDX(*expN*)

Optional CDX(*expN,alias*)

Description CDX returns the name of the multiple index file in the current work area, or a specified work area. The argument *expN* designates the index order number.

Operational rules Each index file is given an order number, depending on the order that it was opened. The SET INDEX TO and USE INDEX commands open the indexes. The first file in the list is the structural index (same name as data file), or 1.

If the number in the argument is larger than the number of index files open, then CDX( ) returns a null string. CDX( ) returns the name of appropriately numbered multiple indexes in the current file, unless a second argument is provided. The optional alias can be either the alias name or work area. Work areas are designated from 1 through 25, or A through J. If no file is open in the designated area, CDX( ) returns a null string. If the designated alias name does not exist, CDX( ) returns an error message.

Use TAG( ) to return the tag names from within an index. Use NDX( ) to return index file names.

See also: TAG( ) p. 380

CEILING(*expN*)

Description CEILING returns the argument, rounded up with 0 decimal places. In other words, this function always returns an integer that is greater than the argument, unless the argument is an integer.

Operational rules If the argument is a negative number, it returns a number closer to zero. This function is useful in cases where you must round up all numbers that have decimal places.

Examples

```
. ? CEILING(5.2)
    6
. ? CEILING(5.6)
    6
. ? CEILING(- 5.2)
   -5
. ? CEILING(- 5.6)
   -5
```

See also: FLOOR( ) p. 309
ROUND( ) p. 361

CHR(*expN*)

Description CHR( ) shows the character that corresponds to the number in the argument.

Operational rules Each key on a computer keyboard has a number that corresponds to it. These numbers are called ASCII codes (pronounced as-kee). Almost all microcomputers use the ASCII codes when storing information.

The CHR( ) function is useful for displaying special characters on the computer and printer, such as graphics characters, the bell tone, and printer control codes.

Table 4-1 shows the codes for the numbers 0 through 127, which are standard among all ASCII computers. Following this chart, you can see that CHR(65) is an *A*, while CHR(97) is *a*. The first 32 numbers represent characters, such as the backspace (BS) and escape (ESC), which cannot be printed. Therefore the CHR( ) of numbers between 1 and 32 are blank.

```
. ? CHR(65)
A
. ? CHR(7) + "That answer is invalid, try again." && message beeps
That answer is invalid, try again.
```

See also: ASC( ) p. 277

Table 4-1. Standard ASCII codes that correspond to CHR(0) through CHR(127).

0 NUL	16 DLE	32 SP	48 0	64 @	80 P	96 '	112 p
1 SOH	17 DCI	33 !	49 1	65 A	81 Q	97 a	113 q
2 STX	18 DC2	34 "	50 2	66 B	82 R	98 b	114 r
3 ETX	19 DC3	35 #	51 3	67 C	83 S	99 c	115 s
4 DOT	20 DC4	36 $	52 4	68 D	84 T	100 d	116 t
5 ENQ	21 NAK	37 %	53 5	69 E	85 U	101 e	117 u
6 ACK	22 SYN	38 &	54 6	70 F	86 V	102 f	118 v
7 BEL	23 ETB	39 '	55 7	71 G	87 W	103 g	119 w
8 BS	24 CAN	40 (	56 8	72 H	88 X	104 h	120 x
9 HT	25 EM	41)	57 9	73 I	89 Y	105 i	121 y
10 LF	26 SUB	42 *	58 :	74 J	90 Z	106 j	122 z
11 VT	27 ESC	43 +	59 ;	75 K	91 [	107 k	123 {
12 FF	28 FS	44 ,	60 <	76 L	92 \	108 l	124 |
13 CR	29 GS	45 -	61 =	77 M	93]	109 m	125 }
14 SO	30 RS	46 .	62 >	78 N	94 ^	110 n	126 ~
15 SI	31 US	47 /	63 ?	79 O	95 _	111 o	127 DEL

CHRSAW( )

Optional CHRSAW(expN)

Description CHRSAW is used only in programs. It returns a value of .T. if the keyboard buffer has a character present.

Operational rules The optional parameter causes CHRSAW to wait up to expN seconds for the input. CHRSAW returns .F. if expN seconds has passed (or no seconds if the optional parameter is not used) and the keyboard has no input in its buffer. The buffer has input if it receives any during the expN period, or if anything has previously entered it.

Example

```
@ 15, 1 SAY "Enter Your Selection: " GET CHOICE
IF .NOT. CHARSAW(60)
   ?"Wake up!! Hurry up and choose a selection!"
ELSE
   READ
ENDIF
```

CHRTRAN(expC1,expC2,expC3)

Description CHRTRAN changes expC1 by replacing all occurrences of characters found to match a character in expC2 with the corresponding character in expC3.

Operational rules If expC2 has more characters than expC3, the extra characters in expC2 are deleted from expC1. If expC2 has fewer characters than expC3 then the extra expC3 characters are ignored.

Examples

```
.? CHRTRAN("hill","hi","ma")     && 'h' replaced with 'm', 'i' with 'a'
mall
.? CHRTRAN("Ken is glad.","gl","s")
Ken is sad.
```

CMONTH(expD)

Description CMONTH returns the name of the month, given a date expression.

Operational rules The three ways to enter a date as an argument are:

1. Enclose the date in curly brackets: {12/5/89}
2. Use the CTOD function: CTOD("12/5/2010")
3. Reference a field name or memory variable.

The date is assumed to be in the 1900s when two digits are used for the year, otherwise you must enter four digits for the year.

An invalid date as the argument generates an error message.

Examples

. ? CMONTH({9/6/60})
September
. ? CMONTH(CTOD("12/25/89"))
December

See also: CTOD( ) p. 291
DOW( ) p. 296
DTOC( ) p. 296

CNTBAR(expC)

Description   CNTBAR returns the number of options in pop-up *expC*.

Operational rules   A pop-up is created and named with the DEFINE POPUP command, and activated with ACTIVATE POPUP. *expC* is the name of the pop-up.

See also: ACTIVATE POPUP p. 142
DEFINE POPUP p. 168

CNTPAD(expC)

Description   CNTPAD returns the number of options in menu *expC*.

Operational rules   A menu is created and named with the DEFINE MENU command, and activated with ACTIVATE MENU. The *expC* is the name of the menu.

See also: ACTIVATE MENU p. 141
DEFINE MENU p. 166

COL( )

Description   COL( ) returns the current column number position of the cursor.

Operational rules   The COL( ) function is used in conjunction with the @...SAY...GET command that places a display in a particular position on the screen or printed page. The @ command places the display on the screen using the following syntax:

@ row, col SAY expression

For instance, the command:

    @ 5,30 SAY "HI THERE"

would display the words HI THERE on the fifth row on the screen, in column 30. The cursor is then positioned at the end of the expression, so the COL() function would return 38 after printing the expression in this example. This allows you to use the COL() function to display an expression on the screen relative to another expression.

Examples The following program prints a message after the expression Mstring (assuming it is of variable lengths). If Mstring places the cursor too far to the right, the program places the message on the next line, otherwise it is placed right next to Mstring:

    @ 5,30 SAY Mstring
    IF COL() > 68
       @ 5, COL() SAY "Y)es or N)o"
    ELSE
       @ 6, 30 SAY "Y)es or N)o"
    ENDIF

This program prints a 5-character string continuously until it reaches the end of the screen:

    DO WHILE COL() < 75
       @ 10, COL() SAY Mstring
    ENDDO

The operator $ can also be used with the @...SAY...GET command interchangeably with COL(). For instance the following commands are valid:

    @ 5,30 SAY Mstring
    @ 5, $ SAY "Y)es or N)o"

The difference between COL() and $ is that COL() can also be used in a conditional statement, as in the two previous examples.

See also: PCOL( ) p. 344
            PROW( ) p. 350
            ROW( ) p. 362

COS(expN)

Description COS returns the cosine of an angle, given in radians.

Operational rules The cosine represents the x-axis value at any point on a circle, so it is always between −1 and 1. See the ACOS() section for a figure of a circle with quadrants marked.

In Quadrant I, cos(x) decreases from 1 to 0. In Quadrant II, cos(x) decreases from 0 to −1. In Quadrant III, cos(x) increases from −1 to 0. In Quadrant IV, cos(x) increases from 0 to 1.

The argument *expN* must be between 0 and 2pi.

Examples

```
? COS(PI( ))
    0
? COS(0)
    1
```

See also: SIN( ) p. 367
TAN( ) p. 380

CTOD(*expC*)

Description CTOD converts the expression, entered as a string that looks like a date, into a date that can be used for calculations.

Operational rules Variables that are date type can be used to calculate the difference between two dates. For instance, subtracting 5/1/89 from 5/20/89 gives 19, the number of days between the two dates. This type of calculation is often used in accounts aging reports and with personnel database applications.

The character expression in the arguments must be MM/DD/YY, unless the format has been changed with SET DATE or SET CENTURY. The date is assumed to be in the 1900s when two digits are used for the year, otherwise you must enter four digits for the year. Any date between January 1, 1582, and December 31, 9999, can be used.

Beginning with FoxPro, you can substitute the curly brackets ({}) for the CTOD function.

Examples

```
. ? CTOD("12/25/89") − CTOD("9/6/89")
110
. ? {12/25/89} − {9/6/89}
110
```

The following program uses the CTOD function to create a blank date for input with the @...SAY...GET command.

```
Bdate = CTOD(" / / ")
@ 5,1 SAY "Enter Date:" GET Bdate
```

See also: DATE( ) p. 292
DTOC( ) p. 296

CURDIR( )

Optional CURDIR(expC)

Description CURDIR returns the current directory of the specified drive as a character string.

Operational rules The optional parameter is a drive letter. If the optional parameter is not specified, then CURDIR gives the current directory of the default drive. If no such drive exists, the function returns null. If no directory is in use (i.e., you are in the root), the function returns \.

Examples

```
&& if we are currently in C:\foxpro\
.? CURDIR( )
\FOXPRO\
.? CURDIR("D")
\DATA\
```

DATE( )

Description DATE returns the system date as a date that can be used for calculations.

Operational rules Variables that are date type can be used to calculate the difference between two dates. For instance, subtracting 5/1/89 from 5/20/89 gives 19, the number of days between the two dates.

The system date is kept through DOS, and can be set with the DATE command at the DOS prompt. Many computers come with battery clocks that keep the system date current at all times.

The SET CENTURY and SET DATE commands change the way that the date is displayed. The default is MM/DD/YY.

Examples

```
.? {12/25/89} – DATE( )
210
```

The following program uses the DATE( ) function to create a date for input with the @...SAY...GET function.

```
Mdate = DATE( )
@ 5,1 SAY "Enter Date:" GET Mdate
```

See also: SET DATE p. 251
SET CENTURY p. 247
CTOD( ) p. 291

DAY(expD)

Description DAY returns the number of a day of the month, given a date expression.

Operational rules The three ways to enter a date as an argument are:

1. Enclose the date in curly brackets: {12/5/89}
2. Use the CTOD function: CTOD("12/5/2010")
3. Reference a field name or memory variable.

The date is assumed to be in the 1900s when two digits are used for the year, otherwise you must enter four digits for the year.

Examples

```
. ? DAY({9/6/89})
6
. ? DAY(CTOD("12/25/89"))
25
```

See also: CTOD( ) p. 291
 DOW( ) p. 275
 MONTH( ) p. 338

DBF( )

Optional DBF(alias)

Description DBF returns the name of the database file in the current work area, or a specified work area.

Operational rules Use the IN keyword with the USE command to choose the work area before opening a file. The valid work areas are 1 through 10, or A through J. The file name is the default alias, although you can provide a different one by using the ALIAS keyword with the USE command.

Examples

```
. USE Journal IN 1
. USE Account IN 2 ALIAS COA
. ? DBF( )
C:JOURNAL.DBF
. ? DBF(COA)
C:COA.DBF
```

See also: USE p. 241
 ALIAS( ) p. 275
 NDX( ) p. 339

DELETED( )

Optional DELETED(*alias*)

Description DELETED returns .T. if the current record in a specified file is marked for deletion.

Operational rules A record can be marked for deletion in one of two ways:

1. By using the DELETE command.
2. By pressing Ctrl – U while in Edit or Browse mode.

While there are deleted records in a database, the SET DELETED ON command can be used so that all deleted records are ignored when listing, reporting, editing, etc.

Examples

```
. SELECT 1
. USE Journal
. USE Coa IN 2
. GOTO 5
. ? DELETED( )
.F.
. ? DELETED(COA)
.T.
```

See also: PACK p. 209
RECALL p. 218
SET DELETED p. 252

DIFFERENCE(*expC,expC*)

Description DIFFERENCE returns a number that estimates how much two strings sound alike. The SOUNDEX( ) code (described next) is used to calculate the difference.

Operational rules In brief, the SOUNDEX( ) code is a four-digit code, made up of the following:

1. The first digit is the first character of the string.
2. After the first digit of the string, all occurrences of the letters *a, e, h, i, o, u, w,* and *y* are ignored.
3. It assigns a number to the remaining letters. For example, the letters *b, f, p,* and *v* equal 1. The letters *c, g, j, k, q, s, x,* and *z* equal 2, and so forth.

For example, the word *humbug*, is coded as H512. Additional rules to soundex coding are described under the SOUNDEX( ) section.

The DIFFERENCE( ) function compares the SOUNDEX codes of two strings. If the SOUNDEX codes are the same, DIFFERENCE returns a 4. If none of the characters in the SOUNDEX codes match, DIFFERENCE returns a 0. Each character in common returns a 1.

Examples

```
. ? DIFFERENCE("HUMBUG","HAMBURGER")
    3
. ? DIFFERENCE("TINY","LITTLE")
    1
. USE CLIENTS
. LIST Lname FOR DIFFERENCE("BALISTRERI",Lname) > 3
    4 Balestreros
    8 Balistreri
   10 Balosteri
   20 Balestri
```

See also: SOUNDEX( ) p. 368

DISKSPACE( )

Description DISKSPACE returns the number of bytes available on the current disk drive.

Operational rules Certain file operations in FoxPro require as much free space on disk as there is room in the file. Two of these functions are the PACK command and the MODIFY STRUCTURE command. Use DISKSPACE( ) before running either of these two commands.

Additional functions that can be used to calculate disk space are RECCOUNT( ) (number of records in the file) and RECSIZE (number of bytes used by each record). When using these functions, keep in mind that the header record uses up an additional 2000 bytes at the top of the file.

The current drive can be changed with the SET DEFAULT TO command.

Examples This example shows a program that checks whether there is room on the disk to run the PACK routine before executing the command:

```
IF DISKSPACE( ) < (RECCOUNT( ) * RECSIZE( )) + 2000
    ? "There is not enough room to run the PACK routine"
    WAIT
ELSE
    PACK
ENDIF
```

See also: RECCOUNT( ) p. 357
RECSIZE( ) p. 359

DMY(*expD*)

Description DMY converts a date to the character string of DD Month YY, where the month is spelled out.

Operational rules The DMY conversion shows the day as a one or two digit number, the month is spelled out, and the year is two digits. To show the year as four digits, use the SET CENTURY ON command. For example, the date 5/15/89 would be displayed as 15 May 89 in the DMY format.

Examples

. ? DMY({9/6/89})
6 September 89
. ? DMY(CTOD("12/25/89"))
25 December 89

See also: CTOD( ) p. 291

DOW(*expD*)

Description DOW returns the numeric value of the day of the week of the date expression.

Operational rules The three ways to enter a date as an argument are:

1. Enclose the date in curly brackets: {12/5/89}
2. Use the CTOD function: CTOD("12/5/2010")
3. Reference a field name or memory variable.

The DOW returns a number with two decimal places. To change the number of decimals, use the SET DECIMAL TO command.

Examples

. ? DOW(DATE( ))
  9.00
. ? "This contract, commencing ", CMONTH(DATE( )), STR(DOW(DATE( )),2)
This contract, commencing January 12

See also: CTOD( ) p. 291
            DATE( ) p. 292

DTOC(*expD*)

Optional   DTOC(*expD*,1)
Description DTOC converts the expression, entered as a date, to a string that looks like a date in MM/DD/YY format.

Operational rules The date is assumed to be in the 1900s when two digits are used for the year, otherwise you must enter four digits for the year. Any date between January 1, 100, and December 31, 9999, can be used.

The optional argument causes the date to appear in YYYYMMDD form, which is very useful for indexing files by DTOC( ). Notice that indexing by the DTOC( ) function without the optional argument does not sort dates in chronological order (05/01/90 will come before 12/31/89).

Examples

```
. ? DTOC(DATE( ))
02/20/89
. HEADING = "Date" + DTOC(DATE( )) + "     MONTHLY REPORT"
. ? HEADING
Date: 02/20/89       MONTHLY REPORT
. USE SALES
. INDEX ON DTOC(SALES_DAT,1) + PONUM TO SALESDAT
. LIST SALES_DAT, PONUM
```

Record #	SALES_DAT	PONUM
3	12/27/89	A1001
4	12/27/89	A1001
1	12/27/89	B2000
5	12/29/89	A2001
2	01/03/90	A1005
7	01/03/90	B2002
6	01/05/90	A1001
8	01/05/90	A2001

See also: SET DATE p. 251
            CTOD( ) p. 291

DTOR(*expN*)

Description DTOR converts a number, representing an angle measured by degrees, into radians.

Operational rules Fractions of a degree, usually represented by minutes and seconds, must be represented by decimals. For instance, 45 minutes should be depicted as .75 degrees.

The figure in the ACOS( ) section shows a circle with points marked in radians (0 to pi). This helps illustrate the conversion of degrees to radians.

Use the SET DECIMALS command to change the number of decimals which appear in the answer. The RTOD( ) function is used to conversely change radians to degrees.

Examples

. ? DTOR(50)
.87
. ? DTOR(PI( )/2)
.03

See also: ACOS( ) p. 271
           RTOD( ) p. 363

DTOS(*expD*)

Description DTOS converts a date to a character expression, but unlike the DTOC function, which returns a character in MM/DD/YY format, the DTOS character can be used for sorting because it is in the format YYYYMMDD.

Operational rules The DTOS( ) function, introduced in FoxPro, is useful when you need to index on both a date and character string added together. The DTOS( ) function returns a character in the YYYYMMDD format regardless of the SET CENTURY COMMAND.

When entering the expression, you can use a field, memory variable, or date entered using {}. This function is equivalent to the DTOC( ) function used with the optional argument of 1.

Examples

. ? DTOS({12/25/89})
19891225
. USE CHECKS
. INDEX ON DTOS(Chk_date) + Acct
. LIST Chk_date, Acct

Record #	Chk_date	Acct
3	12/27/89	A1001
4	12/27/89	A1001
1	12/27/89	B2000
5	12/29/89	A2001
2	01/03/90	A1005
7	01/03/90	B2002
6	01/05/90	A1001
8	01/05/90	A2001

Notice that the DTOC function (without the optional parameter) could not be used in place of DTOS for this index, because the dates in January would precede the dates in December.

See also: CTOD( ) p. 291
           DTOC( ) p. 296

EMPTY(*expr*)

Description EMPTY returns a logical true (.T.) if the expression, which can be of any type, is empty.

Operational rules Each type of expression evaluates as empty according to the following table of values:

Data type	Is empty when
Character	No characters other than spaces.
Numeric	0
Date	" / / "
Logical	.F.
Memo	No contents.

```
. USE SALES
. LIST FOR EMPTY(CHK_DATE) .OR. EMPTY(ACCT)
Record #   Chk_date   Acct
    1        / /      A1001
    4      12/27/91
    7        / /
```

EOF( )

Optional EOF(*alias* or *expN*)

Description EOF returns a logical true (.T.) when the record pointer is at the end of a file and is then moved one more record forward. This function is useful in programs where the database (either indexed or nonindexed) is being read sequentially.

Operational rules The SKIP command moves the record pointer forward one record. The last record in a nonindexed file is the record number returned by RECCOUNT( ). The last record in an indexed file is the record reached with the command GO BOTTOM. When SKIP is used to go one record past this record, the record number becomes RECCOUNT( ) + 1, and EOF( ) is set to .T.

The two situations where the EOF( ) returns true are:

1. When the pointer is at the bottom record, and SKIP 1 is issued.
2. When the bottom record is being edited, and the user presses PgDn.

If the pointer is already at the end of file, and the SKIP command is issued again, FoxPro returns an End of File Encountered error message. If no file is opened in the current work area, EOF( ) returns a logical false (.F.).

The optional *alias* can be either the alias name or work area. Work areas are designated from 1 to 25, or A through J.

Examples

```
. USE MAILLIST
. GOTO BOTTOM
. SKIP 1
. ? EOF( )
.T.

GOTO TOP
DO WHILE .NOT. EOF( )
  ? LNAME,FNAME
  SKIP 1
ENDDO
```

See also: BOF( ) p. 284
RECCOUNT( ) p. 357
SKIP p. 235

ERROR( )

Description   ERROR returns the number corresponding to the error that has just occurred. The ON ERROR command must be active for this function to work.

Operational rules   The ON ERROR command is given at the beginning of a program, but waits until an error occurs before performing. When ON ERROR is triggered by an error, the command can call a program, a procedure, or a user-defined function. The syntax for the command is ON ERROR *command*.

The ERROR( ) function can be used in conjunction with the program that ON ERROR branches to. The program can display different directions to the user, depending on the error that has occurred. The MESSAGE( ) function can also be helpful in this routine, as it displays the error message that would appear if the ON ERROR( ) command was not present.

If the ON ERROR command is not active, errors in programs display the Cancel, Suspend, Ignore? error message.

To clear the number returned by ERROR( ), use the RETURN or RETRY command.

Examples   The following program calls an error routine command named Errtrap:

Mailprog.PRG

```
ON ERROR DO Errtrap
USE MAILLIST
SET PRINT ON
```

```
DO WHILE .NOT. EOF( )
  ? LNAME, FNAME
  SKIP
ENDDO
```

Errtrap.PRG

```
DO CASE
  SET PRINT OFF
  CASE ERROR( ) = 126 .OR. ERROR( ) = 125
    ? "Please put your printer on line. "
    WAIT
    SET PRINT ON
    RETRY
  CASE ERROR( ) = 114
    ? "The index is corrupted, please reindex the file"
    WAIT
    RETURN TO MASTER
  OTHERWISE
    ? "The following error has occurred: ", MESSAGE( )
    WAIT
    RETURN TO MASTER
ENDCASE
```

The routine Errtrap checks for a printer error (126 or 125) which signifies that the printer is off-line. If that is the case, the program pauses until the user sets the printer on. Error 114 reports a corrupted index file, so the user is instructed to reindex the file. All other error codes return the user to the main program that called Mailprog.PRG.

See also: ON ERROR p. 200
MESSAGE( ) p. 334
RETRY p. 223

EVALUATE expC

Description EVALUATE performs the same type of macro substitution as the & function, but is faster. You can include it any time that you are using a string memory variable with a command that doesn't expect quotes around the string. Examples of these commands are FIND, USE, and other commands that expect a file name.

This function can also be used for referencing fields or memory variables, because field and variable names do not have quotes around them.

Operational rules The macro substitution can be used with a character memory variable, or as a prefix or a suffix to a literal string.

The first example shows an EVALUATE command being used with a memory variable to open a file. It must be used because otherwise the command would be given as USE Mfile, and FoxPro would look for a file named MFILE instead of MAILLIST.

The second example shows the function used for referencing fields in a database. The third example shows the function used as a prefix and a suffix to a literal.

Examples

```
. Mfile = "MAILLIST"
. USE EVALUATE("Mfile")

. ACCEPT "Enter the field to list: " TO Mfield
Enter the field to list: LNAME
. LIST EVALUATE("Mfield")
Smith
Jones
Miller
```

Beginning with FoxPro, there is another way that you can open a file with a memory variable that is faster than macro substitution. If you begin the file name with the character string of the drive, and/or the directory, you can simply use the memory variable. The following command is valid:

```
. USE "C:\" + Mfile
```

See also: & p. 267

EXP(*expN*)

Description   The EXP() function returns the number e raised to the *expN* power.

Operational rules   The value of e is approximately 2.7182818. The EXP function is the inverse of the natural logarithm LOG(). The *expN* can be a numeric field or memory variable, or the actual value.

Examples

```
. ? EXP(1)
  2.72
. SET DECIMALS TO 6
. ? EXP(1)
  2.7182825
```

See also: SET DECIMALS p. 251
           LOG( ) p. 327

FCLOSE(expN)

Description The FCLOSE() function closes a file that has been opened with FCREATE() or FOPEN().

Operational rules The FCREATE() command is a low-level command that creates a file, most often from a program. The file is given a number, called the "file handle". The number must be passed in the parameter when using the FCLOSE command. The FCLOSE function is used to close this type of low level file to save it to disk. If the file cannot be closed, FCLOSE() returns a logical false (.F.), otherwise it returns logical true (.T.).

Examples

```
. FNUM = FOPEN("MAINFRAM.DTA")
1
. CLOSED = FCLOSE(FNUM)
.T.
```

See also: FOPEN( ) p. 309
FCREATE( ) p. 303

FCOUNT( )

Optional FCOUNT(*alias*)

Description FCOUNT returns the number of fields in a database.

Operational rules The optional *alias* can be either the alias name or work area. Work areas are designated from 1 to 25, or A through J.

Examples

```
. SELECT 1
. USE Journal
. USE Coa IN 2
. GOTO 5
. ? FCOUNT( )
5
. ? FCOUNT("COA")
10
```

See also: FIELD( ) p. 306

FCREATE(expC)

Optional FCREATE(*expC,expN*)

Description The FCREATE() function creates a file and opens it for use.

Operational rules The FCREATE( ) command is a low-level command that creates a file, most often from a program. The FCREATE( ) function returns a number, called the file's *handle*. Designate the name of the file using the parameter *expC*. If the file already exists, it will be overwritten. If the file cannot be created, FCREATE( ) returns −1.

The optional argument *expN* allows you to set a DOS attribute. The available attributes are:

0	Read / Write (default)
1	Read only
2	Hidden
3	Read only / Hidden
4	System
5	Read only / System
6	System / Hidden
7	Read only / Hidden / System

Examples

```
. OPENED = FCREATE("LISTED.DTA")
    1
```

See also: FCLOSE( ) p. 303
          FOPEN( ) p. 309

FEOF(*expN*)

Description The FEOF( ) function checks if the file pointer is at the end of a file opened with FCREATE( ) or FOPEN( ).

Operational rules The FCREATE( ) and FOPEN( ) commands are low-level commands that open a file, most often from a program. The file is given a number, called the *file handle*. The number must be passed in the parameter when using the FEOF( ) function. FEOF( ) returns logical true (.T.) if the pointer is at the bottom of the file, otherwise it returns logical false (.F.).

Examples

```
. FNUM = FOPEN("MAINFRAM.DTA")
    1
. MTOP = FSEEK(FNUM,0)     && Go to top of file
    0
. ? FEOF(FNUM)     && If true, then the file is empty
    .T.
```

See also: FOPEN( ) p. 309
          FCREATE( ) p. 303

FERROR( )

Description The FERROR function checks whether the last low-level file operation was successfully completed. If it was not successful, it returns the error that occurred.

Operational rules The FCREATE( ) and FOPEN( ) commands are low-level commands that open a file, most often from a program. FERROR( ) is used after issuing one of the functions that uses a low-level file. The following functions can all be tested with the FERROR function: FCREATE( ), FOPEN, FCLOSE( ), FSEEK( ), FEOF( ), FFLUSH( ).

The FERROR( ) function returns 0 if no error occurred. Otherwise, it can return any of the following errors:

2	File not found.
4	Too many files open.
5	Access denied.
6	Invalid file handle given.
8	Out of memory.
25	Seek error.
29	Disk full.
31	Error opening file or general failure.

Examples A segment of Fileit.prg, which opens a file

```
MHAND = FCREATE("LISTFILE.DTA")
IF FERROR( ) = 29
    ? "Disk full - you must erase some files. "
    WAIT
ENDIF
```

See also: *FOPEN( ) p. 309*
             FCREATE( ) p. 303

FFLUSH(*expN*)

Description The FLUSH function completely closes a file opened with one of the low-level file operations.

Operational rules The FCREATE( ) and FOPEN( ) commands are low-level commands that open a file, most often from a program. The file is given a number, called the *file handle*. The number must be passed in the parameter when using the FLUSH( ) function. The FLUSH( ) function flushes the memory buffers of all file data, and writes it to disk. It is a good idea to use this function when closing a file, because it reduces the chance of data loss if the computer is shut down before exiting FoxPro.

See also: *FCLOSE( ) p. 303*

FGETS(*expN*)

Optional FGETS(*expN,expN*)
Description The FGETS function returns a character string from a file opened with one of the low-level file operations.
Operational rules The first parameter *expN* is the file handle. FGETS( ) always starts at the byte where the file pointer is positioned. The optional second parameter is the number of bytes to be returned. If the optional parameter is not given, it returns the next 254 bytes, or the bytes between the file pointer and next carriage return, whichever is shorter.

See also: FREAD( ) p. 311

FIELD(*expN*)

Optional FIELD(*expN,alias*)
Description The FIELD( ) function returns the name of the specified field, designated by the number. Each field is numbered sequentially in the data file structure.
Operational rules You can see the number of each field when creating, modifying, or displaying the structure. The FIELD( ) returns the name as an uppercase string. If the number in the argument is greater than the number of fields in the database, FIELD( ) returns a null string ("").

If no file is opened in the current work area, FIELD( ) returns a null string. The optional *alias* can be either the alias name or work area. Work areas are designated from 1 to 10, or A through J.

Examples

```
. USE MAILLIST
. ? FIELD(1)
LNAME
```

```
Showfld.PRG
SET TALK OFF
USE Maillist
Rnd = 1
DO WHILE "" < > FIELD(Rnd)
   ? FIELD(Rnd)
   Rnd = Rnd + 1
ENDDO
```

Showfld output
LNAME

FNAME
ADD
CITY
ST
ZIP

See also: RECSIZE( ) p. 359
            RECCOUNT( ) p. 357

FILE(expC)

Description   The FILE( ) function returns a logical true (.T.) when a file with the name *expC* exists on the disk. The name is not case sensitive, but the extension must be included.

Operational rules   Unless the drive and directory are entered in the character expression, the function searches the default drive and directory. This is the drive that the user was on when going into FoxPro. The default drive can be changed after entering FoxPro, using SET DEFAULT, and the default directory can be changed using SET PATH.

Examples

```
. ? FILE("Maillist.DBF")
.T.
. ?FILE("d:\FILES\Journal.DBF")
.T.

Openfile.PRG
SET TALK OFF
IF FILE("MAILLIST.DBF")
   USE Maillist
ELSE
   ? "The MAILLIST.DBF file is not found on the disk."
   WAIT
   QUIT
ENDIF
```

See also: SET DEFAULT p. 251
            SET PATH p. 259

FILTER( )

Optional   FILTER(*alias*)
Description   The FILTER function returns the current filter conditions on a file.

Operational rules FILTER( ) returns the filter condition as a string. The filter condition for all currently open files can also be seen with the DISPLAY STATUS command.

If no file is opened in the current work area, FILTER( ) returns a null string. The optional *alias* can be either the alias name, or work area. Work areas are designated from 1 to 25, or A through J.

Examples

```
. USE MAILLIST IN 1
. SET FILTER TO ZIP = "92"
. SELE 2
. ? FILTER(1)
ZIP = "92"
```

FKLABEL(*expN*)

Description The FKLABEL( ) returns the name which has been given to the specified function key.

Operational rules SET FUNCTION (or the full-screen SET command) allows you to program the function keys. You can program 9 function keys (F2 through F10), 9 Shift – function keys, and 10 Ctrl – function keys.

The SET FUNCTION command can be issued one of two ways. The more common is SET FUNCTION *key label*. (For instance, SET FUNCTION F2 TO "Modify Command"). The second way is SET FUNCTION *expN*, where each key is designated by a number. (For instance, SET FUNCTION 1 TO "Modify Command"). The FKLABEL( ) function returns the function key assigned to each number.

The F1 key is not assignable, because it is used as the Help key. Therefore, the numbers start with F2 = 1, F3 = 2, and so forth.

Examples

```
. ? FKLABEL(1)
F2
```

See *also*: SET FUNCTION p. 255

FKMAX( )

Description The FKMAX( ) returns the number of keys on the current keyboard that can be programmed.

Operational rules SET FUNCTION (or the full-screen SET command) allows you to program the function keys. The maximum number of programmable keys is 28: 9 function keys (F2 through F10), 9 Shift – function keys, and 10

Ctrl – function keys. Function keys F11 and F12 are not programmable through FoxPro.

This command is used primarily with applications that are not going to be run on typical IBM-compatible keyboards.

Examples

```
. ? FKMAX( )
28
```

See also: SET FUNCTION p. 255

FLOOR(expN)

Description   FLOOR returns the argument, rounded down to 0 decimal places. In other words, this function always returns an integer that is less than or equal to the argument.

Operational rules   This function is useful in cases where you must round down all numbers that have decimal places. Negative numbers return a number less than the argument by rounding to the next smaller number.

Examples

```
. ?FLOOR(5.2)
    5
. ? FLOOR(5.6)
    5
. ? FLOOR(- 5.2)
   -6
. ? FLOOR(- 5.6)
   -6
```

See also: CEILING( ) p. 286
            ROUND( ) p. 361

FOPEN(expC)

Optional   FOPEN(expC,expN)

Description   The FOPEN( ) function opens a file. This is one of the low-level commands used for opening nondatabase files.

Operational rules   The FOPEN( ) command is a low-level command that opens a file, most often from a program. The FOPEN( ) function returns a number, called the *file handle*. Designate the name of the file using the parameter *expC*. If the file cannot be opened, FOPEN( ) returns – 1.

The optional argument *expN* allows you to set a DOS attribute. The available attributes are:

0   Read / Write   (default)
1   Read only
2   Hidden

Examples

```
. OPENED = FOPEN("LISTED.DTA")
     1
```

See also: FCREATE( ) p. 303

FOUND( )

Optional   FOUND(*alias* or *expN*)

Description   The FOUND( ) function returns a logical .T. if the most recent positioning command (FIND, SEEK, LOCATE, or CONTINUE) was successful.

Operational rules   The FOUND( ) function can be used at the dot prompt or in programs, to show whether a record that matches the search criteria has been found. All of the positioning commands move the record pointer to the first record that matches the criteria. The FIND and SEEK commands require the database to be indexed on the search criteria, and are much faster than the LOCATE command.

FOUND( ) returns the search status of the current file, unless an argument is provided. The optional argument can be either the alias name, or work area. Work areas are designated from 1 through 10, or A through J.

When searching for a record, the entire key field does not have to match. For instance, the command SEEK "SM" finds the first occurrence of a name beginning with SM (for instance, SMITH). The SET EXACT ON command turns off this ability to check only the number of characters in the comparison string. With the EXACT ON, the criteria must be the exact length of the key field(s) in question. For instance, if that particular field is a length of 12 characters, only SEEK "SMITH" returns FOUND( ).

Examples   These commands perform a search on a nonindexed file. In this example, only one record matches the criteria.

```
USE Maillist
LOCATE FOR Lname = "SMITH"
? FOUND( )
    .T.
CONTINUE
? FOUND( )
    .F.
```

This program performs a search and edit on an indexed file:

```
USE Maillist INDEX Mailname
ACCEPT "Enter Name to Edit" TO Mname
SEEK Mname
IF FOUND( )
   EDIT
ELSE
   ? "Name not found"
   WAIT
ENDIF
```

See also: CONTINUE *p. 153*
FIND *p. 180*
LOCATE *p. 192*
SEEK *p. 228*

FPUTS*(expN,expc)*

Optional FPUTS*(expN,expC,expN)*

Description The FPUTS function writes a character string into a file that has been opened with one of the low-level file operations. The character string has a carriage return placed at the end.

Operational rules The first parameter *expN* is the *file handle*. FPUTS( ) writes the character string at the byte where the file pointer is positioned. The optional third parameter is the number of bytes to be written. FPUTS( ) returns the number of bytes written to the file.

This file is equivalent to the FWRITE( ) function, except it always appends a carriage return to the end of the string.

See also: FREAD( ) *p. 311*

FREAD(*expN,expN*)

Description The FREAD function returns a character string from a file opened with one of the low-level file operations.

Operational rules The first parameter *expN* is the *file handle*. FREAD( ) always starts at the byte where the file pointer is positioned. The second parameter is the number of bytes to be returned. The FREAD( ) function returns the bytes specified, or the bytes between the file pointer and end of file, whichever is shorter.

This function is much like the FGETS() function with the optional number of bytes parameter, except that FREAD() reads past carriage returns when they are within the specified number of bytes.

See also: FGETS( ) p. 306

FSEEK(*expN,expN*)

Optional   FSEEK(*expN,expN,expN*)

Description   The FSEEK function moves the file pointer within a file that has been opened with one of the low-level file operations.

Operational rules   The first parameter *expN* is the *file handle*. The second parameter is the number of bytes to be moved. To move the pointer forward, use a positive number; move backward with a negative number.

If the third parameter is not used, FSEEK() moves the pointer starting at the beginning of the file. To move it from a different position, use the following values as the third parameter:

0   Start from beginning of the file (default)
1   Start from current file pointer position
2   Start from the end of the file

See also: FREAD( ) p. 311

FSIZE(*field*)

Optional   FSIZE(*field,alias*)

Description   The FSIZE function returns the length of a specified field.

Operational rules   This function can be used with any type of field. The difference between the FSIZE() function and the LEN(*field*) is that LEN() can only be used with character fields.

If no file is opened in the current work area, FSIZE() returns a zero. The optional *alias* can be either the alias name or work area. Work areas are designated from 1 to 25, or A through J.

Examples

```
. USE MAILLIST
. ? FSIZE("LNAME")
20
. SELECT 2
. ? FSIZE("LNAME")
0
. ? FSIZE("LNAME",1)
20
```

See also: RECSIZE( )p. 359

FULLPATH(*file*)

Optional FULLPATH(*file*,1)
FULLPATH(*file*,1,*file2*)

Description The FULLPATH( ) function returns the path where *file* exists.

Operational rules Unless the optional argument is used, the function searches the default and all directories in the FoxPro path. If the optional argument, 1 (or any other number), is used, the function searches all directories in the DOS path. If the file does not exist in the designated path, the function returns the name of the file and the default directory.

If *file2* is included, the function returns the path relative to the two files, *file1* and *file2*.

Examples

```
. ? FULLPATH("Maillist.DBF")
D:\FILES\MAILLIST.DBF
```

See also: SET DEFAULT p. 251
SET PATH p. 259

FV(*payment,rate,term*)

Description The FV( ) function returns the future value of fixed periodic payments with a compounded interest rate. This is the function that answers the question, "If I put $250 a month in an account that pays 10 percent interest, how much will I have at the end of 10 years?"

Operational rules As with all of the FoxPro financial functions, keep in mind that if the rate is given as an annual percentage rate (as it most often is), and the periods are monthly (as they most often are), then the interest rate must be divided by 12, and the term must be in months (years times 12).

Payments are assumed to be made at the end of each period. The formula to calculate the future value if the payments are made at the beginning of each period is:

FV(pmt,rate,term)*(1 + rate)

The term must be at least one. The following formula is used to calculate the future value:

pmt * (((1 + rate)^ term) – 1/rate)

Examples The function in the example calculates the future value of periodic payments of $250 for 10 years placed in an account paying 10 percent interest, compounded monthly:

```
? FV(250,.1/12,10*12)
    51211.24
```

See also: PAYMENT( ) p. 343
            PV( ) p. 252

FWRITE(*expN,expC*)

Optional   FPUTS(*expN,expC,expN*)

Description   The FWRITE function writes a character string into a file that has been opened with one of the low-level file operations.

Operational rules   The first parameter *expN* is the *file handle*. FWRITE( ) writes the character string at the byte where the file pointer is positioned. The optional third parameter is the number of bytes to be written. FWRITE( ) returns the number of bytes written to the file.

This file is equivalent to the FPUTS( ) function, except that FPUTS always appends a carriage return to the end of the string.

See also: FPUTS( ) p. 311

GETBAR(*expC,expN*)

Description   GETBAR returns the name of the option positioned at *expN* in menu *expC*.

Operational rules   A menu is created and named with the DEFINE MENU command, and activated with ACTIVATE MENU. The *expC* is the name of the menu. The *expN* is the physical position of the option in the menu.

See also: DEFINE MENU p. 166

GETENV(*expC*)

Description   GETENV( ) returns the status of current DOS settings such as PATH, PROMPT, and COMPSPEC.

Operational rules   DOS has a group of commands that change the DOS working environment. These commands include PROMPT, which changes the appearance of the DOS system prompt, and PATH, which tracks the subdirectories that should be searched when a command is issued. Your DOS manual has a list of these commands. They are often automatically issued through the Autoexec.bat file.

The argument must be given as a string or string variable. It can be upper or lowercase, but must match the particular DOS system command.

Examples   The function in the example checks the existing path set up in the DOS working environment.

    ? GETENV("PATH")
    C:\;C:\DOS;C:\WP

See also: OS( ) p. 341

GETFILE( )

Optional GETFILE(*expC,expC*)
Description The GETFILE( ) function displays the Open File dialog box, allowing the user to choose a file from the list.
Operational rules The function returns the name of the file chosen, returned as a character string. If no file is chosen, it returns a null string.

The first optional parameter *expC* can be one or more extensions that determine the types of files to be listed. If more than one extension is listed, separate them with semicolons (;). The extension parameter must be surrounded by quotes (″). To display all files in the directory, use the null string (″″) for this parameter.

The second optional parameter is a message to display the Open File dialog box. This parameter must be a character string.

Examples
```
. DATA = GETFILE("DBF","CHOOSE A FILE")
. USE &DATA
```

GETPAD(*expC,expN*)

Description GETPAD returns the number of the option positioned at *expN* in pop-up *expC*.
Operational rules This function is needed when the MOVER keyword has been included when the pop-up was defined. MOVER allows the options in the pop-up to be positioned in an order other than their numeric order.

A pop-up is created and named with the DEFINE POPUP command, and activated with ACTIVATE POPUP. The *expC* is the name of the pop-up.

The *expN* is the physical position of the option in the pop-up.

See also: DEFINE POPUP p. 168

GOMONTH(*expD,expN*)

Description The GOMONTH( ) function adds a certain number of months to the specified date.
Operational rules The function returns the date *expN* months after *expD*. If *expN* is negative, the function subtracts the months from the date.

Examples
```
. WEDDATE = {9/16/90}
. MAILDATE = GOMONTH(WEDDATE, -2)
```
07/16/90

HEADER( )

Optional HEADER(alias)
Description HEADER returns the size of the header record in the database file.
Operational rules This function returns the length of a header. This function can be used in conjunction with the RECSIZE( ) and RECCOUNT( ) functions to find the total number of bytes used by a file. The following formula will return the number of bytes used by the data in the database:

HEADER + (RECCOUNT( ) * RECSIZE( )) + 1

The optional *alias* can be either the alias name or work area. Work areas are designated from 1 through 10, or A through J. If no file is open in the designated area, HEADER( ) returns zero. If the designated alias name does not exist, HEADER( ) returns an error message.

Examples

```
. USE Maillist
. LIST STRUCTURE
Structure for database: D:MAILLIST.DBF
Number of data records:        6
Field  Field Name  Type        Width
  1    LNAME       Character    10
  2    FNAME       Character    10
** Total **                     21

. ? HEADER( ) + (RECSIZE( ) * RECCOUNT( ) + 1)    && calculate file size
225
```

See also: RECSIZE( ) p. *359*
RECCOUNT( )p. *357*

IIF(*condition,x,y*)

Description The IF( ) function tests a condition, returning x if the condition is true, and y if the condition is false.
Operational rules A simple explanation of this function is to use the English translation, "If this condition is true, do this (x), otherwise do this (y)." The condition must be a logical formula or logical variable.
Conditional statements usually use one or more of the following operators:

    =   equal
    <   less than
    < = less than or equal

```
>      greater than
>=     greater than or equal
<>     not equal
$      substring search
```

.AND. Both conditions must be true.
.OR.   Either condition may be true.

For instance, IIF(Sex="F","FEMALE","MALE") states, "If the variable Sex equals F, then display FEMALE, otherwise display MALE.

The expressions, x and y can be character, numeric, logical, or date. However, both expressions must be of the same type.

The IIF( ) function can save you space in your programs, because in one line it can take the place of the five-line IF...ELSE...ENDIF command. However, in many cases the IF command must be used, because the IIF( ) function cannot be used to issue commands based on a condition. Following is an example of the IF command replaced by the one-line IIF( ) function:

```
IF Results = "P"
   ? "Positive"
ELSE
   ? "Negative"
ENDIF
```

or as an IIF function:

```
? IIF(Results = "P","Positive","Negative")
```

The IIF function can also be used in the contents of a report created with the report generator, or a label created with the label generator.

In instances where more than two conditions must be run, you can nest IIF ( ) functions. An example is a grading application where (in English): "If score >= 90, then return A, otherwise, if score >= 80, then return B, otherwise return a C." (In this case, C is the lowest grade possible). The comparable FoxPro function for this case is:

```
IIF(Score >= 90,"A",IIF(Score >= 80,"B","C"))
```

Examples The following are all valid uses of the IIF( ) function:

```
IIF(Grade > 70, "PASS","FAIL")      (contents of a report column)
? IIF(Sex = "M","Male",IIF(Sex = "F","Female",""))
Tax = IIF(State = "CA" .AND. Taxable = "Y",Price*.06,0)
```

See also: IF p. 184

INKEY( )

Optional INKEY(*expN*)

Description INKEY( ) returns a number that represents the most recent key pressed on the keyboard. Unlike the INKEY function in some other programming languages such as BASIC, the FoxPro INKEY does not pause and wait for the user to type something, unless the optional argument is used.

Operational rules When the INKEY( ) function is used, the key that the user presses is not displayed on the screen, as with all other interactive commands. Also, INKEY( ) can detect the exact keystroke pressed (such as a Ctrl key combination, or an arrow key), unlike the other commands.

If the user has typed several characters, the INKEY( ) function returns the first character in the typeahead buffer, and removes it from the buffer.

The optional numeric argument *expN* determines how long INKEY( ) pauses to receive the keystroke. If there is no argument, INKEY reads the most recent key pressed.

INKEY does not return the values of Alt function key combinations because these keystrokes are handled by the macro interpreter.

For values 0 through 255, the number is the ASCII value that corresponds to the keystroke. Function keys and their Ctrl and Shift combinations are represented by negative numbers. Alt key combinations with letters are also negative, and there is no differentiation between uppercase and lowercase with Alt keys.

If the key pressed is between 40 and 126, the CHR( ) function of the INKEY displays the character pressed. For instance, the function

```
CHR(INKEY(20))
```

returns the letter A if uppercase A (INKEY value 65) is pressed.

Examples The program below pauses and waits for the user to press a key. The program responds with three different displays depending if the ↑, ↓, or other key is pressed.

```
Pressed = INKEY(20)
DO CASE
   CASE Pressed = 5
      ? "Going UP!"
   CASE Pressed = 24
      ? "Going DOWN!"
   OTHERWISE
      ? "Please press the up or down arrow!"
ENDCASE
```

See also: ON KEY p. 202
  CHR( ) p. 287
  READKEY( ) p. 355

INLIST(expr1,expr2,expr3 ...)

Description INLIST returns .T. if *expr1* is found in the list of expressions following it.

Operational rules All expressions in the arguments must be of the same type (numeric, character, or date). The INLIST function is equivalent to the following criteria selection:

expr1 = *expr2* .OR. *expr1* = *expr3* .OR. . . .

Examples

.Fruit = "apple"
.? INLIST(FRUIT,"pear","banana","orange")
.F.

. USE CLIENTS
. LIST FOR INLIST(AMT, 100, 250, 500)

NUMBER	CLIENT	AMT
4	Smith	100
6	Miller	100
7	Jones	500

INSMODE( )

Optional INSMODE(expL)

Description This function automatically turns on and off the Insert key (to insert mode or back to typeover mode).

Operational rules INSERT(.T.) switches the Insert mode on, and INSERT(.F.) switches it off. If the parameter is given, INSERT( ) returns the mode before the change. If the optional parameter is left out, INSERT( ) returns the state of the Insert key without changing mode.

Examples

.? INSERT(.T.)
.T. (if Insert was already on)
.? INSERT( )
.T. (if the Insert is on)

See also: CAPSLOCK( ) p. 285

INT(expN)

Description The INT( ) function returns the numeric expression, truncated at the decimal point.

Operational rules The INT() function ignores all numbers that are right of the decimal point, and returns the integer value of the number. To round numbers to zero decimal places, use the ROUND() function with zero decimal places. The INT(5.6) is equal to 5, while the ROUND(5.6,0) is equal to 6.

Examples

```
. ? INT(5.2)
    5
. ? INT(5.6)
    5
. ? INT(- 5.6)
   -5
```

See also: CEILING( ) p. 286
FLOOR( ) p. 309
ROUND( ) p. 361

ISALPHA(expC)

Description The ISALPHA() function returns logical true (.T.) if the character expression in the argument begins with a letter.

Operational rules The ISALPHA() function returns true if the first character of the string is an upper or lowercase letter, a through z. All other cases return logical false (.F.)

The function that tells whether a variable is a character string or a numeric (or other type), is the TYPE() function.

Examples The following program allows the user to edit a record. The user can pull up the record by entering the record number, or a last name for seeking. The ISALPHA() function checks whether the first character of the seek string begins with a letter or a number. If it is a number, the GOTO *record number* command is used, otherwise, a SEEK is performed.

```
ACCEPT "Enter a name or record number " TO Search
IF ISALPHA(Search)
   SEEK Search
ELSE
   GOTO VAL(Search)
ENDIF
EDIT
```

See also: ISDIGIT( ) p. 321

ISCOLOR( )

Description The ISCOLOR( ) function returns logical true (.T.) if the computer has the ability to display color.

Operational rules The ISCOLOR( ) function checks whether the computer has a color graphics adapter. This function can be used in programs that will be run on several computers. By checking if ISCOLOR is true, the program can set screen colors on or leave them off. The command to change the colors is SET COLOR TO.

The one problem with changing the colors even if a color graphics adapter is present is that sometimes the computer has the adapter, but not a color terminal. In these cases, when the colors are turned on, the screen can become unreadable.

Examples The following program checks whether there is a color adapter. If there is, it then asks the user whether the console is a color console (in case there is a monochrome console on a color graphics computer):

```
IF ISCOLOR( )
   ACCEPT "Can this console display colors? " TO Colorit
   IF UPPER(Colorit) = "Y"
      SET COLOR TO G/B, GR+/N
   ENDIF
ENDIF
```

See also: SET COLOR p. 249

ISDIGIT(*expC*)

Description The ISDIGIT( ) function returns logical true (.T.) if the character expression begins with a digit (0 – 9).

Operational rules This is the companion function to ISALPHA, which returns true (.T.) if the expression begins with a letter. The function that tells whether a variable is a character string or a numeric (or other type), is the TYPE ( ) function.

See also: ISALPHA( ) p. 320

ISLOWER(*expC*)

Description The ISLOWER( ) function returns logical true (.T.) if the character expression in the argument begins with a lowercase letter.

Operational rules The ISLOWER() function returns true if the first character of the string is a lowercase letter, A through Z. All other cases return logical false (.F.)

Examples

```
. ? ISLOWER("John")
.F.
. ? ISLOWER("john")
.T.
. ? ISLOWER("")
.F.
. ? ISLOWER("55")
.F.
```

See also: ISUPPER( ) p. 322

ISUPPER(expC)

Description   The ISUPPER() function returns logical true (.T.) if the character expression in the argument begins with a uppercase letter.

Operational rules   The ISUPPER() function returns true if the first character of the string is an uppercase letter, A through Z. All other cases return logical false (.F.)

Examples

```
. ? ISUPPER("John")
.T.
. ? ISUPPER("john")
.F.
. ? ISUPPER("")
.F.
. ? ISUPPER("55")
.F.
```

See also: ISLOWER( ) p. 321

KEY(expN)

Optional   KEY(expN,alias)
             KEY(.cdx file,expN)

Description   The KEY() function returns the expression that the specified index file was keyed on.

Operational rules   KEY() Returns the key expression of the current index file. This is the same expression displayed in DISPLAY STATUS. The *expN* determines which index key to return. Indexes are numbered in the order they were opened with the USE or SET INDEX TO command.

KEY( ) shows the display for the numbered index of the current file, unless an argument is provided. The optional alias can be either the alias name or work area. Work areas are designated from 1 through 25, or A through J.

If the optional clause *.cdx file* is used, key returns index key expressions for particular tags in a multiple index file. Tags are numbered in the order they were created in the multiple index file.

See also: ORDER( ) p. 341
INDEX p. 185

LASTKEY( )

Description   LASTKEY( ) returns a number that represents the most recent key pressed on the keyboard in response to an interactive command.

Operational rules   LASTKEY( ), like the INKEY( ) function, can detect the exact keystroke pressed (such as a Ctrl key combination, or an arrow key), unlike other interactive commands such as READ and ACCEPT.

The LASTKEY function is different than INKEY( ), however, in that it reads the key pressed in the last interactive command (such as READ or ACCEPT), while INKEY( ) pauses to receive the keystroke (or captures it during a noninteractive command). The READKEY( ) function, which also captures keystrokes, is different in that it is only used with full-screen commands, and it returns a different value depending on whether data was changed or not.

For values 0 through 255, the number is the ASCII value that corresponds to the keystroke. Function keys and their Ctrl, Shift, and Alt combinations are represented by negative numbers.

Examples   The following program instructs the user to press Escape to abort the program and return to the main menu. The LASTKEY function reads whether that key was pressed. The following keys (and their LASTKEY values) can be used to exit a full-screen command without the user having to press Enter through each field: PgDn (3), PgUp (18), Ctrl – End (23), and Esc (27):

```
*     Mailing List Program
PRN = "P"
ZSORT = "A"
@ 1,1 SAY "Press ESC to Return to Main Menu"
@ 3,1 SAY "Display on Printer or Screen? (P/S) " GET prn
@ 5,1 SAY "Sort by Zip or Alpha? (A/Z) " GET Zsort
READ
IF LASTKEY( ) = 27
   CLEAR
```

```
    ? "Returning to Master Menu"
    RETURN
ENDIF
DO MAILLIST
```

See also: ON KEY p. 202
         INKEY( ) p. 318
         READKEY( ) p. 355

LEFT(expC,expN)

Description The LEFT( ) function returns the first *expN* letters of a string.

Operational rules The LEFT( ) function returns a substring of *expC*. This can be helpful in retrieving first initials of names, or printing variables on forms where there is not enough room for the entire string to print. There is no difference between the LEFT( ) function and the SUBSTR*(string,start- number,length)* function where the *start-number* is 1.

If the number *expN* is larger than the length of the string, the result is the string itself. If the number is 0, the function returns the null string.

FoxPro, unlike previous versions, allows you to perform the LEFT( ) function on a memo field.

Example

```
? LEFT("California",5)
Calif
? LEFT("California",0)
    (a null string)

MM = "11-Nov-89"
? LEFT(MM,2)
11
? LEFT("Hello",9)
Hello
```

See also: SUBSTR ( ) p. 372
         RIGHT( ) p. 360

LEN(expC)

Description The LEN function returns the number of letters in a string.

Operational rules The LEN( ) function is often used with coding schemes such as product codes, where codes of one length are treated differently than codes of another length. LEN( ) can also be used to check data entry that should be a certain length, such as zip codes or employee numbers.

A null string returns the length of 0. The LEN( ) of a database field will always be the length of the field itself. To calculate the length of the entry, take the LEN( ) function of the TRIM( ) of the field.

FoxPro, unlike previous versions, allows you to perform the LEN( ) function on a memo field. LEN( ) returns the exact length of the memo field entry without having to use the TRIM( ) function.

Example The following example assumes that Lname is the name of a field that is 25 characters long.

```
? Lname
Smith
? LEN(Lname)
    25
? LEN(TRIM(Lname))
    5
```

See also: TRIM( ) p. 382

LIKE(expC,expC)

Description LIKE returns a .T. if the two character expressions match. The first expression, however, can contain wildcard operators.

Operational rules The first character expression can include any combination of the two wildcards:

* *   Represents any group of characters.
* ?   Represents any one character.

For instance, the string SM?TH* represents SMITH, SMOTHERS, SMITHSONIAN, and SMYTHE.

Unlike DOS, which uses the same wildcard operators, the asterisk (*) can be placed anywhere within the string. DOS only allows the asterisk at the end of the string. For instance, SM*TH represents both SMITH and SMOOTH.

The LIKE( ) function returns logical true (.T.) if the two strings match. The function is case sensitive, so SM?TH does not match Smith. The SOUNDEX( ) function is like this function, except it compares the SOUNDEX codes attributed to each character expression to estimate how much the two strings sound alike.

Examples

```
. ? LIKE("Go?f*","Golfing")
.T.
. ? LIKE("GO?F*","GOOFIER")
.T.
. ? LIKE("GO?F?","GOOFIEST")
.F.
```

```
. ? LIKE("Go?f*","GOOFIER")
.F.
. USE Clients
. LIST LNAME, FNAME FOR LIKE("J*NSON*",LNAME)
 4    JOHNSON    JILL
 8    JONSON     JANE
10    JANSONS    JAMES
20    JENSON     JULIE
```

See also: SOUNDEX( ) p. 368

LINENO( )

Description   LINENO returns the number of the next line of a program that is about to occur.

Operational rules   The LINENO( ) function is useful in two situations:

1. The ON ERROR command.
2. The Debug window.

Use LINENO( ) with the ON ERROR command when an error is trapped. Using LINENO( ), the error routine can display the line number where the error occurred.

Debug is a full-screen environment that can be displayed while running a program. Debug displays a variety of information and can be very helpful in catching programming errors. When the LINENO( ) function is used in the Breakpoint window of the Debug environment, control is returned to the Debug window at the bottom of the screen.

Examples   The following program calls an error routine command named Errtrap:

```
Mailprog.prg
ON ERROR DO Errtrap
USE Maillist
DO WHILE .NOT. EOF( )
   ? Lname, Fname
   SKIP
ENDDO

Errtrap.prg
CLEAR
? "An error has just occurred. The error is:",MESSAGE( )
? "and it occurred on line", LINENO( )
WAIT
RETURN TO MASTER
```

The routine Errtrap is automatically called any time an error occurs. The MESSAGE( ) function displays the error message, while LINENO( ) shows the line number that the error occurred in. The user then returns to the main program that called Mailprog.prg.

See also: ON ERROR p. 200

LOCFILE(expC)

Optional   LOCFILE(*expC,file extension list,open file dialog prompt*)

Description   The LOCFILE( ) function locates a file on the disk and returns the name with its path.

Operational rules   The function returns the name of the file chosen, returned as a character string. If no file is chosen, it returns a null string.

The first parameter, *expC*, can include a path or not. If the file is not found in the designated path, FoxPro searches the default directory and then the FoxPro path. If the file cannot be found, it displays the Open File dialog box, allowing the user to search for it.

The second parameter, *file extension list*, might be one or more extensions that determine the types of files to be listed. If more than one extension is listed, separate them with semicolons (;). The extension parameter must be surrounded by quotes (''). To display all files in the directory, use the null string ('''') for this parameter. DOS wild cards (* and ?) can be used in the file extension list.

The third optional parameter is a message to display above the dialog box. This parameter must be a character string.

Use the function GETFILE( ) to bring up the Open File dialog box automatically.

See also: GETFILE( )   p. 315

LOG(expN)

Description   The LOG function returns the number e base x, or natural logarithm.

Operational rules   e is approximately 2.7182818. The LOG( ) function returns:

e^x

or, in English: e raised to the x power. A zero or negative value returns an error message. The EXP( ) function is the inverse of the natural logarithm.

Examples

. ? LOG(5)
  1.61
. ? LOG(− 5)
  error message
. ? LOG(2.7182818)
  1.02

See also: EXP( ) p. 302

LOG10(*expN*)

Description   The LOG10( ) function returns the base 10 exponent of the numeric expression x. This is called the *command logarithm*.

Operational rules   The LOG10( ) function returns x in the following formula:

expN = 10^x

For instance, the logarithm of 100 is 2, because 10^2 is 100.

A zero or negative value returns an error message.

Examples

. ? LOG10(5)
  0.70
. ? LOG10(100)
  2.00

To calculate the antilog of an expression:

. Mem = LOG10(3) + LOG10(3)
  .95
. ? 10^ Mem
  9

See also: EXP( ) p. 302

LOWER(*expC*)

Description   The LOWER( ) function converts all the letters in a string to lowercase letters.

Operational rules   The companion function is UPPER( ), which converts all letters in the expression to uppercase. Numbers and other nonalphabetical characters are not affected.

Examples

? LOWER("Hello")
hello
? LOWER("HELLO")
hello

To convert a string to proper case (first letter uppercase, and all other letters lowercase):

Fname = "JOHN"
? UPPER(LEFT(Fname,1)) + LOWER(SUBSTR(Fname,2))
John

See also: SUBSTR( ) p. 372
            UPPER( ) p. 383

LTRIM(*expC*)

Description   The LTRIM( ) function removes all leading spaces from a string.

Operational rules   The companion function is TRIM( ), which removes all trailing blanks from an expression. The LTRIM( ) function is often used to trim off leading spaces created by the STR( ) function which converts numbers to a character string.

Examples

? LTRIM(" Hello")
Hello

? LEN(TRIM(LTRIM(" Hello ")))
5

Donation = 500
? "Thank you for the donation of $" + LTRIM(STR(Donation)) + " to us."
Thank you for the donation of $500 to us.

See also: TRIM( ) p. 382
            STR( ) p. 370

LUPDATE( )

Optional   LUPDATE(*alias* or *expN*)

Description   The LUPDATE( )function returns the date that the file was last updated.

Operational rules The LIST FILES command shows the last date that a database file was updated (as well as the number of records and the byte size of the database). The DIR command from DOS shows the same date.

Because the date is based on the DOS system date, the computer must have a battery clock or the date must be set with the DATE command. Otherwise, the date will reflect the DOS BIOS date, which is January 1, 1980, in many computers.

LUPDATE( ) returns the last update date of the current file, unless an argument is provided. The optional *alias* can be either the alias name or work area. Work areas are designated from 1 through 10, or A through J. If no file is open in the designated area, LUPDATE( ) returns a blank date.

Examples This program displays the last date that the file was updated, and verifies it with the user, before continuing the program:

```
USE Maillist
? "This file was last updated on ", LUPDATE( )
WAIT
DO Mailedit
```

See also: DBF( ) p. 293
         RECCOUNT( ) p. 357

MAX(*expr,expr* ...)

Description The MAX( ) function compares a list of expressions, and returns the largest value. The arguments can be numeric, character, or date.

Operational rules When the arguments are dates, the later date is considered greater. When the arguments are strings, its value is designated by its ASCII code value. Therefore, S is greater than A, and a is greater than Z.

To calculate the maximum value of a field in a FoxPro file, use the MAX argument of the CALCULATE command.

Examples

```
Max_wage = 45000
Income = 60000
? MAX(Max_wage,Income)
60000

? MAX("Apple","Banana")
Banana
? MAX("Pear","banana")
banana
```

The following function displays 12/25/89 until the system date is set to a date later than December 25, 1989:

> ? MAX(DATE( ),{12/25/89})
> *12/25/89*

See also: MIN( ) p. 335

MDX(*expN*)

Optional MDX(*expN,alias*)

Description MDX returns the name of the multiple index (.CDX) file in the current work area, or a specified work area. The argument *expN* designates the index order number.

Operational rules Each index file is given an order number, depending on the order that it was opened. The SET INDEX TO and USE INDEX commands open the indexes. The structural index file (same name as the data file) is 1.

If the number in the argument is larger than the number of index files open, then MDX( ) returns a null string. MDX( ) returns the name of appropriately numbered index in the current file, unless a second argument is provided. The optional alias can be either the alias name or work area. Work areas are designated from 1 through 25, or A through J. If no file is open in the designated area, MDX( ) returns a null string. If the designated alias name does not exist, MDX( ) returns an error message.

The CDX( ) function is equivalent to MDX( ).

Examples

> . USE Maillist INDEX Name,Zip,Code
> . ? MDX(1)
> *NAME.NDX*
> . SET ORDER TO 2
> . ? NDX(1)
> *ZIP.NDX*

See also: SET ORDER TO p. 258
          USE p. 241

MDY(*expD*)

Description MDY converts the expression, entered as a date, to a string that looks like a date in the written format Month, Day, Year (such as September 16, 1990).

Operational rules The character string returned by the MDY function only shows two digits for the year, unless the SET CENTURY command is ON.

The three ways to enter a date as an argument are:

1. Enclose the date in curly brackets: {12/5/89}
2. Use the CTOD function: CTOD("12/5/2010")
3. Reference a field name or memory variable.

The date is assumed to be in the 1900s when two digits are used for the year, otherwise you must enter four digits for the year. Any date between January 1, 1582, and December 31, 9999, can be used.

Examples

. ? MDY(DATE( ))
September 16, 89
. SET CENTURY ON
. ? MDY({09/16/89})
September 16, 1989

. HEADING = "Date: " + MDY(Repdate) + "   MONTHLY REPORT"
. ? HEADING
Date: February 20, 1989   MONTHLY REPORT

See also: SET CENTURY p. 247
    CTOD( ) p. 291
    DATE( ) p. 292

MEMLINES(*memo field*)

Description MEMLINES returns the number of lines in the memo of the current record.

Operational rules The argument is the name of the memo field and can include an alias. MEMLINES( ) returns the number of lines of the memo at the current record, so the pointer must be set at the desired record.

The command SET MEMOWIDTH TO determines the width of the memo display. FoxPro automatically word wraps the memo according to the MEMOWIDTH. The default is 50 characters. When the memowidth is changed, the memo is automatically displayed with the new margin, so the MEMLINES( ) might also change.

Notice that the argument is not a character expression. It is the name of a field, so it does not have to be surrounded by quotes. Therefore, if you are using a memory variable as the expression, you can use the macro substitution sign (&).

Examples

```
. USE Maillist
. ? Comments
```
    Joe's Garage is one of our happiest clients.
They may always be used as a referral, although try not to give their name out more than once a month.

```
. ? MEMLINES(Comments)
3

. SET MEMOWIDTH TO 30
```
    Joe's Garage is one of
our happiest clients. They may
always be used as a referral,
although try not to give their
name out more than once a
month.

```
. ? MEMLINES(Comments)
6
. Mfield = "Comments"
. ? MEMLINES(&Mfield)
6
```

See also: SET MEMOWIDTH p. 257

MEMORY( )

Description   MEMORY returns the amount of RAM available in the current application.

Operational rules   The MEMORY( ) function returns the amount of RAM available in units of 1024 bytes (or 1 kilobyte). For instance, a MEMORY( ) of 5 is equal to 5 kilobytes, or 5125 RAM.

The three instances when FoxPro might need additional RAM are:

1. Applications that use menus and windows.
2. Extra memory must be allocated for some arrays.
3. The RUN/! command, which must load Command.com, needs an additional 25 kilobytes of memory.

The companion function to MEMORY( ) is DISKSPACE( ), which returns the disk space available.

Examples

```
. ? MEMORY( )
60
```

See also: DISKSPACE( ) p. 295

MENU( )

Description   MENU returns the name of the most recent menu activated.

Operational rules   The command that activates a bar menu is ACTIVATE MENU. A *bar menu* is a menu that pops up on the screen. The user chooses the desired option by navigating through menu with the arrow keys and pressing Enter at the desired pad. The MENU( ) function returns the name of only the most recent menu activated.

To create a bar menu, you must use the commands DEFINE MENU and DEFINE PAD. DEFINE MENU assigns a name to the menu, and DEFINE PAD is used to define the prompt and coordinates of each pad within the menu.

The companion function PAD( ) returns the name of the pad most recently chosen.

Examples

```
. ? MENU( )
Main
```

See also: ACTIVATE MENU p. 141
          DEFINE MENU p. 166
          DEFINE PAD p. 167

MESSAGE( )

Description   MESSAGE returns the message corresponding to the error that has just occurred. The ON ERROR command must be active for this function to work.

Operational rules   The ON ERROR command is given at the beginning of a program, but waits until an error occurs before performing. When ON ERROR is triggered by an error, the command can call a program, a procedure, or a user-defined function. The syntax for the command is ON ERROR *command*.

The MESSAGE( ) function can be used in conjunction with the program that ON ERROR branches to. The program can display directions to the user, including the error that occurred. The ERROR( ) function is similar to MESSAGE( ), except it returns the error number.

If the ON ERROR command is not active, errors in programs behave like errors at the dot prompt, with the Cancel, Edit, Help message. To clear the message returned by MESSAGE( ), use the RETURN or RETRY command.

Examples   The following program calls an error routine command named Errtrap:

Mailprog.prg

ON ERROR DO Errtrap
USE Maillist
DO WHILE .NOT. EOF( )
  ? Lname, Fname
  SKIP
ENDDO
Errtrap.prg

CLEAR
? "The following error has occurred. Please call your service "
? "representative if you do not understand it."
?
? "Error Message: " + MESSAGE( )
?
? "You will be returning to the main menu."
WAIT
RETURN TO MASTER

See also: ON ERROR p. 200
           RETRY p. 223
           RETURN p. 224
           ERROR( ) p. 300

MIN(*exp,exp* ...)

Description   The MIN( ) function compares a list of expressions and returns the smallest value. The arguments can be numeric, character, or date.

Operational rules   When the arguments are dates, the less recent date is considered less. When the arguments are strings, its value is designated by its ASCII code value. Therefore, *A* is less than *K*, and *Z* is less than *a*.

To calculate the minimum value of a field in a FoxPro file, use the MIN argument of the CALCULATE command.

Examples

Min_ wage = 45000
Income = 60000

```
? MIN(Max_wage,Income)
    45000
? MIN("Apple","Banana")
Apple
? MIN("apple","Banana")
Banana
```

The following function displays today's date until the system date is set beyond December 25, 1989. It will display that date from then on:

```
? MIN(DATE( ),{12/25/89})
09/16/89
```

See also: MAX( ) p. 330

MLINE(*memo field,expN*)

Optional   MLINE(*memo field,expN,offset from beginning of the line*)

Description   MLINE returns a specific line of text in the memo of the current record.

Operational rules   The arguments are the name of the memo field and the line number to be returned. MLINE returns a character string. As always when working with MEMO fields, the pointer must be set at the desired record.

If the optional third argument is used, the offset from the beginning of the memo field is used for finding the line to return. This is most often used in conjunction with _mline system function. _mline tracks the offset from line one of the memo each time that MLINE( ) is called. Using _mline as the optional third argument (and 1 as the second argument, *expN*) greatly speeds up the performance of the MLINE( ) function.

The command SET MEMOWIDTH TO determines the width of the memo display. FoxPro automatically word wraps the memo according to the MEMOWIDTH. The default is 50 characters. When the memowidth is changed, the memo is automatically displayed with the new margin, so the contents of each line is altered, changing the value returned by MLINE.

Examples

```
USE MAILLIST
. ? Comments
    Joe's Garage is one of our happiest clients. They may always be used as a
referral, although try not to give their name out more than once a month.

. ? MLINE(Comments,2)
```

referral, although try not to give their name out more than once a month.

```
. SET MEMOWIDTH TO 30
. ? Comments
    Joe's Garage is one of our happiest clients.
They may always be used as a referral, although try not to
give their name out more than once a month.

. ? MLINE(Comments,2)
They may always be used as a referral, although try not to
```

The following program allows the user to print a memo field on a 4-inch long index card. If the field is too long, it pauses and lets the user put a new card in the printer.

```
USE Maillist
SET MEMOWIDTH TO 55
Line = 1
SET PRINT ON
DO WHILE Line < MEMLINES(Comments)
  ? MLINE(Comments,Line)
  Line = Line + 1
  IF Line = 20
    EJECT
    SET PRINT OFF
    ? "Put a new index card in"
    WAIT
    SET PRINT ON
    Line = Line + 1
  ENDIF
ENDDO
```

See also: SET MEMOWIDTH p. 257
             MLINE( ) p. 336

MOD(*expN,expN*)

Description   The MOD(x,y) function returns the remainder of x/y (*modulo*). For instance, the MOD(5,2) is 1 because 5 divided by 2 equals to 2 with 1 left over.

Operational rules   The MOD function can be helpful in finding every nth occurrence of a number. For instance, in the sequence 1, 6, 11, 16, etc., each of the numbers have a modulo of 1 when y is 5.

y cannot be a 0 because a denominator of zero is an infinite number. If y is negative, then the MOD( ) returns a negative answer.

Examples

```
. ? MOD(5,2)
    1
. ? MOD(11, - 3)
   - 1
```

See also: FLOOR( ) p. 309

MONTH(expD)

Description   MONTH returns the number of the month, given a date expression.

Operational rules   The three ways to enter a date as an argument are:

1. Enclose the date in curly brackets: {12/5/89}
2. Use the CTOD function:CTOD("12/5/2010")
3. Reference a field name or memory variable.

The date is assumed to be in the 1900s when two digits are used for the year, otherwise you must enter four digits for the year.

Examples

```
. ? MONTH({9/6/89})
9
. ? MONTH(CTOD("12/25/89"))
12
```

See also: CTOD( ) p. 291
            DAY( ) p. 293

MRKBAR(pop-up name,expN)

Description   MRKBAR returns .T. if the option positioned at *expN* is marked.

Operational rules   An option within a pop-up is marked using the SET MARK OF command. The pop-up is named with the command DEFINE POPUP. The *expN* is the number of the bar in the pop-up.

See also: SET MARK OF p. 257

MRKPAD(*menu name,pad name*)

Description   MRKPAR returns .T. if option *pad name* is marked.
Operational rules   A pad within a menu is marked using the SET MARK OF command. The menu is named with the command DEFINE MENU. The pad is named with the command DEFINE PAD.

See *also*:   SET MARK OF p. 257

NDX(*expN*)

Optional   NDX(*expN, alias*)
Description   NDX returns the name of the index file in the current work area or a specified work area. The argument *expN* designates the index order number.
Operational rules   Each index file is given an order number, depending on the order that it was opened. The SET INDEX TO and USE INDEX commands open the indexes. The first file in the list is the master index, or 1. The SET ORDER TO command can be used to change the order of currently opened index files.

If the number in the argument is larger than the number of index files open, then NDX( ) returns a null string. NDX( ) returns the name of appropriately numbered index in the current file, unless a second argument is provided. The optional alias can be either the alias name or work area. Work areas are designated from 1 through 25, or A through J. If no file is open in the designated area, NDX( ) returns a null string. If the designated alias name does not exist, NDX( ) returns an error message.

Use CDX( ) or MDX( ) to return the names of multiple index files.

Examples

```
. USE Maillist INDEX Name,Zip,Code
. ? NDX(1)
NAME.NDX
. SET ORDER TO 2
. ? NDX(1)
ZIP.NDX
```

See *also*:   SET ORDER TO p. *258*
             USE p. *240*

NUMLOCK( )

Optional NUMLOCK(expL)

Description This function automatically turns on and off the NumLock key (to set NumLock on or back to NumLock off).

Operational rules NUMLOCK(.T.) switches the NumLock on, and NUMLOCK(.F.) switches it off. If the parameter is given, NUMLOCK( ) returns the mode before the change. If the optional parameter is left out, NUMLOCK( ) returns the state of NumLock without changing mode.

Examples

```
.? NUMLOCK(.T.)
.T.     (if NumLock was already on)
.? NUMLOCK( )
.F.     (if NumLock is off)
```

See also: CAPSLOCK( ) p. 285

OBJNUM(*var*)

Optional OBJNUM(var,expN)

Description The OBJNUM( ) function returns a GET object's number.

Operational rules When the @...GET and @...EDIT commands are used, each object (field, check box, push button, pop-up, etc.) is numbered in the order that the cursor passes through it using a READ statement. OBJNUM returns the number, given the variable or field name.

The optional argument *expN* is the READ level of the object. Multiple READ levels occur when UDFs are used in the WHEN or VALID clauses. If the UDF contains a READ, there are now multiple READs. FoxPro supports up to four nested READs.

See also: @SAY... GET p. 125

OCCURS(*expC,expC*)

Description The OCCURS( ) function returns the number of times a substring occurs within a character string.

Operational rules The arguments are entered as OCCURS(*substring, character string*). If the substring does not occur within the character string, the function returns zero.

Examples

```
. ? OCCURS("p","apple")
2
. ? OCCURS(" ",City)      && where City is "San Juan Capistrano"
2
```

See also: AT( ) p. 280

ORDER( )

Optional   ORDER(alias)

Description   ORDER returns the name of the master index file or master tag in the current work area or a specified work area.

Operational rules   Each index file is given an order number, depending on the order that it was opened. The SET INDEX TO and USE INDEX commands open the indexes. The first file in the list is the master index or 1. The SET ORDER TO command can be used to change the order of currently opened index files or order of tags within a multiple index file.

The master file or tag is the key used with the FIND and SEEK commands. It also determines the sorted order when using LIST or SKIP.

ORDER( ) returns the name of the primary index or tag in the current file, unless a second argument is provided. The optional alias can be either the alias name or work area. Work areas are designated from 1 through 25, or A through J. If no file is open in the designated area, ORDER( ) returns a null string. If the designated alias name does not exist, ORDER( ) returns an error message.

Examples

```
. USE Maillist INDEX Name,Zip,Code
. ? ORDER( )
Name
. SET ORDER TO 2
. ? ORDER("Maillist")
Zip
```

See also: SET ORDER TO p. 258
            USE p. 240

OS( )

Description   OS returns the name and version of the operating system that FoxPro is running on.

Operational rules   This function can be used to determine whether certain DOS operations can be performed with the RUN/! command.

Examples

```
. ? OS( )
DOS 3.10
```

See also: VERSION( ) p. 385

PAD( )

Description   PAD returns the name of pad most recently selected from a bar menu.

Operational rules   The command that activates a bar menu is ACTIVATE MENU. A bar menu is a menu that pops up on the screen and the user chooses the desired option by navigating through the menu with the arrow keys, and pressing Enter at the desired pad. The PAD( ) function returns the name of only the most recent pad activated.

To create a bar menu, you must use the commands DEFINE MENU and DEFINE PAD. DEFINE MENU assigns a name to the menu, and DEFINE PAD is used to define the prompt and coordinates of each pad within the menu.

The companion function, MENU( ), returns the name of the menu most recently activated.

Examples   This example assumes that a bar menu has been recently activated. The options are Print Report, Listing, and Labels:

```
. ? PAD( )
Labels
```

See also: ACTIVATE MENU p. 141
DEFINE MENU p. 166
DEFINE PAD p. 167

PADC(*expr,expN*)
PADL(*expr,expN*)
PADR(*expr,expN*)

Optional   PAD(expr,expN,expC)

Description   The PAD functions return a string of *expN* length, which displays the expression *expr* with padding. The padding is filled from the left or right, or it is centered, depending on the function used.

Operational rules   PADL( ) pads from the left, PADR( ) from the right, and PADC( ) displays *expr* centered in the padding.

If *expN* is less than the length of *expr*, then the function truncates it to that length. The optional argument *expC* defines the character to use for padding. If it is omitted, the space is used.

The PADC( ) function, which was introduced with FoxPro, can be used in place of the following command to center a title on the screen or on a page (assuming the screen is 80 characters wide):

```
. Mtitle = "This is the Title"
. ? SPACE(40 – LEN(Mtitle)/2)) + Mtitle
                        This is the Title
```

Examples

```
. ? PADC("This is the Title",80)
                        This is the Title

. ? PADC("This is the Title",60," – ")
          ------------------------------------This is the Title------------------------------------

. ? PADL("This is the Title",60,"-")
------------------------------------------------------------------------------------------------------------- This is the Title
```

See also: STUFF( ) p. 371

PARAMETERS( )

Description   PARAMETERS( ) returns the number of parameters passed to the last procedure called.

Operational rules   Programs can call routines, called *procedures*. Procedures can receive parameters passed to them using the PARAMETER command. Parameters can also be passed to user-defined functions, defined with the FUNCTION command.

See also: PARAMETERS p. 209

PAYMENT(*principal,rate,term*)

Description   The PAYMENT function returns the fixed payment on a loan of *principal* at an interest rate of *rate* for *term* periods. This is the function that answers the question, "What will be my monthly payment on a $75,000, 30-year fixed loan with a 10% interest rate?"

Operational rules   The PAYMENT returns the amount of the periodic payment assuming the interest rate and term are in periodic amounts. Because most fixed loans have monthly periods, the interest and term often must be adjusted. For instance, suppose if the payments are to be made monthly, but the interest rate and term are given in annual terms, such as a 10% annual rate for 30 years.

In this case, divide the annual interest rate by 12 and multiply the yearly term times 12. FoxPro uses the following formula to calculate the PAYMENT:

$$\text{princ} * (\text{int}/(1 - (1 + \text{int})^{-n}))$$

where

   princ = principal
   int   = interest rate
   n   = term

As with all financial functions dealing with annuities (fixed payments), payments are assumed to be made at the end of each period. The formula to calculate the term if the payments are made at the beginning of each period is:

   PAYMENT(*princ,rate,term*)/(1 + *rate*)

Example This function calculates the monthly payment on a 30-year fixed rate loan of $75,000 at a 10% interest rate:

   . Pmt = PAYMENT(75000,.1/12,30*12)
   658.18

The next formula calculates the total paid over the 30 years: pmt * term * 12. Running this calculation is not advised for those with weak stomachs or newly purchased homes:

   . ? Pmt * 12 * 30
   236944.32

See also: PV( ) p. 352

PCOL( )

Description   PCOL( ) returns the column number position where the printer head currently is.

Operational rules   The PCOL( ) function is used in conjunction with the @...SAY...GET command that places a display in a particular position on the screen or printed page. The @ command places the display on the screen using the following syntax:

   @ *row,col* SAY *expression*

For instance, the command:

   @ 5,30 SAY "HI THERE"

would display the words HI THERE on the fifth row on the screen, in column 30. When the command SET DEVICE TO PRINT has been given, all @...SAY commands are sent to the printer.

After each @...SAY, the cursor is then positioned at the end of the expression. Therefore, the PCOL( ) function would return 38 after printing the expression in the example. This allows you to use the PCOL( ) function to display an expression on the screen relative to another expression.

Examples The following program prints a message after the expression Mstring (assuming it is of variable lengths). If Mstring places the cursor too far to the right, the program places the page number on the next line, otherwise it is placed right next to Mstring:

```
SET DEVICE TO PRINT
@ 5,30 SAY Mstring
IF PCOL( ) < 68
    @ 5, PCOL( ) SAY "Page: " + PAGNUM
ELSE
    @ 6, 1 SAY "Page: " + PAGNUM
ENDIF
```

This program prints a string continuously until it reaches the end of the screen:

```
DO WHILE PCOL( ) < 75
    @ 10, PCOL( ) + SAY Mstring
ENDDO
```

The operator $ can also be used with the @...SAY...GET command interchangeably with PCOL( ). For instance, the following commands are valid:

```
@ 5,30 SAY Mstring
@ 5, $ SAY "Y)es or N)o"
```

The difference between PCOL( ) and $ is that PCOL( ) can also be used in a conditional statement, as in the last two examples. Also, $ can be used to relatively address the screen or printer, while PCOL( ) can only be used with the printer, and COL( ) can only be used with the screen.

See also: COL( ) p. 289
            PROW( ) p. 350

PI( )

Description The PI function returns the number *pi* (approximately 3.1415926). This value is used in engineering and drafting calculations, often in conjunction with trigonometric functions (COS, SIN, ACOS, etc.) The ratio between the circumference of a circle and its diameter is always pi.

Operational rules Because it is a constant, there are no arguments to the PI function. The function is usually entered in formulas, such as:

PI( )*3^2 The area of the circle with radius of 3.
COS(PI( )) The cosine of the half circle.

Examples

```
. SET DECIMALS TO 5
. ? PI( )
3.14159
```

The formula below calculates the area of a circle with a 5 inch radius:

```
. ? PI( ) * 5^2
78.53982
```

See also: COS( ) p. 290
            SIN( ) p. 367

POPUP( )

Description POPUP returns the name of the most recent pop-up menu activated.

Operational rules The command that activates a pop-up menu is ACTIVATE POPUP. A pop-up menu is a menu that pops up on the screen with a specific message. The POPUP( ) function returns the name of only the active pop-up menu. Once the menu is deactivated, it is erased from the screen, and the screen is restored to its previous contents.

To create a pop-up menu, you must use the commands DEFINE POPUP. This command assigns the coordinates and prompts of the menu. To create a pop-up menu where the user can make selections, use the DEFINE BAR command in conjunction with DEFINE POPUP.

The companion function, BAR( ), returns the number of the bar most recently chosen.

Examples

```
. ? POPUP( )
MAIN
```

See also: ACTIVATE POPUP p. 142
            DEFINE POPUP p. 168
            DEFINE BAR p. 163

PRINTSTATUS( )

Description PRINTSTATUS returns logical true (.T.) if the printer is on-line.

Operational rules This function can be used to determine whether a command that sends output to the printer will print. Examples of these commands are SET PRINT ON, SET DEVICE TO PRINT, Ctrl – P, or any of the commands that accept the TO PRINT clause.

The four main reasons that the printer is not on-line are:

1. The printer is not turned on.
2. The printer's on-line toggle is not on.
3. The cable between the printer and computer is disconnected.
4. The computer is not set to send output to the correct printer port. Use the MODE command from DOS to change this setting.

When a print command is given and the printer is not on-line, FoxPro responds with the message Printer not Ready (125) or Printer is either not connected or turned off (126). The PRINTSTATUS( ) function is helpful in circumventing these errors.

Examples The following program checks the print status before running a report to the printer:

```
IF .NOT. PRINTSTATUS( )
    ? "The printer is not on or is not connected. Please turn it "
    ? "on-line, and try to run this option again. "
    WAIT
    RETURN
ENDIF
REPORT FORM Maillist TO PRINT
```

See also: SET PRINTER ON p. 259

PRMBAR(*pop-up name,expN*)

Description PRMBAR returns the prompt of the bar positioned at *expN*.

Operational rules The bar within a pop-up is given a prompt using the DEFINE BAR command. The pop-up is named with DEFINE POPUP. The *expN* is the number of the bar in the pop-up.

Hot keys and other special characters in the prompt are not returned with this function.

See also: DEFINE POPUP p. 168

PRMPAD(*menu name,pad name*)

Description PRMPAD returns the prompt of *pad name* within menu *menu name*.

Operational rules The pad within a menu is given a name using the DEFINE PAD command. The menu is named with DEFINE MENU.

Hot keys and other special characters in the prompt are not returned with this function.

See also: DEFINE PAD p. 167

PROGRAM( )

Description PROGRAM returns the name of the program that was running when the last error occurred.

Operational rules This command can be used at the dot prompt, in a program, or in the debugger. To use PROGRAM( ) from the dot prompt, the program must be suspended. This function is very useful when used in conjunction with the ON ERROR command.

The ON ERROR command is given at the beginning of a program, but waits until an error occurs before performing. When ON ERROR is triggered by an error, the command can call a program, a procedure, or a user-defined function. The syntax for the command is ON ERROR *command*.

The PROGRAM( ) function can be used in conjunction with the program that ON ERROR branches to. The program can display different the program that was being run when the error occurred. The MESSAGE( ) function can also be helpful in this routine, as it displays the error message that would appear if the ON ERROR( ) command was not present.

Examples The following program calls an error routine command named Errtrap:

```
Mailprog.prg
ON ERROR DO Errtrap
USE Maillist
SET PRINT ON
DO WHILE .NOT. EOF( )
   ? Lname, Fname
   SKIP
ENDDO

Errtrap.prg
SET PRINT OFF
```

```
? "An error has occurred. "
? "The error is: ", MESSAGE( )
?
? "It occurred in the program: ",PROGRAM( )
? "on line :",LINENO( )
WAIT
RETURN TO MASTER
```

See also: ON ERROR *p. 200*
           MESSAGE( ) *p. 334*
           LINENO( ) *p. 326*

PROMPT( )

Description PROMPT returns the name of prompt selected in the currently defined pop-up menu.

Operational rules The command that activates a pop-up menu is ACTIVATE POPUP. A pop-up menu is a menu that pops up on the screen with a specific message. To create a pop-up menu, you must use the commands DEFINE POPUP. This command assigns the coordinates and prompts of the menu. To create a pop-up menu where the user can make selections, use the DEFINE BAR command in conjunction with DEFINE POPUP.

The companion function, BAR( ), returns the number of the bar most recently chosen. The function POPUP( ) returns the name of the current pop-up menu. If there is no menu current, PROMPT( ) returns a null string.

Examples

```
. ? PROMPT( )
```
Run Report

See also: ACTIVATE POPUP *p. 142*
           DEFINE POPUP *p. 168*
           DEFINE BAR *p. 163*

PROPER(*expC*)

Description The PROPER( ) function converts the letters in a string so that the first letter of each word is capitalized and all the rest are lowercase.

Operational rules The companion functions are UPPER( ) and LOWER( ), which convert all letters in the expression to upper or lowercase. Numbers and other nonalphabetical characters are not affected.

Examples

. ? PROPER("JULIE ANN SMITH")
Julie Ann Smith

See also: LOWER( ) p. 328
UPPER( ) p. 383

PROW( )

Description   PROW( ) returns the row number position where the printer head currently is.

Operational rules   The PROW( ) function is used in conjunction with the @...SAY...GET command that places a display in a particular position on the screen or printed page. The @ command places the display on the screen using the following syntax:

@ row,col SAY *expression*

For instance, the command:

@ 5,30 SAY "HI THERE"

would display the words HI THERE on the fifth row on the screen, in column 30. When the command SET DEVICE TO PRINT has been given, all @...SAY commands are sent to the printer.

After each @...SAY, the cursor is then positioned at the end of the expression. Therefore, the PROW( ) function would return 5 after printing the expression in the example. This allows you to use the PROW( ) function to keep track of the rows printed and place page breaks accordingly.

Examples   The following program prints a phone directory. Each name uses two lines: One for the name, and one for the phone number. Each time printer head reaches the 55th line, the program ejects a page, and reprints the title:

```
USE Maillist
SET DEVICE TO PRINT
@ 1,1 SAY "Phone Listing "
DO WHILE .NOT. EOF( )
   IF PROW( ) > 55
      EJECT
      @ 1,1 SAY "Phone Listing "
   ENDIF
   @ PROW( )+2,1 SAY Fname + Lname
```

```
    @ PROW( )+1,1 SAY Phone
    SKIP
ENDDO
```

The operator $ can also be used with the @...SAY...GET command interchangeably with PROW( ). For instance, the following commands are valid:

```
DO WHILE .NOT. EOF( )
    @ $+2,1 SAY FNAME + LNAME
    @ $+1,1 SAY PHONE
    SKIP
ENDDO
```

The difference between PROW( ) and $ is that PROW( ) can also be used in a conditional statement, as in the two examples above. Also, $ can be used to relatively address the screen or printer, while PROW( ) can only be used with the printer, and ROW( ) can only be used with the screen.

See also: COL( ) p. 289
          PCOL( ) p. 344
          ROW( ) p. 362

PUTFILE( )

Optional PUTFILE(expC,expC, ...)

Description The PUTFILE( ) function displays the Save As dialog box, allowing the user to choose a file from the list.

Operational rules The function returns the file name chosen, returned as a character string. If no file name is chosen, it returns a null string.

The first optional parameter is a message to display above the dialog box. This parameter must be a character string.

The second optional parameter is the default file name to display in the text box.

The third parameter, expC, is the extension to be used as the default of the file name. If more than one extension is listed, separate them with semicolons (;). The first extension is the one that will be appended, however.

Examples

```
. Data = PUTFILE("Name of ASCII file","MAILLIST","DTA")
. COPY TO &Data SDF
```

See also: GETFILE( ) p. 315

PV(*principal,rate,term*)

Description The @PV function returns the present value on a loan with fixed payments at an interest rate of *rate* for *term* periods.

Operational rules The PV returns the amount of the present value assuming the interest rate and term are in periodic amounts. Because most fixed loans have monthly periods, the interest and term often must be adjusted. For instance, if the payments are monthly, but the interest rate and term are annual, divide the annual interest rate by 12 and multiply the yearly term times 12. FoxPro uses the following formula to calculate the PV:

$$pmt * ((1 - (1 + int)^{-n}))/int$$

where

    pmt = periodic payment
    int = interest rate
    n   = term

As with all financial functions dealing with annuities (fixed payments), payments are assumed to be made at the end of each period. The formula to calculate the term if the payments are made at the beginning of each period is:

PV(*pmt,int,term*)*(1+*int*)

This function is the companion to PMT, which returns the payment given principal, interest and term. The PV answers the question, "How much can I borrow if my loan will be 30-year fixed, 10% interest rate, with a monthly payment of $500?". The other present value function, NPV, finds the value based on an interest rate and a range of variable payments.

Example The following example calculates the principal on a 30-year fixed rate loan with payments of $500 at a 10% interest rate. Because the interest and term are in annual figures, the arguments in the @PV formula divide the annual interest by 12 and multiply the annual term times 12:

    . ? PV(500,.1/12,30*12)
    56975.41

The next example calculates the principal left on the same loan after 2 years of payments:

    . ? PV(500,.1/12,2*12)
    10835.43

RAND( )

Optional RAND(expN)

Description RAND returns a number between 0 and 1 that changes each time you request the function.

Operational rules Because it is a constant, there are no arguments to the RAND function. The optional numeric argument is used as a seed to create a new random number sequence.

The default seed is 100001. Although this function is named after the "random" expression, the sequence of numbers returned from a series of RAND( )'s is always the same if started from the same seed. However, if you use a negative number as the argument, the seed is taken from the system clock.

Although the number returned by RAND is less than 1, you can get larger numbers. First choose the highest and lowest numbers you would like to generate. Create a formula that multiplies RAND by the highest minus lowest number, and then adds the lowest number.

RAND( )   A random number between 0 and 1.
RAND( )*5+1   A number between 1 and 6.

The RAND is used in some statistical modeling applications as well as computer games. (Random numbers are often used to ensure that the game does not start the same way every time.)

Example

```
. ? RAND( )
  0.47
. ? RAND( )
  0.80
. ? RAND( )
  0.88
```

The following sequence starts with a seed taken from the system clock:

```
. ? RAND(-5)
  0.55
. ? RAND( )
  0.62
. ? RAND( )
  0.53
```

RAT(expC,expC)

Optionals RAT(expC,memofield name)
             RAT(expC,expC,expN)

Description The RAT function returns the position where one string appears within another starting from the end of the string.

Operational rules The arguments are entered as RAT(*substring,string to search*). The function is very useful for finding key words within comments or addresses, or for finding the last word in a full name or address. If the substring does not exist in the string, the function returns 0.

The optional third argument, *expN*, searches for the *expN*th occurrence (backwards) of substring in the string to search.

Example

```
. ? RAT(" ","555 Main Street")
      9
```

The example below shows how the RAT can be used in conjunction with the SUBSTR function to extract last names from fields that contain the entire name. The arguments of the SUBSTR are SUBSTR(*string,start number*). Therefore, the function in D1 states, "extract the end of the Name field, starting one character after the position of the last space."

```
. USE CLIENTS
. LIST OFF NAME
NAME
Mr. John Smith
Bonnie Miller
Mr. and Mrs. Tom Jones
. LIST OFF SUBSTR(NAME, RAT(" ",NAME)+1)
Smith
Miller
Jones
. REPLACE ALL LNAME WITH SUBSTR(NAME, RAT(" ",NAME)+1)
```

See also: SUBSTR p. 372

RATLINE(*expC,expC*)

Description The RATLINE function returns the line number in a memo field where the last occurrence of the substring appears.

Operational rules The arguments are entered as RATLINE(*substring,memo-field*). The function is used for finding key words within narrative entries. If the substring does not exist in the memo, the function returns 0.

Use this function in conjunction with the MLINE( ) function, which returns any line from the memo as a character string.

Example The following example assumes that the database has a memo field named Notes:

```
. STORE RATLINE("camp fund",NOTES) TO MEMOLN
    12
. ? MLINE(NOTES,MEMOLN)
```
Phone call 12/15/90: probably the last time we discuss the camp fund

See also: ATLINE( ) p. 282
            MLINE( ) p. 336

RDLEVEL( )

Description   RDLEVEL( ) returns the current READ level.

Operational rules   Multiple READ levels occur when UDFs are used in the WHEN or VALID clauses. When a UDF contains a READ, there are multiple READs. FoxPro supports up to four nested READs.

See also: @SAY...GET p. 125

READKEY( )

Description   READKEY( ) returns a number that represents the most recent key pressed on the keyboard to exit a full-screen command.

Operational rules   The full-screen commands that READKEY can detect are: APPEND, BROWSE, CHANGE, CREATE, EDIT, INSERT, MODIFY, and READ. READKEY( ), like the INKEY( ) function, can detect the exact keystroke pressed (such as a Ctrl key combination, or an arrow key), unlike other interactive commands, such as READ and ACCEPT.

The READKEY function is different than INKEY( ), however, in that it only reads the key pressed in the last full-screen command (such as READ or ACCEPT), while INKEY( ) pauses to receive the keystroke (or captures it during a noninteractive command). The value returned by READKEY is different depending on whether any data was changed during the command. The LASTKEY( ) function, which also captures keystrokes, is different in that it is used with any type of interactive command, such as ACCEPT, and it returns the same value whether or not data was changed.

The following Table 4-2 lists all READKEY return values. Notice that there are only codes for those keystrokes that exit from a full-screen command.

Table 4-2. READKEY return values.

Key	No-update	Update
Backspace, left arrow Ctrl – H, Ctrl – S	0	256
Right arrow, Ctrl – D, Ctrl – L	1	257
Home, Ctrl – A	2	258
End, Ctrl – F	3	259
Up arrow, Ctrl – E, Ctrl – K Shift – Tab	4	260
Down arrow, Ctrl – X, Tab, Ctrl – Enter, Ctrl – J	5	261
PgUp, Ctrl – R	6	262
PgDn, Ctrl – C	7	263
Ctrl – U	10	266
Ctrl – N	11	267
Esc, Ctrl – Q	12	-
Ctrl – End, Ctrl – W	14	270
Enter, Ctrl – <right arrow> Ctrl – M	15	271
Ctrl – Home, Ctrl –]	33	289
Ctrl – PgUp, Ctrl – -	34	290
Ctrl – PgDn, Ctrl – ^	35	291
F1	36	292

Examples The program below instructs the user to press Esc to abort the program and return to the main menu. The READKEY function reads whether that key was pressed.

```
*  Mailing List Program
DO WHILE .T.

  PRN = "P"
  ZSORT = "A"
  @ 1,1 SAY "Press ESC to Return to Main Menu, PgDn for Help"
  @ 3,1 SAY "Display on Printer or Screen? (P/S) " GET PRN
  @ 5,1 SAY "Sort by Zip or Alpha? (A/Z) " GET ZSORT
  READ
  IF READKEY( ) = 12         && if ESC, return to menu
    CLEAR
    ? "Returning to Master Menu"
    RETURN
  ENDIF
  IF READKEY(*) = 7 .OR. READKEY = 263     && if PgDn, run Help
    CLEAR
```

```
        DO HELPER
        LOOP
    ENDIF
    DO MAILLIST
    EXIT
ENDDO
```

See also: ON KEY *p. 202*
INKEY( ) *p. 318*
LASTKEY( ) *p. 323*

RECCOUNT( )

Optional RECCOUNT(*alias*)

Description RECCOUNT returns the number of records in a database file.

Operational rules This function returns the number of records in a file, as displayed on the LIST FILES directory. This is the same number received by running the COUNT command without any options. However, the COUNT command takes a much longer time to return the same answer.

RECCOUNT( ) always returns the total number of records, regardless of whether the commands SET DELETED or SET FILTER have been turned on.

RECCOUNT( ) returns the number of records in the current file unless an argument is provided. The optional *alias* can be either the alias name or work area. Work areas are designated from 1 through 25, or A through J. If no file is open in the designated area, RECCOUNT( ) returns zero. If the designated alias name does not exist, RECCOUNT( ) returns an error message.

Examples The example here assumes that Journal.dbf has 20 records and that Coa.dbf has 8 records:

```
. SELECT A
. USE Coa
. SELECT B
. USE Journal
. ? RECCOUNT( )
  20
. ? RECCOUNT("A")
  8
. ? RECCOUNT(1)
  8
```

See also: DBF( ) *p. 293*
RECSIZE( ) *p. 359*

RECNO( )

Optional RECNO(*alias*)

Description RECNO returns the number of the record where FoxPro is currently positioned.

Operational rules This function returns the record number of the current record, except in the following occasions:

RECNO( ) =	when
0	no current file
1	no records in database
1	record pointer is at BOF( )
RECCOUNT( )+1	record pointer is at EOF( )

RECNO( ) returns the number of records in the current file unless an argument is provided. The optional *alias* can be either the alias name or work area. Work areas are designated from 1 through 25, or A through J. If the designated alias name does not exist, RECNO( ) returns an error message.

Examples

```
.USE Coa
. GO 5
```
COA: Record No 5
```
. ? RECNO( )
    5
. GO BOTTOM
```
COA: Record No 8

See also: DBF( ) p. 293
RECSIZE( ) p. 359

RECNO(0)

Description RECNO(0) is used after a SEEK in an indexed database, where a matching record was not found. RECNO(0) finds the next closest match.

Operational rules This function returns the record number of the record that is closest to the SEEK value.

```
. USE Maillist INDEX Mnames
. SEEK "SMITH"
. ? FOUND( )
.F.
. GOTO RECNO(0)
. ? LNAME
```
SMYTHE

RECSIZE( )

Optional   RECSIZE(alias)

Description   RECSIZE returns the size of a record in the database file.

Operational rules   This function returns the length of a record, which is the total of the lengths of each field plus 1. This is the number displayed during the CREATE or MODIFY STRUCTURE commands. The following formula returns the number of bytes used by the data in the database:

RECCOUNT( ) * RECSIZE( ) + 1

All database files have a header record at the top of the file. The length of the header record is returned with the HEADER( ) function.

RECSIZE( ) returns the length of the records in the current file unless an argument is provided. The optional *alias* can be either the alias name or work area. Work areas are designated from 1 through 10, or A through J. If no file is open in the designated area, RECSIZE( ) returns zero. If the designated alias name does not exist, RECSIZE( ) returns an error message.

Examples

```
. USE Maillist
. LIST STRUCTURE
Structure for database: D:MAILLIST.DBF
Number of data records:    6

Field  Field name   Type       Width
  1    LNAME        Character  10
  2    FNAME        Character  10
** Total **                    21
. ? RECSIZE( )
  21
. FILESIZE = HEADER + (RECSIZE( ) * RECCOUNT( ) + 1)
  225
```

See also: RECCOUNT( ) p. 357

RELATION(*expN*)

Optional   RELATION(expN,alias)

Description   The RELATION function returns the *expN*th relation set into a file.

Operational rules   RELATION( ) returns the relationship as a string. The relationships for all currently open files can also be seen with the DISPLAY STATUS command.

If no file is opened in the current work area or no relations have been set, RELATION( ) returns a null string. The optional *alias* can be either the alias name or work area. Work areas are designated from 1 to 10, or A through J.

Examples

```
. USE MAILLIST IN 1
. USE STATENAM INDEX STATENAM IN 2
. SELE 1
. SET RELATION TO STATE INTO STATENAM

. ? RELATION(1)
STATE
. ? RELATION(1,"STATNAM")
        && null string
```

REPLICATE(*expC,expN*)

Description REPLICATE( ) returns a character string that is *expC*, repeated *expN* number of times.

Operational rules This function is useful when creating lines for report headings and section breaks. The character string can be more than one character, but the resulting character string cannot be more than 254 characters.

The SPACE( ) function is equivalent to using REPLICATE( ) with " " as the character argument.

Examples

```
. ? REPLICATE("-",40)
```

```
. ? REPLICATE("yeah ",3)
yeah yeah yeah

. ? REPLICATE("* ",10)
* * * * * * * * * *
```

See also: SPACE( ) p. 369

RIGHT(*expC,expN*)

Description The RIGHT( ) function returns the last *expN* letters of a string.

Operational rules The RIGHT( ) function returns a substring of *expC*. There is no difference between the RIGHT( ) function and the SUBSTR(*string,start-number,length*) function where the start-number is the *expN*, and the length is to the end of the string.

If the number *expN* is larger than the length of the string, the result is the string itself. If the number is 0, the function returns the null string.

FoxPro, unlike previous versions, allows you to perform the RIGHT( ) function on a memo field.

Example

```
? RIGHT("California",5)
     ornia
? RIGHT("California",0)
       (null string)

MM = "11-Nov-89"
? RIGHT(MM,2)
89

? RIGHT("Hello",9)
Hello
```

See also: LEFT( ) p. 324
            SUBSTR( ) p. 372

ROUND(*expN,expN*)

Description   The ROUND function returns the number *expN* rounded to n number of decimal places.

Operational rules   The first argument is the number that you are rounding. The second argument is the number of decimal places to be rounded.

To truncate at the decimal (always rounding down), use the INT( ) function. Numbers display with less decimal places (see SET DECIMAL TO), but they calculate the decimals that do not show.

If the second argument is a negative number, the number rounds to multiples of 10, 100, etc. For instance, rounding to −1 places returns a multiple of 10, and rounding to −2 places returns a multiple of 100.

Example

```
. ? ROUND(5.22,0)
     5
. ? ROUND(5.29,1)
     5.3
. ? ROUND(− 5.22,0)
     −5
. ? ROUND(8, − 1)
     10
. ? ROUND(125, − 2)
     100
```

See also: INT( ) p. 319
SET DECIMAL TO p. 251

ROW( )

Description ROW( ) returns the row number position where the cursor is currently positioned.

Operational rules The ROW( ) function is used in conjunction with the @...SAY...GET command that places a display in a particular position on the screen or printed page. The @ command places the display on the screen using the following syntax:

@ row,col SAY expression

For instance, the command:

@ 5,30 SAY "HI THERE"

would display the words HI THERE on the fifth row on the screen, in column 30.

After each @...SAY, the cursor is then positioned at the end of the expression. Therefore, the ROW( ) function would return 5 after printing the expression in the example. This allows you to use the ROW( ) function to keep track of the rows displayed on the screen.

Examples The following program displays a list of information on the screen. Each name can use one or two lines: If the name does not have a phone number, the program does not print one. Each time the screen fills with names down to row 22, the program pauses, and waits for the user to press a key to continue.

```
USE Maillist
@ 1,1 SAY "Mailing List "
DO WHILE .NOT. EOF( )
   IF ROW( ) > 22
      WAIT
      CLEAR
      @ 1,1 SAY "Mailing List "
   ENDIF
   @ ROW( )+2,1 SAY Fname + Lname
   IF Phone < >
      @ ROW( )+1,1 SAY Phone
   ENDIF
   SKIP
ENDDO
```

The operator $ can also be used with the @...SAY...GET command interchangeably with ROW( ). For instance, the following commands are valid:

```
DO WHILE .NOT. EOF( )
   @ $+2,1 SAY FNAME + LNAME
   @ $+1,1 SAY PHONE
   SKIP
ENDDO
```

The difference between ROW( ) and $ is that ROW( ) can also be used in a conditional statement, as in the two previous examples. Also, $ can be used to relatively address the screen or printer, while PROW( ) can only be used with the printer, and ROW( ) can only be used with the screen.

See also: COL( ) p. 289
PCOL( ) p. 344
PROW( ) p. 350

RTOD(*expN*)

Description   RTOD converts a number representing an angle measured by radians into degrees.

Operational rules   Fractions of a degree, usually represented by minutes and seconds, are to be represented by decimals. For instance, 45 minutes is depicted as .75 degrees.

The figure in the ACOS( ) section shows a circle with points marked in radians (0 to pi). This helps illustrate the conversion of degrees to radians.

Use the SET DECIMALS command to change the number of decimals that appear in the answer. The DTOR( ) function is used to conversely change degrees to radians.

Examples

```
. ? RTOD(PI( )/2)
  90
. ? X1 = 45.75
  45.75
. ? RTOD(X1)
  2621.28
```

See also: ACOS( ) p. 271
DTOR( ) p. 297
SET DECIMALS p. 251

RTRIM(*expC*)

Description The RTRIM( ) function removes all trailing spaces from a string.

Operational rules The RTRIM( ) function is often used to trim off the blanks at the end of a field, because the display commands do not do this automatically. It is also often used with the SEEK command to ensure that there are no blanks at the end of the string being searched for.

The only command that automatically trims trailing spaces when displaying expressions is the LABEL command.

The companion function to RTRIM( ) is LTRIM( ), which removes all leading spaces from an expression. RTRIM( ) is identical to the TRIM( ) function.

Examples The first example shows how fields are displayed when the RTRIM( ) is not used. The second example shows how RTRIM( ), when used in conjunction with a comma, leaves one space between the two strings. The third example shows how RTRIM( ), when used in conjunction with a plus sign, leaves no spaces between the two strings:

```
. USE Maillist
. ? FNAME,LNAME
```
John   Smith

```
. ? RTRIM(FNAME),LNAME
```
John Smith

```
. ? RTRIM(FNAME)+LNAME
```
JohnSmith

See also: LTRIM( ) p. 329

SCHEME(*expN*)

Optional SCHEME(*expN,expN*)

Description The SCHEME( ) function returns the colors set from the command SET COLOR TO.

Operational rules The argument *expN* refers to the color scheme number. If you omit the optional second argument, it returns the entire color pair listing for the desired scheme. The *expN* in the second argument refers to the pair number in the listing.

Examples

```
. ? SCHEME(1,1)
```
B/R

See also: SET COLOR TO p. 249

SCOLS( )

Description The SCOLS( ) function returns the number of columns on the console currently being used.

Operational rules A standard console displays 80 characters across the screen. However, some programs change the number, usually allowing more than 80 characters to be displayed. This function can be very useful in determining how reports and other listings will be displayed.

See also: SROWS( ) p. 369

SECONDS( )

Description The SECONDS( ) function returns the system time in number of seconds since midnight.

Operational rules Divide the value returned from the SECONDS( ) function by 60 to get the number of minutes since midnight. Divide the value returned by the function by 360 to get the number of hours since midnight.

Examples

. ? SECONDS( )
12099.122

See also: TIME( ) p. 381

SEEK(*expr*)

Optional SEEK(*expr,alias*)

Description The SEEK( ) function looks up a record in an indexed database.

Operational rules The SEEK( ) function returns logical true (.T.) if the expression is found in the index, otherwise it returns false (.F.). At this time, the record pointer is moved to the record that matches, otherwise it is moved to the end of the file (EOF( )).

The SEEK( ) function, which was introduced with FoxPro, can be used in place of the SEEK command, which moves the record pointer, followed by the FOUND( ) function, which states whether a match was found.

SEEK( ) performs the lookup on the current file, unless the second argument is provided. The optional *alias* can be either the alias name or work area. Work areas are designated from 1 to 10, or A through J.

Examples The example is a program that looks for a name in an indexed database, and edits the record that matches. If no records match, a message is displayed. Notice that the SEEK( ) function replaces the use of the SEEK command followed by the FOUND( ) function, as used in previous versions of Fox (FoxPlus and FoxBASE):

```
USE Maillist INDEX Mailname
ACCEPT "Enter Last Name of Person to Edit " TO Mlname
IF SEEK(Mlname)
   EDIT
ELSE
   ? "NO MATCHING RECORDS FOUND!"
   WAIT
ENDIF
```

See also: FOUND( ) p. *310*
SEEK p. *228*

SELECT( )

Description The SELECT( ) function returns the highest work area number that is currently not selected.

Operational rules The use of this function can ensure that the area being selected is not currently being used. SELECT( ) returns the highest unselected work area, with 1 being the lowest and 10 the highest.

If SET COMPATIBLE is off, the SELECT( ) function returns the number of the currently selected work area.

Examples The following example opens two files, and then opens a third file named Batch in the next available work area:

```
. USE Coa IN 10
. USE Jnl IN 2
. ? SELECT( )
9
. USE Batch IN SELECT( )
```

See also: USE p. *240*

SET(expC)

Description The SET( ) function returns the current status of a particular SET command.

Operational rules The argument for this function is the name of the SET command. Examples are: BELL, CARRY, MEMOWIDTH, STATUS, and other SET commands. The argument is not case sensitive.

The SET( ) function returns ON or OFF, depending on the current status of the command. Some SET commands, such as MEMOWIDTH return an integer. For some commands that can be set as an integer or on/off, the function only returns the on/off status. For commands that have a setting other than on/off or an integer, the function returns an error.

Examples

```
. ? SET("memowidth")
   60
. ? SET("STATUS")
ON
. ? SET("Carry")
OFF
```

See also: SET commands chapter 3

SIGN(*expN*)

Description   The SIGN( ) function returns a number that represents whether the argument is a positive number, negative number, or zero.

Operational rules   SIGN( ) returns a 1 for positive numbers, a −1 for negative numbers, and a 0 for zero. This function, which was introduced with Fox-Pro, replaces the following function:

IIF(X > 0,1,IIF(X < 0, − 1,0))

Examples

```
. ? SIGN(55)
   1
. ? SIGN(0)
   0
. ? SIGN(−55)
   −1
```

See also: IIF( ) p. 316

SIN(*expN*)

Description   SIN( ) returns the sine of an angle.

Operational rules   The sine represents the y-axis value at any point of the circle with radius pi/2. Therefore it is always between −1 and 1.

It is often better to use memory variables as the argument, because the function then uses 20-place numeric accuracy. You can change the number of decimal points displayed in the answer with the SET DECIMALS command.

Examples

? SIN(0)
　0
? SIN(PI( )/6)
　.5

See also:　ASIN( ) p. 277
　　　　　ACOS( ) p. 271
　　　　　COS( ) p. 290

SOUNDEX(expC)

Description　The SOUNDEX( ) function returns a code that is used for determining how much two strings sound alike.

Operational rules　In brief, the SOUNDEX( ) code is a four-digit code, made up of the following:

1. The first digit is the first character of the string.
2. After the first digit of the string, all occurrences of the letters a, e, h, i, o, u, w, and y are ignored.
3. It assigns a number to the remaining letters:

   b, f, p, and v = 1
   c, g, j, k, q, s, x, z = 2
   d, t = 3
   l = 4
   m, n = 5
   r = 6

4. If two letters next to each other have the same code, it only uses the code of the first letter.
5. It stops at the first character that is not a letter. If the first character of the string is not a letter, it returns 0000.

The companion function, DIFFERENCE( ), calculates the difference between the SOUNDEX( ) codes of two strings.

Examples

. ? SOUNDEX("HUMDINGER")
H535

You can index a file on the soundex code of a name to help look up names when you do not know the exact spelling:

. USE Clients
. INDEX ON SOUNDEX(Lname) TO Clisound

. SEEK SOUNDEX("Balisteri")
. ? FNAME,LNAME
John Ballestros

See also: DIFFERENCE( ) p. 294

SPACE(*expN*)

Description   The SPACE( ) function returns a string of spaces with length *expN*.

Operational rules   The SPACE( ) function is often used to pad a string on the left so that it displays at a certain position. The argument can be any number between 0 and 254.

Examples   The example displays the character string in the center of an 80-character screen. The PADC( ) function performs this same function:

. Title = "Income Projection"
. Padding = (80/2) – LEN(Title)/2   && PAD = screen/2 – title-length/2
. ? SPACE(Padding) + Title
Income Projection

See also: LEN( ) p. 324

SQRT(*expN*)

Description   The SQRT function returns the square root of the argument.

Operational rules   A negative argument returns an error message, as it is impossible to take the square root of a negative number. Either the ABS or IF functions can be used to circumvent this problem:

SQRT(ABS(Amount))   && Squareroot of the absolute value
IIF(Amount<0,0,SQRT(Amount))   && 0 if Amount < 0

Examples

. ? SQRT(100)
  10.00
. ? SQRT(ABS(–100))
  10.00

See also: ABS( ) p. 269

SROWS( )

Description   The SROWS( ) function returns the number of rows on the console currently being used.

Operational rules A standard console displays 25 rows down the screen. However, some programs change the number, and some special consoles are longer. This function can be very useful in determining how reports and other listings will be displayed depending on the number of rows being displayed.

See also: SCOLS( ) p. 365

STR(*expN*)

Optional   STR(expN,length,decimals)
Description   The STR function returns the number x as a string representing the number.
Operational rules   This function is helpful when used to display a number with a specified width. The *length* argument represents the length of the string, including decimal points and places. If the number is longer than the requested length, the STR( ) function returns asterisks.

The *decimal* argument represents the number of digits left of the decimal point. If the number has more decimal places than requested, STR( ) rounds it.

The default length is 10. The default decimal places is 0.

The companion function is the VAL( ) function, which converts a string to a numeric value.

Example

```
. ? STR(5,6,2)
5.00
. ? STR(5,6)
    5
```

The following example uses the LTRIM( ) (trim off leading blank spaces) to left justify a number.

```
. Owe = 500
. ? "You have 10 days to send the $" + LTRIM(STR(Owe)) + " that you owe."
You have 10 days to send the $500 that you owe.
```

See also: VAL( ) p. 384

STRTRAN(*expC1,expC2,expC3*)

Optional   STRTRAN(expC1,expC2,expC3,expN1,expN2)
Description   The STRTRAN function replaces the occurrences of *expC2* in *expC1* with *expC3*.
Operational rules   STRTRAN( ) performs a "find and replace" function using the following arguments: STRTRAN(*expression to replace in, string to find, string to replace it with*).

The optional first numeric argument tells the function to replace at the *expN1*th occurrence of *expC2* in *expC1*. If it is omitted, the function starts at the first occurrence. The optional second numeric argument tells the function to replace *expN2* times. If it is omitted, the function replaces all occurrences of *expC2*.

Example In the following example, all occurrences of Los Angeles are replaced with L.A. in order to save room for more comment space:

```
. USEMAILLIST
. LIST COMMENTS FOR "LOS ANGELES" $ COMMENTS
```

Record #	COMMENTS
4	OUR DEALER IN LOS ANGELES
6	CONTACT TO LOS ANGELES POLITICIANS
8	VOTED "LOS ANGELES MAN OF THE YEAR"

```
. REPLY all comments with STRTRAN(COMMENTS,"LOS ANGELES", "L.A.")
. LIST COMMENTS FOR "L.A." $ COMMENTS
```

Record #	COMMENTS
4	OUR DEALER IN L.A.
6	CONTACT TO L.A. POLITICIANS
8	VOTED "L.A. MAN OF THE YEAR"

See also: STUFF( ) p. *371*

STUFF(*expC1,expN1,expN2,expC2*)

Description   The STUFF function replaces a portion of *expC1* with *expC2* in a specified position.

Operational rules   STUFF( ) removes the *expN2* number of characters from *expC1*, starting at position *expN1*. Then it takes *expC2*, and places it within *expC1* at the *expN1* position.

If *expN1* is greater than the length of *expC1*, then STUFF appends *expC2* to the end of *expC1*. If *expN2* is zero, then no characters are eliminated from *expC1*, and *expC2* is simply inserted into the string.

The STUFF( ) function, which was introduced with FoxPro, can be used in place of the following command:

```
. Oldstring = "I am happy"
. Newstring = LEFT(Oldstring,5) + " very" + SUBSTR(Oldstring,5)
I am very happy
```

In this case, Oldstring is *expC1*, " very" is *expC2*, and 5 is *expN1*. *expN2* is zero because no characters are eliminated from *expC1*.

The STUFF( ) function is not supported in memo fields.
Example

```
. mm = "I am happy"
. ? stuff(mm,6,0,"very ")
I am very happy
. ? stuff(mm,6,5,"hungry")
I am hungry
```

To replace all occurrences of the word Exxon with Arco in a character field named Desc:

```
. SET FILTER TO "Exxon" $ Desc
. REPLACE Desc WITH STUFF(Desc,AT("Exxon",Desc),5,"Arco")
```

See also: REPLACE p. 220
            LEFT( ) p. 324
            SUBSTR( ) p. 372

SUBSTR(expC,start position)

Optional   SUBSTR(expC,start position,number of characters)
Description   The SUBSTR function returns the rest of the string expC, starting at the *start position*.
Operational rules   If the third argument is given, the SUBSTR( ) function returns a substring of that length. When no third argument is entered, the answer ends at the last character of expC. If the third argument is larger than the number of characters left in the string, then the third argument is ignored. If the number is 0, the function returns the null string.

If the second argument is larger than the number of characters in expC, an error occurs. This is also true of negative numbers in the argument.

FoxPro, unlike previous versions, allows you to perform the SUBSTR( ) function on a memo field.
Example

```
. ? SUBSTR("California",5,3)
for
. ?SUBSTR("California",5)
fornia
. ? SUBSTR("California",0)
    (a null string)
. MM = "11-Nov-89"
. ? SUBSTR(MM,4,3)
Nov
```

See also: LEFT( ) p. 324
RIGHT( ) p. 360

SYS(*expN*)

Description The FoxPro SYS( ) functions each return information regarding system status. The argument is a number that designates the type of information to be obtained.

SYS(1)

This function returns a character string which displays the system date in Julian date form.

    . ? SYS(1)
    2448101
    . ? SYS(10,SYS(1))
    07/28/90

SYS(2)

SYS(2) returns a character string that displays the number of seconds that have passed since midnight.

    . ? SYS(2)
    9235
    . ? VAL(SYS(2))/(60*60)
    2.50
    . ! TIME
    Current time is: 2:30:00

SYS(3)

SYS(3) returns a file name that does not exist in the current directory. Use this function for creating files to ensure that you are not writing over existing files.

    . REPORT FORM MAILLIST TO FILE SYS(3)+".TXT"

SYS(5)

SYS (5) returns the default disk drive. This is set with the SET DEFAULT TO when it is not the drive that FoxPro was logged in from.

```
. SET DEFAULT TO D:\DATAFILE
. ? SYS(5)
D:
```

SYS(6)

SYS(6) returns the device that the SET PRINTER TO command outputs to. The default is PRN:, although it can be set to the screen or to a file.

```
. ? SYS(6)
PRN:
```

SYS(7)

Optional SYS(7,*expN*)

SYS(7) returns the name of the current format (.FMT) file. Use the optional argument to designate a work area other than the current one.

```
. SET FORMAT TO ADDNAMES
. ? SYS(7)
D:\DATAFILE\ADDNAMES
```

SYS(9)

SYS(9) returns the FoxPro serial number as a character string. This is the same number that displays on the initial FoxPro screen.

```
. ? SYS(9)
XPPX100
```

SYS(10)

This function converts a Julian date number, as returned by SYS(1) into a readable date character string. SYS(10) returns the date in MM/DD/YY format.

```
. ? SYS(10,SYS(1))
07/28/90
```

SYS(11,*expD*) or SYS(11,*expC*)

This function converts a date character string, or a date expression into the Julian date number. The number returned is the same as that displayed in the

SYS(1) function for the current date.

```
. ? SYS(11,"7/28/90")
2448101
. ? SYS(11,{7/28/90})
2448101
```

SYS(12)

This function returns the number of available memory as a character string. This is useful before calling an application (such as the RUN/! command) where you need a certain amount of memory to run it. The number is returned in bytes.

SYS(13)

The SYS(13) function tells whether the printer is online. If it is not, it returns the character string OFFLINE.

```
IF SYS(13) = "OFFLINE"
    ? "Please put your printer on-line "
    WAIT
ENDIF
SET PRINT ON
```

SYS(14,*expN*)

Optional SYS(14,*expN*,*expN*)

SYS(14) function shows the key that the specified index file was indexed on. This function displays the same string as that shown in the DISPLAY STATUS command. The first numeric argument, *expN*, is the index file number (the master being 1). The second numeric argument is optional. It designates the work area for the index file. If this is omitted, the current work area is used.

```
. USE MAILLIST INDEX MAILNAME, MAILZIP
. ? SYS(14,1)
LNAME
. SELECT 2
. USE STATENAM
. ? SYS(14,2,1)
ZIP
```

SYS(15,expC1,expC2)

SYS(15) looks up the value of the character string *expC2* in the table file designated in *expC1*. The function returns the value found in the table at the position of *expC2*. This function is most often used when working with foreign letters where the high bit has been set to 1.

SYS(16)

Optional SYS(16,*expN*)

This function returns the name of the program where the error occurred. Use this program in routines that catch errors with the ON ERROR command. The optional argument designates how many programs to go back from the program where the error occurred. Therefore, if the program you are currently running has an error in it, you can display the programs that called this one.

```
. ? SYS(16)
ADDNAME.PRG
. ? SYS(16,1)
EDMENU.PRG
. ? SYS(16,2)
MAINMENU.PRG
```

SYS(17)

SYS(17) returns the number of the processor being used. The most common are 8086/88, 80286, 80386, and 80486.

SYS(18)

This function works exactly like the VARREAD( ) function, which returns the name of the variable that the user was editing immediately before exiting. SYS(18) works in conjunction with the ON KEY = routine command which triggers a program or procedure when a particular key is pressed.

The following program displays context-sensitive help:

```
USE Maillist
ON KEY = 315 DO Helpit
@ 1,1 SAY "Press F1 to get help for a particular field"
@ 3,1 GET Code
@ 4,1 GET Desc
READ
```

```
Helpit.Prg
DO CASE
  CASE SYS(18) = "CODE"
    ? "Help for Code Field"
  CASE SYS(18) = "DESC"
    ? "Help for Desc Field"
ENDCASE
RETURN
```

SYS(23)

SYS(23) returns the character representation of the number of EMS (extended memory) being used by FoxPro. The number will be composed of 16K segments. If no EMS memory is being used, it returns the null string ("").

SYS(24)

SYS(24) returns the character representation of the number of EMS (extended memory) that FoxPro is limited to. The limit of EMS memory is set in the Config.fp file. If no EMS memory limit has been set, it returns the null string ("").

The following functions, SYS(100) through SYS(103) are designed for correcting the settings after an error.

SYS(100)

SYS(100) returns the current setting of the CONSOLE. It either returns ON (the default) or OFF (set with the SET CONSOLE OFF command).

SYS(101)

SYS(101) returns the current DEVICE setting. It either returns SCREEN (the default) or PRINT (set with the SET DEVICE TO command).

SYS(102)

SYS(102) returns the current PRINT setting. It either returns OFF (the default) or ON (set with the SET PRINT ON command).

SYS(103)

SYS(103) returns the current TALK setting. It either returns OFF or ON (set with the SET TALK command).

SYS(2000,*expC*)

Optional SYS(2000,*expC*,1)

SYS(2000) returns the first file that matches the skeleton entered as *expC*. Use the optional argument of 1 to show the next file that matches:

    . ? SYS(2000,"MAILLIST.*")
    MAILLIST.DBF
    . ? SYS(2000,"MAILLIST.*",1)
    MAILLIST.DBT

SYS(2001,*expC*)

Optional SYS(2001,*expC*,1)

This function works much like the SET( ) function, which returns the status of the specified SET option. SYS(2001) is different, however, in that it returns more of the SET options. SET( ) only returns options that have ON/OFF settings.

Use the optional argument of 1 with options that have both an ON/OFF setting and other settings (such as SET ALTERNATE TO *file* and SET ALTERNATE ON). The argument of 1 causes SYS(2001) to return the ON/OFF setting, where omitting the argument returns the other setting.

SYS(2002)

Optional SYS(2001,*expC*,1)

This function turns the cursor on and off. The argument of 1 turns it on. Omitting the argument turns the cursor off.

SYS(2003)

SYS(2003) returns the name of the default drive and directory:

    . ? SYS(2003)
    D:\FoxPro\DATA

SYS(2005)

SYS(2005) returns the name of the currently active resource file.

   . ? SYS(2005)
   D:\FoxPro\FOXUSER.DBF

SYS(2006)

SYS(2006) returns the current graphics card and console being used.

   . ? SYS(2006)
   CGA/Color

SYS(2007,expC)

SYS(2007) returns the checksum value of character string *expC*. Check sums are used in comparing two strings.

SYS(2013)

   SYS(2013) returns the FoxPro System menu names. The string is returned as a space delimited string that contains the names of each menu bar and menu pop-up options. Examples of menu names are _msystem, _mwindow, etc.

SYS(2014,*file name*)

   SYS(2014) returns the minimum file path between the current directory and the file *file name*. To find the relative minimum file path between two files, use SYS(2014,*file 1*,*file 2*).

SYS(2015)

   SYS(2015) returns a unique procedure name. The name is 10 characters and begins with an underscore.

SYS(2016)

   SYS(2016) returns the last SHOW GETS WINDOW window name. SHOW GETS...WINDOW *window name* refreshes GETs in a particular window. SYS(2016) returns the name of the last window used.

TAG(expN)

Optional TAG(.cdx file,expN,alias)

Description TAG returns the tag names from a multiple index file in the current work area, or a specified work area.

Operational rules Each tag in a multiple index file is given an order number, depending on the order that it was created. Use TAG() to return the tag names from within an index. Use NDX() to return index file names.

You only need to use the .cdx file clause if more than one multiple index file is open.

The optional alias can be either the alias name or work area. Work areas are designated from 1 through 25, or A through J. If no file is open in the designated area, TAG() returns a null string. If the designated alias name does not exist, TAG() returns an error message.

See also: CDX( ) p. 286

TAN(expN)

Description TAN() returns the tangent of an angle. The tangent is cos x divided by sin x.

Operational rules A circle is marked with points in radians (0 to pi). The cosine represents the x-axis value at any point, and the sine represents the y-axis value at any point. The tangent, therefore, is @SIN(x)/@COS(x). This ratio can be any number other than PI( )/2 or 3PI( )/2, which have sine values of 0.

Examples

```
. TAN(0)
  0
. TAN(30*PI/180)
  .5
```

See also: COS( ) p. 290
            SIN( ) p. 367

TARGET(expN)

Optional TARGET(expN,alias)

Description The TARGET function returns the file name of the target in the expNth relation set into a file.

Operational rules TARGET() returns the file name as a string. The relationships for all currently open files can also be seen with the DISPLAY STATUS command.

If no file is opened in the current work area or no relations have been set, TARGET( ) returns a null string. The optional *alias* can be either the alias name or work area. Work areas are designated from 1 to 25, or A through J.

Examples

```
. USE MAILLIST IN 1
. USE STATENAM INDEX STATENAM IN 2
. SELE 1
. SET RELATION TO STATE INTO STATENAM
. ? TARGET(1)
STATENAM
. ? TARGET(1,"B")
&& returns null string
```

TIME( )

Description TIME returns the system time as a character string.

Operational rules The system time is kept through DOS and can be set with the TIME command at the DOS prompt. Many computers come with battery clocks that keep the system time current.

The TIME( ) format is hh:mm:ss. Use the SET HOURS command to determine whether the time is displayed on a 12-hour or 24-hour clock.

Examples

```
. ? TIME( )
16:35:36
```

See also: DATE( ) p. 292

TRANSFORM(*exp,picture string*)

Description The TRANSFORM function returns expression *exp* formatted with a PICTURE format.

Operational rules The PICTURE formats are used to display numbers, strings, logicals, and dates in a set format. They are usually used in conjunction with the @...SAY command. Examples of a few picture formats:

Variable	Format	will print as
5000	"###,###.##"	5,000.00
5000	"$ ####.#"	$5000.0
"hello"	"@!"	HELLO

The TRANSFORM function allows these picture formats to be used in commands other than @...SAY. This command is often used with any of the DISPLAY commands, and in the report generator.

Example

```
. MM = 66000
. ? TRANSFORM(MM,"###,###.##")
66,000.00

. PIC = "$ #,###,###"
. ? TRANSFORM(MM,PIC)
$66,000
```

See also: @SAY...GET p. 125

TRIM(expC)

Description   See the RTRIM( ) function.

TYPE(exp)

Description   TYPE returns a code that signifies the type of variable of *exp*.
Operational rules   TYPE( ) returns one of the following codes:

Code	Type of variable
C	Character
N	Numeric
D	Date
L	Logical
M	Memo
U	Undefined

This function is useful when checking whether a certain variable exists in a file.

Examples

```
. USE Mail
. ? TYPE("ZIP")
  C
. MM = TYPE("ZIPCODE")
  U
```

See also: DATE( ) p. 292

UPDATED( )

Description   The UPDATED( ) function tells whether any of the expressions to be edited in the last @...GET statement were changed.

Operational rules This function must be used after the READ command. If any of the variables or fields from the last set of @...GETs were changed, the function returns true (.T.).

Examples The following program has a Lookup Address option. If the user changes anything on the address screen, a field named UPDATE_DAT gets updated with today's date:

```
USE MAILLIST INDEX MAILNAME
@ 3,1 SAY "Lookup Address Screen"
@ 6,1 SAY " Name:" GET NAME
@ 7,1 SAY "Address:" GET ADD
@ 8,1 SAY " City: " GET CITY
@ $,$+2 SAY "State: " GET STATE
@ $,$+2 SAY "Zip: " GET ZIP
READ
IF UPDATED( )
   REPLACE UPDATE_DAT WITH DATE( )
ENDIF
```

See also: READKEY( ) p. 355

UPPER(*expC*)

Description The UPPER( ) function converts all the letters in a string to uppercase letters.

Operational rules The companion function is LOWER( ), which converts all letters in the expression to lowercase. Numbers and other nonalphabetical characters are not affected.

Examples

```
? UPPER("Hello")
HELLO
? UPPER("hello")
HELLO
```

See also: LOWER( ) p. 328

USED(*expr*)

Description The USED( ) function tells whether a database is currently being used in the specified work area.

Operational rules The use of this function can ensure that the area being selected is not currently being used. The argument can be the work area designated by the numbers 1 to 10, or letters A through J.

Examples

```
. USE Coa IN 10
. USE Jnl IN 2
. ? USED(2)
.T.
. ? USED("C")
.F.
```

See also: SELECT( ) p. 366

VAL(expC)

Description The VAL function returns the character *expC* as a number.

Operational rules This function is helpful when used to read the numeric value of a character string. If the string has no numbers in it, the VAL( ) function returns zero. VAL( ) reads the numeric characters in the string until it reaches a nonnumeric character.

The companion function is the STR( ) function, which converts a numeric value to a string. The SET DECIMALS command can be used to change the number of decimal places displayed.

Example

```
. ? VAL("5")
  5.00
. ? VAL("500 West Street")
  500
```

See also: STR( ) p. 370

VARREAD( )

Description The VARREAD( ) function returns the name of the variable that the user was editing immediately before exiting.

Operational rules This function is used in conjunction with the full-screen function @...GET and READ. When the user exits the screen with one of the following keys: Esc, PgDn, Ctrl – End, or ON KEY, the user can be placed in any variable on the screen. The VARREAD( ) function returns a character string of the name of the variable.

This function can be used to create context-sensitive help screens.

Examples The following program displays context-sensitive help.

```
USE Maillist
ON KEY = 315 DO Helpit
```

```
@ 1,1 SAY "Press F1 to get help for a particular field"
@ 3,1 GET Code
@ 4,1 GET Desc
READ

Helpit.Prg
DO CASE
  CASE VARREAD( ) = "CODE"
    ? "Help for Code Field"
  CASE VARREAD( ) = "DESC"
    ? "Help for Desc Field"
ENDCASE
RETURN
```

See also: ON KEY p. 202
              READ p. 216
              READKEY( ) p. 355

VERSION( )

Description   The VERSION( ) function returns the version number of Fox-Pro currently being used.

Operational rules   The version is always the same as the number displayed at the FoxPro sign-on message.

Examples

```
. ? VERSION( )
FoxPro Rev 1.0
```

WCHILD( )

Description   The WCHILD( ) function returns the number and names of child windows.

Operational rules   It is possible to place a window (the child) inside of another window (the parent). To do this, use the IN or IN WINDOW clause in any of the commands that allow a window to be placed within another. The child window must be smaller than the parent and stay within the parent window's boundaries.

If no argument is given, WCHILD( ) returns the parent window name of the current window. For other windows, use the name of the child window as the argument. If there is no parent window, the null string is returned.

See also: WPARENT( ) p. 387

WCOLS( )

Optional WCOLS(expC)

Description The WCOLS( ) function returns the number of columns available in the specified window.

Operational rules If no argument is given, the function returns the number of columns in the current window. Otherwise, use the name of the window as the optional argument.

See also: WROWS( ) p. 387

WEXIST(expC)

Description The WEXIST( ) function tells whether the specified window exists.

Operational rules Use the name of the window as the argument. The function returns true (.T.) as long as the window exists. The window need not be activated to exist. Use the WVISIBLE( ) function to see if a window is currently activated.

See also: WVISIBLE( ) p. 387

WONTOP( )

Optional WONTOP(expC)

Description The WONTOP( ) function tells which window is frontmost.

Operational rules If no argument is given, the function returns the name of the frontmost window as a character string. The optional argument is the name of a particular window. When the argument is used, the function returns true (.T.) if the window is frontmost.

See also: DEFINE WINDOW p. 170
          WEXIST( ) p. 386

WOUTPUT( )

Optional WOUTPUT(expC)

Description The WOUTPUT( ) function tells which window currently has output being directed to it.

Operational rules If no argument is given, the function returns the name of the window displaying output. The optional argument is the name of a particular window. When the argument is used, the function returns true (.T.) if the window is frontmost.

See also: WEXIST( ) p. 386

WPARENT( )

Description The WPARENT( ) function returns the name of the parent window.

Operational rules It is possible to place a window (the child) inside of another window (the parent). The child window must be smaller than the parent and stay within the parent window's boundaries.

If no argument is given, WPARENT( ) returns the parent window name of the current window. For other windows, use the name of the child window as the argument. If there is no parent window, the null string is returned.

See also: WCHILD( ) p. 385

WROWS( )

Optional WROWS(expC)

Description The WROWS( ) function returns the number of rows available in the specified window.

Operational rules If no argument is given, the function returns the number of rows in the current window. Otherwise, use the name of the window as the optional argument.

See also: WCOLS( ) p. 386

WVISIBLE(expC)

Description The WVISIBLE( ) function tells whether the specified window is currently activated.

Operational rules Use the name of the window as the argument. The function returns true (.T.) as long as the window is currently activated. The ACTIVATE WINDOW command displays the window on the screen (activates it). The DEACTIVATE WINDOW command takes the window off the screen.

See also: WEXIST( ) p. 386

YEAR(expD)

Description   YEAR returns the number of the year, given a date expression.
Operational rules   The three ways to enter a date as an argument are:

1. Enclose the date in curly brackets: {12/5/89}
2. Use the CTOD function: CTOD("12/5/2010")
3. Reference a field name or memory variable.

Examples

```
. ? YEAR({9/6/89})
1989
. ? YEAR(CTOD("12/25/89"))
1989
```

See also: DAY( ) p. 293
           MONTH( ) p. 338

5

System memory variables

THE SYSTEM MEMORY VARIABLES ARE SPECIAL FUNCTIONS THAT ALLOW YOU TO change certain characteristics of your FoxPro program. Many of these variables pertain to printing characteristics, such as the page length used by the report generator.

System memory variables return the current settings, although they can also be used to change these settings. For instance, the page length variable is _plength. To display the current page length setting, use:

    ? _plength

To change the current setting, change the value of the system memory variable. The following command changes the page length from the 66-line default to the 84 lines needed for legal length paper:

    _plength = 84

The following is a list of the system memory variables.

_alignment

Description This variable determines the alignment of the output displayed through the ? command. The default is left alignment. The choices are LEFT, RIGHT, and CENTER. The right margin setting (_rmargin) determines the placement of centered and right-aligned materials. This variable can only be changed when the wrap function (_wrap) is set to true (.T.).

Example

    . _wrap = .T.
    . _alignment = "RIGHT"
    . ? "Date: ",DATE( )

Date: 12/31/89

_box

Description This variable determines whether or not boxes are displayed. Boxes are defined with the DEFINE BOX command. If _box is set to true (.T.), the boxes display. Otherwise, they do not. This variable does not affect boxes displayed with the @...TO command. The default is true (.T.)

_indent

Description This variable determines the number of spaces that the first line is indented for output displayed through the ? command. The default is 0 spaces. The choices are any number up to the right margin setting. The _indent may be less than the left margin. In fact, it may be up to the negative of the _lmargin setting.

This variable can only be changed when the wrap function (_wrap) is set to true (.T.).

Example

```
. _wrap = .T.
. _rmargin = 30
. _indent = 5
. mm = "This is a test of the word wrap function with indent."
    This is a test of
  the word wrap function
    with indent.
```

_lmargin

Description This variable determines the left margin for output displayed through the ? command. The default is 0 spaces. The choices are any number from 0 to 254. This variable can only be changed when the wrap function (_wrap) is set to true (.T.).

Example

```
. _wrap = .T.
. _lmargin = 25
. mm = "This is a test of the word wrap function with a large left margin."
            This is a test of the word wrap function
            with a large left margin.
```

_mline

Description Each time the MLINE( ) function is called, _mline stores the number of the memo line offset. Using _mline as the optional third argument in MLINE( ) (and one as the second argument) greatly speeds up the performance of the MLINE( ) function.

_padvance

Description This variable determines the method used for advancing the paper with the EJECT command. The default is FORMFEED. The choices are FORMFEED and LINEFEED.

The FORMFEED setting causes the paper to advance the same number of lines as the form-feed button on the printer. This can cause a problem if the internal workings of the printer are not set for the correct page length. The LINEFEED setting ensures that the paper advances the correct number of lines according to the page length set with the _plength variable (default 66 lines).

This command only affects the EJECT command. Displaying function CHR(12) sends a form feed regardless of the _padvance setting.

_pageno

Description This variable determines the page number to print on a REPORT FORM or other printed output (except output created with the @ commands). The default _pageno is 1. For output other than report forms, FoxPro tracks the current page number depending on the page length set through _plength, and the number of lines printed. This variable can be used to change the number printed on the first and preceding pages on a report.

_pbpage

Description This variable determines the page to begin printing for a REPORT FORM or other printed output. The default _pbpage is 1. This variable can be used if a printout was aborted after a certain number of pages, and you do not want to print those pages again. A _pbpage number greater than _pageno skips the pages before _pbpage by not printing them to the screen or printer.

_pcolno

Description This variable determines the column position of the output displayed through commands other than the @ commands. This variable can be used to change the column position of text to be displayed. Changing the _pcolno number has different effects depending on whether the output is being sent to the printer.

If SET PRINT is ON and _wrap is false (.F.), then lowering _pcolno causes the last printed text to be overstruck by the new text. If SET PRINT is OFF, or it is ON and _wrap is false (.T.), then lowering _pcolno causes the last printed text to be replaced by the new text.

Example The following program causes the word strike-out to appear as the following:

This function will ~~strike-out~~ some text.

Strike.Prg
```
_wrap = .F.
SET PRINT ON
? "This function will strike-out"
_pcolno = _pcolno - 10
?? "- - - - - - - - - - -"
?? "some text."
?
```

_pcopies

Description This variable determines the number of copies of a PRINTJOB to be printed. The default _pcopies is 1. This command can only be used for printing with the PRINTJOB or REPORT FORM commands. You must set _pcopies for issuing the PRINTJOB command.

_pdriver

Description This variable determines the current printer driver. The default is set through the Config.db file. Printer drivers determine such print characteristics as boldface, underlining, and italics. These characteristics can be set with the STYLE argument of the ? command, or through the report generator.

Printer drivers are files with a .PR2 extension. The extension does not need to be included when changing the _pdriver.

Example The following command sets the printer driver for an Epson LX-80:

```
. _pdriver = "LX80"
```

_pecode

Description This variable determines the control codes sent at the end of a PRINTJOB. The default _pecode is a null string.

This command is often used in conjunction with the _pscode which sends out a certain control code before printing. After the PRINTJOB is finished, the printer can be set back to its default mode. Otherwise, all subsequent printing is printed with the _pscode style.

This variable can only be used for printing with the PRINTJOB or REPORT FORM commands.

Example In this example, the report prints in condensed print, but then sets the printer back to normal pitch. The example is for an Epson printer where

CHR(15) sends the printer into condensed mode, while CHR(18) sets it to 10 pitch:

    _pscode = "{15}"
    _pecode = "{18}"
    REPORT FORM Maillist TO PRINT

_peject

Description This variable determines when an eject is sent within a PRINTJOB. The default _peject is BEFORE. The choices are BEFORE, AFTER, BOTH, and NONE. This command can only be used for printing with the PRINT-JOB or REPORT FORM commands.

_pepage

Description This variable determines the page to end printing for a REPORT FORM or other printed output. The default _pepage is 32,767 or the last page of the output, whichever comes first. This variable can be used to reprint an output without printing all the way to the end. A _pepage number less than the number of pages of the entire printout skips the last pages by not printing them to the screen or printer.

_pform

Description This variable determines the print form file. Print form files set characteristics such as _pageno, _pcopies, _pscode, etc., for report and label forms. You can change all these settings with one command by placing them in a print form file, and then changing _pform before issuing the REPORT FORM or LABEL FORM command. Printer form files have a .PRF extension. The extension does not need to be included when changing the _pform.

Example The following command sets the print form file to the file Month.prf:

    . _pform = "MONTH"
    . REPORT FORM Journal

_plength

Description This variable determines the page length for printed output. The default is 66. If the page length is different than that set within the mechanism of the printer, this command does not always cause the page length to advance correctly with the EJECT command. To ensure that the page ejects correctly, set _padvance to LINEFEED before issuing EJECT.

_plineno

Description This variable determines the line position of the output displayed through commands other than the @ commands. The default _plineno is 0. FoxPro keeps track of this number as it prints each line. Users of previous FoxPro versions were forced to increment the line numbers with a repetition of ? commands because there was no _plineno variable.

_ploffset

Description This variable determines the left side of the screen and print page. The default is 0 spaces. This is the same variable changed with the SET MARGIN TO command.

This variable is different than the _lmargin variable, because it determines the column to begin counting left for the _lmargin. In other words, you can change the _ploffset, and all _lmargin changes will change relatively. If _ploffset is 0 and the _lmargin is 5, the display then begins in column 5 of the screen. If _ploffset is 10 and the _lmargin is still 5, the display then begins in column 15 of the screen.

_ppitch

Description This variable determines the current printer pitch. The default _ppitch is DEFAULT, which is equivalent to the setting in the printer mechanism. The choices are PICA, ELITE, CONDENSED, and DEFAULT. This command can only be used if the correct printer driver is set, otherwise the pitch must be changed by sending character strings to the printer using the ? command or _pscode variables.

_pquality

Description This variable determines the current mode of the printer. The default _pquality is false (.F.), or draft mode. The choices are true (.T.), which is letter quality and false (.F.), which is draft mode. This command can only be used if the correct printer driver is set, otherwise the quality must be changed by sending character strings to the printer using the ? command or _pscode variables.

_pretext

Description This variable determines a character expression sent at the beginning of each line in a text merge. This variable is only used when outputting text with \ and \\ commands. Use Tabs as the _pretext character to indent areas of programming output.

_pscode

Description This variable determines the control codes sent at the beginning of a PRINTJOB. The default _pscode is a null string.

This variable can only be used for printing with the PRINTJOB or REPORT FORM commands.

Example In this example, the report prints in condensed print. The example is for an Epson printer where, CHR(15) sends the printer into condensed mode.

```
_pscode = "{15}"
REPORT FORM Maillist TO PRINT
```

_pspacing

Description This variable determines the line spacing. The default is single spacing, or 1. The choices are 1, 2, and 3. This variable affects all outputs except those created with the @ commands.

_pwait

Description This variable determines whether FoxPro pauses between pages so the user can put in a new piece of paper. This is needed for printing on separate sheets of paper when there is no sheet feeder or paper bin. The default value is false (.F.). The choices are false (.F.), which is no pausing, and true (.T.), which turns on the wait mode.

This variable can only be used with any command that sends information to the printer. It pauses at each occurrence after the EJECT command and at each point that the _plength is reached.

_rmargin

Description This variable determines the right margin for output displayed through the ? command. The default is 80 spaces. The choices are any number from 1 to 254, although the right margin must be at least 1 space greater than the _lmargin setting. This variable can only be changed when the wrap function (_wrap) is set to true (.T.).

Example

```
. _wrap = .T.
. _rmargin = 25
. mm = "This is a test of the word wrap function with a small right margin."
```

This is a test of the
word wrap function with
a small right margin.

_tabs

Description This variable determines the tab settings for output displayed through the ? command. The tabs are only affected when the tab character, CHR(9) is displayed.

The default tab setting is every 8 spaces, or 8, 16, 24, ... The choices are any series of numbers separated with commas. This variable can be changed whether the wrap function (_wrap) is set to true (.T.) or false (.F.).

Changing this variable is equivalent to changing the tab settings in the Config.db file.

Example

```
. ? "Col 1",CHR(9),"Col 2", CHR(9),"Col 3"
Col 1     Col 2     Col 3
. _tabs = "15,30,45"
Col 1          Col 2          Col 3
```

_tally

Description Certain FoxPro commands process a group of records. When TALK is set ON, the number of records processed is displayed on the screen. After any one of the following commands is run, _tally stores the number of records processed:

APPEND FROM	COUNT	PACK	SORT
AVERAGE	DELETE	REINDEX	SUM
CALCULATE	INDEX	REPLACE	TOTAL
COPY TO	JOIN	SQL SELECT	UPDATE

_tallytime

Description Certain FoxPro commands process a group of records. These commands also track the number of seconds for the command to be executed. After any one of the commands listed above in the _tally section is run, _tallytime stores the number of seconds it took to process.

_text

Description This variable determines the name of a file where each line of the text merge is output. Low-level files are non-database files often used by programs, FCREATE( ) creates low-level files, and FOPEN( ) opens an existing file. The _text is only used when outputting text with the \ and \\ commands.

Set _text to − 1 to stop text output into the current file (without closing it) and begin outputting to another one. This makes it easier to output to several files at once.

Examples

```
SET TEXTMERGE TO Nametag
\ HI MY NAME IS
\
\ <Fname>,<Lname>
File1 = _text
_text = -1
SET TEXTMERGE TO Letter
\ Dear <Fname>,
\
\ You are invited to our FoxPro seminar, December 10, 1991.
CLOSE ALL
```

_wrap

Description This variable determines the word wrap is on. When _wrap is true (.T.), text that is longer than the area between the left and right margins automatically wraps to the second line, breaking between words.

The default is false (.F.). The choices are true (.T.), which turns word-wrap on, and false (.F.), which turns it off. The _lmargin, _rmargin, _indent, and _alignment variables are only effective when _wrap is true (.T.).

6
FoxPro programming

IN THIS CHAPTER, THE SUBJECT OF PROGRAMMING IS ADDRESSED. THE PRIMARY intent of this book is to provide information in a reference-based manner. All commands and functions are presented in other sections, many of which are used here. For a more in-depth survey of FoxPro programming, you might wish to acquire an additional publication, although the material here might be adequate enough for your needs.

First the editor is discussed. The attention then turns toward programming, where a few basics are mentioned. Finally, an example program for managing a mailing list database is presented and analyzed in detail.

Since the early days of dBASE II, programming in a database language has rapidly evolved from being somewhat awkward to being sophisticated and powerful. The main idea was to allow a sequence of commands (normally executed from the command window) to be executed in succession, while providing some programming constructs for decision making and control. This is still true, but the tools at the programmer's disposal have much improved.

Using the editor

FoxPro has its own built-in editor for editing program files. The editor can be invoked in two ways: MODIFY COMMAND followed by a file name can be entered at the command window, or a file can be selected or created from the File menu. To save a little bit of typing when at the command menu, remember that you only need to type the first four letters of the command, so MODI COMM can be entered instead of MODIFY COMMAND.

To create a program file from the File menu, choose New, and then Program. To open an existing file, choose Open, and go to the Type box to choose Program. You can then choose the desired program file from a list.

If you wish to use another program such as WordStar or WordPerfect to edit your files, you can modify the Config.fp file. Add the additional line TEDIT = *editor*, where *editor* is the name of the program you wish to use to edit files (e.g., WS or WP).

Editing keys

Basic cursor keys function as you would expect when editing files. A table appears below for all editing keys:

Key	Description
Arrow keys	Move left, right, up, down.
Ctrl – →	Move one word to the right.
Ctrl – ←	Move one word to the left.
Home	Go to the beginning of the line.
End	Go to the end of the line.
Tab	Go to the next tab.
Shift – Tab	Go to the previous tab.
PgUp	Move up one screen.
PgDn	Move down one screen.
Ctrl – PgUp	Go to the beginning of the file.
Ctrl – PgDn	Go to the end of the file.
Ctrl – Backspace	Delete word.
Ins	Toggle insert/typeover modes.
Esc	Exit editor without saving work.

All other editing is done through the Edit menu. Through this menu you can "cut and paste" and find occurrences of certain strings or a particular line. To use the Cut and Paste commands, you need to select text. To do this, highlight the area by holding down the Shift key and pressing the arrows to highlight, or if you have a mouse, double-click it and drag it over the area. To delete an area, simply highlight it and then press the Delete key.

Indentation

You can set the editor to indent automatically when you edit files. After pressing Return on a line, the cursor appears immediately below the first nonspace character in the previous line. If the ← is now pressed, the cursor jumps back to the end of the previous line, and does not move to the empty space to the left. Just remember this—pressing Shift – Tab allows you to move to the left, specifically to the previous tab setting. Forgetting this fact can result in experiencing some annoyance. The Enable automatic indent option from the Edit, Preferences menu can be used to turn indentation ON or OFF.

Copying and moving text

For both operations, first go to the beginning of the desired block of code. Highlight the area (using the mouse or Shift – arrow combinations). After the entire area is highlighted, pull up the Edit menu.

To copy the text, choose Copy. This places the text in the *clipboard*, a temporary storage location in memory. Then move to the area that you want the text copied to, and choose Paste. This places the text from the clipboard at the cursor's position. The text stays in the clipboard until something else is placed there, so you can call the Paste command more than once to copy something several times.

To move the text, choose Cut. This places the text in the clipboard, and deletes it from the current area of the file. Then move to the area that you want the text moved to, and choose Paste. As with the Copy command, this places the text from the clipboard at the cursor's position.

Other features

A few other features are mentioned here.

The Go To Line option allows you to jump to the specified line number of the program and continue editing. This is useful when compiling programs because FoxPro notifies you on what line number the error occurred.

You can print your program while it is open by simply opening the File menu and choosing Print.

Modular design programming

In programming, it is often easier to complete a large task by breaking it down into smaller, more manageable tasks. This is known as *modular programming*. Each module of a program is dedicated to performing one operation, which makes designing and debugging a much easier process.

To execute a program from the command menu, enter the DO command followed by the desired filename. If the file has been modified, it is compiled first. Within your programs, you can also include DO commands, having programs call other subprograms, while all public variables are still retained in memory for use of the subprograms.

A more structured approach is to use procedures. A *procedure* is found in a program file that does not necessarily bear its name, as in the aforementioned method. A procedure begins with the keyword PROCEDURE followed by the procedure name. The lines of code to execute are next, and the procedure is terminated by a RETURN statement. For example, a procedure to print Hello, world appears below:

```
PROCEDURE Hello
    ? "Hello World"
RETURN
```

To execute this within a program, the line DO Hello is included.

There is another species of animals called *procedure files*. We do not go into detail here, but basically it is a file of procedures that your programs can call with the DO command, after first setting SET PROCEDURE TO followed by the name of the file that contains all the procedures.

Procedures can also have parameter passing, but that is not discussed here.

Setting up the FoxPro environment

When the highest level program is executed, usually the first lines of programming code set up the environment. These include CLEAR ALL to release existing variables in memory and close any open files, and many SET commands. Several SET commands are available; these can be found in the command reference section of this book. They allow you to do things like suppress system responses to commands in order to keep the screens neat (SET TALK OFF).

Memory variables

After setting up the environment, variables should be initialized. You can have a statement like x = y appear for the first time x is used, but it is better style to assign x to a constant when it is declared, rather than another variable. In addition, in @SAY...GETs, the memory variable following the GET is expected to already exist. In the memory variable's declaration, the variable can be set to some default constant like 0 (for type numeric), today's date or null dates (for type date), or a string of spaces of a specified length (for type character).

You can initialize memory variables in two ways. You can either use the assignment statement (x = 0), or use the STORE command (STORE 0 TO x). The STORE method might seem more verbose, but it offers the advantage of having the ability to assign the same value to more than one variable at a time.

To assign x, y, and z to 0 using assignment statements, you would enter:

```
x = 0
y = 0
z = 0
```

Using the STORE command instead, you could enter the following:

```
STORE 0 TO x,y,z
```

Memory variable arrays are a very useful feature of FoxPro. They can be either one- or two-dimensional arrays. The number of elements in the array must be included in the declaration. For example, to declare an array names for 20 entries and 2 elements (last name and first name) for those 20 entries, enter:

```
DECLARE names[20,2]
```

Assignments to the names array can now be made:

```
name[1,1] = "Lambert"
name[1,2] = "Julie"
```

The elements of an array can have different types. You can copy the contents of a record to an array using the COPY TO ARRAY command. Similarly, new records can be added by inserting values into an array and using the APPEND FROM ARRAY command. These two commands allow you to shorten up the length of your programs a bit by performing several actions in just one statement.

Memory variables and fields

One concern that can be frustrating for first-time programmers is using field names from data files and memory variables together in programs. Naming a memory variable the same name as a field is never a good idea. The important thing to remember is that STORE and assignment statements change the value of memory variables only. To change the value in a field, the REPLACE command must be used.

The format of the REPLACE command is:

REPLACE *field* WITH *value*

where *value* is a constant or expression of variables or fields. Observe the following program excerpt:

```
USE Names
STORE "Fred" to Mname
REPLACE Fname WITH Mname
? Fname
```

Assume the field Fname exists in the database Names.dbf. The file is open and is at the first record. Fred is initialized to the memory variable name. The field name in the current record is replaced with the contents of the memory variable name, Fred.

To avoid confusion, good database programming style precedes memory variables with an M that are to be used as temporary variables for fields.

Decision making

The two tools available to facilitate decision making are IF statements and CASE statements.

The IF command uses the following format:

IF *condition*
   list of commands
ENDIF

The IF statement processes the commands between the IF and ENDIF only if the condition is true (.T.). It is considered good programming style to indent (3 or 4 spaces) all of the commands between the IF and ENDIF statements. IF statements can also have ELSE statements within them. The format for this type of command would be:

IF *condition*
   list of commands
ELSE
   list of commands
ENDIF

In this case, the commands between the IF and ELSE are performed if the condition is true (.T.), otherwise the command between the ELSE and ENDIF are performed.

The DO CASE command uses the following format:

DO CASE
   CASE *condition*
      list of commands
   CASE *condition*
      list of commands
   CASE *condition*
      list of commands
etc.
ENDCASE

The DO CASE statement processes the commands after the first CASE condition which is true (.T.). This command is useful in situations where several conditions can exist, such as choosing one of five options from a menu.

For more information on the IF...ENDIF and DO CASE commands, look them up in chapter 2, the commands chapter.

Loops

The three looping mechanisms are DO WHILE...ENDDO, FOR...ENDFOR, and SCAN...ENDSCAN.

The DO WHILE command uses the following format:

DO WHILE *condition*
   list of commands
ENDDO

The DO WHILE statement keeps processing the commands between the DO and ENDDO until the condition is no longer true (.T.).

The FOR command uses the following format:

FOR *memvar = expN1* TO *expN2*
   list of commands
ENDFOR

The FOR statement keeps processing the commands between the FOR and ENDFOR a set number of times (from *expN1* to *expN2*).

The SCAN command uses the following format:

SCAN
   list of commands
ENDSCAN

The SCAN statement moves through a database file and processes the commands between the SCAN and ENDSCAN for each record in the file. This command can use a scope or FOR *condition* statement to only process records that match a specified condition.

Again, for more information look these statements up in chapter 2 about the commands.

The People sample application

Here is a sample application to introduce some typical programming techniques. A database named People is used. It contains mailing list information, phone number, the date it was entered, and a numeric field for a dollar amount of potential business to be obtained from this person. The structure is:

Field	Field name	Type	Width	Dec
1	lname	Character	20	
2	fname	Character	15	
3	address	Character	30	

4	city	Character	20	
5	state	Character	2	
6	zip	Character	10	
7	phone	Character	14	
8	ent_date	Date	8	
9	poten	Numeric	8	2

The file is indexed by Lname in the file Name.idx.

To improve readability in the program listings provided, the conventions used for capitalization are:

- All FoxPro keywords are in upper case.
- Memory variables and field names are in lower case.
- Procedures and files begin with a capital letter followed by lower case letters.

A simple program for maintaining the file

Before going on to a modular designed program, here is a single program file that handles opening the People database, adding records, editing records, and running a report. The program is not as sophisticated as the application that follows it, but it does contain many of the basic commands and standards used in FoxPro programs:

Pmain.prg:

```
* Set-up environment
SET TALK OFF
SET STATUS OFF

* Open People database
USE People INDEX Name

* Repeat Until "Exit" is selected from menu
choice = "0"
DO WHILE choice # "4"
   CLEAR
   TEXT

      PEOPLE DATABASE PROGRAM
      1) Insert Entries
      2) Edit Entries
      3) Run a Report
      4) Exit
```

```
          ENDTEXT
          ACCEPT "     Enter Selection: " TO choice
          CLEAR
          DO CASE
            CASE choice = "1"
              APPEND

                 * Find name in index, and edit
            CASE choice = "2"
              ACCEPT "Enter Last Name of Record to Edit " TO mname
              SEEK mname
              EDIT

                 * Turn on print mode if desired, and list report
            CASE choice = "3"
              ACCEPT "List to Screen or Printer? (S/P) " TO prnt
              IF UPPER(prnt) = "P"
                SET PRINT ON
              ENDIF
              REPORT FORM Plist
              IF UPPER(prnt) = "P"
                SET PRINT OFF
              ELSE
                WAIT
              ENDIF
          ENDCASE
        ENDDO
        QUIT
```

Notice the comments that introduce each section of the program. Comment lines must begin with asterisks (*). You can also use asterisks in front of a line of code that you temporarily want the program to ignore, such as SET PRINT ON. It is very important to comment your programs, no matter how simple they can seem. Comments not only help you when going back to the program to edit or add additional features, but they are essential in helping someone else understand your coding.

The SET TALK OFF command at the top of Pmain.prg is needed so that Fox-Pro does not display each memory variable as it is assigned. This also suppresses the TALK messages displayed during commands such as INDEX, REPLACE, and SEEK.

Next, the USE command opens the database along with the index file, ensuring that the data is in alphabetical order. The memory variable choice holds the number of the menu option that the user chooses. Following good programming standards, we initialize the memory variable by making it equal to a constant, in this case zero.

The DO WHILE choice # 4 command ensures that the menu is not being displayed after each option is run, until the user presses 4 as the selection. The TEXT command then displays all text between TEXT and ENDTEXT. In this case, the text is the menu. The ACCEPT command displays the prompt for the user's selection and waits for input. The memory variable choice becomes equal to whatever the user types.

We use the DO CASE command instead of IF...ENDIF because it is more efficient in instances where more than two conditions exist. In this case, there are three possible conditions (DO CASE statements). The first case, choice = "1", simply calls the APPEND command. This is a very simplistic way to add records, as it calls the plain-looking Append screen. The more sophisticated application in the next section sets up a custom-designed screen for inserting records.

The second case, choice = "2", asks the user for the last name of the record to be edited. Because the database is indexed on Lname, we use the SEEK command to find the name. Using the SEEK command (which requires an indexed file) can be much faster than using the LOCATE command, especially with large databases. Notice that there are no provisions in case the user types in a name that is not found in the database. If this happens, the Edit command will be positioned at the top record of the index. The editing program in the next section includes a routine that handles this situation.

The third case, choice = "3", turns on the printer if the user so desires. It then calls a report that has already been formatted from the Report menu. The reports name is Plist. This report lists all records in the database, in alphabetical order because the index is open.

The rest of this chapter covers a program that handles much of the same functions as this simple program. However, it is much more sophisticated. The main menu utilizes pop-up menus, the editing screens utilize custom designed screens instead of the basic Edit command layout, and the reports allow the user to build a criteria for filtering out names. Because each of the modules takes many lines of programming, the application is broken up into separate .PRG files, starting with the Main menu program.

The Main program

In the highest-level program (the one executed first that calls other subprograms), the environment for the entire application is set up, and the main menu is put into action. The program is first listed, and then discussed.

Main.prg:

```
* Set-up environment
SET TALK OFF
SET HEADING OFF
SET STATUS OFF
SET SCOREBOARD OFF
SET BELL OFF
CLEAR ALL

* Open People database
USE People INDEX Name
* Do menu definition
DO Def_Main
* Repeat Until "Exit" is selected from menu
DO WHILE BAR( ) # 10
   CLEAR
   ACTIVATE POPUP main
ENDDO
RETURN

PROCEDURE Def_Main
   DEFINE POPUP main FROM 1,30 to 12,50
   DEFINE BAR 1 OF main PROMPT " PEOPLE DATABASE" SKIP
   DEFINE BAR 3 OF main PROMPT " Insert Entries"
   DEFINE BAR 4 OF main PROMPT " Edit Entries"
   DEFINE BAR 5 OF main PROMPT " Delete Entries"
   DEFINE BAR 6 OF main PROMPT " Report"
   DEFINE BAR 7 OF main PROMPT " Labels"
   DEFINE BAR 8 OF main PROMPT " Pack"
   DEFINE BAR 10 OF main PROMPT " Exit"
   ON SELECTION POPUP main DO Main_opt
RETURN

PROCEDURE Main_opt
   DO CASE
      CASE BAR( ) = 3
         DO Insert
      CASE BAR( ) = 4
         DO Edit
      CASE BAR( ) = 5
         DO Delete
      CASE BAR( ) = 6
         DO Report
      CASE BAR( ) = 7
         DO Labels
```

```
            CASE BAR( ) = 8
                DO Packem
            CASE BAR( ) = 10
                RETURN TO MASTER
        ENDCASE
    RETURN
```

The first command executed command, CLEAR ALL, releases memory variables (if they exist) from memory, closes all files, and sets the work area to 1. In other words, any leftover garbage from previous work is cleaned up.

The SET commands used are the typical ones that many applications use. They ensure that FoxPro messages are not printed on the display to mess up the screen, that column headings do not appear when using the LIST command, and that the somewhat annoying BELL is turned OFF.

Next, the USE command opens the database for adding, editing, or listing records.

Now we discuss a new feature of FoxPro, pop-up menus. The three components of the menus are the definition, the activation, and the actions to take based on the menu's result.

The *definition* is put in procedure Def_Main. The DEFINE POPUP command names the pop-up menu and gives the placement and dimensions of the menu. DEFINE BAR is used to describe the lines in the menu. For BAR 1, the keyword SKIP is included at the end so that PEOPLE DATABASE appears as a heading and not as an option that can be selected. There is no BAR 2 definition so that a line is skipped between the heading and the options. ON SELECTION POPUP determines what procedure to execute after an option has been selected. If no DO *procedure* follows, the course of action to take is to do nothing, and execution of the program continues following the line in which the menu was activated.

After being defined, a menu can be activated with the ACTIVATE POPUP command. After execution of subprograms, control automatically returns to the pop-up menu.

The actions to take appear in procedure Main_opt. The function BAR( ) contains the value of the bar last selected. Typically a CASE statement appears to select the course of action next.

The menu normally can be deactivated by pressing Escape or by using the DEACTIVATE POPUP command. In this case, however, after pressing Escape the menu is deactivated and then reactivated because of the DO WHILE BAR( ) # 10 loop.

Do not be misled by the DO WHILE BAR # 10 (# means "does not equal") loop. As stated above, when returning from each subprogram such as Insert, the menu remains in control. However, if in a subprogram (or its subprograms) and

RETURN TO MASTER is encountered, the flow of control shifts to the line following the ACTIVATE POPUP command in the main program, as opposed to returning to the menu as it normally would. RETURN TO MASTER can be used anywhere, and it basically shifts control to the highest-level calling program without having to retrace level by level. Therefore, the DO WHILE loop reactivates the menu after a subprogram uses RETURN TO MASTER.

Use this as a model for your pop-up menus, and the DO WHILE part for your main menu. Compactly:

```
DO Def_Main ACTIVATE POPUP main
PROCEDURE Def_Main
   DEFINE POPUP main FROM .. TO ..
   DEFINE BAR 1 OF main PROMPT ......
   :
   ON SELECTION POPUP main DO Main_opt
RETURN
 PROCEDURE Main_opt
   DO CASE
      :
   RETURN
```

The Insert program

The Insert program allows new records to be inserted into the database. The program follows:

```
Insert.prg:
DEFINE WINDOW again FROM 10,26 TO 14,54
DEFINE WINDOW insert FROM 6,10 TO 19,60
ACTIVATE WINDOW insert
* Repeat forever
DO WHILE .T.
   * Initialize variables
   STORE SPACE(20) TO mlname,mcity
   STORE SPACE(15) TO mfname
   STORE SPACE(30) TO maddress
   STORE " " TO mstate
   STORE SPACE(10) TO mzip
   STORE SPACE(14) TO mphone
   STORE { / / } TO ment_date
   STORE 0 TO recnum,mpoten
   STORE "Y" TO yn
   * Obtain values
```

```
      @ 1,1 SAY " Last Name:" GET mlname
      @ 2,1 SAY "First Name:" GET mfname
      @ 3,1 SAY "  Address:" GET maddress
      @ 4,1 SAY "     City:" GET mcity
      @ 5,1 SAY "     Sate:" GET mstate PICTURE "!!"
      @ 6,1 SAY "      Zip:" GET mzip PICTURE "99999-9999"
      @ 7,1 SAY "    Phone:" GET mphone PICTURE "(999) 999-9999"
      @ 8,1 SAY "Entry Date:" GET ment_date
      @ 9,1 SAY " Potential:" GET mpoten PICTURE "99999.99"
      @ 11,1 SAY "Press ESC To Abort"
      READ
      * See if Escape was pressed
      IF LASTKEY( ) = 27
         DEACTIVATE WINDOW insert
         RETURN
      ENDIF
      * Add new record
      APPEND BLANK
      * Replace field values
      REPLACE lname WITH mlname, fname WITH mfname, ;
         address WITH maddress, city WITH mcity, ;
         state WITH mstate, zip WITH mzip, ;
         phone WITH mphone, ent_date WITH ment_date ;
         poten WITH mpoten
      * See if user wants to continue insertions
      ACTIVATE WINDOW again
      @ 1,1 SAY "Insert Another? (Y/N):" GET yn PICTURE "!"
      READ
      DEACTIVATE WINDOW again
      IF yn < > "Y"
         DEACTIVATE WINDOW insert
         RETURN
      ENDIF
   ENDDO
```

Windows are used here for a clean-looking entry screen that can be laid over the menu. The first two lines define two windows, Again and Insert, and give their coordinates. Each time this program is executed from the main menu, the windows are redefined. This does not hurt anything, but we could have had the definitions appear in the Main program so they are only executed once.

Next the Insert window is activated. Now when printing is done to the screen, it is bounded by the window, and coordinates are now relative within the window, not the entire screen. In other words, @ 0,0 appears at 0,0 within the window, but is at 7,11 on the screen.

A DO WHILE .T. loop appears next. The .T. denotes the Boolean value true as the loop condition, so the loop is instructed to repeat indefinitely. However, the loop can be left by two methods: By an EXIT command, in which case the next command to execute is the command following ENDDO; or by the RETURN command, to RETURN to the calling program.

The program is structured to allow many insertions to be made without having to go back to the main menu. Thus, the variables are initialized within the loop, otherwise on subsequent insertions the previous values appear. The memory variables are initialized to reflect the definitions of the fields that appear in the database that they replace.

@SAY...GETs are used to obtain the new record's values. The PICTURE clauses are used to format variables into their desired appearances.

It is nice to allow users the opportunity to abort an operation if the users change their minds or press the wrong key. The LASTKEY( ) function returns the ASCII value of the last key that was pressed in exiting a READ. We can check if Escape was pressed here, and if so deactivate the Insert window, and return to the main menu. Escape's ASCII value is 27.

Pressing Escape does not always halt program execution. It depends where in the program you currently are. Pressing Escape in a READ exits the READ. Pressing Escape when selecting a pop-up menu option deactivates the menu. If executing other statements that do not involve a built-in FoxPro procedure, then the current program is interrupted.

After obtaining user input, we can now create a new record to hold the data. The APPEND BLANK command creates an empty record at the end of the database and becomes the current record. The REPLACE command is employed to transfer the values in the memory variables into the proper fields in the record. Several fields in a record can be replaced at once, separated by commas. In the program, note that semicolons appear at the end of the line. The semicolons tell FoxPro that the command continues on the next line.

Finally, the user is given the opportunity to insert another record. The Again window is activated and the user is prompted. Whether the user answered yes or no, the window is no longer needed, so it is immediately deactivated. If the answer was not Y for yes, the Insert window is deactivated, and we return to the main menu. Otherwise the end of the loop is encountered, and the program loops back to the top and obtains the next record.

Insert using arrays

An alternative Insert program is presented to demonstrate using arrays and how they can shorten the length of your programs somewhat. APPEND FROM ARRAY creates a new record with the contents of the specified array. The code follows:

```
* Declare the array named stuff, 9 elements
DECLARE stuff[9]
DEFINE WINDOW again FROM 10,26 TO 14,54
DEFINE WINDOW insert FROM 6,10 TO 19,60
ACTIVATE WINDOW insert
* Repeat forever
DO WHILE .T.
   STORE SPACE(20) TO stuff[1],stuff[4]
   STORE SPACE(15) TO stuff[2]
   STORE SPACE(30) TO stuff[3]
   STORE " " TO stuff[5]
   STORE SPACE(10) TO stuff[6]
   STORE SPACE(14) TO stuff[7]
   STORE { / / } TO stuff[8]
   STORE 0 TO recnum,stuff[9]
   STORE " " TO yn
   @ 1,1 SAY " Last Name:" GET stuff[1]
   @ 2,1 SAY "First Name:" GET stuff[2]
   @ 3,1 SAY "   Address:" GET stuff[3]
   @ 4,1 SAY "      City:" GET stuff[4]
   @ 5,1 SAY "      Sate:" GET stuff[5] PICTURE "!!"
   @ 6,1 SAY "       Zip:" GET stuff[6] PICTURE "99999-9999"
   @ 7,1 SAY " Phone:" GET stuff[7] PICTURE "(999) 999- 9999"
   @ 8,1 SAY "Entry Date:" GET stuff[8]
   @ 9,1 SAY " Potential:" GET stuff[9] PICTURE "99999.99"
   @ 11,1 SAY "Press ESC To Abort"
   READ
   * See if Escape was pressed
   IF LASTKEY( ) = 27
      DEACTIVATE WINDOW insert
      RETURN
   ENDIF
   * Add new record
   APPEND FROM ARRAY stuff
   * See if user wants to continue insertions
   ACTIVATE WINDOW again
   @ 1,1 SAY "Insert Another? (Y/N):" GET yn PICTURE "!"
   READ
   DEACTIVATE WINDOW again
   IF yn < > "Y"
      DEACTIVATE WINDOW insert
```

        RETURN
      ENDIF
    ENDDO
    RETURN

The Edit program

With the Edit program, existing records can be retrieved and modified. Here is the program:

```
Edit.prg:
* Initialize memory variables
STORE SPACE(20) TO mcity
STORE SPACE(15) TO mfname
STORE SPACE(30) TOmaddress
STORE " " TO mstate
STORE SPACE(10) TO mzip
STORE SPACE(14) TO mphone
STORE { / / } TO ment_date
STORE 0 TO reccnt,mpoten
DEFINE WINDOW err FROM 10,20 to 14,60
DEFINE WINDOW edit FROM 6,10 to 19,60
DEFINE WINDOW key FROM 4,35 TO 21,75
ACTIVATE WINDOW key
* Repeat forever
DO WHILE .T.
   * Clear part of window
   @ 2,0 CLEAR TO 15,36
   STORE 0 TO recnum
   STORE SPACE(20) TO mlname
   * Get desired name
   @ 0,1 SAY "Enter Last Name:" GET mlname
   @ 15,1 SAY "Press ESC To Abort"
   READ
   * See if Escape was pressed.
   IF LASTKEY( ) = 27
      DEACTIVATE WINDOW key
      RETURN
   ENDIF
   mlname = TRIM(mlname)
   SEEK mlname
   * Error if not found
```

```
IF .NOT. FOUND( )
   ACTIVATE WINDOW err
   @ 1,1 SAY "Not Found! Press Any Key To Continue."
   WAIT ""
   DEACTIVATE WINDOW err
   LOOP
ENDIF
* List all matches
DO WHILE lname = mlname
   @ 2,0 CLEAR TO 15,36
   @ 1,0
   reccnt = 0
   SCAN WHILE lname = mlname .AND. reccnt < 10
      LIST NEXT 1 TRIM(lname)+ ", " + TRIM(fname)
      reccnt = reccnt + 1
   ENDSCAN
   IF lname = mlname
      ?
      WAIT
   ENDIF
ENDDO
@ 13,0 SAY " Enter Record # To Edit:" GET recnum RANGE 1,RECCOUNT( )
@ 15,0 SAY " Press ESC To Abort"
READ
* See if Escape was pressed.
IF LASTKEY( ) = 27
   DEACTIVATE WINDOW key
   RETURN
ENDIF
* Goto the record, assign fields to memory variables.
GOTO recnum
mlname = lname
mfname = fname
maddress = address
mcity = city
mstate = state
mzip = zip
mphone = phone
ment_date = ent_date
mpoten = poten
ACTIVATE WINDOW edit
@ 1,1 SAY " Last Name:" GET mlname
```

```
   @ 2,1 SAY "First Name:" GET mfname
   @ 3,1 SAY " Address:" GET maddress
   @ 4,1 SAY " City:" GET mcity
   @ 5,1 SAY " Sate:" GET mstate PICTURE "!!"
   @ 6,1 SAY " Zip:" GET mzip PICTURE "99999-9999"
   @ 7,1 SAY " Phone:" GET mphone PICTURE "(999) 999-9999"
   @ 8,1 SAY "Entry Date:" GET ment_date
   @ 9,1 SAY " Potential:" GET mpoten PICTURE "99999.99"
   @ 11,1 SAY "Press ESC To Abort"
   READ
   * See if Escape was pressed.
   IF LASTKEY( ) = 27
      DEACTIVATE WINDOW edit
      LOOP
   ENDIF
   REPLACE lname WITH mlname, fname WITH mfname, ;
      address WITH maddress, city WITH mcity, ;
      state WITH mstate, zip WITH mzip, ;
      phone WITH mphone, ent_date WITH ment_date, ;
      poten WITH mpoten
      DEACTIVATE WINDOW edit
ENDDO
```

First, the variables are initialized. They do not need to be part of a loop here as they were in Insert.

Three windows are defined. One is for a record not found error, one for editing, and one for selecting which record to edit.

After the window is activated, a DO WHILE .T. loop appears so that users can edit records for as long as they so desire. The window is cleared of its previous contents, and the user is prompted to enter the last name of the person to look up. Here again as in Insert, the Escape key is checked after a READ.

Next mlname is trimmed to remove trailing spaces, which is very important for string comparisons. The default in string comparisons is to compare the two strings only up to the length of the string on the right. For example, if the following is typed at the command window:

```
? "program" = "pro"
.T.
```

a value of true is returned. FoxPro considers these two strings equivalent. However the following returns false:

```
? "program" = "pro    "
.F.
```

The spaces are not ignored.

The SEEK command also functions this way. If mlname = "D", SEEK goes through the database indexed on lname and stops at the first occurrence of a last name beginning with D. This is useful if the user is unsure of the spelling or does not want to type in a long name. Just the first few letters can be entered.

After executing a SEEK, the function FOUND( ) is true if SEEK found a match, otherwise it is false. If no names match the mlname pattern, the err window is activated, and an error message is displayed. WAIT "" causes the program to wait until a key is pressed by the user. Normally WAIT has its own error message, but you can instruct it to print your own, in this case "" indicates not to print anything. After a key is pressed the window is deactivated, and LOOP causes the flow of the program to jump to the instruction immediately following DO WHILE .T..

The next part is a bit tricky. If SEEK was successful, the DO WHILE lname = mlname loop is executed. The idea here is to list all the records that match mlname. Because the database is indexed on the last name, all the records that meet the lname = mlname condition will appear one after another.

First, part of the window is cleared, the cursor is positioned @ 1,0 in the window, and a counter, reccnt, is set to 0.

A SCAN WHILE loop then appears within the DO WHILE loop. The SCAN WHILE loop is a new FoxPro construct, and used here in the following:

SCAN WHILE *condition*
   :
ENDSCAN

has the same meaning as:

DO WHILE *condition* .AND. .NOT. EOF( )
   :
  SKIP
ENDDO

The SCAN's *condition* in the Edit program is to loop as long as the lname field in the current record equals mlname, up to ten times by keeping track of reccnt.

Within the SCAN WHILE loop, one record's lname and fname fields are displayed, and the record counter (reccnt) is incremented.

If reccnt is equal to 10, the loop exits. A check is made to see if lname equals the new current record. If so, more records are going to have to be displayed, so a line is skipped and a WAIT is issued to allow the user to see the existing records so far.

Although we are now outside the SCAN WHILE loop, we are still inside the DO WHILE loop. Because lname = mlname, the process repeats; the window is cleared, and the next 10 records are scanned, and so on.

After listing all matching records, the user can select which person to edit by their record number. The @SAY...GET statement uses the RANGE clause to ensure that nonexistent record numbers are not entered. RECCOUNT( ) is equal to the number of records in the database.

If the Escape key was not pressed, we GOTO the record number chosen by the user. Next, memory variables are assigned the values in these fields.

The rest should look familiar; it is similar to Insert. The Edit window is activated, and the values are edited and replaced. Encountering ENDDO causes the program flow to jump back to the top of the loop, where another entry can be retrieved.

Edit with arrays

Just as two different Insert programs were shown, two Edit programs are demonstrated as well. Once again the second version uses an array. The COPY TO ARRAY command copies the contents of the current record into the specified array. The program follows:

```
* Declare an array named stuff, 9 elements
DECLARE stuff[9]
STORE SPACE(20) TO mlname
DEFINE WINDOW err FROM 10,20 to 14,60
DEFINE WINDOW edit FROM 6,10 to 19,60
DEFINE WINDOW key FROM 4,35 TO 21,75
ACTIVATE WINDOW key
DO WHILE .T.
   @ 2,0 CLEAR TO 15,36
   STORE 0 TO recnum
   STORE SPACE(20) TO mlname
   * Get desired name
   @ 0,1 SAY "Enter Last Name:" GET mlname
   @ 15,1 SAY "Press ESC To Abort"
   READ
   * See if Escape was pressed.
   IF LASTKEY( ) = 27
      DEACTIVATE WINDOW key
      RETURN
   ENDIF
   mlname = TRIM(mlname)
   SEEK mlname
   * Error if not found
   IF .NOT. FOUND( )
      ACTIVATE WINDOW err
```

```
        @ 1,1 SAY "Not Found! Press Any Key To Continue."
        WAIT ""
        DEACTIVATE WINDOW err
        LOOP
    ENDIF
    * Display all matches
    DO WHILE lname = mlname
        @ 2,0 CLEAR TO 15,36
        @ 1,0
        reccnt = 0
        SCAN WHILE lname = mlname .AND. reccnt < 10
            LIST NEXT 1 TRIM(lname) + ", " + TRIM(fname)
            reccnt = reccnt + 1
        ENDSCAN
        IF lname = mlname
            ?
            WAIT
        ENDIF
    ENDDO
        @ 13,0 SAY " Enter Record # To Edit:" GET recnum RANGE 1,RECCOUNT( )
        @ 15,0 SAY " Press ESC To Abort"
        READ
        * See if Escape was pressed.
        IF LASTKEY( ) = 27
            DEACTIVATE WINDOW key
            RETURN
    ENDIF
        * Goto the record, assign fields to memory variables.
        GOTO recnum
        COPY NEXT 1 TO ARRAY stuff
        ACTIVATE WINDOW edit
        @ 1,1 SAY " Last Name:" GET stuff[1]
        @ 2,1 SAY "First Name:" GET stuff[2]
        @ 3,1 SAY "   Address:" GET stuff[3]
        @ 4,1 SAY "      City:" GET stuff[4]
        @ 5,1 SAY "      Sate:" GET stuff[5]
        @ 6,1 SAY "       Zip:" GET stuff[6]
        @ 7,1 SAY "     Phone:" GETstuff[7]
        @ 8,1 SAY "Entry Date:" GET stuff[8]
        @ 9,1 SAY " Potential:" GET stuff[9]
        @ 11,1 SAY "Press ESC To Abort"
        READ
        * See if Escape was pressed.
```

```
      IF LASTKEY( ) = 27
         DEACTIVATE WINDOW edit
         LOOP
      ENDIF
      REPLACE lname WITH stuff[1], fname WITH stuff[2], ;
         address WITH stuff[3], city WITH stuff[4], ;
   state WITH stuff[5], zip WITH stuff[6], ;
   phone WITH stuff[7], ent_date WITH ment_date, ;
   poten WITH mpoten
      DEACTIVATE WINDOW edit
         ENDDO
```

The Delete program

The Delete program is very similar to Edit. The program appears here:

```
Delete.prg:
* Initialize
STORE SPACE(15) TO mfname
STORE 0 TO reccnt
DEFINE WINDOW err FROM 10,20 to 14,60
DEFINE WINDOW delete FROM 6,15 to 10,60
DEFINE WINDOW key FROM 4,35 TO 21,75
ACTIVATE WINDOW key
DO WHILE .T.
   @ 2,0 CLEAR TO 15,36
   * Initialize variables
   STORE SPACE(20) TO mlname
   STORE "N" to yn
   STORE 0 TO recnum
   @ 0,1 SAY "Enter Last Name:" GET mlname
   @ 15,1 SAY "Press ESC To Abort"
   READ
   * See if Escape key was pressed.
   IF LASTKEY( ) = 27
      DEACTIVATE WINDOW key
      RETURN
   ENDIF
   mlname = TRIM(mlname)
   SEEK mlname
   * Error if not found
   IF .NOT. FOUND( )
      ACTIVATE WINDOW err
```

```
      @ 1,1 SAY "Not Found! Press Any Key To Continue."
      WAIT ""
      DEACTIVATE WINDOW err
      LOOP
   ENDIF
   * List all matches
   DO WHILE lname = mlname
      @ 2,0 CLEAR TO 15,36
      @ 1,0
      reccnt = 0
      SCAN WHILE lname = mlname .AND. reccnt < 10
         LIST NEXT 1 TRIM(lname) + ", " + TRIM(fname)
         reccnt = reccnt + 1
      ENDSCAN
      IF lname = mlname
         ?
         WAIT
      ENDIF
   ENDDO
   @ 13,0 SAY " Enter Record # To Delete:" GET recnum RANGE 1,RECCOUNT( )
   @ 15,0 SAY " Press ESC To Abort"
   READ
   * See if Escape was pressed
   IF LASTKEY( ) = 27
      DEACTIVATE WINDOW key
      RETURN
   ENDIF
   * Goto the record, assign fields to memory variables.
   GOTO recnum
   mlname = lname
   mfname = fname
   * Last chance prompt
   ACTIVATE WINDOW delete
   @ 0,1 SAY TRIM(lname) + ", " + TRIM(fname)
   @ 2,1 SAY "Delete: Are You Sure? (Y/N):" GET yn PICTURE "!"
   READ
   IF yn = "Y"
      DELETE
   ENDIF
   DEACTIVATE WINDOW delete
ENDDO
```

Again, it is similar to Edit, only the record selected is to be deleted not edited. An Are You Sure? prompt appears with the record in the Delete window to verify the user's selection.

Keep in mind that when records are "deleted," they are marked for deletion only. They are physically removed from the database only when a PACK is performed.

Report

Both the Report and Labels program try to emphasize how to use previously created reports in programs, the scopes of variables, and how to obtain the criteria to filter those reports with. The Report program appears here:

```
Report.prg:
* Initialize variables
STORE SPACE(20) TO mlname, mcity
STORE SPACE(15) TO mfname
STORE SPACE(30) TO maddress
STORE " " TO mstate
STORE SPACE(10) TO mzip
STORE SPACE(14) TO mphone
STORE { / / } TO ment_date
STORE 0 TO mpoten1
STORE 99999.99 TO mpoten2
STORE "" TO criteria
* Get criteria
DO Crit
SET FILTER TO &criteria
* Get destination
DO Dest
REPORT FORM Peorep
SET PRINT OFF
SET FILTER TO
WAIT
CLEAR
RETURN
```

When memory variables are declared in FoxPro, they can be accessed by the program in which they were declared, or by the subprograms that the current program calls. If a memory variable is declared in a subprogram that was called, the program that called it cannot access the variable.

This point is mentioned here because in Report two subprograms are called, Crit, to obtain criteria, and Dest, to select the print destination. We wanted Crit to return a criteria that we can use in this program. Because we are not using procedures with parameter passing, the memory variables must be declared here. The Crit program is discussed later.

After Crit is executed, the memory variable criteria contains the criteria for the report. To use this information, the SET FILTER TO &criteria command is used. Note that criteria is preceded with an ampersand (&), making criteria a macro. This means "substitute &criteria with the contents of criteria, and execute this statement." For example, if mac = "DO MAIN", typing &mac at the command window executes Main.

Next Dest is executed to select where to output the report, to the screen or printer.

We assume a report exists called Peorep, created in the Reports section of the Control Center. See the reports section in chapter 6 for creating reports. The report Peorep is run.

Afterwards, if the printer was selected, SET PRINT OFF deselects it. No harm is done in saying SET PRINT OFF if it was not previously set on.

The filter condition is removed with SET FILTER TO command followed by nothing. WAIT pauses execution, CLEAR clears the screen, and finally the program returns.

Crit

Crit allows users to set a filter condition that is entered into the memory variable criteria. The program follows:

```
Crit.prg:
DEFINE WINDOW crit FROM 6,10 TO 21,60
ACTIVATE WINDOW crit
@ 0,1 SAY " ENTER CRITERIA:"
@ 2,1 SAY " Last Name:" GET mlname
@ 3,1 SAY "First Name:" GET mfname
@ 4,1 SAY " Address:" GET maddress
@ 5,1 SAY " City:" GET mcity
@ 6,1 SAY " Sate:" GET mstate PICTURE "!!"
@ 7,1 SAY " Zip:" GET mzip PICTURE "99999-9999"
@ 8,1 SAY " Phone:" GET mphone PICTURE "(999) 999-9999"
@ 9,1 SAY "Entry Date:" GET ment_date
@ 10,1 SAY " Potent > =:" GET mpoten1 PICTURE "99999.99"
@ 11,1 SAY " Potent < =:" GET mpoten2 PICTURE "99999.99"
@ 13,1 SAY "Press ESC To Abort"
READ
* See if Escape was pressed
```

```
      IF LASTKEY( ) = 27
         DEACTIVATE WINDOW crit
         RETURN TO MASTER
      ENDIF
      * Trim all variables
      mlname = TRIM(mlname)
      mfname = TRIM(mfname)
      maddress = TRIM(maddress)
      mcity = TRIM(mcity)
      mstate = TRIM(mstate)
      mzip = TRIM(mzip)
      mphone = TRIM(mphone)
      * For each variable, check and see if it was used,
      * and if so, add it to criteria
      DO CASE
         CASE LEN(mlname) > 0
            criteria = criteria + "lname = mlname .AND."
         CASE LEN(mfname) > 0
            criteria = criteria + "fname = mfname .AND."
         CASE LEN(mcity) > 0
            criteria = criteria + "city = mcity .AND."
         CASE LEN(mstate) > 0
            criteria = criteria + "state = mstate .AND."
         CASE LEN(mzip) > 0
            criteria = criteria + "zip = mzip .AND."
         CASE LEN(mphone) > 0
            criteria = criteria + "phone = mphone .AND."
         CASE DAY(ent_date) > 0
            criteria = criteria + "ent_date = ment_date .AND."
         CASE mpoten1 > 0
            criteria = criteria + "poten > = mpoten1 .AND."
         CASE mpoten2 < 99999.99
            criteria = criteria + "poten < = mpoten2 .AND."
      ENDCASE
      * Get rid of last " .AND."
      criteria = LEFT(criteria, LEN(criteria) – 6)
      DEACTIVATE WINDOW crit
      RETURN
```

The first part of the program is not anything new. There are two "poten" fields, allowing a range of potential values to be entered.

Here is how it works. Only those memory variables where an entry has been made are counted toward the criteria. If more than one field is filtered on, they are ANDed together.

After input is read, all string variables are trimmed to remove trailing spaces. The CASE statement checks each variable to see if it has an entry. An entry will exist if the length of the variable is greater than 0. If an entry does exist, it is added to criteria. .AND. appears at the end of all the strings to allow all the conditions to be ANDed together.

The last " .AND." is removed by the LEFT( ) function. LEFT( ) takes the substring of criteria starting at the left and continuing for length of criteria minus 6 characters, the length of " .AND.".

Dest

The Dest program selects the destination for report output. The program appears here:

```
Dest.prg:
* Do menu definition Do Def_dest
ACTIVATE POPUP dest
RETURN
PROCEDURE Def_dest
   DEFINE POPUP dest FROM 10,55 TO 16,70
   DEFINE BAR 1 OF dest PROMPT " PRINT TO" SKIP
   DEFINE BAR 3 OF dest PROMPT " Screen"
   DEFINE BAR 4 OF dest PROMPT " Printer"
   DEFINE BAR 5 OF dest PROMPT " Abort"
   ON SELECTION POPUP dest DO Destpop
RETURN

PROCEDURE Destpop
   DO CASE
      CASE BAR( ) = 4
         SET PRINT ON
      CASE BAR( ) = 5
         RETURN TO MASTER
   ENDCASE
   DEACTIVATE POPUP
RETURN
```

The pop-up menu is similar to the Main program's main menu.

If Printer is selected, the printer is set on. Selecting screen does nothing, for the output appears on the screen anyway. The last option allows the user to abort the entire operation, and returns control to the main program via RETURN TO MASTER.

DEACTIVATE POPUP deactivates the most recently activated pop-up menu, in this case the menu Dest.

Labels

The Labels program is exactly like the report program, except that the REPORT FORM command is replaced with a LABEL FORM command, assumed to already exist. The program appears here:

```
Labels.prg:
* Initialize variables
STORE SPACE(20) TO mlname, mcity
STORE SPACE(15) TO mfname
STORE SPACE(30) TO maddress
STORE " " TO mstate
STORE SPACE(10) TO mzip
STORE SPACE(14) TO mphone
STORE { / / } TO ment_date
STORE 0 TO mpoten1
STORE 99999.99 TO mpoten2
STORE "" TO criteria
* Get criteria
DO Crit
SET FILTER TO &criteria
* Get destination
DO Dest
LABEL FORM Peolab
SET PRINT OFF
SET FILTER TO
WAIT
CLEAR
RETURN
```

Packem

The Packem program is a brief program that uses the PACK command to remove those records marked for deletion from the database. The code is as follows:

```
Packem.Prg:
CLEAR
SET TALK ON
```

```
@ 1,1 SAY "One moment, please..."
PACK

SET TALK OFF
WAIT
CLEAR
RETURN
```

Recall that in Main.prg we SET TALK OFF. Packing can take quite a while for large databases. Not seeing anything change on the screen for a long time can sometimes cause anxiety. SET TALK ON allows users to see the process take place. Afterwards the talk is set off again.

7

Using the Screen Builder

AN IMPORTANT ADDITION TO FOXPRO 2.0 IS THE SCREEN BUILDER, A VERY powerful screen generator. This chapter contains an exercise that shows how to create a custom screen using the Screen Builder. Following the exercise is a listing of the Screen Builder options.

Designing a custom screen

This section shows how to create a custom screen for a database of high school students. Figure 7-1 shows an example of how the finished entry screen will look. The Screen Builder makes it easy to create screen layouts by providing a "view screen" that lets you move information around, add prompts and boxes, and add other embellishments without using the normal FoxPro programming commands. In addition, you can place controls (push buttons, radio buttons, pop-up menus, check buttons, or lists) on the screen.

To create the screen in the next section, follow these steps:

1. Enter the Screen Builder and load the fields.
2. Move the fields around and change the prompts.
3. Attach formatting statements to the fields.
4. Create sections that use push buttons and check boxes.
5. Generate the Screen Code file.

The database to be used in the Screen Builder is MADISON.DBF. Create this file with the following structure:

Field Name	Type	Width	Dec
LNAME	Character	15	
FNAME	Character	15	

SOC_SEC	Character	11
GPA	Numeric	4
SEX	Character	1
CLASS	Numeric	4
SPORTS	Logical	1
POLIT	Logical	1
ACAD	Logical	1
OTHER	Logical	1

Make sure that this file is open before entering the Screen Builder.

```
                     ┌─────────────────────┐
                     │  MADISON HIGH SCHOOL│
                     │   STUDENT DATABASE  │
                     └─────────────────────┘

    First Name:  ANDY              Last:  ADAMS

           GPA:  3.00       Social Sec:  777-33-2222

         Class:  1990              Sex:  M



    Extra-Curricular Activities:

    [ ] Sports    [ ] Politics   [ ] Academics   [ ] Other Clubs
```

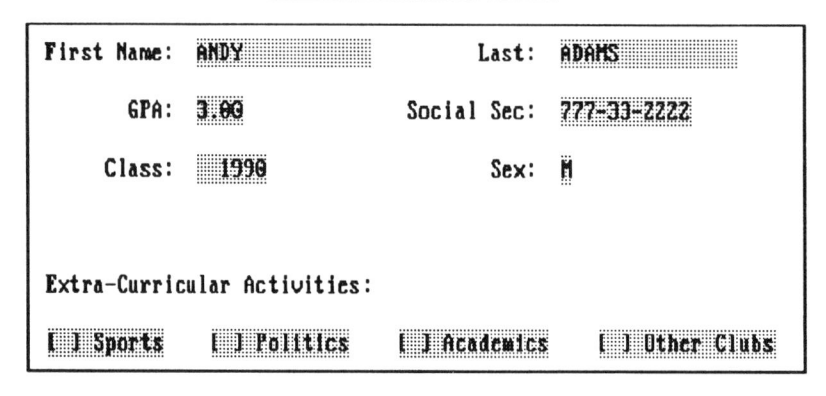

`<Next Record> <Prev. Record> < Continue > < Exit >`

Fig. 7-1. A screen created with the Screen Builder.

Starting the Screen Builder

You can enter the Screen Builder in two ways:

1. To enter from the command line, enter CREATE SCREEN. (You can include an optional file name.)
2. Choose New... from the File menu. Then choose the screen radio button.

For this example, use the first method, as it allows you to name the screen from the start. At the command window, type CREATE SCREEN MADISON and press Enter. You are now in the Screen Builder. From this screen you can change prompts, move objects around, and place in controls such as radio buttons and check boxes. Notice that there is a new menu option, Screen, to the right of the Window option.

Designing the screen

Loading fields Because this example creates a database edit screen, it begins with the command that loads some or all fields from the current file. To load the first six fields in the database:

1. Choose the Quick Screen option from the Screen menu.
2. Check the Fields... box.
3. From the dialog box that appears, choose the first six fields from the database, by moving to the field with the ↓ and then pressing Enter.
4. The fields selected should now be: Lname, Fname, Soc_Sec, GPA, Sex, and Class.
5. Choose OK to exit the dialog box, and then OK again to exit the Quick Screen box.

The six fields should now be loaded into the top left corner of the screen. Press the Tab key several times. Notice that the cursor stops at each prompt and each field. Each item that it stops at is called an *object*. Objects can be one of four types:

- *Fields* Fields or memory variables to display or edit.
- *Graphics* Boxes or lines.
- *Controls* Push buttons, radio buttons, check boxes, pop-ups, or lists.
- *Text* Any text on the screen, such as prompts, headings, etc.

To edit an object or to move it to a different place on the screen, you must be currently positioned at that object. In the next two steps, the fields are moved around, and then the text objects (prompts for each field) are edited.

An alternate way to load fields on the screen is to choose them one at a time. To do this, move to the area where the field is to go, and choose Field... from the Screen menu. Then choose the Get... option. At this point, you can choose the field from a list of names or type it in. The other options in this dialog box are explained further on in this chapter, under the Formatting section.

Moving objects To move an object, the following steps must be taken:

1. Go to the object.
2. Press the spacebar (or click the mouse).
3. Use the arrows (or mouse) to drag the field to the desired position.
4. Press the spacebar (or click the mouse outside the object).

Start by Tabbing to the Lname field box labeled 1: lname.... Use the steps above to move it to the right and down a row. As you drag the field, notice the status line at the top of the screen shows your row and column. Drag the field to row 1, column 40, so that it is right of the Fname field. Repeat this step for the other fields until your screen looks like the one in Fig. 7-2.

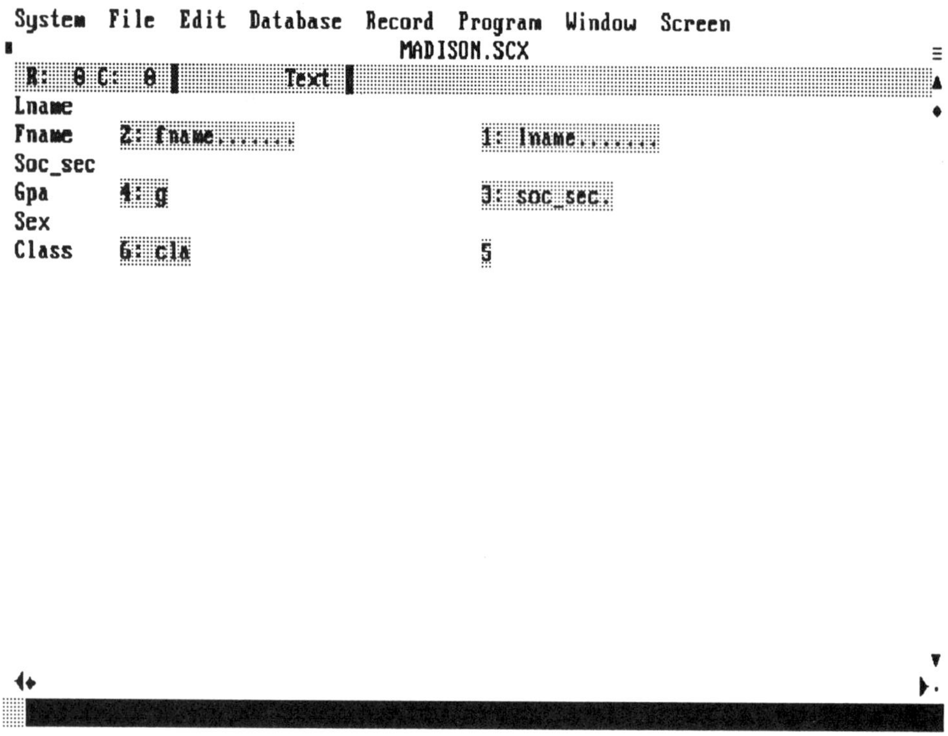

432 Using the Screen Builder

```
System  File  Edit  Database  Record  Program  Window  Screen
                             MADISON.SCX
 R:  0  C:  0          Text
Lname
Fname    2: fname......            1: lname......
Soc_sec
Gpa      4: g                      3: soc_sec.
Sex
Class    6: cla                    5
```

Fig. 7-2. Any type of object can be moved within the screen.

Moving multiple objects Often a group of objects must be moved. To do this, the entire area surrounding the objects must be selected, which is best done by drawing a *marquee* (dashed line) around the group. To do this, the following steps must be taken:

1. Go to a corner of the group area, but not within any object.
2. Press the spacebar (or press the mouse button).
3. Use the arrows (or mouse) to drag the marquee around the group.
4. Press Enter (or release the mouse button). The area is now selected.

To move the fields to the center of the screen, start by moving the cursor one row and a couple of spaces to the left above the Fname field box (row 0, column 8). Use the steps above to draw a marquee around all of the field boxes (do not include the field prompts in the selection area). Now drag it down five rows and to the right until it is centered. Finish by pressing Enter or releasing the mouse button. Figure 7-3 shows the fields after being moved.

The next step is to draw a marquee around the field names up in the top left corner of the screen and delete the entire area. To do this, start by moving the cursor to the right of the Lname prompt (row 0, column 8). Use the steps above to draw a marquee around the prompt area (the dotted line will cover the first

```
System  File  Edit  Database  Record  Program  Window  Screen
                            MADISON.SCX
   R: 12 C: 66          Move
Lname
Fname
Soc_sec
Gpa
Sex      ..................................................
Class    .                                                 .
         .   2: fname                  1: lname            .
         .                                                 .
         .   4: g                      3: soc_se           .
         .                                                 .
         .   6: cla                    5                   .
         .                                                 .
         ..................................................
```

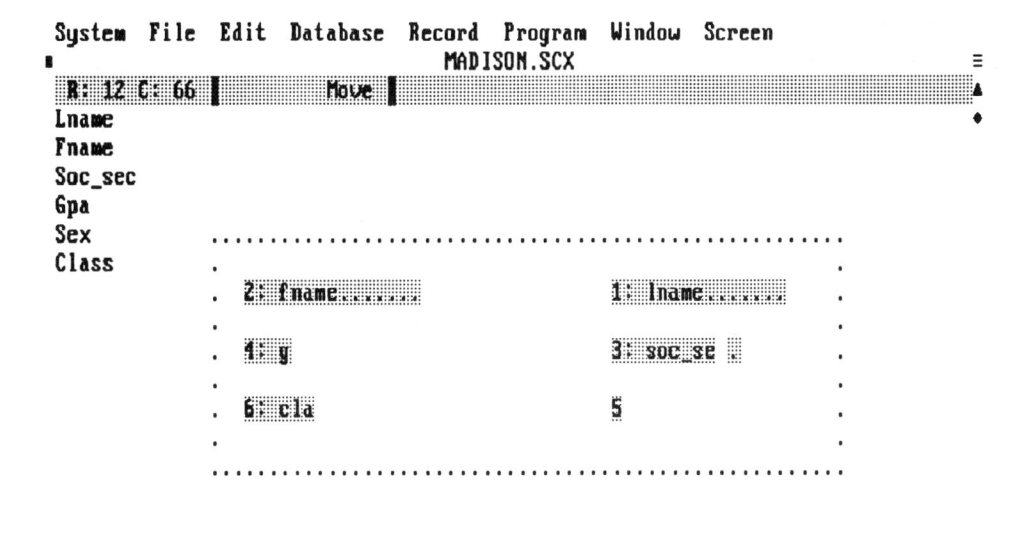

Fig. 7-3. The marquee allows a group of objects to be moved.

letter of each field name in column 0). Finish by pressing Enter or releasing the mouse button. Now the entire area is selected. Press Delete to delete it.

Adding text to the screen The next step is to add prompts in front of each field. Because each prompt is considered a text object, you must press Enter after typing it. To enter the first prompt:

1. Move 13 characters to the left of the Fname field box.
2. Type First Name:.
3. Press Enter.

Type in the rest of the text so that all prompts reflect those of Fig. 7-4. Remember, if a text object is not placed exactly where you want, you can select it and drag it to the correct spot.

Placing a box on the screen Boxes help draw attention to particular fields and areas of the screen. To place a box on the screen, the following steps must be taken:

1. Move where the top left corner of the box is to be positioned.
2. Press Ctrl – B (or choose Box from the Screen menu).
3. Adjust the size by dragging it to the right and down.

434 Using the Screen Builder

   4. Press Enter (or release the mouse button).
   5. If desired, change the type of box (Double Line, Character, Filled, etc.) by pressing Enter while in it.

To place the box around the heading, move one row above and a little to the left of the MADISON HIGH SCHOOL heading. Press Ctrl – B. Use the arrows (or mouse) to drag the box down and to the right, surrounding the area with a single-line box. Press Enter (or release the mouse button). To change the box to a double line, move anywhere on the border of the box and press Enter. From this menu choose the Double line radio button. You can also use any other character for the border by choosing Character.

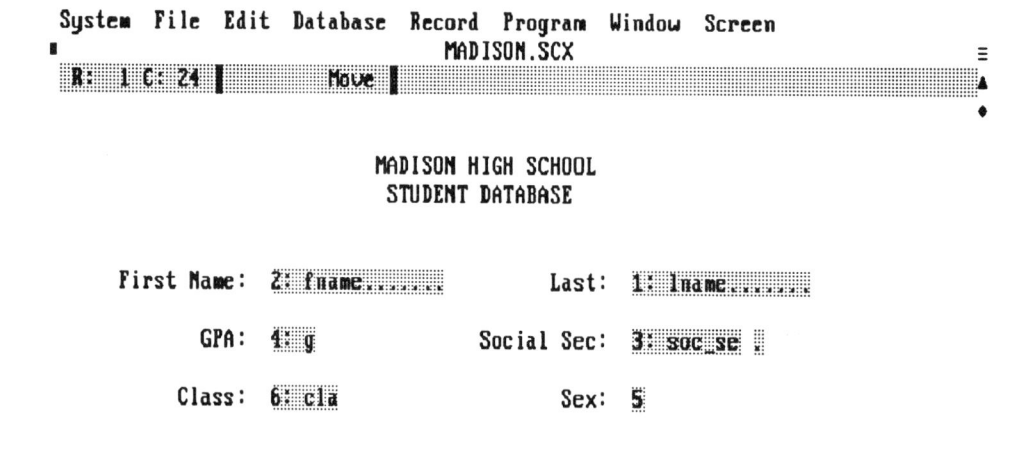

```
System  File  Edit  Database  Record  Program  Window  Screen
                              MADISON.SCX
  R:  1  C: 24          Move



                      MADISON HIGH SCHOOL
                       STUDENT DATABASE


           First Name:  2: fname          Last:  1: lname

                  GPA:  4: g         Social Sec:  3: soc_se

                Class:  6: cla              Sex:  5
```

Fig. 7-4. The screen with modified prompts.

   To move a box, remember that it is an object (in this case a graphic object), so you can select it and drag it to a different spot. To resize a box, move to the border and press Ctrl – spacebar. Use the arrows to resize the box. Only the bottom right corner can be resized.
   Formatting the fields to be edited   You can specify data editing options for each expression on the screen. This places restrictions on what the user can

enter for that particular field or memory variable. The steps for setting a format are:

1. Move to the field object.
2. Press Enter (this pulls up the Format dialog screen).
3. This screen allows you to either choose a format from the Format... push button or enter a template next to Format....
4. If desired, choose from the Range, Valid, Message, and/or other check boxes.

The first format placed in the example is to restrict the first and last names to all uppercase letters. To start, move to the Fname field box and press Enter. Choose the Format... push button. From the checklist of editing options, choose To Upper Case. Finish by pressing OK to exit the Format... options, and then OK again to exit the Format dialog. Repeat this step with the Lname field.

The next format is to set a range limit between 0 and 4 for GPA scores. Move to the GPA field box and press Enter. Choose the Upper... option. Change the radio button to Expression. In the text box enter 4 and press Ctrl – Tab to exit. Finish by pressing OK to exit the Upper... options. Next, choose the Lower... option. Again, change the radio button to Expression and enter 0 in the text box. Finish by pressing OK to exit the Lower... options, and then OK again to exit the Format dialog.

The format for Social Security number is entered as a template of ###-##-####. The # forces the entry to be numeric, and the hyphens should be placed as a "mask" in the entry area. See the @SAY...GET section in chapter 2 for a list of all format template options. Move to the Soc_Sec field box and press Enter. Move to the box next to the Format... option. In the box enter ###-##-####. Finish by pressing OK twice.

A message will appear at the bottom of the screen when the user moves to the Class field. Move to the field box and press Enter. Choose the Message... option. Change the radio button to Expression. In the text box enter: "Type a year between 1956 and 1998" (include the quotes). Press Ctrl – Tab to exit. Finish by pressing OK through both screens.

A validity check is performed on the Sex field, to make sure that the user has entered an M or F. Move to the field box and press Enter. Choose the Format... push button. From the checklist of editing options, choose To Upper Case. Finish by pressing OK to exit the Format... options. Then choose Message... and change the radio button to Expression. In the text box type "Enter M or F". Press OK to exit the Message... screen. Next, choose Valid... and change the radio button to Expression. In the text box enter Sex $ "MF" (the entry must be a logical expression that evaluates to True or False). Finish by pressing OK through both screens.

Placing controls on the screen You can place check boxes, pop-up menus, and other types of interfaces on the screen. In this section four check boxes are created for enter Extra-Curricular Activities. Then, push buttons are added to ask the user what to do next: go to the next record, the previous record, or quit.

Check boxes Check boxes can only be used for expressions that are logical or numeric. If logical, the expression returns .T. when the user checks the box, .F. when left blank. If numeric, the expression returns 1 if the users check the box, 0 if not. The steps for setting up a check box are:

1. Move to the area where the box will go.
2. Choose Check Box... from the Screen menu (or press Ctrl – K).
3. Enter a prompt for the box, and the field or memory variable to be edited.
4. If desired, set Messages, Valid clauses, and other options.

The first check box is for the Sports field. To start, move six rows below the Class and Sex fields. Choose Check Box... from the Screen menu. Under the Check Box prompt, enter Sports. Then under Variable, select Choose.... Select the Sports field. Finish by pressing OK through both screens.

Repeat the steps until the four check boxes are on the screen, laid out as displayed in Fig. 7-5. Finish off by entering the text Extra-Curricular Activities two lines above the boxes.

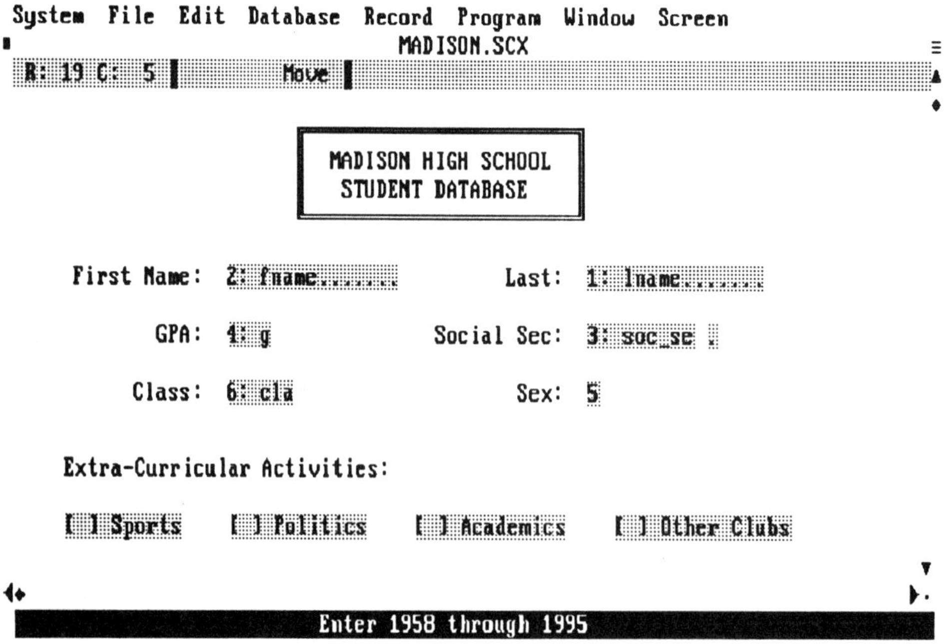

Fig. 7-5. Check boxes work best for logical fields.

Selecting an object Throughout a session with the Screen Builder you might need to edit the settings of particular objects. To do this, move to the object and press Enter. Depending on the type of object, one of the following dialog boxes will appear, allowing you to make changes. The object types and their corresponding dialogs are:

- Fields   Field dialog box that sets editing characteristics.
- Graphics   Dialog box that allows for changes in graphic characters.
- Controls   Dialog box for that particular control.
- Text   Dialog box that allows for a comment to be entered.

All dialogs allow comments to be entered. These comments are saved with the screen file, and do not appear anywhere else.

Reordering fields You might have noticed that the field numbers are not ordered left to right. Because the Fname field is number two, it is currently sequenced after the Lname field, even though it should now be the first field in the entry screen. To change the editing order of fields:

1. Select all fields objects on the screen (see the section "Moving Multiple Objects" above).
2. Choose Reorder Fields from the Screen menu.
3. Fields will now be numbered left to right, top to bottom.

Screen code setup Each time that the screen is run, it is important to make sure that a CLEAR command is issued first. Through the Screen Layout menu you can set initial commands that are always run when the screen is called. You can also set "cleanup" commands that run when the screen is terminated. To set the command:

1. Choose Screen Layout from the Screen menu.
2. Choose Setup... and then OK. This brings up the Setup area where you can place initial commands.
3. In the editing box, type CLEAR and then exit by pressing Ctrl – Enter.

The Screen Layout dialog is also the area that allows you to size and position the screen (if it is not to be full size), add clauses to the READ command, and change environment settings.

One last embellishment Finish the screen by adding a box around all of the field prompts:

1. Move one line above and several characters left of the First Name: prompt.
2. Press Ctrl – B.
3. Size the box so that it appears around all the fields (see Fig. 7-6).

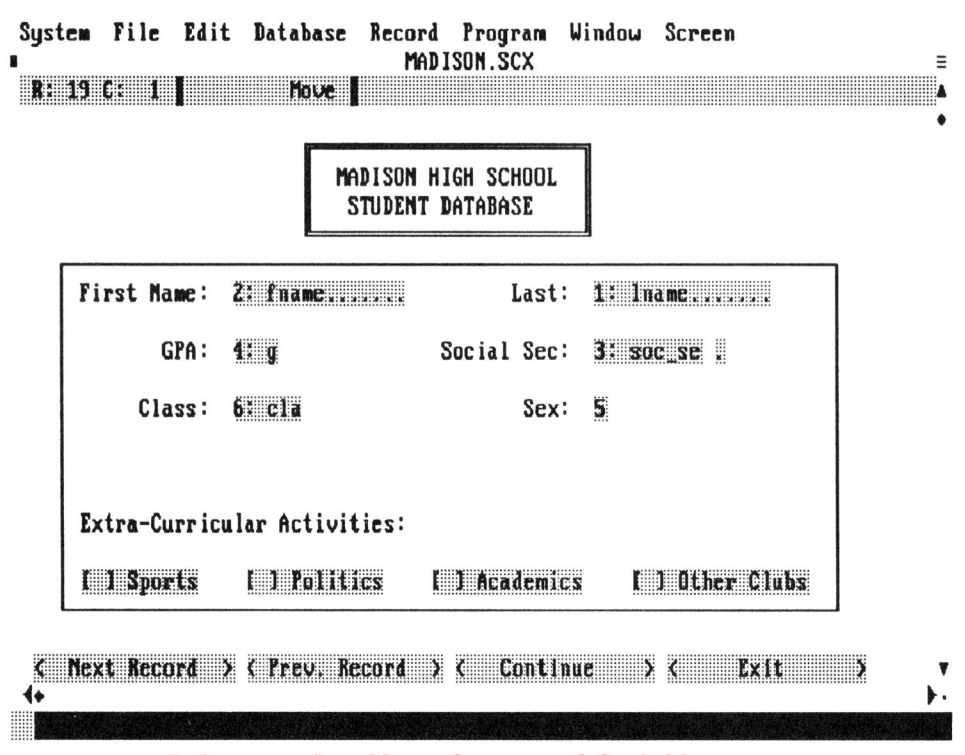

Fig. 7-6. Finish the screen by adding a box around the fields.

Saving the screen

All of the definitions of the screen are contained in the screen file, which has an .SCX extension. This file is a database which can be viewed and/or edited. To open an .SCX file, simply call USE *file name* where the *file name* is the screen file (remember to type in the .SCX extension).

A screen file cannot be run by FoxPro, but it can be used to generate a Fox-Pro program. You must save your screen if you are to generate the program. To save the MADISON.SCX file:

1. Choose Save from the File menu (or Press Ctrl – W)
2. If you have not named the file yet, it asks for a name.

Creating a second screen

The bottom of Fig. 7-6 shows four push buttons that allow the user to choose what to do when done editing the current record. They are labeled Next, Previous, Current, and Exit. These options are going to be created on a second screen panel, separate from MADISON.SCX. By placing them in their own screen file, two things are accomplished. First, because the options are generally used in any editing situation, this second screen can be used in conjunction with other screens in the future. Secondly, the user is able to get down to the push buttons by pressing PgDn, Ctrl – End, or Esc because there is a READ statement placed between each screen. If the push buttons were part of the MADISON.SCX screen, the user could only get to the bottom by passing through every one of the fields.

The second screen panel is named BOTT.SCX. To create it, enter CREATE SCREEN BOTT from the command screen. Now, place the push buttons on the bottom of the screen, following the directions below.

Push buttons   Push buttons are most often used when the user is choosing an action to be performed. Common push buttons in dialog boxes are Cancel (abort the dialog) and OK (save the dialog selections and exit). A group of push buttons evaluate to one answer, as only one can be chosen by the user. The answer can be stored in a field or memory variable expression. The variable can be numeric or character. The steps for setting up a push button are:

1. Move to top left corner of the push button area.
2. Choose Push Button... from the Screen menu (or press Ctrl – H).
3. Enter the prompts for the push buttons, and then the name of the field or memory variable to hold the answer.
4. If desired, set Messages, Valid clauses and other options.

The push buttons should be placed at the bottom of the screen, allowing the user to choose to go to the next record, the previous record, or exit. To start, move down to row 19, column 1. Choose Push Button... from the Screen menu. Under the Push Button prompts, enter the following list:

Next Record
Prev. Record
Continue
Exit

Select the Terminating check box, as the user will be done with the screen when they reach these push buttons at the bottom. Then type the field name Mselect in the box next to Choose.... Finish by pressing OK.

Mselect is the name of a numeric memory variable that holds the user's selection. If the user chooses the first push button (Next Record), Mselect is one, and so on. If the variable has been declared as a character, it is equivalent to the prompt chosen. If the variable has not been declared before the screen is run, FoxPro creates it as a numeric variable with a value of 0.

Push Buttons default to being laid out horizontally, although you can choose a Vertical orientation instead. You can also change the spacing between the buttons. To define a default push button, enter \! before the prompt.

Hot keys Hot keys may be set within push buttons, radio buttons, and check boxes. This section explains how to define a hot key for each prompt created above. To define a hot key, place \ before the appropriate letter in the prompt. To edit the prompts:

1. Move to one of the push buttons at the bottom of the screen.
2. Press Enter (this brings up the push button setup screen).
3. Change the prompts to: <Next Record, \<Prev. Record, \<Continue, and \<Exit.
4. Finish by pressing OK.

The second screen is now finished. Save it by pressing Ctrl – W.

Generating code

Once the screens have been designed, you must generate a program that can run them. In this example, the two screens are generated into one program named MADISON.PRG, with a READ command between each. To generate a program, the steps are:

1. Open the .SCX file of the first (or only) screen to be generated.
2. Choose Generate... from the Program menu.
3. If more than one screen panel is to be generated, add the screen names to the list.
4. If desired, set options for automatic opening and closing of files, multiple READs and comments for the program.

To generate the code for MADISON.PRG, do the following:

1. Open MADISON.SCX file by entering MODIFY SCREEN MADISON from the Command screen.
2. Choose Generate... from the Program menu.
3. The BOTT.SCX screen is also part of this program, so choose Add Select Bott.SCX from the list.
4. Under Code Options, erase the two Open and Close File check boxes. If these options were left on, the program would re-open the file each pass through the screen, preventing the record pointer from being able to move to next and previous records.
5. Choose the Multiple READs check box, because placing a READ after the first screen panel allows the user to press any screen exiting key to get to the second panel.
6. The output file is given the same name as the open screen file, with a .PRG (or .SPR) extension. The Generate... dialog should now match that of Fig. 7-7.
7. Press <<Generate>>.

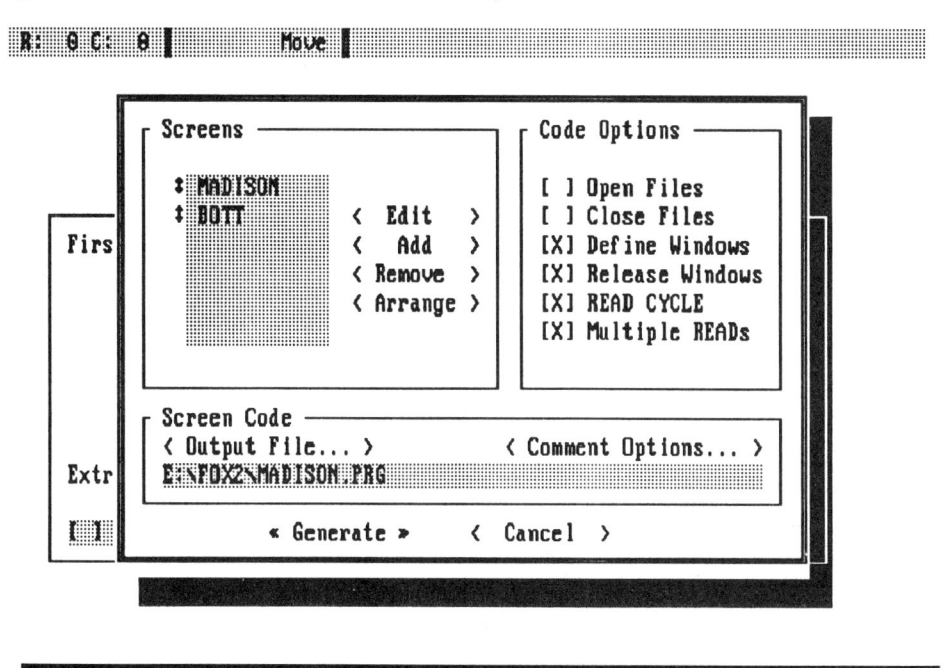

Fig. 7-7. The Generate... dialog box.

The program that has been generated, MADISON.SPR, contains all of the directives to running the screens created in the Screen Builder. You can open a .SPR file by typing MODIFY COMMAND from the command window, or choosing Open... from the File menu and then changing the Type to Program. Example of source code from the MADISON.SPR file:

```
#REGION 1
@ 6,5 SAY "First Name:"
@ 6,42 SAY "Last:"
@ 8,12 SAY "GPA:"
@ 6,18 GET madison.fname SIZE 1,15 DEFAULT " " PICTURE "@!"
@ 6,49 GET madison.lname SIZE 1,15 DEFAULT " " PICTURE "@!"
@ 8,18 GET madison.gpa SIZE 1,4 RANGE 0,4 DEFAULT 0
```

Running a program

The program MADISON.SPR sets up the screen layout, but it does not have all the commands to run the menu options (Next Record, Prev. Record, Continue, and Exit). Create the following program, EDITMAD.PRG, which calls the Madison screen. To do this, type MODIFY COMMAND EDITMAD from the command window and type in the following code:

```
*** Editmad.prg
*** Edits MADISON.DBF by calling the MADISON.SPR screen

mselect = 0
USE Madison INDEX Names && Open the Madison database
DO WHILE mselect < > 4
  DO Madison.SPR
  DO CASE
    CASE mselect = 1 .AND. .NOT. eof( )
      SKIP
    CASE mselect = 2 .AND. .NOT. bof( )
      SKIP - 1
  ENDCASE
ENDDO
```

To run the program you must have some names already added to the database. To do this, type APPEND from the command window and enter three or four test records. The next step is to index the file by the Lname field. To do this, type INDEX ON LNAME TO NAMES from the command window. Finally, run the editing program by typing DO EDITMAD from the command window or choosing Do... from the Program menu.

Try changing the values of certain fields, especially those where masks and ranges are set. To get to the bottom of the screen, press Enter through every field or press PgDn or Ctrl - End. Choose Next Record to skip to the next name in the database. After testing the screen, choose Exit to return to the command window.

The Editmad program contains a simple loop that runs the MADISON.SPR screen for record editing until the user decides to exit. The mselect memory variable is the same name as the variable defined by the push buttons. Therefore, it returns one if Next Record is chosen, a two if Prev. Record is chosen, etc. This is why the program skips to the next record when mselect is one. When the user sets mselect to four by choosing Exit, the program exits the DO WHILE loop.

Although the editing program seems quite limited, several embellishments can be added to make it much more powerful. For instance, a push button of Seek Record at the bottom of the screen can call a routine that asks for a last name and then go directly to the name by calling the SEEK command.

Other control objects

In addition to the two control objects described in the exercise above, push buttons and check buttons, you can create four others. These are radio buttons, check boxes, pop-ups, lists, and invisible buttons.

Radio buttons are much like push buttons in that only one can be chosen from a group. The main difference is that a dot appears next to the currently chosen button, and when the user chooses a different one the dot is automatically removed. To set up radio buttons, follow the directions above for setting up push buttons.

Pop-ups allow the user to choose an item from a list. The list of items only appears when the user moves to the pop-up object. Again, only one choice can be made, so setting up pop-ups is much like setting the push buttons in the example above. When entering pop-up prompts using the screen generator, you can type in the prompts (list pop-up) or define an array pop-up.

Lists also allow the user to choose an item from a list. The list, unlike a pop-up, appears on the screen at all times. The list's contents can be from an array, an existing pop-up, the names of the fields from a data file's structure, the contents of a certain field from each record in an open file, or a list of files which follow a certain skeleton (such as *.DBF). You can resize a list by moving to the list, pressing the Ctrl – spacebar and using the arrow keys, or Ctrl – clicking with the mouse.

Invisible buttons work just like push buttons, except you do not define prompts for them. Instead, they are typically placed on top of text.

Design screen commands

The following commands are available in the Screen Builder while editing a screen. Each of these commands can also be chosen from the Screen menu.

Control key	Description
Ctrl – B	Creates a box.
Ctrl – F	Creates a field object.
Ctrl – T	Creates a text object.
Ctrl – H	Creates push buttons.
Ctrl – N	Creates radio buttons.
Ctrl – K	Creates check boxes.
Ctrl – O	Creates pop-ups.
Ctrl – L	Creates a list.
Ctrl – I	Creates invisible buttons.

8

Using the Menu Builder

ALONG WITH THE SCREEN BUILDER, THE MENU BUILDER IS ANOTHER FOXPRO 2.0 addition that makes program generation easier. This chapter contains an exercise that shows how to create a custom menu using the Menu Builder.

Designing a custom menu

This section shows how to create a custom menu that maintains and prints a database of high school students. Figure 8-1 shows how the finished menu will look. The Menu Builder makes it easy to create the bounce-bar menu and its associated pop-ups. It lets you assign commands to each option, and then it generates a program that runs the menu.

All the definitions of the menu are contained in the menu file, which has a .MNX extension. This file is a database that can be viewed and/or edited. To open an .MNX file, simply call USE *file name* where the *file name* is the menu file (remember to type in the .MNX extension).

To create the menu, follow these steps:

1. Enter the Menu Builder.
2. Create the bounce-bar menu that shows along the top.
3. Create a pop-up for each menu option.
4. Assign commands and procedures to be run for each pop-up option.
5. Generate a program file that runs the menu.

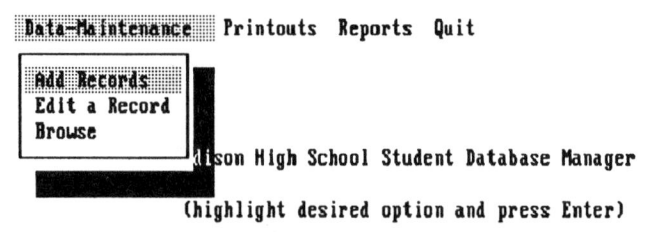

```
  Data-Maintenance  Printouts  Reports  Quit
  ┌─────────────┐
  │ Add Records │
  │ Edit a Record│
  │ Browse      │
  └─────────────┘son High School Student Database Manager

         (highlight desired option and press Enter)
```
Fig. 8-1. A menu created with the Menu Builder.

The database to be used in the Screen Builder is MADISON.DBF, the same file used in the previous chapter. If you have not created it yet, do so with the following structure:

Field name	Type	Width	Dec
LNAME	Character	15	
FNAME	Character	15	
SOC_SEC	Character	11	
GPA	Numeric	4	2
SEX	Character	1	
CLASS	Numeric	4	
SPORTS	Logical	1	
POLIT	Logical	1	
ACAD	Logical	1	
OTHER	Logical	1	

Starting the Menu Builder

You can enter the Menu Builder in two ways:

1. To enter from the command line, enter CREATE MENU. (You can include an optional file name)
2. Choose New... from the File menu. Then choose the Menu radio button.

For this example, use the first method, as it allows you to name the screen from the start. At the command window, type CREATE MENU MADISON and press Enter. You are now in the Menu Builder. Notice that there is a new menu option, Menu, to the right of the Window option.

Designing the screen

Defining menu pads Because this example creates a bounce-bar menu where each option has a corresponding pop-up, the first step is to assign prompts and results to each pad in the bounce-bar menu.

1. At the Prompt Box, enter \<Data-Maintenance. The \ causes the letter D to be a hot key.
2. Press ↓ to get to the next prompt area. Submenu is being left as the Result default, because this pad brings up a submenu pop-up. Also, do not go into the Create Result section, because the pop-up is created in the next section of this exercise.
3. Enter the other three prompts: \<Printouts, \<Reports, and \<Quit.
4. At this point, the Menu Builder screen should look like Fig. 8-2.

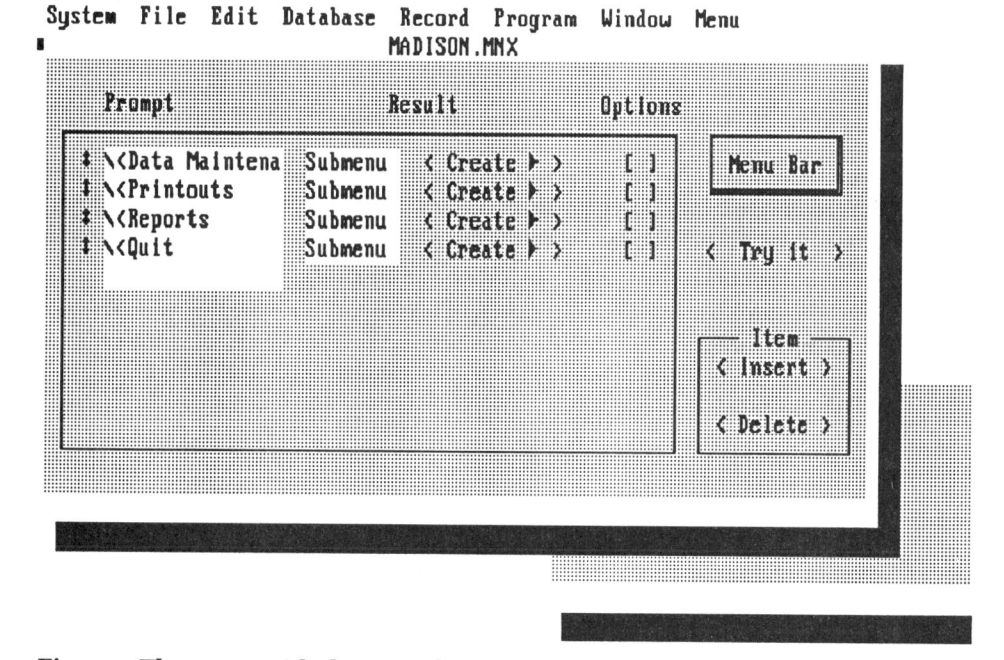

Fig. 8-2. The menu with the menu bars entered.

In the example above, all four results were set to Submenu. However, each pad can be set to one of the following results:

- Submenu   Allows definition of a pop-up submenu for the pad.
- Command   Allows entry of a command that is run when this option is chosen. The command can be any FoxPro command, including a call to a program. If the command is longer than the Result box, the box scrolls horizontally.
- Procedure   Allows entry of a group of commands that is run when this option is chosen. The code generator assigns this procedure a unique name.

- **Pad Name** Allows entry of a defined pad name (including any of FoxPro system bar menu names).

Defining a submenu option The next step is to set up the pop-up menu for the first pad, Data-Maintenance. To enter the first pop-up:

1. Move to the Data-Maintenance Submenu Create option and press Enter. It now shows an area for designing the first pop-up.
2. At the Prompt Box, enter \<Add Records.
3. Leave Command as the Result default, because this pad runs a command.
4. In the Result box, type in the command APPEND. When this pop-up bar is chosen, the APPEND command is run automatically.

Defining a submenu procedure The next step is to write a procedure that is run every time that Edit a Record is chosen from the Data-Maintenance pop-up.

1. Press ↓ to get to the next prompt.
2. At the Prompt Box, enter \<Edit a Record.
3. Press Enter at the Command option and choose Proc.
4. Now choose Create, which brings up a text area for entering a procedure. Type in the following procedure:

    ```
    CLEAR
    ACCEPT "Enter a Last Name to Search for: " TO Mlname
    LOCATE FOR upper)(Lname) = upper(Mlname)
    EDIT
    ```

5. Press Ctrl – Enter when done.
6. Press ↓ and enter the third prompt \<Browse.
7. Leave Command as the default, and in the Result box, type in the command BROWSE.
8. At this point the Menu Builder screen should look like Fig. 8-3.
9. Return to the menu bar definition screen, by choosing the pop-up (the box with double lines around the right and bottom). Select the Menu Bar option from the pop-up.

Setting up the Printout submenus. Setting up the Printout and Submenu pop-ups are essentially the same step as that of Data-Maintenance. To enter the Printouts pop-up:

1. Move to the Printout submenu Create option and press Enter.
2. At the prompt box, enter the following prompts and results:

Prompt	Result
\<Mailing Labels Command	LABEL FORM Madison TO PRINT

```
\ <Listing Proc
CLEAR
LIST Fname,Lname,Class,GPA
WAIT
```

3. Return to the menu bar definition screen by pulling up the pop-up. Select the Menu Bar option.

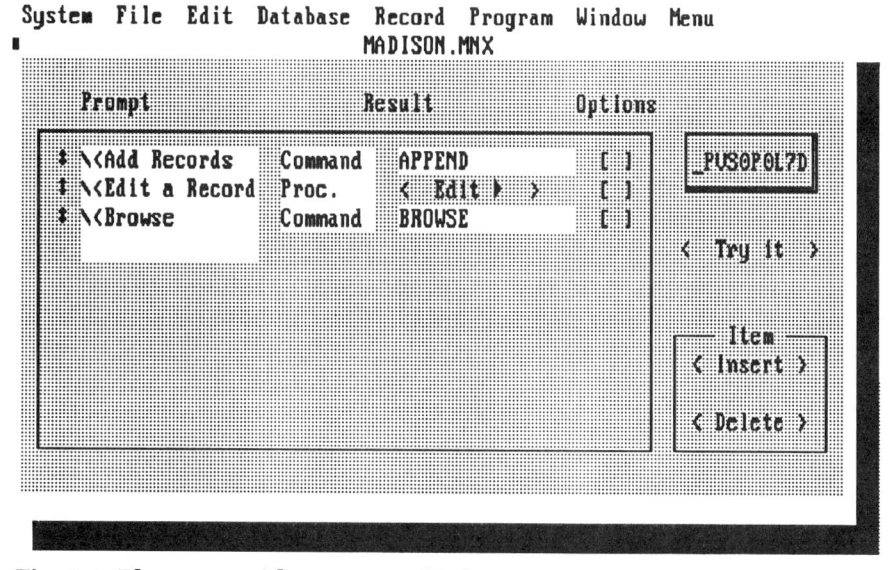

Fig. 8-3. The menu with pop-ups added.

Options check box Notice the Options check box next to each menu pad and submenu option. Choosing this box brings up the Options dialog box. This box allows you to specify the following:

- *Comment* A comment stored in the .MNX database.
- *Shortcuts* Allows definition of a shortcut key. This is different from a hot key, in that a shortcut must be a valid key label (such as Alt – F). For pop-up options, a shortcut text can be defined so that it shows next to the prompt.
- *Mark* A check mark character is placed before the option. The diamond is the default character, although you can define any character as the check mark.
- *Skip For* Allows a logical expression to be entered. When the logical expression is true (.T.), the option is disabled.

Setting up the Report submenus The Report submenu takes advantage of a few of the options. To enter the Report pop-up:

1. Move to the Reports submenu Create option and press Enter.

2. At the prompt box, enter the following prompts and results:

Prompt	Result
\\<Summary Command	REPORT FORM MADSUM TO PRINT
\\<Detail Command	REPORT FORM MADDET TO PRINT

3. Move to the \\<Summary Options check box and press Enter.
4. Choose the Shortcut... check box.
5. At the Key Label: box, press Alt – S and then choose OK. Choose OK again to exit the dialog box. When the menu is run, the \\<Summary bar can now be chosen by the hot key (S) or the shortcut key, Alt – S.
6. Move to the \\<Detail Options check box and press Enter.
7. Choose the Skip For... check box.
8. At the Skip For *expL* box, enter the following logical expression: .NOT. FILE("MADDET.FRX").
9. Choose OK, and then choose OK again to exit the dialog. The \\<Detail bar is disabled if the report form MADDET.FRX is not found.
10. Return to the menu bar definition screen by pulling up the pop-up. Select the Menu Bar option.

Defining the Quit option The Quit option is simply a command that quits FoxPro.

1. Move to the Quit submenu option and change it to Command.
2. At the Result box, enter QUIT. The option should look like this:

   \\<Quit   Command   QUIT

Menu code setup Each time that the menu is run, it is important to make sure that the data file is opened. Through the General Options... menu you can set initial commands that are always run when the screen is called. You can also set "cleanup" commands that run after the screen is defined. To set the command:

1. Choose General Options... from the menu.
2. Choose Setup... and then OK. This brings up the Setup area where you can place initial commands.
3. In the editing box, enter the following command:

   USE Madison INDEX Names

4. Exit by pressing Ctrl – Enter.

Menu code cleanup The program that generates the menu defines all menu pads and pop-ups, but it does not actually activate the menu. The final step is to add the ACTIVATE MENU command in the cleanup procedure. Through the General Options..., menu you can set final commands that are run after the menu has been defined. To set the command:

1. Choose General Options... from the menu.
2. Choose Cleanup... and then OK. This brings up the Cleanup area where you can place initial commands.
3. In the editing box, enter the following commands:
   ACTIVATE MENU _msysmenu
4. Exit by pressing Ctrl – Enter.

The Menu Builder names the main menu _msysmenu.

Saving the menu

The menu information is saved in a file with a .MNX extension. A screen file cannot be run by FoxPro, but it can be used to generate a FoxPro program. You must save your screen if you are to generate the program. To save the MADISON.MNX file:

1. Choose Save from the File menu.
2. If you have not named the file yet, it asks for a name.

Generating code

Once the menu has been designed, you must generate a program that defines the menus and run them. FoxPro gives the program a .MPR extension. The menu is generated a named MADISON.MPR. To generate the code for MADISON.MPR, do the following:

1. Choose Generate... from the Program menu.
2. Give the output file the same name as the menu file, with a .MPR extension.
3. Press <<Generate>>.

The program that has been generated, MADISON.MPR, contains all of the directives to running the screens created in the screen builder. You can open an .MPR file by typing MODIFY COMMAND from the command window, or choosing Open... from the File menu and then setting the Type to Program. Example of source code from the MADISON.MPR file:

```
DEFINE POPUP Data MARGIN RELATIVE SHADOW COLOR SCHEME 4
DEFINE BAR 1 OF Data PROMPT " \ <Add Records"
DEFINE BAR 2 OF Data PROMPT " \ <Edit"
DEFINE BAR 3 OF Data PROMPT " \ <Browse"
```

ON SELECTION BAR 1 OF Data APPEND ON SELECTION BAR 2 OF Data;
DO _pvt0jaxq9 IN MADISON.MPR

Running the menu

To exit the Menu Builder, press Ctrl – W or Ctrl – Enter. The program is ready to try out. From the command window, enter the following: DO MADISON.MPR. The menu shown resembles the one in Fig. 8-1 at the beginning of the chapter. Highlight the different menu pads. Notice that it automatically places a shadow behind each pop-up. Notice that the Report menu option, Detail Report, is disabled because the report MADDET.FRX does not exist. Choose one of the pop-up options, such as Browse. When you exit the option, the program goes back to the command window.

Once you have run the menu, the menu options at the top of the screen are now the Madison options, not the system menu. To bring the system menu back up, enter the following command:

SET SYSMENU TO DEFAULT

Running a program generated from Screen Builder

The program MADISON.MPR sets up the menu layout, but it does not have the commands to return to the menu after running an option. Create the program MADMENU.PRG, to call the Madison menu and return to it after each option. To do this, type MODIFY COMMAND Madmenu from the command window and type in the following code:

```
*** Madmenu.prg
*** Maintains and Prints MADISON.DBF by calling the MADISON.MNX menu

DO WHILE .T.      && create endless loop (quit is the only exit)
  CLEAR
  @ 5,15 SAY "Madison High School Student Database Manager"
  @ 7,16 SAY "(highlight desired option and press Enter)"
  DO Mad.MPR
ENDDO
```

To run the program you should have some names already added to the database. If there are no names in it, type APPEND from the command window and enter three or four test records. If the index has not been created, do this by typing INDEX ON LNAME TO NAMES from the command window. Finally, run the menu program by typing DO MADMENU from the command window or by choosing Do... from the Program menu.

Notice how the screen title is shaded when each pop-up is brought up.

Although the menu program seems quite limited, several embellishments could be added to make it much more powerful. For instance, the Append and Edit routines could call up customized format screens using the SET FORMAT TO command. The Report and Print routines could have procedures that ask the user whether they want their output to the screen or printer. These routines could also ask the user for sort order or selection criteria before printing. See the programming chapter for examples of these types of routines.

9

Using the RQBE window

THE FIRST SQL (STANDARD QUERY LANGUAGE) COMMAND TO BE ADDED TO FoxPro is SELECT which was introduced with version 2.0. SELECT is a very powerful command which can take the place of many FoxPro commands. For instance, one SELECT command can perform the function of five commands such as USE, SET FILTER TO, SET INDEX, BROWSE, and SET RELATION.

The SELECT command is quite complex, and it takes awhile to learn all of its clauses and features. However, FoxPro has a window which allows you to easily put together the pieces of the command. This RQBE (Relational Query By Example) window lets you set filters, the FOR conditions; set the output format (browse, display, report format, labels, etc.); set the index order; and set relations.

Setting query conditions

This section uses the COMPANY.DBF database in examples of several queries in the RQBE window. The database holds records of companies that have made purchases at a computer store. The Amount field contains the total of all purchases per client. If you are following along with this exercise hands-on, create this file and add the following records:

Company.DBF

Record #	NAME	CODE	CITY	AMOUNT
1	Joe's Tacos	A01	San Diego	1000
2	Jill's Advertising	A02	La Jolla	5000
3	Computers R Us	B01	San Diego	8000
4	Sausedo Systems	A05	San Jose	6000
5	Jetson Electronics	B02	Glendale	0

To run a query, the following steps will be taken:

1. Open the RQBE window.
2. Specify the database(s) to be used in the query.
3. Select fields to appear in the query results.
4. Change output format and order, if desired.
5. Specify selection criteria.
6. Execute the query.

Opening the RQBE window

You can enter the RQBE window in two ways:

- To enter from the command line, enter CREATE QUERY. (You can include an optional file name).
- Choose New... from the File menu. Then choose the Query radio button.

For this example, use the first method, as it allows you to name the screen from the start. At the command window, type CREATE QUERY COMPANY and press Enter. You are now in the RQBE window, displayed in Fig. 9-1. Notice that there is a new menu option, RQBE, to the right of the Window option.

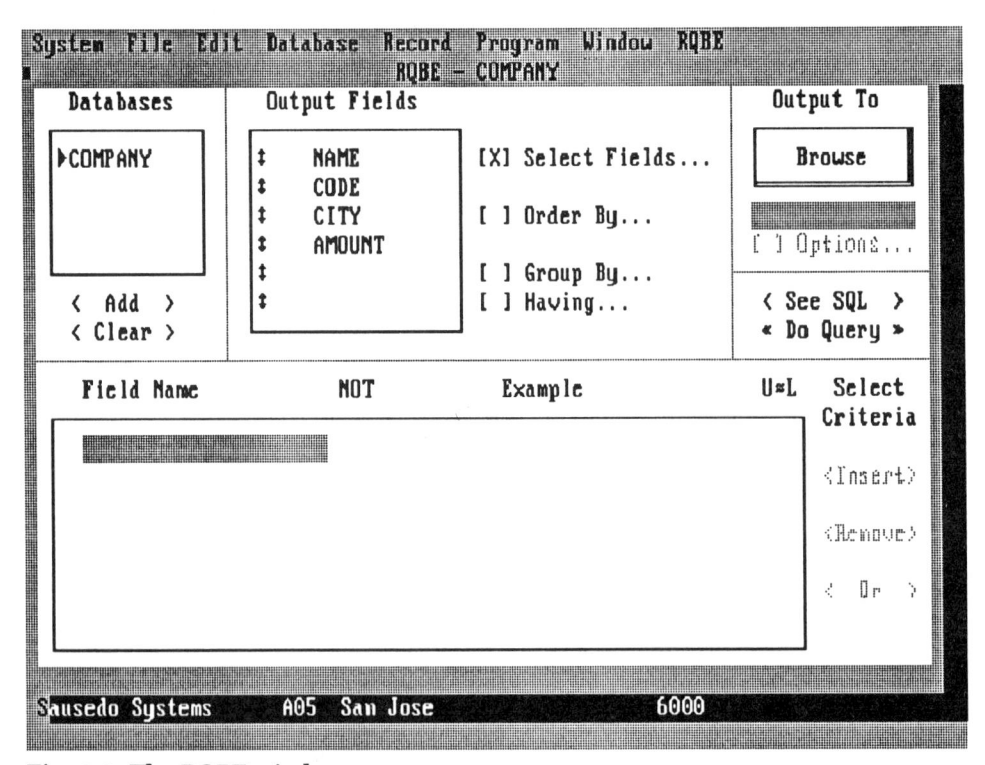

Fig. 9-1. The RQBE window.

Creating a query

Specifying the database(s) If no database is open in the current selection area, the Select database list appears, allowing you to choose the database for the query. If a database is currently open, that file becomes the selected data file for the RQBE window. If more than one data file is open, only the file in the current selection area is chosen.

Because COMPANY.DBF is open, the RQBE window automatically chooses it as the data file. Further on in this chapter is an example where multiple files are opened and then joined, using the Add option.

Specifying the output fields The default is for all fields to display in the query output. In this example, all fields are selected, so no changes are made. However, details of the Select Fields options are explained.

To change the fields that are displayed, choose the Select Fields... check box. This brings up the Select Fields dialog pictured in Fig. 9-2. Although all fields from the current database are automatically chosen, you can choose Remove All to remove all fields from the Selected Output list. To remove a particular field, highlight it and select it by pressing the spacebar and choosing Remove. To use the mouse, simply double click on the field. You can select fields one at a time

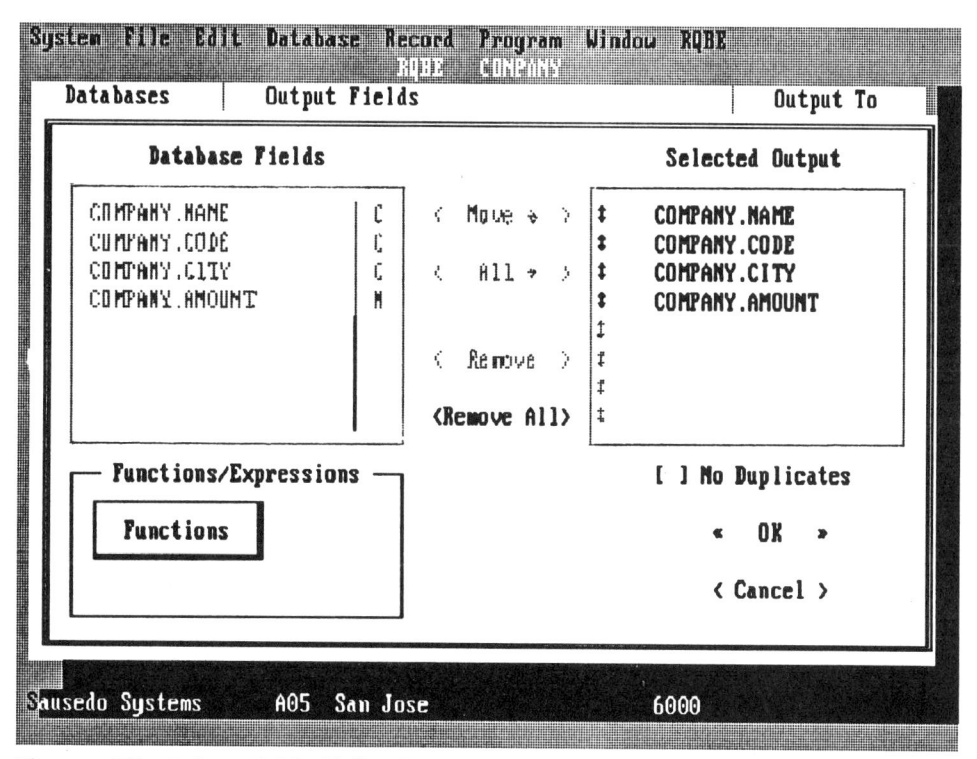

Fig. 9-2. The Select Fields dialog box.

by selecting them from the Database Fields list. To select all fields, choose All – >.

The following functions can be included in the query output:

COUNT( )
SUM( )
AVG( )
MIN( )
MAX( )

To choose a function, pull up the Functions pop-up and choose one of the listed functions (all functions except COUNT( ) can be performed on numeric fields only). An alternate method for entering functions is to move to the Text box in the Functions/Expressions box and enter the function. To place the function in the Selected Output list, choose Move – >. You cannot select memo fields for the output.

To adjust the order of the Selected Output fields, highlight the desired field. Then hold down Ctrl, and then press ↑ or ↓ in the direction to move the field. To adjust the order using the mouse, point to the double-headed arrow at the left of the field and drag the field to the new location.

The No Duplicates check box allows you to eliminate any duplicate records from the output. Duplicate records are defined as records that have identical entries in just the fields shown in the Selected Output list.

To exit the dialog, choose OK.

Specifying the output order The default is for all fields to display in record number order. In this example, the database is ordered alphabetically by Client Name. Choose the Order By... check box. This brings up the Order By dialog box. Highlight the Name field and press Enter (or double click with the mouse).

If desired, multiple fields can be used in the sort order. This is most often needed when the primary field is not unique and many records share the same primary key. If multiple keys are chosen, and the fields must then be re-ordered, highlight the desired field. Then hold down Ctrl, and then press ↑ or ↓ in the direction to move the field. To adjust the order using the mouse, point to the double-headed arrow at the left of the field and drag the field to the new location. To remove a particular field, highlight it and select it by pressing the spacebar and choosing Remove. To use the mouse, simply double click on the field.

You can choose ASCENDING or DESCENDING order (the default is ascending). If the Ignore Case check box is chosen, it does not differentiate between uppercase and lowercase letters. Exit the dialog box by choosing OK.

Specifying the output to format A query can output to a Browse window, a Display (list, report form or label form), a Table/DBF (new file containing results), or Cursor (temporary database that can be used until the database is closed). To choose the desired output, pull up the Output To pop-up. The default for the query output is the Browse screen.

In this example, the Browse screen is used for the output, so no changes are made. However, details of the other outputs are explained.

The Table/DBF option asks for a file name for the new file that is to be created. Running this type of query performs a function similar to the COPY TO *file name* FOR *criteria* command.

If the Display option is chosen, the Options... check box should then be selected. This brings up the RQBE Display Options dialog. The dialog allows one of the following three radio buttons to be selected: Screen Display, Report, or Label. If Report or Label is chosen, the form name must be selected. To choose an existing form, select the Report/Label Form Name check box to bring up the file list of form names. If the form has not been created yet, enter the name in the text box below the check box.

Many of the report or label form's options can be set in this dialog box. There are check boxes for Preview, Summary, Report Heading, and Pause Between Screens. If Quick Report is chosen, a RQBE quick report can be created and saved right from this dialog.

The output default is for the display to be sent to the screen. To send to the printer, choose the To Printer check box (you can then choose whether to suppress the console display). To send to file, choose the To File check box and choose an existing file name or enter a new name in the text box.

The Cursor output creates a temporary file that contains just the output fields, and records that match the criteria. The file appears in the View window and can be used for browsing, reporting, etc. When the database is closed, the file is not saved on disk. Exit the dialog by choosing OK.

Selection criteria

The bottom half of the RQBE screen is the area where selection criteria is entered. The first criteria example is a selection that finds all records from "San Diego". To specify a selection, the following must be done:

1. Choose a field from the Field Name pop-up.
2. Choose the type of comparison (Like, Exactly Like, More Than, Less Than, Between, or In).
3. Enter the criteria example.
4. If desired, choose the check box that tells RQBE to ignore differences between uppercase and lowercase.

When choosing the field, the pop-up that appears allows you to choose a field name from any of the files chosen. If the *expression...* option is chosen, the dialog allows you to choose a Math, String, Logical, or Date function. If the NOT box is checked, the query finds the opposite of the criteria asked for.

Comparison types After the NOT box, one of the following comparison types must be chosen:

- *Like* Works like the equal sign with SET EXACT OFF. When searching on character fields, if the example is n characters long, it only searches on the first n characters of the field. For instance, in the criteria of City LIKE S, because the example is one letter long, it compares against just the first letter of City, finding records from San Diego, San Jose, etc.
- *Exactly Like* Works like the equal sign with SET EXACT ON. When searching on character fields, the example must be exactly the same number of characters as the field. For instance, if the field name is City and the example is "San Diego", no records would be found because the City field is 15 characters wide. For a San Diego record to match, the criteria would have to be City EXACTLY LIKE "San Diego   ".
- *More than* Works like the greater than sign (>). With character fields, this finds letters that come after the example. For example, Name MORE THAN R would find records whose company names begin with the letters S through Z. Remember that lowercase letters are greater than uppercase, unless case is being ignored.
- *Less Than* Works like the less than sign (<). With character fields, this finds letters that come before the example.
- *Between* Works like *field >= expr* .AND. *field <= expr* without having to use two lines of criteria. The example must be a range separated with the word AND. The example can be numeric or character, but if it is character the example expressions must be surrounded by quotes. For instance, Amount BETWEEN 5000 AND 8000 would find all records with amounts greater than or equal to 5000 and less than or equal to 8000.
- *In* Works like *field $ value list*. The example can be a list of values separated with commas. For example, City IN San Diego, La Jolla would find all records from San Diego or La Jolla.

Entering the example The example is the expression used in the comparison. If it is a character, the quotes are not necessary unless the Between comparison is being used.

Multiple criteria If multiple lines of criteria are used, the default is that they are connected with AND. This creates a *selective search* where both criteria must be true for a record to be found. The alternate method is to use an OR connection, also called a *non-selective search*. In OR searches, either criteria can be true for a record to match. To create a nonselective connection, enter the first criterion and then choose < Or > from the dialog. This separates the two lines of criteria with an = = = = OR = = = = divider line.

Editing criteria To delete a criterion highlight that row and choose Remove. To place a criterion over an existing criterion, move to the row where the new criterion is to be placed, and choose Insert. To rearrange the order of criteria, highlight the criterion to move, hold down Ctrl, and press ↑ or ↓ in the direction to move it.

Follow the steps above to create the following criteria:

Field name	NOT	Example	U = L
COMPANY.CITY	[ ]	Like	San Diego

Below are examples of other criteria and the records that would be found with each:

CITY		Like	S	(records from any city beginning with S)
CITY		Like	S	(records where City begins with S) AND
NAME		Like	J	(company Name begins with J)
CITY		Like	S	(records where City begins with S OR)
= = OR = =				(company Name begins with J)
NAME		Like	J	

AMOUNT Between 5000 AND 10000   (records between 5000 and 10000)

CODE   In   A01,B01,C01   (records where the code is A01, B01, or C01)

The SQL SELECT command

The RQBE window constructs a SQL SELECT command. Each option modifies the clauses used in the command. Choose See SQL to see the syntax used for the query.

An example of a SELECT command constructed by the RQBE window is:

```
SELECT *;
  FROM COMPANY;
  WHERE COMPANY.NAME = "J";
    AND COMPANY.CITY = "San Diego";
  INTO CURSOR COMPANY_A
  BROWSE NOMODIFY PREFERENCE COMPANY_A
```

Exit the SQL screen by pressing Ctrl – W or Ctrl – Enter. For more information on the syntax of the SELECT command, see the listing in chapter 2.

Running the query

To run the query, choose Do Query. The output is in browse mode, unless you have chosen a different format. Before it shows the output, it shows how many records were selected and the number of seconds it took to run the query.

Joining multiple databases

Multiple databases can be used in the RQBE window. A relationship must be set between the fields that join the two files together. Unlike the SET RELATION command, which also joins files together, indexes do not have to be created or open for the join option to work.

An example of a file that could be joined to COMPANY.DBF is a data file named TAXES.DBF, which tracks the sales tax being charged in the following cities:

Record #	City	Tax
1	San Diego	.06
2	La Jolla	.07
3	San Jose	.05

To see the sales tax next to the record of each company, the files can be joined. The City field is the shared field, which is used for joining the records. Shared fields do not have to have the same name.

To join the files, choose Add from the RQBE window. Choose Taxes.DBF from the list of files. The Join Condition dialog box then appears. Choose the first pop-up, which lists the fields from the Taxes file. Choose Taxes.City. Leave LIKE as the comparison default (you can also join with the Exactly Like, More Than, and Less Than comparisons). In the last pop-up, choose Company.City. The files are now connected by the City fields. Notice that the Ignore Upper/Lower Case check box allows the connection to not be case sensitive.

Now choose Do Query. The Browse screen now shows the corresponding tax from TAXES.DBF next to each record in the Company file.

Saving the query

All of the definitions of the query are contained in a query file, which has a .QPR extension. This file is a program file that contains the SELECT command and all of the options chosen in the RQBE window. You must save your query if you are going to use it again. To save the COMPANY.QPR file:

1. Choose Save from the File menu.
2. If you have not named the file yet, it asks for a name.

Exiting the RQBE window

To exit the RQBE window, press Ctrl – W or Ctrl – Enter. This also saves the .QPR file. You can then run the query at any time from the command window, by entering the following: DO Company.QPR. To bring up an existing query in the RQBE window, either:

- Choose MODIFY QUERY *file name* from the command window, or
- Choose Open... from the File menu, and change the database type to Query.

10

The 10 most important additions to FoxPro 2.0

WITH THE ADVENT OF FOXPRO 2.0, INTRODUCED, LATE 1991, THE PROGRAM has been greatly enhanced. The most important additions are discussed in this chapter.

Increased speed

FoxPro version 2.0 is simply faster than previous versions. The program is also smaller, it only uses 280K or RAM, so there is more room in memory for your programs and operations.

SQL SELECT

The SELECT command is FoxPro's first foray into SQL (Standard Query Language). One command can take the place of five or six normal commands. For instance, the following command opens files, sets a relation, filters out records that don't match a criteria, selects the fields to be output, and selects the sort order. This one command takes the place of USE, SET RELATION, SET FIELDS TO, SET FILTER TO, and SET INDEX.

```
SELECT COMPANY.NAME,COMPANY.CITY,TAXES.RATE;
   FROM COMPANY,TAXES;
   WHERE TAXES.CITY = COMPANY.CITY;
     AND COMPANY.STATE = "CA";
   ORDER BY COMPANY.NAME;
   INTO CURSOR COMPANY_A
```

RQBE window

As noted above, the SELECT command is very powerful. It is also very complex, and it takes awhile to become comfortable with all of its clauses and features. However, FoxPro 2.0 has a window that helps you easily put together the pieces of the command. This RQBE (Relational Query By Example) window lets you set filters, set the output format, set the index order, and set relations.

The Rushmore technology

Rushmore is an access technique that permits certain selections to run much faster than earlier FoxPro versions. Some complex database operations run hundreds and even thousands of times faster than before. In general, any command using the FOR clause will run much faster under Rushmore. The default is for Rushmore to be activated, although there are situations where it must be deactivated. These situations are with commands that modify the field that is being used in the selection.

Improved index files

FoxPro's index files have improved in two ways. First, you can create multiple index (.CDX) files. This allows several keys, or "tags," to be contained in one file. Secondly, you can create compact index files. *Compact indexes* create files as small as $1/6$ the size of normal indexes. Because of the smaller size, compact index operations also run much faster. If you are trying to maintain compatibility with FoxPlus or Fox/Mac indexes, you should disable the compact index.

Extended Version

FoxPro's Extended Version utilizes all available extended memory. Full multi-user capabilities are supported. With this version, the number of indexes, windows, and browse sessions are limited only to memory. You should have at least 1.5 megabytes of memory to use the Extended Version.

Screen Builder

The Screen Builder is a very powerful, but easy-to-use screen generator. The Screen Builder provides a view screen that makes it easy to move around objects, add prompts and boxes, and other embellishments without using the normal FoxPro commands. In addition, you can easily place controls (push buttons, radio buttons, pop-up menus, check buttons, and lists) on the screen.

Menu Builder

The Menu Builder is another 2.0 addition that makes program generation easier. With the menu builder you can design a bounce-bar menu and each of its associated pop-ups. It lets you assign commands to each option, and then generates a program that runs the menu.

Application Program Interface

The External Routine API (Application Program Interface) allows programmers to create routines in C and 80 x 86 assembly language. To use this capability, simply call the SET LIBRARY TO command to open an external routine library. More than one library can be opened at a time.

New commands and functions

FoxPro 2.0 has over 100 new and enhanced commands and functions. Many of these help with setting controls (pop-ups, menu bars, buttons, etc.). Some have to do with the new index options. Other commands make text merging easier. There are a whole new set of commands and functions that manipulate arrays. In addition, the BROWSE command has many new features.

A

Setting parameters with Config.fp

YOU CAN CHANGE MANY OF FOXPRO'S DEFAULT SETTINGS BY USING THE CONFIG.FP file. This file contains one or more commands that change such things as the editor used for MODIFY COMMAND, the TALK and BELL settings, colors, and data formats. By placing these commands in CONFIG.FP, you avoid having to issue the SET command from the command window.

CONFIG.FP must be an ASCII file. You can create and edit it using MODIFY COMMAND or any other text editor. When FoxPro is started up, it searches for the file in the current directory. If it doesn't find it, it searches for it throughout the DOS path.

Each line in the file changes a setting. The line must be entered in the following format:

item = value

The *item* is a FoxPro keyword, and the *value* is the setting that you have chosen. It is not case sensitive, and spaces are ignored. For instance, the following lines are all valid:

```
BELL = OFF
tedit = ws
Confirm = on
```

The following items are available for use in the CONFIG.FP file:

Item	**Value**	**Default**
ALTERNATE	*file name*	
AUTOSAVE	OFF/ON	OFF
BELL	ON/OFF	ON

Item	Value	Default
BELL	*freq,duration*	512,2
BLINK	ON/OFF	ON
BORDER	*attribute*	SINGLE
CARRY	OFF/ON	OFF
CENTURY	OFF/ON	OFF
CLEAR	ON/OFF	ON
CLOCK	OFF/ON	OFF
CLOCK	*coord*	0,69
COLOR	OFF/ON	
COLOR	*color attrib*	
COLOR SET	*color set name*	
COLOR OF BOX	*color attrib*	
COLOR OF FIELDS	*color attrib*	
COLOR OF INFORMATION	*color attrib*	
COLOR OF NORMAL	*color attrib*	
COLOR OF MESSAGES	*color attrib*	
COLOR OF TITLE	*color attrib*	
COLOR OF SCHEME	*color pair list*	
COMMAND	*command*	
COMPATIBLE	OFF/ON	OFF
CONFIRM	OFF/ON	512,2
CONSOLE	OFF/ON	ON
CURRENCY	*char*	SINGLE
CURRENCY	*position*	OFF
DATE	*format*	OFF
DEBUG	OFF/ON	ON
DECIMALS	0 to 18	OFF
DEFAULT	*drive*	0,69
DELETED	OFF/ON	OFF
DEVELOPMENT	OFF/ON	ON
DEVICE	SCREEN/PRINT	SCREEN
DISPLAY	*type*	Installed
ECHO	OFF/ON	OFF
EMS	ON/OFF/*kb of ram*	ON
ESCAPE	OFF/ON	ON
EXACT	OFF/ON	OFF

Item	Value	Default
EXCLUSIVE	OFF/ON	ON
Fnum	char string	
FULLPATH	OFF/ON	ON
HEADING	OFF/ON	ON
HELP	OFF/ON	ON
HELP	file name	FOXHELP
HOURS	12/24	12
INDEX	extension	.IDX
INTENSITY	OFF/ON	ON
LABEL	extension	.LBL
LOGERROR	OFF/ON	ON
MARGIN	0 to 254	
MARK	char	'/'
MEMOWIDTH	8 to 32,000	50
MVARSIZ	1 to 64	6
MVCOUNT	128 to 3600	256
MENUS	OFF/ON	ON
MOUSE	1 to 10	5
NEAR	OFF/ON	OFF
ODOMETER	1 to 32767	100
PATH	path	
POINT	char	'.'
PRINT	OFF/ON	OFF
REPORT	extension	.FRX
RESOURCE	OFF/ON	ON
RESOURCE	file name	FOXUSER
SAFETY	OFF/ON	ON
SEPARATOR	char	','
SPACE	OFF/ON	ON
STATUS	OFF/ON	ON
STEP	OFF/ON	OFF
TALK	OFF/ON	ON
TABS	char string	null string
TEDIT	MODIFY COMMAND editor name	
TIME	<0 to 1000000>	6000
TMPFILES	<drive:>	
TYPEAHEAD	<0 to 32000>	20
UNIQUE	OFF/ON	OFF
WP	MEMO editor name	

B

Color schemes and color pairs

THERE ARE THREE WAYS TO CHANGE THE FOXPRO COLOR SETTINGS (OR highlighting if you have monochrome). You may use the Color Picker from the Window menu; issue SET COLOR from the command window or from a program; or use the COLOR item in CONFIG.FP. To set colors, you must be familiar with color pairs and color schemes.

Each color scheme refers to the colors being used in a particular part of Fox-Pro. For instance, scheme 1 is for the underlying screen, 2 is for user-defined menus and pop-ups, 3 for the system menu bar, etc. Below is a listing of the color schemes:

Scheme	Description
1	Usr Wind: underlying screen, user-defined widows, clock
2	Usr Menus: user-defined menus and pop-ups
3	Menu Bar: system menu bar
4	Menu Pops: system menu bar pop-ups
5	Dialogs: dialogs and system messages
6	Diag Pops: pop-ups and lists that appear within dialogs
7	Alerts: error message screens
8	Windows: command, text edit, debug, trace, etc.
9	Window Pops: pop-ups that appear in windows
10	Browse: browse window
11	Report: report window

You can set up to 24 schemes, so scheme 12 through 24 are color layouts for your own use. These last 12 schemes all default to the colors set with scheme 1.

Each color scheme is made up of 10 pairs of colors. In some schemes, not all 10 pairs are used. The first number of the pair represents the color of the text, the second number the background. The numbers are separated with a slash, and each pair is separated with a comma. The colors are represented by:

Color	Symbol	Color	Symbol
Black	N or blank	Red	R
Blue	B	Magenta	RB
Green	G	Brown	GR
Cyan	BG	Yellow	GR+
Blank	X	White	W
Gray	N+		

Place the + after a symbol to designate an enhanced color. The following is an example of the SET COLOR OF SCHEME command:

SET COLOR OF SCHEME 1 TO b/g,gr+/r,r,b/g,w/g,,,,g/w,gr+/w

The following table shows the item within each scheme area that gets set by the corresponding color pair.

Color Pair	Usr Wind Scheme 1	Usr Menus Scheme 2	Menu Bar Scheme 3	Menu Pops Scheme 4	Dialogs Scheme 5
1	SAY field		Disabled pads	Disabled opt.	Normal text
2	GET field	Enabled opt.	Enabled pads	Enabled opt.	Text box
3	Border	Border	Border	Border	Border
4	Title,active	Menu Titles	Title	Title	Title
5	Title,idle	Message	Message	Message	Message
6	Selected item	Selected opt.	Selected pad	Selected opt.	Selected item
7	Clock	Hot Key	Hot Key	Hot Key	Hot Key
8	Shadow	Shadow	Shadow	Shadow	Shadow
9	Enabled ctrl.	Enabled ctrl.	Enabled ctrl.	Enabled ctrl.	Enabled ctrl.
10	Disabled ctrl.	Disabled ctrl.	Disabled ctrl.	Disabled ctrl.	Disabled ctrl.

Dlog Pops Scheme 6	Alert Scheme 7	Windows Scheme 8	Wind Pops Scheme 9	Browse Scheme 10	Report Scheme 11
Disable opt.	Normal text	Normal text	Disabled opt.	Other records	Text & B full
Enabled opt.	Text box	Text box	Enabled opt.	Curr. field	Report field
Border	Border	Border	Border	Border	Border

Dlog Pops Scheme 6	**Alert Scheme 7**	**Windows Scheme 8**	**Wind Pops Scheme 9**	**Browse Scheme 10**	**Report Scheme 11**
Title	Title	Title,act	Title	Title,act	Title,act
Message	Message	Title,idle	Message	Title,idle	Title,idle
Selected opt.	Selected item	Selected text	Selected opt.	Selected text	Selected item
Hot Key	Hot Key	Hot Key	Hot Key	Curr. record	Band A, empty
Shadow	Shadow	Shadow	Shadow	Shadow	Shadow
Enabled ctrl.	Enabled ctrl.	Enabled ctrl.	Enabled ctrl.	Enabled ctrl.	Band A, full
Disabled ctrl.	Disabled ctrl.	Disabled ctrl.	Disabled ctrl.	Disabled ctrl.	Band B, empty

C

System menu names

EACH OF THE SYSTEM MENU BARS AND POP-UP OPTIONS HAS A FOXPRO NAME. These names are used with commands such as SET SYSMENU, which controls the System menu bar during program execution.

The menu itself is named _msysmenu. The System menu pads and their names are:

Pad	Name
System	_msm_systm
File	_msm_file
Edit	_msm_edit
Database	_msm_data
Record	_msm_recrd
Program	_msm_prog
Window	_msm_windo

The System menu pop-up names are:

Pop-up	Name
System	_msystem
About FoxPro…	_mst_about
Help…	_mst_help
Macros…	_mst_macro
1st Separator	_mst_sp100
Filer	_mst_filer
Calculator	_mst_calcu
Calendar	_mst_diary
Spec. Chars.	_mst_specl

ASCII Chart	_mst_ascii
Capture	_mst_captr
Puzzle	_mst_puzzl

The File menu pop-up names are:

Pop-up	Name
File popup	_mfile
New...	_mfi_new
Open...	_mfi_open
Close	_mfi_close
Close All	_mfi_clall
1st Separator	_mfi_sp100
Save	_mfi_save
Save as...	_mfi_savas
Revert	_mfi_revrt
2nd Separator	_mfi_sp200
Printer Setup...	_mfi_setup
Print...	_mfi_print
3rd Separator	_mfi_sp300
Quit	_mfi_quit

The Edit menu pop-up names are:

Pop-up	Name
Edit popup	_medit
Undo	_med_undo
Redo	_med_redo
1st Separator	_med_sp100
Cut	_med_cut
Copy	_med_copy
Paste	_med_paste
Clear	_med_clear
2nd Separator	_med_sp200
Select All	_med_slcta
3rd Separator	_med_sp300
Goto Line...	_med_goto
Find...	_med_find
Find Again	_med_finda
Replce/Fnd Again	_med_repl
Replace All	_med_repla
4th Separator	_med_sp400
Preferences	_med_quit

The Database menu pop-up names are:

Pop-up	Name
Database popup	_mdata
Setup…	_mda_setup
Browse	_mda_brow
1st Separator	_mda_sp100
Append from…	_mda_appnd
Copy to…	_mda_copy
Sort…	_mda_sort
Total…	_mda_total
2nd Separator	_mda_sp200
Average…	_mda_avg
Count…	_mda_count
Sum…	_mda_sum
Calculate…	_mda_calc
Report…	_mda_reprt
Label …	_mda_label
3rd Separator	_mda_sp300
Pack	_mda_pack
Reindex	_mda_rindx

The Record menu pop-up names are:

Pop-up	Name
Record popup	_mrecord
Append	_mrc_appnd
Change	_mrc_chnge
1st Separator	_mrc_sp100
Goto…	_mrc_goto
Locate…	_mrc_locat
Continue…	_mrc_cont
Seek…	_mrc_seek
2nd Separator	_mrc_sp200
Replace…	_mrc_repl
Delete…	_mrc_delet
Recall…	_mrc_recal

The Program menu pop-up names are:

Pop-up	Name
Program popup	_mprog
Do…	_mpr_do

1st Separator	_mpr_sp100
Cancel	_mpr_cancl
Resume	_mpr_resum
2nd Separator	_mpr_sp200
Echo	_mpr_echo
Step	_mpr_step
Talk	_mpr_talk
3rd Separator	_mpr_sp300
Compile…	_mpr_compl
Generate…	_mpr_gener
FoxDoc	_mpr_docum
FoxGraph	_mpr_graph

The Window menu pop-up names are:

Pop-up	Name
Window popup	_mwindow
Hide	_mwi_hide
Hide All	_mwi_hidea
Show All	_mwi_showa
Clear	_mwi_clear
1st Separator	_mwi_sp100
Move	_mwi_move
Size	_mwi_size
Zoom up	_mwi_zoom
Minimize down	_mwi_min
Cycle	_mwi_rotat
Color…	_mwi_color
2nd Separator	_mwi_sp200
Command	_mwi_cmd
Debug	_mwi_debug
Trace	_mwi_trace
View	_mpr_view

D

Foxhelp categories

EACH OF THE CATEGORIES IN THE HELP FILE, FOXHELP.DBF HAS A TWO-LETTER code in the Class field. These codes can be used with the SET HELPFILTER command to find information on a particular subject.

The two-letter Class codes are:

Category

General:	Abbreviation
What's new	wn
Compatibility	cm
Configuration	cf
Error messages	em
Commands:	
Database (fields, indexes, relations, etc.)	db
Environment (Set commands, screen, etc.)	en
Errors and debugging	er
Event handlers (ON ERROR, ON KEY, etc.)	eh
File management	fm
Keyboard and mouse	km
Memory variables and arrays	mv
Menus and pop-ups	mp
Printing	pr
Program execution	pe
Structured programming	sp
SQL	sq
Text merge	tm
Windows	wi

Interface	in
Multi-user	mu

Functions:

Character	ch
Numeric	nu
Date and time	dt
Logical	lo
Database (fields, indexes, relations,etc.)	db
Data conversion	dc
Environment	en
File management	fm
Keyboard and mouse	km
Low-level	ll
Memory variables and arrays	mv
Menus and pop-ups	mp
Windows	wi
Printing	pr
Multi-user	mu

System memory variables (Sysmemvar):

Desk Accessories	da
Printing	pr
Interface	in
Text Merge	tm
System menu names	sn

Interface:

Dialogs	di
General	ge
Menus	me
Windows	wi

Index

% operator, 268-269

= command, 140

* (NOTE) command, 199

& function, 267-268
&& (NOTE) command, 199

\ \ command, 123, 124
\ command, 123, 124

? command, 124
?? command, 124
??? command, 125

@...BOX command, 128
@...CLEAR command, 128-129
@...EDIT Text Edit Region, 137-138
@...GET Check Boxes, 129
@...GET Invisible Boxes, 129, 130
@...GET Lists command, 130-132
@...GET Pop-ups, 132-134
@...GET Push Buttons, 134-135
@...GET Radio Buttons, 135-137
@...MENU command, 138-139
@...PROMPT command, 139-140
@...TO command, 140
@SAY...GET, 125-128, 402, 413, 419

_alignment, 389
_box, 390
_indent, 390
_lmargin, 390
_mline, 390
_padvance, 391
_pageno, 391
_pbpage, 391
_pcolno, 391-392
_pcopies, 392
_pdriver, 392
_pecode, 392-393
_peject, 393
_pepage, 393
_pform, 393
_plength, 393
_plineno, 394
_ploffset, 394
_ppitch, 394
_pquality, 394
_pretext, 394
_pscode, 395
_pspacing, 395
_pwait, 395
_rmargin, 395
_tabs, 396
_tally, 396
_tallytime, 396
_text, 396-397
_wrap, 397

A

absolute values, ABS( ), 269
ACCEPT command, 141, 408
access levels, show level, ACCESS( ), 269-270
ACCESS( ), 269-270
ACOPY( ), 270-271
ACOS( ), 271-272
ACTIVATE MENU command, 141-142, 450-451
ACTIVATE POPUP, 142, 410, 411
ACTIVATE SCREEN command, 142-143
ACTIVATE WINDOW command, 143
ADEL( ), 272
ADIR( ), 272-273
AELEMENT( ), 273-274
AFIELDS( ), 274
AINS( ), 275
ALEN( ), 276
alerts, 6
ALIAS( ), 275
ALLTRIM( ), 276
angles
    radians, DTOR( ), 297-298
    radians, RTOD( ), 363
APPEND BLANK command, 143-144, 413
APPEND command, 143, 408, 442, 452
APPEND FROM ARRAY command, 145, 403, 413
APPEND FROM command, 144-145
APPEND MEMO command, 145
Application Program Interface (API), 467
applications (see programming)
arc tangent, ATAN( ) and ATAN2( ), 281, 283
arccosine, ACOS( ), 271-272

483

archived files, 108
arcsine, ASIN( ), 277-278
arrays (see also records)
  copy file information to array, ADIR( ), 272-273
  create, DECLARE command, 162-163
  database structure copied to array, AFIELDS( ), 274
  edit records, Edit With Arrays program, 419-421
  elements, copy, ACOPY( ), 270-271
  elements, delete, ADEL( ), 272
  elements, insert, AINS( ), 275
  elements, number of, ALEN( ), 276
  elements, row-column position, AELEMENT( ), 273-274
  elements, row-column position, ASUBSCRIPT( ), 279-280
  elements, search, ASCAN( ), 276-277
  get array values from records, SCATTER TO, 227
  memory variables, 403
  put array values in records, GATHER FROM, 182-183
  records, copy, COPY TO ARRAY, 156, 157, 419
  records, move records to file, APPEND FROM ARRAY, 145, 413
  single- vs. multi-dimensional, 162-163
  sorting, ASORT( ), 278-279
ASC( ), 277
ASCAN( ), 276-277
ASCII codes, 116-117, 287
  character for number, CHR( ), 287
  number of character, SYS(15), 376
  show number for character, ASC( ), 277
ASIN( ), 277-278
ASORT( ), 278-279
ASUBSCRIPT( ), 279-280
AT( ), 280-281
ATAN( ), 281
ATC( ), 281-282
ATCLINE( ), 282
ATLINE( ), 282-283
ATN2( ), 283
attributes, file, 107-108
AVERAGE command, 146

averaging, 74-75
  AVERAGE command, 146
  memory variables, 75

B
backup copies, text, 89
BAR( ), 283, 410
BELL, 47, 246, 410, 469, 470
BETWEEN( ), 283-284
binary files
  delete, RELEASE command, 219
  load into memory, LOAD, 192
  run, CALL command, 150
BOF( ), 284-285
borders
  boxes, DEFINE BOX, 166
  set, SET BORDER, 247, 470
  windows, DEFINE WINDOW, 170
bounce-bar menus (see also Menu Builder)
  activate, DEFINE MENU, 166
  character or box before option, DEFINE MENU, 166
  character or box before option, DEFINE PAD, 168
  check mark before option, MRKBAR( ), 338
  check mark before option, MRKPAD( ), 339
  check mark before option, SET MARK OF, 257, 471
  color selection, DEFINE MENU, 167
  color selection, DEFINE PAD, 168
  create, MENU BAR, 193
  current menu displayed, MENU( ), 334
  display, ACTIVATE MENU, 141-142, 450-451
  erase from screen, DEACTIVATE MENU, 162
  hot key assignment, DEFINE MENU, 166
  hot key assignment, DEFINE PAD, 168
  message displayed, DEFINE PAD, 168
  name, DEFINE MENU, 166
  options, name, GETBAR( ), 314
  options, number of available options, CNTPAD( ), 289
  options, number of selected pad, PAD( ), 342
  options, selection, ON SELECTION MENU, 208
  options, selection, ON SELECTION PAD, 208
  options, setting, DEFINE PAD, 167-168
  options, setting, Menu Builder, 447-448
  prompts, PRMPAD( ), 348
  prompts, setting, Menu Builder, 447-448
  submenu display, ON PAD, 206
  window placement, DEFINE MENU, 166
boxes
  border coordinates, DEFINE BOX, 166
  borders, SET BORDER, 247, 470
  check boxes, 5
  check boxes, create, @...GET Check Boxes, 129
  check boxes, Screen Builder, 436
  clear box, @...CLEAR command, 128-129
  control boxes, Screen Builder, 436
  dialog boxes, 3-6
  display, _box, 390
  draw box, @...BOX command, 128
  draw box, @...TO command, 140
  invisible boxes, create, @...GET Invisible Boxes, 129, 130
  reports using, 22-23
  Screen Builder, 433-434, 437-438
  text boxes, 5
break points, debugging, 43-44
BROWSE command, 146-149, 455, 467
Browse menus, 51-56, 63-67
  add records, 54, 67
  delete records, 53-54, 66-67
  grid on/off, 52, 65
  list fields, 52, 64-65
  move fields, 53, 66
  partitions, 53, 65-66
  relationships of files, 54-56
  scrolling, 53, 66
  size of fields, 53, 66
buffers
  flush to disk, FFLUSH( ), 305
  flush to disk, FLUSH, 180
BUILD APP command, 149
BUILD PROJECT command, 149

buttons, dialog box, 4-6

C

CALCULATE command, 150
calculated fields, 77-78
  create, BROWSE command, 147
  reports, Calculate dialog box, 25-26
calculator feature, System menu, 114-115
calendar feature, System menu, 115-116
CALL command, 150
CANCEL command, 151
capitalization
  PROPER( ), 349-350
  UPPER( ), 383
CAPSLOCK( ), 285
CASE statements, 404, 410, 426
CDOW( ), 285
CDX( ), 286
CEILING( ), 286
centering lines, 28
CHANGE command, 151
check boxes, 5
  create, @...GET Check Boxes, 129
  create, @...GET Invisible Boxes, 129, 130
  hot key assignment, 129
  Menu Builder, 449
  Screen Builder, 436
checksums, SYS(2007), 379
CHR( ), 287
CHRSAW( ), 288
CHRTRAN( ), 288
CLEAR command, 151, 402, 410, 424, 437, 470
CLEAR READ command, 151-152
clipboard, copy text from screen to clipboard, 117, 401
CLOCK, 47, 470
  position and display, SET CLOCK, 248
CLOSE command, 152
CMONTH( ), 288-289
CNTBAR( ), 289
CNTPAD( ), 289
COL( ), 289-290
COLOR, 470, 473
COLOR OF BOX, 470
COLOR OF FIELDS, 470
COLOR OF INFORMATION, 470
COLOR OF MESSAGES, 470
COLOR OF NORMAL, 470
COLOR OF SCHEME, 470
COLOR OF TITLE, 470

Color Picker, 473
color selection, 473-475
  @SAY...GET command, 127
bounce-bar menus, 167
bounce-bar menus, DEFINE PAD, 168
computer capability, ISCOLOR( ), 321
lists, @...GET Lists command, 131
pop-up menus, DEFINE BAR command, 164
pop-up menus, DEFINE POPUP, 169
pop-ups, @...GET Pop-ups, 133
push buttons, @...GET Push Buttons, 134-135
radio buttons, @...GET Radio buttons, 136-137
SET COLOR commands, 248-250
show selection, SCHEME( ), 364
show selection, SHOW GETS, 232-233
show selection, SHOW OBJECT, 233
text editing regions, @...EDIT Text Edit Region, 138
windows, 170-171
windows, Window Color, 40-42
COLOR SET, 470
columns
  cursor at column number, COL( ), 289-290
  on-screen display, number of, SCOLS( ), 365
  referencing columns, @SAY...GET command use, 126
comma separators, SET SEPARATOR, 261, 471
COMMAND, 470
Command window, windows, 43
commands
  display responses, SET TALK, 263
  display responses, SYS(103), 378
  execution time, _tallytime, 396
Expression Builder, 13-14
show as executed, SET DOHISTORY, 253
show as executed, SET ECHO, 253, 470
show last given commands, LIST HISTORY, 190-191

comments, 199, 407
COMPILE command, 152
compiling programs, 89, 119-120, 152
condition testing, IIF( ), 316-317
conditional processing
  DO CASE, 174-175
  DO WHILE, 174-175
  IF command, 184-185
conditional statements, 316-317
CONFIG.FP file, 469-471
configuration (see environment)
console setting, SYS(100), 377
CONTINUE command, 153
control boxes, Screen Builder, 436
COPY FILE command, 153
COPY INDEXES command, 153-154
COPY MEMO command, 154
COPY STRUCTURE command, 154
COPY TAG command, 155
COPY TO ARRAY command, 156, 157, 403, 419
COPY TO command, 155-156
COPY TO STRUCTURE EXTENDED command, 156
cosine, COS( ), 290-291
COUNT, 157
CREATE command, 157-158
CREATE FROM command, 158
CREATE LABEL command, 158
CREATE MENU command, 159, 446
CREATE PROJECT command, 159
CREATE QUERY command, 160
CREATE REPORT command, 160
CREATE SCREEN command, 161
CREATE VIEW command, 161
Crit program, 424-426
CTOD( ), 291
CURDIR( ), 292
currency, 47, 470
  symbols, SET CURRENCY, 251
cursor
  column number, COL( ), 289-290
  move, 6-7
  on/off, SYS(2002), 378
  row number, ROW( ), 362-363
cut and paste text, 84-86

D

database files (see Database menu; files)

Database menu (*see also* files), 57-82
  FoxPro pop-up names (_mda_xxx), 479
  _msm_data FoxPro name, 477
dates, 47
  calculations, CTOD( ), 291
  calculations, DATE( ), 292
  century prefixes, SET CENTURY, 247, 470
  day-of-month, DAY( ), 293
  day-of-week, DOW( ), 296
  day-of-week, CDOW( ), 285
  DATE, 470
  DATE( ), 292
  delimiters, SET MARK TO, 257, 471
  display, SET DATE, 251
  Julian date, SYS(10) and SYS(11), 374-375
  month-day-year format, DTOC( ), 296-297
  month-day-year format, MDY( ), 331-332
  months, CMONTH( ), 288-289
  months, DMY( ), 296
  months, GOMONTH( ), 315
  months, MONTH( ), 338
  system date, SYS(1), 373
  update date, LUPDATE( ), 329-330
  YEAR( ), 388
  year-month-day format, DTOS( ), 298
DAY( ), 293
DBF( ), 293
DEACTIVATE MENU command, 162
DEACTIVATE POPUP command, 162, 410, 427
DEACTIVATE WINDOW command, 162
DEBUG, 470
debugging, 43-44
  break points, 43-44
  DEBUG command, 470
  display program execution, Window Trace, 44
  line-by-line execution, LINENO( ), 326-327
  show commands as executed, Program Echo, 119
  step-by-step execution, Program Step, 119
  step-by-step execution, SET STEP, 262, 471
  Window Debug commands, 43-44

decimal places
  SET DECIMALS, 251, 470
  SET FIXED command, 254
  SET POINT command, 259, 471
decision-making, IF and CASE statements, 404
DECLARE command, 162-163
default settings (*see* environment)
DEFINE BAR command, 163-165, 410
DEFINE BOX command, 166
DEFINE MENU command, 166
DEFINE PAD command, 167-168
DEFINE POPUP command, 168-170, 410
DEFINE WINDOW command, 170-171
definitions, 410
DELETE command, 171-172
DELETE FILE command, 172
DELETE TAG command, 172-173
DELETED( ), 294, 470
Dest program, 426-427
device setting
  SET DEVICE command, 470
  SYS(101), 377
dialog boxes, 3-6
  check boxes, 5
  pop-ups, 5
  radio buttons, 4
  scrollable lists, 4
  text boxes, 5
  text buttons, 5
diary feature, System menu, 115-116
DIFFERENCE( ), 294-295
DIMENSION command, 173
directories (*see also* files), 45, 54, 102-114
  attributes for files, 107-108
  change current directory, 111
  change current directory, File Open, 33-34
  copy directory, 111-112
  create, DIRECTORY command, 173
  current directory, CURDIR( ), 292
  default, SET DEFAULT, 251-252
  default, SYS(2003), 378
  delete directory, 113
  delete files, 107
  DIRECTORY or DIR command, 173
  drive selection, 110
  make directory, 111

  move directory, 113
  move files, 106-107
  paths, SET PATH, 259, 471
  rename directory, 110
  rename files, 108
  replace files, 106
  size of file, 108-109, 113-114
  sort files, 109-110
  tag files for inclusion, 104
  tag directories for use, 110
  targeting files, 106
  tree structure, 110
DIRECTORY or DIR command, 173
DISKSPACE( ), 295
DISPLAY command, 173, 470
DMY( ), 296
DO CASE command, 174-175, 404, 408
DO command, 174, 401
DO WHILE, 405, 408, 410, 413, 415, 418, 442
DO...ENDDO loop, stop, EXIT command, 178
documentation, FoxDoc, 121
DOW( ), 296
drives, 45, 110
  change, File Open, 33-34
  default, SET DEFAULT, 251-252
  default, SYS(5), 373-374
  default, SYS(2003), 378
  space available, DISKSPACE( ), 295
DTOC( ), 296-297
DTOR( ), 297-298
DTOS( ), 298

E

EDIT command, 176-177
Edit with Arrays program, 419-421
editing/Edit menu, 83-90
  backup copies, 89
  carriage returns/line feeds, 89
  copy, 84-86
  cut and paste, 84-86
  default settings, 89-90
  delete, 87
  end-of-file marker, 89
  FoxPro pop-up names (_med_xxx), 478
  go to specific line, 87
  indentation, 89
  _msm_edit FoxPro name, 477
  program files, 400
  redo un-done changes, 86
  search and replace, 84, 87-89

select, 87
text entry, 83
undo changes, 85
word wrap, 89
EJECT command, 177
EJECT PAGE command, 177
ELSE statements, 404
EMPTY( ), 299
EMS, 470
encrypting program files, 120
end-of-file marker, 89
ENDIF (see IF)
environment settings
  CONFIG.FP file, default settings, 469-471
  On/Off panel, Window menu, 45
  console setting, SYS(100), 377
  current settings, GETENV( ), 314
  current settings, LIST STATUS, 191
  dates, SYS(1), 373
  dates, SYS(10) and SYS(11), 374-375
  default drive, SYS(5), 373-374
  device setting, SYS(6), 374
  device setting, SYS(101), 377
  extended memory, SYS(23) and SYS(24), 377
  format file names, SYS(7), 374
  graphics card, SYS(2006), 379
  macros, 102
  memory available, SYS(12), 375
  On/Off panel, Window menu, 45
  print setting, SYS(102), 377
  printer on-line, SYS(13), 375
  processor name, SYS(17), 376
  programming settings, 402
  serial number of FoxPro, SYS(9), 374
  system memory variables, 389-397
  System menu, 98-117
  system status, SYS( ), 373
  talk setting, SYS(103), 378
  time, SYS(2), 373
  version number of FoxPro, 98, 250, 385, 466
EOF( ), 299-300
ERASE command, 178
error trapping, 120
  alerts/warning, 6
  data-entry errors, ON READERROR, 207
  file operations, FERROR( ), 305

message of error, MESSAGE( ), 334-335
name of program with error, PROGRAM( ), 348-349
name of program with error, SYS(16), 376
ON ERROR command, 200-201
save compilation errors, SET LOGERRORS, 257
show error number, ERROR( ), 300-301
ERROR( ), 300-301
EVALUATE( ), 301-302
EXCLUSIVE, 471
EXIT command, 178, 413
exponents, EXP( ), 302
EXPORT TO command, 178-179
Expression Builder, 13-14
expressions/expression lists
  complex expressions, 14
  empty, EMPTY( ), 299
  Expression Builder, 13-14
  evaluate, = command, 140
  evaluate, BETWEEN( ), 283-284
  functions, 14
  memory variables, 14-15
  memory variables, create, GETEXPR, 183
  on-screen display (@SAY...GET), 125-128
  Report Expression dialog box, 23-24
  search for expression, INLIST( ), 319
  send expression to printer (??? command), 125
  show changes, UPDATED( ), 382-383
  show contents (? and ?? commands), 124
  space between expressions, SET SPACE, 262
extended memory, SYS(23) and SYS(24), 377
extended version, FoxPro, 466
extensions, file, 33-34
EXTERNAL command, 179

F

FCLOSE( ), 303
FCOUNT( ), 303
FCREATE( ), 303-304
FEOF( ), 304
FERROR( ), 305
FFLUSH( ), 305
FGETS( ), 306
FIELD( ), 306-307

fields (see also files; records), 48, 50, 60, 62, 69, 73
  add, 69
  averaging, 74-75
  calculated fields, 77-78
  calculated fields, BROWSE, 147
  clear, 51, 62
  copy, 71
  count, FCOUNT( ), 303
  define, File New Database, 11-12
  define, SET FIELDS, 254
  delete, 51, 62, 69
  display, 50, 62
  formatting, Screen Builder, 434-435
  length of field, FSIZE( ), 312
  loading fields, Screen Builder, 431
  memory variable use, 403
  move, 50, 53, 62, 66
  name, FIELD( ), 306-307
  reordering, Screen Builder, 437
  reports including fields, 23-27
  select, 50, 62
  select, BROWSE, 147
  size, 53, 66
  sorting, 72
  summing, 76-77
  width of field, 26-27
FILE( ), 307
files and File Menu (see also fields; records), 9-36, 102-114, 405, 428
  access levels, show, ACCESS( ), 269-270
  alternate file names, 46
  archived, 108
  attributes, 107-108
  averaging, 74-75
  Browse menu, 63-67
  choose from list, PUTFILE( ), 351
  clear, CLEAR, 151
  close, CLOSE command, 152
  close, FCLOSE( ), 303
  close, FFLUSH( ), 305
  close, File Close, 34
  close, File Quit, 36
  close, QUIT command, 216
  combine, JOIN command, 187-188
  compile, 89
  copy file-information to array, ADIR( ), 272-273
  copy, 69-71
  copy, COPY FILE, 153

488 Index

files and File Menu (cont.)
  copy, structure only, COPY STRUCTURE, 154
  copy, structure only, COPY TO STRUCTURE EXTENDED, 156
  copy, to directory, 105-106
  create, CREATE command, 157-158
  create, CREATE FROM command, 158
  create, FCREATE( ), 303-304
  create, File New, 10-1
  create, SYS(3), 373
  current, USED( ), 383-384
  Database menu, 57-82
  default settings, Files panel, Window menu, 45
  delete, 107
  delete, changes only, File Revert, 35
  delete, DELETE FILE, 172
  delete, packing, 81-82
  delete, SET DELETED command, 252, 470
  Dest (printer destination) program, 426-427
  directories (see directories)
  display, DISPLAY command, 173, 470
  display, TYPE command, 239
  drive selection, 110
  drive/directory currently used, CURDIR( ), 292
  drive/directory location, SET DEFAULT, 251-252
  editing, 107
  end-of-file marker, 89
  end-of-file marker, FEOF( ), 304
  error checking, FERROR( ), 305
  export, EXPORT TO, 178-179
  extensions, 33-34
  field manipulation (see fields)
  File Menu, 9-36
  Filer accessory, System menu, 102-114
  filters, FILTER( ), 307-308
  formatting, 51, 63
  FoxPro pop-up names (_mfi_xxx), 478
  hidden, 108
  index files (see index files)
  joining, JOIN command, 187-188
  joining, RQBE window, 462
  labels (see labels)
  list, DIRECTORY command,173
  list, LIST FILES, 190
  location, LOCFILE( ), 327
  _msm_file FoxPro name, 477
  match to skeleton, SYS(2000), 378
  memos, add existing memo, APPEND MEMO, 145
  move, 106-107
  name, _text, 396-397
  name, DBF( ), 293
  name, FILE( ), 307
  open, 9, 54, 58, 407
  open, & function, 268
  open, EVALUATE( ), 302
  open, FGETS( ), 306
  open, File Open, 33-34
  open, FOPEN( ), 309-310
  open, FPUTS( ), 311
  open, FREAD( ), 311-312
  open, FSEEK( ), 312
  open, FWRITE( ), 314
  open, GETFILE( ), 315
  open, SELECT command, 229-232
  open, USE command, 240-241
  output to, \ commands, 123, 124
  output to, SET DEVICE command, 252, 470
  overwrite protection, SET SAFETY, 261, 471
  paths, 45-46
  paths, FULLPATH( ), 313
  paths, SYS(2014), 379
  PRG file, create, File New Program, 12
  printing (see printing)
  read-only, 107
  record manipulation (see records)
  relationships, 54-56
  relationships, RELATION( ), 359-360
  relationships, SELECT command, 229-232
  relationships, SET RELATION, 260
  rename, 108
  rename, RENAME command, 219
  replace within directory, 106
  reports (see reports)
  resource files, 46
  resource files, current, SYS(2005), 379
  resource files, SET RESOURCE, 260-261, 471
  save, File Save, 34
  save, File Save As, 35
  scrolling, 53, 66
  search, 104-105
  size of file, 108-109, 113-114
  sort, 58, 71-73, 109-110
  sort, INDEX ON, 185-186
  sort, SELECT command, 230-232
  store output, SET ALTERNATE, 245-246, 469
  structure, 48, 58, 405
  structure, change, 58
  structure, change, MODIFY STRUCTURE, 198
  structure, COPY STRUCTURE, 154
  structure, copy to array, AFIELDS( ), 274
  structure, COPY TO STRUCTURE EXTENDED, 156
  structure, File New Database, 11-12
  structure, list, LIST STRUCTURE, 191
  subtotals, TOTAL command, 238-239
  system files, 108
  tag for directory inclusion, 104
  targeting, 106
  targeting, TARGET( ), 380-381
  text editing region (see text editing regions)
  totals calculation, 73-74, 76-77
  totals calculation, SUM, 237
  tree structure of directory, 110
  undefined-reference location, EXTERNAL command, 179
  update, date of update, LUPDATE( ), 329-330
Files panel, Window menu, 45
FILTER( ), 307-308
filtering
  Crit program, 424-426
  FILTER( ), 307-308
  position of filter condition, SELECT command, 230-232
financial functions
  future value, FV( ), 313-314
  payment amount, PAYMENT( ), 343-344
  present value, PV( ), 352
FIND command, 180
FKLABEL( ), 308
FKMAX( ), 308-309
FLOOR( ), 309
FLUSH command, 180

footers, 16
FOPEN( ), 309-310
For clause, adding records, 68, 70-71
FOR command, 180-181, 405, 455, 456
FOR...ENDFOR loop, 405
  stop, EXIT command, 178
foreign language characters, 116
form feeds
  _padvance, 391
  _peject, 393
  EJECT command, 177
  EJECT PAGE command, 177
format files and formatting
  BROWSE command, 148-149
  fields, Screen Builder, 434-435
  labels, 31-32
  name, SYS(7), 374
  reports, 80
  reports, Format dialog box, 24-25
  SET FORMAT TO command, 254
FOUND( ), 310-311, 418
FoxDoc documentation, 121
FoxGraph graph generator, 121
FoxHelp, 46, 98-99
  access, HELP command, 184
  categories, 481-482
  show help screens on error, SET HELP, 256
  subset of help topics displayed, SET HELPFILTER, 255
FPUTS( ), 311
FREAD( ), 311-312
FSEEK( ), 312
FSIZE( ), 312
FULLPATH( ), 313, 471
FUNCTION command, 181-182
function keys
  assign values, SET FUNCTION, 255
  maximum number programmable, FKMAX( ), 308-309
  name of key, FKLABEL( ), 308
functions
  = command use, 140
  user-defined, create, FUNCTION command, 181-182
future value, FV( ), 313-314
FWRITE( ), 314
FXP files (see programming)

G

GATHER FROM command, 182-183
GET command, size of display, @SAY...GET command, 127
GETBAR( ), 314
GETENV( ), 314
GETEXPR command, 183
GETFILE( ), 315
GETPAD( ), 315
GOMONTH( ), 315
GOTO command, 183-184, 419
graphics card, SYS(2006), 379
graphs, FoxGraph generator, 121

H

hard drive (see drives)
headers
  create, SET HEADING command, 255, 471
  print, ON PAGE command, 206, 207
  programming, 16, 17
  size of header, HEADER( ), 316
help (see FoxHelp)
HELP command, 184
hidden files, 108
HIDE WINDOW command, 184
hot keys
  bounce-bar menu assignment, 166, 168
  check box assignment, 129
  macro assignment, 100
  pop-up menu assignment, 132, 163-164, 169
  push button assignment, 134
  radio button assignment, 136
  Screen Builder, 440
HOURS, 471

I

IF command, 184-185
IF statements, 404
IF...ENDIF, 408
IIF( ), 316-317
indentation, 20, 89
  program files, 400
index files (see also sorting techniques), 12-15, 49-51, 57-59, 60-61, 466
  change key, 50, 61
  copy, COPY INDEXES, 153-154
  create, 49, 61
  create, File New Index, 12-15
  delete, 50, 61
  find record, FIND command, 180
  key, 13
  key, SYS(14), 375
  key, show , KEY( ), 322-323
  limit records for selection, 49, 61
  multiple index files, 13, 58
  multiple index files, name, MDX( ), 331
  name, CDX( ), 286
  name, NDX( ), 339
  name, ORDER( ), 341
  open, 49, 60
  open, SET INDEX TO, 256, 407, 471
  open, USE command, 241
  order of sorting, 50, 62
  order of sorting, SET ORDER, 258
  records, find, 94
  recreate open files, REINDEX, 218
  save, 49, 61
  search for record, SEEK( ), 365-366
  single index files, 13, 58
  sorting, 13, 58
  sorting, INDEX ON command, 185-186
  tags, 58
  tags, copy tags, COPY TAG command, 155
  tags, delete, DELETE TAG, 172-173
  tags, name, TAG( ), 380
  unique records only, SET UNIQUE, 264, 471
INDEX ON command, 185-186, 452
INKEY( ), 318
INLIST( ), 319
INPUT command, 186-187
INSERT command, 187
Insert mode/typeover mode, INSMODE( ), 319
Insert Records program, 411-413
Insert Using Arrays program, 413-415
INSMODE( ), 319
integers, INT( ), 319-320
interest rates
  future value, FV( ), 313-314
  payment amount, PAYMENT( ), 343-344
  present value , PV( ), 352
invisible boxes, create, @...GET Invisible Boxes, 129, 130
invisible buttons, Screen Builder, 443
ISALPHA( ), 320
ISCOLOR( ), 321

ISDIGIT( ), 321
ISLOWER( ), 321-322
ISUPPER( ), 322

J

JOIN command, 187-188
joining files, RQBE window, 462
Julian dates (see dates)

K

KEY( ), 322-323
keys, index files, 13, 322-323, 375
KEYBOARD command, 188
keyboards/keyboard buffers
  add characters, KEYBOARD command, 188
  character is/is not present, CHRSAW( ), 288
  clear, CLEAR command, 151
  command entry from keyboard, 3
  cursor movement, 6-7
  keypress displayed, INKEY( ), 318
  keypress displayed, LASTKEY( ), 323-324
  keypress displayed, READKEY( ), 355-357
  typeahead buffer, 47
  typeahead buffer, SET TYPEAHEAD, 264, 471

L

LABEL FORM command, 189, 427
labels, 29, 32, 80-81, 471
  create, 80, 471
  create, CREATE LABEL command, 158
  create, File New Label, 29-30
  create, LABEL FORM command, 189, 471
  delete custom layouts, 32
  Expression Builder use, 30-31
  For and While clauses, criteria for label selection, 81
  formatting and layout, 31-32
  formatting and layout, MODIFY LABEL, 196
  Labels program, 427
  previewing page before printing, 30
  printing, 81
  sample label, 81
  save, 32, 80-81
  scope of records, 81

trimming extra characters/spaces, TRIM( ), 31
LASTKEY( ), 323-324, 413
LEFT( ), 324, 426
LEN( ), 324-325
libraries, external, SET LIBRARY, 256-257, 467
light-bar menus (see also bounce-bar menus; menus; pop-up menus)
  activate, MENU TO command, 195
  create, @...PROMPT, 139-140
LIKE( ), 325-326
line-drawing, REPLICATE( ), 360
LINENO( ), 326-327
LIST, 410
LIST command, 173, 189-190, 410
LIST FILES command, 190
LIST HISTORY command, 190-191
LIST STATUS command, 191
LIST STRUCTURE command, 191
lists
  color of list, 131
  create, @...GET Lists, 130-132
  programming, 18
  records in file, LIST command, 189-190
  Screen Builder, 443
  scroll bar to right of list, 131
  scrollable lists, dialog boxes, 4
  size of list, 130
  width of list, 130
LOAD command, 192
loans
  payment amount, PAYMENT( ), 343-344
  present value, PV( ), 352
LOCATE command, 192, 408
LOCFILE( ), 327
log files, programming, 120
logarithms, LOG( ) and LOG10( ), 327-328,
LOGERROR, 471
LOOP command, 418
loops (see also FOR), 405, 413, 418
  leave loop, EXIT, 178
  run loop x times, FOR command, 180-181
LOWER( ), 328-329
LTRIM( ), 329
LUPDATE( ), 329

M

macros, 99-102

create, 99-101
create, record, 101
delete, clear and clear all, 101-102
hot key assignment, 100
load into memory, RESTORE MACROS, 222
name, 100
replace or overwrite, 100
restore, 102
run, PLAY MACRO, 211
save, 100, 102
save, SAVE MACROS, 225
set defaults, 102
substitution function, EVALUATE( ), 301-302
substitution function, & function, 267-268
margins, 20, 471
maximum values, MAX( ), 330-331
MDX( ), 331
MDY( ), 331-332
MEMLINES( ), 332-333
memo fields
  add existing memo, APPEND MEMO, 145
  copy, COPY MEMO, 154
  edit, MODIFY MEMO, 196
  edit, @SAY...GET command, 127
  edit, SET WINDOW, 265
  number of lines, MEMLINES( ), 332-333
  specific line, MLINE( ), 336-337
  specific line, _mline, 390
  substring location, ATCLINE( ), 282
  substring location, ATLINE( ), 282-283
  width, SET MEMOWIDTH, 257, 471
memory
  available memory, MEMORY( ), 333-334
  available memory, SYS(12), 375
  clear memory, CLEAR, 151
  extended memory, SYS(23) and SYS(24), 377
  flush buffers to disk, FFLUSH( ), 305
  flush buffers to disk, FLUSH, 180
  macros, load, RESTORE MACROS, 222
  memory variables, create, STORE command, 236-237

Index 491

memory variables, delete, RELEASE, 219
memory variables, load, RESTORE, 221
memory variables, save, SAVE command, 226
menu placed on stack, PUSH MENU, 215
menu placed on stack, PUSH POPUP, 215, 216
menu pulled from stack, POP MENU, 210-211
menu pulled from stack, POP POPUP, 211
windows, load, RESTORE WINDOW, 223
memory variables, 14-15, 402-403
  arrayed, 403
  averaging, 75
  clear, CLEAR ALL, 410
  clear, CLEAR command, 151
  counting records, 76
  create, ACCEPT command, 141
  create, GETEXPR command, 183
  create, INPUT command, 186-187
  create, STORE command, 236-237
  criteria, Crit program, 424-426
  edit, READ command, 216-217
  evaluation, SET TEXTMERGE commands, 263-264
  field use, 403
  get array values from records, SCATTER TO, 227
  pass to program, PARAMETERS command, 209-210
  private declaration, PRIVATE, 212-213
  public declaration, PUBLIC command, 214-215
  put array values in records, GATHER FROM, 182-183
  REPLACE, 413
  save, SAVE command, 226
  system (see system memory variables)
MEMORY( ), 333-334
MENU BAR command, 193
Menu Builder, 445-453, 467
  activate, CREATE MENU command, 159
  code generation, 451-452
  custom-menu design, 445-451
  menu code cleanup, 450-451

menu code setup, 450
option assignment, 447-448
options check box, 449
Printout submenus, 448-449
prompt assignment, 447-448
Quit option, 450
Report submenus, 449-450
running menus, 452
running programs, 452-453
saving menus, 451
startup procedures, 446
submenu options, 448
submenu procedures, 448
MENU command, 193-195
MENU TO command, 195
MENU( ), 334
menus (see also Menu Builder), 2-3, 8, 408, 471
  borders, SET BORDER, 247, 470
  bounce-bar menus (see bounce-bar menus)
  check mark character before option, MRKBAR( ), 338
  check mark character before option, MRKPAD( ), 339
  check mark character before option, SET MARK OF, 257, 471
  clear, CLEAR command, 151
  create, CREATE MENU command, 159
  current menu, MENU( ), 334
  display without activation, SHOW MENU, 233
  editing, MODIFY MENU command, 196
  Expression Builder use, 14
  File menu, 9-36
  keyboard command entry, 3
  light-bar menus (see light-bar menus)
  Menu Builder, 445-453
  mouse command entry, 3
  options, 163
  options, available, CNTPAD( ), 289
  options, name, GETBAR( ), 314
  place on stack, PUSH MENU, 215
  pop-up menus (see pop-up menus)
  prompt within menu, PRMPAD( ), 348
  pull from stack, POP MENU, 210-211
  SET SYSMENU, 477
  submenus, ON BAR command, 199-200
  system menu names, 477-480
  system menu names, SYS(2013), 379
MESSAGE( ), 334-335
messages
  display, SET MESSAGE, 257-258
  errors, MESSAGE( ), 334-335
  on-screen display, @SAY...GET command, 127
minimum values, MIN( ), 335-336
MLINE( ), 336-337
MOD( ), 337-338
MODIFY COMMAND command, 195-196, 399, 451, 452
MODIFY LABEL command, 196
MODIFY MEMO command, 196
MODIFY MENU command, 196
MODIFY PROJECT command, 197
MODIFY QUERY command, 197
MODIFY REPORT command, 197
MODIFY SCREEN command, 197
MODIFY STRUCTURE command, 198
modular design programming, 401-402
MONTH( ), 338
mouse use, 47
  command entry from mouse, 3
  sensitivity setting, SET MOUSE, 258, 471
MOVE POPUP command, 198
MOVE WINDOW command, 198-199
MRKBAR( ), 338
MRKPAD( ), 339
MVARSIZ, 471
MVCOUNT, 471

N

NDX( ), 339
negative numbers, SIGN( ), 367
networks, access levels, show, ACCESS( ), 269-270
NOTE command, 199
numeric display, comma separators, SET SEPARATOR, 261, 471
NUMLOCK( ), 340

O

object code files (see programming)
OBJNUM( ), 340
OCCURS( ), 340-341

ON BAR command, 199-200
ON ERROR command, 200-201
ON ESCAPE command, 201-202
ON KEY command, 202
ON KEY LABEL, 204-206
ON KEY = command, 202-204
ON PAD command, 206
ON PAGE command, 206, 207
ON READERROR command, 207
ON SELECTION BAR command, 207-208
ON SELECTION MENU command, 208
ON SELECTION PAD command, 208
ON SELECTION POPUP command, 209, 410
On/Off panel, Window menu, 45
operating systems, name/version, OS( ), 341-342
ORDER( ), 341
OS( ), 341-342
overwrite protection, SET SAFETY, 261, 471

P

PACK command, 209, 427
Packem program, 427-428
PAD( ), 342
PADC( ), 342-343
PADL( ), 342-343
PADR( ), 342-343
page breaks, create, ON PAGE command, 206, 207
page numbers, _pageno, 391
parameter-settings (see environment)
PARAMETERS command, 209-210
PARAMETERS( ), 343
partitions, Browse windows, 53, 65-66
paths, 45-46
   establish path, SET PATH, 259, 471
   minimum file path, SYS(2014), 379
   show path, FULLPATH( ), 313
   show path, SET FULLPATH, 254
PAYMENT( ), 343-344
PCOL( ), 344-345
People database, sample programming application, 405-428
PI( ), 345-346
picture formats/templates command-use,

   TRANSFORM( ), 381-382
   @SAY...GET command use, 126
PLAY MACRO command, 211
POP MENU command, 210-211
POP POPUP command, 211
pop-up menus (see also Menu Builder), 410
   activate, READ MENU TO, 217-218
   character or box before option, DEFINE BAR, 164
   check mark before options, DEFINE POPUP, 169, 410
   check mark before option, MRKBAR( ), 338
   check mark before option, MRKPAD( ), 339
   check mark before option, SET MARK OF, 257, 471
   clear, CLEAR command, 151
   color selection, DEFINE BAR, 164
   color selection, DEFINE POPUP, 169, 410
   create, @...MENU command, 138-139
   create, MENU command, 193-195
   definitions, 410
   display, ACTIVATE POPUP, 142, 410, 411
   display, SHOW POPUP, 234
   erase from screen, DEACTIVATE POPUP, 162, 410, 427
   hot key assignment, DEFINE BAR, 163-164
   hot key assignment, DEFINE POPUP, 169, 410
   location, DEFINE POPUP, 168-170
   margins around menu, DEFINE POPUP, 169, 410
   message displayed, DEFINE POPUP, 169, 410
   messages displayed, DEFINE BAR, 164
   moving options, DEFINE POPUP, 169, 410
   name, DEFINE POPUP, 168-170, 410
   name, POPUP( ), 346
   options, as files/fields, DEFINE POPUP, 169, 410
   options, location, DEFINE BAR, 164-165
   options, location, DEFINE

    POPUP, 170, 410
   options, location, MENU command, 194
   options, multiple selection, DEFINE POPUP, 170, 410
   options, name, GETBAR( ), 314
   options, number of available options, CNTBAR( ), 289
   options, selection, ON SELECTION BAR, 207-208
   options, selection, ON SELECTION PAD, 208
   options, selection, ON SELECTION POPUP, 209, 410
   options, set, DEFINE BAR, 163-165
   options, show selection number, BAR( ), 283
   options, show selection number, GETPAD( ), 315
   prompts, PRMBAR( ), 347
   prompts, PROMPT( ), 349
   pull from stack, POP POPUP, 211
   push onto stack, PUSH POPUP, 215, 216
   scroll bar to right of menu, DEFINE POPUP, 170, 410
   submenu display, ON PAD, 206
   window placement, DEFINE POPUP, 169, 410
pop-ups, 5
   activate, ON BAR command, 199-200
   color of pop-up, 133
   create, @...GET Pop-ups, 132-134
   define, CREATE SCREEN, 161
   display, ON PAD, 206
   hot key assignment, 132
   move, MOVE POPUP, 198
   resize, SIZE POPUP, 235
   Screen Builder, 443
   size of pop-up, 132
   width of pop-up, 132
POPUP( ), 346
positive numbers, SIGN( ), 367
present value, PV( ), 352
printing and printers, 408
   alignment of output, _alignment, 389
   begin on page x, _pbpage, 391
   column position of printer head, PCOL( ), 344-345
   column position of text, _pcolno, 391-392
   control codes, (??? command), 125

control codes, _pscode, 395
copies, _pcopies, 392
define and set codes/variables, PRINTJOB, 212
Dest (destination) programs, 426-427
display text on screen, TEXT command, 238
end code, _pecode, 392-393
end on page x, _pepage, 393
form feeds, EJECT command, 177
form feeds, EJECT PAGE command, 177
form feeds, _padvance, 391
form feeds, _peject, 393
headers, ON PAGE, 206, 207
indentation, _pretext, 394
line position number of output, _plineno, 394
line spacing, _pspacing, 395
margins, _lmargin, 390
margins, _ploffset, 394
margins, _rmargin, 395
output to printer, File Printer Setup, 36
output to printer, SELECT, 229-232
output to printer, SET DEVICE command, 252, 470
output to printer, SET PRINTER commands, 259, 471
output to printer, SET TEXTMERGE commands, 263-264
output to printer, SYS(6), 374
page breaks, ON PAGE, 206, 207
page length, _plength, 393
page numbers, _pageno, 391
pause between pages, _pwait, 395
pitch, _ppitch, 394
previewing before printing, 20-21, 30
printer on-line test, PRINTSTATUS( ), 347
printer on-line test, SYS(13), 375
printer-driver, _pdriver, 392
print setting, SYS(102), 377
program files, 19, 401
quality setting, _pquality, 394
reports, 80
reports, REPORT FORM, 220-221
row number position of printer

head, PROW( ), 350-351
start print, File Print, 36
PRINTJOB command, 212
PRINTSTATUS( ), 347
PRIVATE command, 212-213
PRMBAR( ), 347
PRMPAD( ), 348
PROCEDURE command, 213-214
procedure files/procedures, 46, 402
  create, PROCEDURE command, 213-214
  name, SYS(2015), 379
  open, SET PROCEDURE, 260
  parameter passing, PARAMETERS( ), 343
processing speed, 465
processors, SYS(17), 376
PROGRAM( ), 348-349
programming and Program Menu, 118-121, 399-428
  Application Program Interface (API), 467
  binary programs (see binary files)
  call, DO command, 174
  cancel command, CANCEL, 151
  cancel execution, Program Cancel, 118
  code generation, Menu Builder, 451-452
  code generation, Screen Builder, 440-441
  command responses shown, SET TALK, 47, 263
  command responses shown, SYS(103), 378
  commands displayed as executed, SET DOHISTORY, 253
  commands displayed as executed, SET ECHO, 253, 470
  comments in program files, 199, 407
  compile, 89, 119-120
  compile, COMPILE, 152
  compile, save errors, SET LOGERRORS, 257
  conditional processing, DO CASE, DO WHILE, IF, 174-175, 184-185
  copying text, 401
  create application, BUILD APP, 149
  create application, File New Program, 12

  Crit program, 424-426
  debugging (see debugging)
  decision-making, IF and CASE statements, 404
  Delete program, 421-423
  Dest program, 426-427
  DO CASE, 174-175
  DO WHILE, 174-175
  documentation, FoxDoc, 121
  Edit program, 415-419
  Edit with Arrays program, 419-421
  editing keys, 400
  editor access, MODIFY COMMAND or File menu, 399
  encryption of program files, 120
  environment settings (see environment)
  error-trapping (see also error-trapping)
  error-trapping, ON ERROR, 200-201
  Escape keypress command, ON ESCAPE, 201-202
  Escape keypress halt, SET ESCAPE command, 253, 470
  execute program, Program Do, 118
  FoxPro pop-up names (_mpr_xxx), 479-480
  go to specific line, 401
  graphing, FoxGraph, 121
  IF command, 184-185
  indentation, 400
  Insert Records program, 411-413
  Insert Using Arrays program, 413-415
  keypress command, ON KEY, 202
  keypress command, ON KEY LABEL, 204-206
  keypress command, ON KEY = commands, 203-204
  Labels program, 427
  line-by-line execution, LINENO( ), 326-327
  log files, 120
  loops, 178, 180-181, 405, 413, 418
  Main program structure, 408-411
  memory variables, 402-403
  Menu Builder, 445-453
  modular design programming 401-402
  moving text, 401

programming and Program (*cont.*)
  _msm_prog FoxPro name, 477
  name of program with error, PROGRAM( ), 348-349
  name of program with error, SYS(16), 376
  optimize/speed-up processing, SET OPTIMIZE, 258
Packem program, 427-428
parameter passing, PARAMETERS( ), 343
pass memory variables, PARAMETERS command, 209-210
pause, SUSPEND, 237-238
pause, WAIT, 242
People sample application, 405-428
pop-up menus, 410
printing, 401
procedure files, 46, 402
procedure files, SET PROCEDURE, 260
procedure names, SYS(2015), 379
processing speed, 465
Program menu, 118-121
resume processing, Program Resume, 118-119
resume processing, RESUME, 223
resume processing, RETRY command, 223-224
return control to calling program, RETURN command, 224, 411
run program, Menu Builder, 452-453
run program, RUN command, 224-225
run program, Screen Builder, 441-442
Screen Builder (*see also* Screen Builder), 121, 429-434
show commands as executed, Program Echo, 119
show commands as executed, Program Talk, 119
step-by-step execution, Program Step, 119
step-by-step execution, SET STEP, 262, 471
subroutines, call, PROCEDURE command, 213-214
update compiled object file, SET DEVELOPMENT, 252, 470
versional differences, SET COMPATIBLE, 98, 250, 385, 466, 470
project files
  create application, BUILD APP, 149
  create, BUILD PROJECT, 149
  create, CREATE PROJECT command, 159
  edit, MODIFY PROJECT, 197
  undefined-reference location, EXTERNAL command, 179
PROMPT( ), 349
prompts
  bounce-bar menu, Menu Builder, 447-448
  menu position, PRMPAD( ), 348
  pause for data entry, ACCEPT command, 141
  pause for data entry, INPUT command, 186-187
  pause for data entry, WAIT command, 242
  pop-up menu, PRMBAR( ), 347
  pop-up menu, PROMPT( ), 349
  show last given command, LIST HISTORY, 190-191
PROPER( ), 349-350
PROW( ), 350-351
PUBLIC command, 214-215
push buttons
  color of button, 134-135
  create, @...GET Push Buttons, 134-135
  hot key assignment, 134
  invisible buttons, 129, 130
  Screen Builder, 439
  size of button, 134
PUSH MENU command, 215
PUSH POPUP command, 215, 216
PUTFILE( ), 351
puzzle feature, System menu, 117
PV( ), 352

Q

queries (*see also* RQBE window), 455-463
create, CREATE QUERY, 160
create, RQBE window, 457-459
edit, MODIFY QUERY, 197
editing selection criteria, RQBE window, 461
multiple selection criteria, RQBE window, 460
query-condition setting, 455-456
RQBE window, 455-463
running, RQBE window, 462
saving, RQBE window, 462-463
SELECT command, 461, 465
selection criteria setting, RQBE window, 459-461
Quick Report feature, 28-29
QUIT command, 216

R

radians of angle, DTOR( ) and RTOD( ), 297-298, 363
radio buttons, 4
  color of button, 136-137
  create, @...GET Radio Buttons, 135-137
  define, CREATE SCREEN, 161
  hot key assignment, 136
  Screen Builder, 443
  size of button, 136
random numbers, RAND( ), 353
RAT( ), 353-354
RATLINE( ), 354-355
RDLEVEL( ), 355
READ command, 216-217, 413, 415, 440
  clear, CLEAR READ, 151-152
  current level, RDLEVEL( ), 355
  display, SHOW GETS, 232-233
  display, SHOW OBJECT, 233
  object number, OBJNUM( ), 340
READ MENU TO command, 217-218
read-only files, 107
READKEY( ), 355-357
RECALL command, 218
RECCOUNT( ), 357, 419
RECNO( ), 358
RECNO(0), 358
records and Record menu (*see also* arrays; fields; files), 91-97
  add, 54, 67-69
  add, APPEND FROM ARRAY, 145, 413
  add, blank, 92, 413
  add, EDIT, 176-177
  add, INSERT, 187
  add, Insert program, 411-413
  append, APPEND BLANK, 143-144, 413
  append, APPEND command, 143, 442
  append, APPEND FROM, 144-145
  append, APPEND FROM ARRAY, 145, 413
  append, @SAY...GET

command, 127
blank records, 92, 143-144
calculations, CALCULATE, 150
carry forward changes, SET CARRY, 247, 470
copy, 69-71
copy, COPY TO ARRAY, 156, 157, 419
copy, COPY TO, 155-156
count, 75-76
count, COUNT, 157
count, RECCOUNT( ), 357
count, SET ODOMOTER, 258
current record number, RECNO( ), 358
delete, 53-54, 66-67, 91-92, 95-96
delete, Delete program, 421-423
delete, DELETE, 171-172
delete, DELETED( ), 294
delete, PACK, 81-82, 209
delete, Packem program, 427-428
delete, ZAP, 242
edit, 92
edit, Edit program, 415-419
edit, EDIT, 176-177
edit, using arrays, Edit with Arrays program, 419-421
fields, select fields, BROWSE, 147
filtering, 51, 63
find (see searching)
FoxPro pop-up names (_mrc_xxx), 479
get array values from records, SCATTER TO, 227
go to specific record, 93
go to specific record, GOTO command, 183-184
grouping for programming, 17-18, 21-22
hold cursor for data entry, SET CONFIRM, 250, 470
index files, find, 94
list, LIST command, 189-190
memo field, number of lines, MEMLINES( ), 332-333
memo field, specific line, MLINE( ), 336-337
memo field, specific line, _mline, 390
move to next, SET SKIP, 261-262, 471
move to next, SKIP, 235, 471
move, LOCATE, 192
_msm_recrd FoxPro name, 477

process all/selected, SCAN command, 226
put array values in records, GATHER FROM, 182-183
Record menu, 91-97
record pointer at end of file, EOF( ), 299-300
record pointer moved back one, BOF( ), 284-285
save, SET AUTOSAVE, 246, 469
scoping, labels, 81
scoping, reports, 79
searching, 91, 93-95
searching, closest match, RECNO(0), 358
searching, CONTINUE command, 153
searching, FIND command, 180
searching, find first match, SEEK, 228, 408
searching, find next match, 93-94
searching, global find and replace, REPLACE, 220, 413
searching, global find and replace, UPDATE, 240
searching, LOCATE command, 192, 408
searching, near matches, SET NEAR, 258, 471
searching, SEEK( ), 365-366
searching, successful search, yes/no, FOUND( ), 310-311
select records, BROWSE, 146
show number of processed records, _tally, 396
show time of processing, _tallytime, 396
size, RECSIZE( ), 359
sort, 72-73
sort, SET FILTER TO, 254
sort, SORT command, 236
total, 73-74
un-delete, 96-97
un-delete, RECALL, 218
update, UPDATE command, 240
RECSIZE( ), 359
REINDEX command, 218
RELATION( ), 359-360
RELEASE command, 219
remainders
  % operator, 268-269
  MOD( ), 337-338
RENAME command, 219
REPLACE command, 220, 403,

407, 413
REPLICATE( ), 360
REPORT FORM command, 220-221, 471
reports, 15-29, 78-80
  add lines, 28
  alphabetic sorting, 17
  bands, 15-16
  boxes, 22-23
  Calculate dialog box, 25-26
  center lines, 28
  create, 78
  create, CREATE REPORT, 160
  create, File New Report, 15-29
  delete lines, 28
  detail band, 16
  display, 18-19
  fields, 23-27
  footers, 16
  For and While clauses, criteria for record selection, 79
  formatting, 80
  formatting, Format dialog box, 24-25
  formatting, MODIFY REPORT command, 197
  grouping records, 17-18, 21-22
  headers, 16-17
  indentation, 20
  layout window, 15
  list creation, 18
  margins, 20
  page layout options, 19-20
  page length, 19
  page numbers, _pageno, 391
  previewing page, 20-21
  printing, 19, 80
  printing, REPORT FORM, 220-221
  Quick Report feature, 28-29
  re-order items, bring to front/send to back, 28
  Report Expression dialog box, 23-24
  Report program, 423-424
  Report submenu, Menu Builder, 449-450
  Reset pop-up, default settings, 26
  saving settings, 79
  scope of records, 79
  Style dialog box, 25
  summary, 16, 22
  text entry steps, 27-28
  title, 16-17, 22
  width of fields in reports, 26-27
resource files, 46

resource files (cont.)
  create, SET RESOURCE, 260-261, 471
  current, SYS(2005), 379
RESTORE command, 221
RESTORE MACROS command, 222
RESTORE SCREEN command, 222-223
RESTORE WINDOW command, 223
RESUME command, 223
RETRY command, 223-224
RETURN command, 224, 411, 413, 427
RIGHT( ), 360-361
ROUND( ), 361-362
rounding numbers
  integers only, INT( ), 319-320
  ROUND( ), 361-362
  rounding down, FLOOR( ), 309
  rounding up, CEILING( ), 286
ROW( ), 362
rows
  cursor at row number, ROW( ), 362-363
  on-screen display, number of, SROWS( ), 369-370
RQBE window, 455-463, 466
  activate, CREATE QUERY, 160
  editing selection criteria, 461
  exiting RQBE window, 463
  joining multiple databases, 462
  multiple selection criteria, 460
  opening RQBE window, 456
  output format specification, 458-459
  output order specification, 458
  query condition setting, 455-456
  query creation, 457-459
  query editing, MODIFY QUERY, 197
  running queries, 462
  saving queries, 462
  SELECT command, 229-232, 455, 461
  selection criteria setting, 459-461
RTOD( ), 363
RTRIM( ), 364
RUN command, 224-225
Rushmore technology, 466

S

SAVE command, 226
SAVE MACROS command, 225
SAVE SCREEN command, 225
SAVE WINDOW command, 226
SCAN, 418
SCAN command, 226-227, 405, 418
SCAN WHILE, 418
SCAN...ENDSCAN loop, 405
  stop, EXIT command, 178
SCATTER TO command, 227
SCHEME( ), 364
SCOLS( ), 365
Screen Builder, 121, 429-443, 466
  boxes, 433-434, 437-438
  check boxes, 436
  code generation, 440-441
  control boxes, 436
  control objects, 442-443
  custom screen design, 427-438
  design-screen commands, 443
  fields, formatting, 434-435
  fields, load, 431
  fields, reordering, 437
  hot keys, 440
  invisible buttons, 443
  lists, 443
  objects, move, 431-433
  objects, select, 437
  pop-ups, 443
  push buttons, 439
  radio buttons, 443
  running programs, 441-442
  save screen, 438
  screen code setup, 437
  secondary screen creation, 438-440
  startup procedures, 430
  text added to screen, 433
screen displays (see also Screen Builder), 429-443
g, SET BLINK, 247, 470
  boxes, border coordinates, DEFINE BOX, 166
  boxes, clear (@...CLEAR command), 128-129
  boxes, draw (@...BOX command), 128
  boxes, draw (@...TO command), 140
  boxes, Screen Builder, 433-438
  clear, CLEAR, 151, 437
  clear, SET CLEAR, 248
  color capability test, ISCOLOR( ), 321
  color selection, SET COLOR...commands, 248-250
  columns displayed on-screen, SCOLS( ), 365
  console setting, SYS(100), 377
  copy text from screen to clipboard, 117, 401
  create, CREATE SCREEN, 161
  cursor column number, COL( ), 289-290
  cursor row number, ROW( ), 362-363
  display, DISPLAY command, 173, 470
  display, LIST command, 173
  display, RESTORE SCREEN, 222-223
  expressions displayed on screen (@SAY...GET), 125-128
  formatting, MODIFY SCREEN, 197
  highlighting, SET INTENSITY, 256, 471
  lines of display, SET DISPLAY, 252-253, 470
  messages, SET MESSAGE, 257-258
  monochrome vs. color, SET DISPLAY, 252-253, 470
  on/off, SET CONSOLE, 250-251, 470
  output to, \ commands, 123, 124
  output to, SET DEVICE command, 252, 470
  rows displayed on-screen, SROWS( ), 369-370
  save layout, SAVE SCREEN, 225
  Screen Builder, 429-443
  screen-code setup, Screen Builder, 437
  scrolling, SCROLL command, 228
  size of display, @SAY...GET command, 127
  text display on-screen, TEXT, 238
SCROLL command, 228
scrollable lists, 4
scrolling, 53, 66, 228
searching/search-and-replace, 84, 87-89, 418-419
  character search and replace, CHRTRAN( ), 288
  editing/Edit menu, 87-89
  elements in array, ASCAN( ), 276-277
  expressions, INLIST( ), 319
  find first match, SEEK command, 228

find next record, CONTINUE command, 153
find record, FIND command, 180
find record, LOCATE command, 192
global find and replace, REPLACE command, 220
global find and replace, UPDATE, 240
near matches, SET NEAR, 258, 471
number search and replace, STRTRAN( ), 370-371
records (see records, searching)
successful search, yes/no, FOUND( ), 310-311
text-search within files, 104-105
SECONDS( ), 365
SEEK command, 228, 407, 408, 418, 442
SEEK( ), 365-366
SELECT command, 229-232, 455, 461, 465
SELECT( ), 366
serial numbers, SYS(9), 374
SET commands, 232-233, 245-265, 402, 410
  CONFIG.FP parameter setting vs., 469-471
  show status, SET( ), 366-367
  show status, SYS(2001), 378
SET ALTERNATE, 245-246, 469
SET ANSI command, 246
SET AUTOSAVE command, 246, 469
SET BELL command, 47, 246, 410, 469, 470
SET BLINK command, 247, 470
SET BORDER command, 247, 470
SET CARRY command, 247, 470
SET CENTURY command, 247, 470
SET CLEAR command, 248
SET CLOCK command, 47, 248, 470
SET COLOR command, 248-249, 473
SET COLOR OF SCHEME, 474
SET COLOR SCHEME, 127
SET COMPATIBLE command, 250, 470
SET CONFIRM command, 250, 470
SET CONSOLE command, 250-251, 470

SET CURRENCY command, 251
SET DATE command, 251
SET DECIMALS command, 251, 471
SET DEFAULT command, 251-252
SET DELETED command, 252, 470
SET DEVELOPMENT command, 252, 470
SET DEVICE command, 252, 470
SET DISPLAY command, 252-253, 470
SET DOHISTORY command, 253
SET ECHO command, 253, 470
SET ESCAPE command, 253, 470
SET EXACT command, 253, 470
SET FIELDS command, 254, 465
SET FILTER TO command, 254, 424, 455, 465
SET FIXED command, 254
SET FORMAT TO command, 254, 453
SET FULLPATH command, 254
SET FUNCTION command, 255
SET HEADING command, 255, 470
SET HELP command, 256
SET HELPFILTER command, 255
SET HOURS command, 256
SET INDEX TO command, 256, 407, 455, 465, 471
SET INTENSITY command, 256, 471
SET LIBRARY command, 256-257, 467
SET LOGERRORS command, 257
SET MARK OF command, 257, 471
SET MARK TO command, 257, 471
SET MEMOWIDTH command, 257, 471
SET MESSAGE command, 257-258
SET MOUSE command, 258, 471
SET NEAR command, 258, 471
SET ODOMETER command, 258, 471
SET OPTIMIZE command, 258
SET ORDER command, 258-259
SET PATH command, 259, 471
SET POINT command, 259, 471
SET PRINTER commands, 259, 407, 424, 471
SET PROCEDURE command, 260, 402

SET RELATION command, 260, 455, 465
SET RESOURCE, 260-261, 471
SET SAFETY command, 261, 471
SET SEPARATOR command, 261, 471
SET SHADOWS command, 261
SET SKIP command, 261-262, 471
SET SPACE command, 262
SET STATUS command, 262, 471
SET STEP command, 262, 471
SET SYSMENU command, 263, 477
SET TALK, 402, 407
SET TALK command, 263, 402, 407, 428
SET TEXTMERGE commands, 263-264
SET TYPEAHEAD command, 264, 471
SET UNIQUE command, 264, 471
SET VIEW command, 264
SET VIEW TO command, 264
SET WINDOW command, 265
SET( ), 366-367
shadowing windows, 41
SHOW GETS command, 232-233
SHOW MENU command, 233
SHOW OBJECT command, 233-234
SHOW POPUP command, 234
SHOW WINDOW command, 234
SIGN( ), 367
sign-on screen, 1-2
sine, SIN( ), 367-368
SIZE POPUP command, 235
SORT command, 236
sorting techniques (see also index files), 17, 58, 71-73, 458
  arrays, ASORT( ), 278-279
  fields, 72
  files, 109-110
  filter records, SET FILTER TO, 254
  index key, 13
  INDEX ON command, 185-186
  order, 50, 62
  records, 72-73
  SELECT command, 230-232
  SORT command, 236
sound effects, 47, 410, 469, 470
  SET BELL command, 246
SOUNDEX( ), 368-369
source code files (see programming)

SPACE, 471
SPACE( ), 369
speed of processing, 465
square roots, SQRT( ), 369
SROWS( ), 369-370
Standard Query Language (SQL), 229, 455, 465
STORE command, 236-237, 402, 403
STR( ), 370
strings
  character search and replace, CHRTRAN( ), 288
  characters as numbers, VAL( ), 384
  characters-testing, ISALPHA( ), 320
  compare, checksum, SYS(200&), 379
  compare, DIFFERENCE( ), 294-295
  compare, LIKE( ), 325-326
  compare, SET ANSI, 246
  compare, SET EXACT, 253, 470
  compare, SOUNDEX( ), 368-369
  length of string, LEN( ), 324-325
  lowercase letters, ISLOWER( ), 321-322
  lowercase letters, LOWER( ), 328-329
  lowercase letters, PROPER( ), 349-350
  number search and replace, STRTRAN( ), 370-371
  number-testing, ISDIGIT( ), 321
  numbers as characters, STR( ), 370
  pad, PADC( )/PADL( )/PADR( ), 342-343
  pad, SPACE( ), 369
  pad, STUFF( ), 371-372
  proper names, PROPER( ), 349-350
  repeat characters, REPLICATE( ), 360
  substring occurrence, OCCURS( ), 340-341
  substring position, AT( ), 280-281
  substring position, ATC( ), 281-282
  substring position, LEFT( ), 324
  substring position, RAT( ), 353-354
  substring position, RATLINE( ), 354-355
  substring position, RIGHT( ), 360-361
  substring position, SUBSTR( ), 372-373
  trim, ALLTRIM( ), 276
  trim, LTRIM( ), 329
  trim, RTRIM( ), 364
  uppercase letters, ISUPPER( ), 322
  uppercase letters, PROPER( ), 349-350
  uppercase letters, UPPER( ), 383
STRTRAN( ), 370-371
STUFF( ), 371-372
styles, reports, Style dialog box, 25
submenus, Menu Builder, 448-449
subroutines (see also programming)
  calling, PROCEDURE command, 213-214
  return control to calling program, RETURN command, 224
SUBSTR( ), 372-373
SUM command, 237
summary, reports, 16, 22
SUSPEND command, 237-238
SYS( ) through SYS(2016), 373-379
system files, 108
system memory variables, 389-397
System menu (see also environment), 98-117
  ASCII codes, 116-117
  calculator feature, 114-115
  calendar/diary feature, 115-116
  copy text from screen to clipboard, 117
  filer accessory (see also files), 102-114
  FoxPro pop-up names (_mst__xxx), 477-478
  help, 98-99
  macros, 99-102
  names, SYS(2013), 379
  on/off, SET SYSMENU, 263
  puzzle feature, 117
  serial numbers, 98
  special characters, 116
  version of FoxPro, 98, 250, 385, 466
  _msm_systm FoxPro name, 477

T

tab setting, _tabs, 396
TABS, 471
TAG( ), 380
tags, index file, 58
  copy, COPY TAG, 155
  delete, DELETE TAG, 172-173
  name, TAG( ), 380
TALK, 407, 471
tangents, TAN( ), 380
TARGET( ), 380-381
TEDIT, 471
text (see also editing/Edit Menu; reports)
  ASCII codes, 116-117
  backup copies, 89
  carriage returns/line feeds, 89
  column position, _pcolno, 391-392
  copy, 84, 85, 86, 401
  copy, from screen to clipboard, 117, 401
  custom screen display, Screen Builder, 433
  cut and paste, 84-86
  default settings, 89-90
  delete, 7-8, 87
  editing/Editing menu, 6, 83-90
  end-of-file marker, 89
  go to specific line, 87
  indentation, 89
  indentation, _indent, 390
  margins, _lmargin, 390
  margins, _ploffset, 394
  margins, _rmargin, 395
  moving, 401
  name output file, _text, 396-397
  output text to screen or file (\ commands), 123, 124
  redo un-done changes, 86
  search and replace, 84, 87-89
  selecting text, 7, 87
  special characters, 116
  text editing regions (see text editing regions)
  text editor, 195
  text entry, 83
  undo changes, 85
  word wrap, 89
  word wrap, _wrap, 397
text boxes, 5
text buttons, 5
TEXT command, 238
text editing regions
  color of region, 138
  create, @...EDIT Text Edit

Region, 137-138
  create, File New File, 12
  scroll bar to right of region, 138
  size of region, 137
text editor, invoke, MODIFY COMMAND, 195-196
time
  SECONDS( ), 365
  SET HOURS command, 256
  SET TIME, 471
  system time, SYS(2), 373
  TIME( ), 381
TIME( ), 381
title, reports, 16-17, 22
TMPFILES, 471
TOTAL command, 238-239
totals, 73-74, 76-77
  SUM command, 237
  TOTAL command, 238-239
tracing execution, debugging, 44
TRANSFORM( ), 381-382
tree structure of directory, 110
TRIM( ), 18, 31, 382
TYPE command, 239
TYPE( ), 382
typeahead buffer (see also keyboards/keyboard buffers), 47

U

undo changes, editing/Edit menu, 85
UPDATE command, 240
UPDATED( ), 382-383
UPPER( ), 383
USE command, 240-241, 407, 410, 455, 465
USED( ), 383-384
user interface, 1-8
  alerts, 6
  cursor movement, 6-7
  dialog boxes, 3-6
  menus, 2-3, 8
  sign-on screen, 1-2
  text deletion, 7-8
  text editing, 6
  text selection, 7
  windows, 1-2
user-defined functions, create, FUNCTION command, 181-182

V

VAL( ), 384
validity testing, @SAY...GET command use, 126-127

variables (see also memory variables, system memory variables)
  return to variable last edited, SYS(18), 376-377
  return to variable last edited, VARREAD( ), 384-385
  type of variable, TYPE( ), 382
VARREAD( ), 384-385
VERSION( ), 385
versional differences, 98, 250, 385, 466
  extended version, 466
  SET COMPATIBLE, 250, 470
View windows, 44
  create, CREATE VIEW, 161
  index files, 49-51
  open, SET VIEW, 264
  retrieve, SET VIEW TO, 264
  settings saved, 161
  Setup dialog box, 47-48
  Structure list box, 48
  work areas, 47

W

WAIT command, 242, 418, 424
warning/alerts, 6
WCHILD( ), 385
WCOLS( ), 386
WEXIST( ), 386
While clause, adding records, 68-69, 71
wildcards, comparing strings, 325-326
windows and Window Menu, 1-2, 37-56, 412-413
  activation test, WVISIBLE( ), 387
  blinking windows, 41
  borders, DEFINE WINDOW, 170
  brightness setting, 41
  change windows, 38
  change windows, Window Cycle, 40
  child windows, WCHILD( ), 385
  color selection, DEFINE WINDOW, 170-171
  color selection, Window Color, 40-43
  columns available, WCOLS( ), 386
  Command window displayed, 43
  coordinate setting, DEFINE WINDOW, 170

  debugging, Window Debug, 43-44
  define, CREATE SCREEN, 161
  display, ACTIVATE SCREEN, 142-143
  display, ACTIVATE WINDOW, 143
  display, SHOW WINDOW, 234
  editing, @SAY...GET command, 127
  enlarge, Window Zoom, 39
  erase from screen, DEACTIVATE WINDOW, 162
  erase remain operative, HIDE WINDOW, 184
  existence test, WEXIST( ), 386
  Files panel, 45
  footers, DEFINE WINDOW, 171
  FoxPro pop-up names (_mwi_xxx), 480
  frontmost window, WONTOP( ), 386-387
  hide/unhide, 37-38
  hide/unhide, Window Hide, 38
  load into memory, RESTORE WINDOW, 223
  memo, edit, SET WINDOW, 265
  move, 37
  move, MOVE WINDOW, 198-199
  move, Window Move, 39
  _msm_window FoxPro name, 477
  name, SYS(2016), 379
  On/Off panel, 45
  output-receiving window, WOUTPUT( ), 387
  parent windows, WPARENT( ), 386
  resize, DEFINE WINDOW, 171
  resize, ZOOM WINDOW, 242-243
  rows available, WROWS( ), 387
  save, SAVE WINDOW command, 226
  shadowing, 41
  shadowing, SET SHADOWS, 261
  show objects, SHOW GETS, 232-233
  shrink, Window Zoom, 39
  sizing, 37-39
  tracing program execution, Window Trace, 44
  View windows (see View windows)
Window menu, 37-56

windows and Window Menu (cont.)
  window-within-window, DEFINE WINDOW, 171
WONTOP( ), 386-387
word wrap, _wrap, 397
work areas
  alias, ALIAS( ), 275
  current file, USED( ), 383-384
  define, SELECT command, 231-232
  file open, DBF( ), 293
  index file named, NDX( ), 339
  index file named, ORDER( ), 341
  open file, USE command, 240-241
  show not-selected area available, SELECT( ), 366
  View window, 47
WOUTPUT( ), 387
WP, 471
WPARENT( ), 386
WROWS( ), 387
WVISIBLE( ), 387

Y
YEAR( ), 388

Z
ZAP command, 242
ZOOM WINDOW command, 242-243